Racial Discrimination

Routledge Research in Race and Ethnicity

1. Racial Discrimination
Institutional Patterns and Politics
Masoud Kamali

Racial Discrimination

Institutional Patterns and Politics

Masoud Kamali

Routledge
Taylor & Francis Group
New York   London

First published 2009
by Routledge
270 Madison Ave, New York, NY 10016

Simultaneously published in the UK
by Routledge
2 Park Square, Milton Park, Abingdon, Oxon OX14 4RN

Routledge is an imprint of the Taylor & Francis Group, an informa business

© 2009 Taylor & Francis

Typeset in Sabon by IBT Global.
Printed and bound in the United States of America on acid-free paper by IBT Global.

Library of Congress Cataloging in Publication Data
Kamali, Masoud.
    Racial discrimination : institutional patterns and politics / by Masoud Kamali. — 1st ed.
        p. cm. — (Routledge research in race and ethnicity ; 1)
    Includes bibliographical references and index.
    1. Racism—Europe.   2. Xenophobia—Europe.   3. Discrimination—
Europe.   4. Ethnic relations—Political aspects.   I. Title.
    HT1521.K36 2008
    305.80094—dc22
    2008013955

ISBN10: 0-415-98987-6 (hbk)
ISBN10: 0-203-89017-5 (ebk)

ISBN13: 978-0-415-98987-9 (hbk)
ISBN13: 978-0-203-89017-2 (ebk)

Contents

vi *Contents*

Acknowledgments

This book would not have been possible without the engagement and contribution of many individuals and research institutions in Europe. I wish to acknowledge the support of the European Commission under its Fifth Framework Programme for the extensive comparative research work conducted within 'The European Dilemma' project. I would like to specially thank the scientific officer of the Commission, Giulia Amaducci, for her significant support during the course of the project. Many researchers and connected individuals have been engaged in this work in different ways, including collecting data and organizing meetings, focus groups, and seminars. They have substantially contributed to this work and I would like to thank all of them, who are too many to name here. I would also like to thank James Milton for his reading and comments at the writing stage.

My special thanks go to the leaders and researchers of the national teams who participated in this project: Ruth Wodak, Michal Krzyżanowski, and Fleur Ulsamer (Austria); Nicos Trimikliniotis (Intercollege, Cyprus); Gerard Delanty and Paul Jones (University of Liverpool, England); John Crowley, Brigitte Beauzamy, and Marie-Cecile Naves (Interdisciplinary Centre for Comparative Research in the Social Sciences, CIR, France); Helena Flam, Axel Philipps, and Björn Carius (Leipzig University, Germany); Carlo Ruzza, Stefano Fella, and Giulia Bigot (University of Trento, Italy); Joanna Kurczewska, Justyna Frelak, and Lena Kolarka-Bobinska (Institute of Public Affair, Poland); and finally, the Swedish research team, Tom R. Bruns, Marcus Carlson, Maja Lilja, and Sami Lipponen (Uppsala University, Sweden). I wish also to specially thank both Tom R. Burns and Maja Lilja for their scientific and administrative contribution to the research project.

Masoud Kamali, February 2008

Introduction

RACISM, XENOPHOBIA, AND DISCRIMINATION

Racism, xenophobia, and discrimination are profound liabilities to European Union identity and development. The ideal is clearly stated: "Racism and xenophobia are diametrically opposed to everything that Europe stands for in terms of human dignity, mutual respect and understanding and citizenship in the broadest sense" (European Commission, Racism and Xenophobia). Yet, the spectre of racism and xenophobia haunts Europe. This spectre derives its rhetorical force from the fact that, on the one hand, contemporary Europe—as represented by the European Union—envisions itself as an open, tolerant, 'multicultural,' democratic community and, on the other, this vision is contradicted by everyday events: persistent stereotyping, stigmatisation, and discrimination at all levels of society; the emergence of political movements and relatively successful political parties espousing racist ideologies; increasing verbal and physical abuse of immigrants and minorities across Europe.

In recent years, geopolitical factors, such as regional economic recessions, increased migration rates in several European countries, and a process of European integration that makes borders more permeable, have made issues of territorial belonging newly relevant in Europe. In this context, movements have emerged that have reemphasised a sense of nationhood and connected it in contentious terms to issues of political representation. A nationalistic populism rooted in perceptions of ethnic community has sparked a rise of xenophobic movements and political parties in several European Union countries, including new member countries such as Poland, along with a concern about attacks on migrants and an increased presence of themes of 'racial identity' in the press. However, although taking new democratic forms, the new nationalist and xenophobic populism is not new and has a long history with its roots in the Crusades and colonialism. Racism and xenophobia is a widespread phenomenon in Europe today. Racism permeates most aspects of social life. As Essed (1991) emphasizes:

> Race relations . . . are a process present in and activated not only at
> the everyday level, but are also pre-structured in a way that transcends
> the control of individual subjects. Everyday racism is the integration
> of racism into everyday situations through practices (cognitive and be-
> havioural) that activate underlying power relations. This process must
> be seen as a continuum through which the integration of racism into
> everyday practices becomes part of the expected, of the unquestioned,
> and of what is seen as normal by the dominant group. When racist
> notions and actions infiltrate everyday life and become part of the re-
> production of the system, the system reproduces everyday racism. . . .
> if we should ignore the permeation of racism throughout the entire so-
> cial system, if we should fail to perceive its integration into the routine
> practices of everyday life, we would miss the point, and we would leave
> racism intact. (p. 50, see also 283)

This occurs in spite of frequent expressions of opposition to it by political
elites—and in spite of the introduction of policies and laws to control it,
such as the antidiscrimination directives of the European Union. It occurs
also in spite of the fact that minorities have rights recognised by the signa-
tories of an array of United Nations and European treaties, conventions,
and declarations. Such rights may include, for example, rights for teaching
'native' languages (or, in some cases, even teaching *in* 'native' languages)
in primary and secondary schools, having periodicals printed in minority
languages, the right to cultural assemblies, and so on. Nevertheless, there
are pervasive indications of unequal treatment in labour markets and in
educational systems, and lack of access to cultural resources, (including
public radio and TV) and relevant policy-making arenas in a reality in
which there is often little or no political representation.

European societies, notwithstanding the increasing attention of the
European Union to antiracist efforts, consistently exhibit high levels of
xenophobia and racism in attitude surveys, a desire to limit immigration
and acceptance of refugees, and a readiness to exclude those defined as
'foreigners' from certain social areas and arenas (e.g., EUMC, 2001; Hargreaves & Leaman, 1995; Wrench & Solomos, 1993). Furthermore, there
is a persistent threat that antipluralistic sociopolitical movements will arise
and establish themselves, introducing a 'racist agenda,' pressuring established parties to shift their position, and blocking or reversing institutional
realignment designed to favour pluralism, equality, and justice. Discrimination on the basis of ethnicity, religion, immigrant-status, or gender is a
persistent and serious human rights violation affecting all of Europe. However, to admit that discrimination is a widespread and serious problem has
been, and seems to continue to be, difficult for most Europeans. Addressing this type of issue has been thus far largely symbolic and rhetorical.

Racism must not be treated as a single concept but instead conceptualised in terms of a combination of social, institutional, and cognitive

factors of differentiation and inequality. Besides the sociocognitive dimension that refers to the shared social cognitions of groups (Van Dijk, 2000), power and institutional arrangements—that is, structural factors—are a second important aspect. Racism may be analyzed in terms of power relations or domination. The dominant group through its access to and/or control over scarce resources, such as residence, nationality, jobs, housing, education, knowledge, health or culture, and capital, reproduces its superiority. The social structure of racism entails institutions, organisations, groups, and their leaders: for example, political leaders and policy makers, political parties, business leaders and organisations, local communities, and NGOs.

Racism as a Particular Type of 'Otherism'

There are many forms and variants of 'racism,' hence the coining of terms such as biological racism, genetic racism, cultural racism, religious racism, and so on. Ethnicity, along with nationality, 'race,' religion, and gender, is an established sociocultural category. Such a category may be linked to visible physical characteristics, such as skin colour, hair type, or anatomical sex that are relatively easy constructions for distinguishing between 'Us' and 'Them,' but also imagined or real 'cultural properties' are used as 'ethnic markers' in the process of 'Otherization.'

Ethnic or 'racial' 'Otherism' entails negative stereotyping, stigmatizing, discriminating, and exclusionary practices with respect to a group or community differentiated and categorised based on their collective traits such as religion, ethnicity, colour of skin, disability, and gender. Problems of stereotyping, stigmatizing, and exclusion are processes that take place in all social groups and communities. By understanding these basic processes, we can better analyze and most effectively address contemporary problems of xenophobia and racism. This view differs, of course, from those who see these problems as largely 'pathological' and as something purely irrational and exceptional. The notion of 'race' or 'ethnicity' are not only part of a classification scheme but part of a model of asymmetric relations in which, for instance, 'white people' and/or 'our ethnicity' rank higher than 'nonwhites' and/or 'other ethnicities' and are treated accordingly.

Xenophobia

In this conception, xenophobia is a particular expression and emotional state of 'Otherism.' In its established definition, xenophobia is presented as 'fear of foreigners.' This definition is rather old and does not express the real state of xenophobia as a social phenomenon engaged in the relationships between those with access to and control over legitimate power means, that is, 'Us,' and those excluded from access to equal life chances, that is, 'Them.' Xenophobia as a form of 'Otherism' is shaped by the logic of exclusion—the separation of 'Us' from 'Them'—and the construction of adversarial frames, requiring a negative identification by which 'Them' becomes not only a feared other but an enemy. Carl Schmitt (1985) generalised such relations of enmity to all of politics, which he believed was always about the fundamental division of 'friends and enemies.' But his reductionist philosophy failed to see that the Us/Them polarity is distinct from the quite different logic of xenophobic politics by which 'Them' becomes first framed and categorised as the opposite poles of 'Us,' and then as an enemy. Xenophobia and racism can be used today interchangeably. The terms 'Xeno-otherism' (discussed and used in this book) and 'xeno-racism' are substitutes to encapsulate many aspects of the new racisms against immigrants and minorities.

'Racial' Discrimination

All societies have ideologies and discourses which discriminate by placing, in a hierarchical order of superiority, groups of people on the basis of sociocultural, religious, physical, or innate hereditary characteristics. In Europe, more recent stereotypes and prejudices are added to earlier forms, for instance against Jews and Roma. In the case of earlier racism, various pseudoscientific arguments were formulated to 'prove' this alleged superiority/inferiority. Van Dijk (1998, 1996) considers racism as a modern ideology. Anthias and Yuval-Davis (1992) point to a number of different forms where racism is expressed as "intersubjective; ideological and systemic" (p. 16). Racism involves ideas about inferiority, superiority, or essential differences of groups of people based on essentialist elements, but it also involves power. As Anthias and Yuval-Davis point out: "Racism involves the ability to impose those beliefs or world views as hegemonic, and as a basic denial of rights and equality" (p. 16).

A transformation of racist ideology has taken place during the post-WWII period. Whilst biological racism is largely discredited, new forms of racism have emerged which are largely based on explicit 'cultural differences.' Balibar (1991) refers to this as 'racisme differentiel' with a focus on cultural differences, not genetic or biological difference. In any general consideration, all forms of 'Otherism' are expressed in types of discourse and practice whose conceptual foundations are based on 'naturalised' notions of the privilege of some in-group members. It entails the unequal treatment of a population, or population group, purely because of particular socially defined characteristics, whether these be physical factors (colour of skin) or beliefs and practices (religious groups, language groups, ethnic communities). Thus, race based on biological traits is only one instance of a much wider phenomenon. All forms of systematic discrimination may be expressed through diverse social processes. These can be economic, political, and cultural projects. The effects can be expressed then in economic, political, and cultural form. One must not be misled by labels and thus obscure the substance of particular discourses, ideologies, and practices, both at institutional and personal group levels. Thus, 'racial' discrimination refers to negative treatment of racialised individuals and groups categorised as the 'Others.'

VARIOUS FORMS OF DISCRIMINATION

The concept of 'racial' discrimination is a suitable analytical tool for understanding those problems which are associated with ethnic inequalities in European societies. Although there have been a wide range of academic and nonacademic debates on the matter of 'racial' discrimination, it has hardly been a subject for systematic and comparative study whereby reliable knowledge about the mechanisms of discrimination, and the reasons that make discrimination a major problem in Europe and 'extended Europe,'[1] can be gained.

Discrimination does not only exist in the form of observable social actions, but also as subtle, hidden, and sometimes unintentional actions that indirectly harm some groups of people in a society (Pincus 1994, 1996). Discriminatory actions can often be based on established routines, norms, rules, and laws that are normally not contested in a society (de los Reyes & Kamali, 2005; Kamali, 2005;).

We need some conceptual clarification when using the concept of discrimination and its different arenas. Discrimination can be divided into the following three categories:

1. individual;
2. institutional; and
3. structural.

Individual discrimination addresses those actions that are conducted by individuals from an ethnic group or/and gender group that intentionally have 'Otherizing' and destructive effects on the members of another ethnic or gender group. However, it is not only the members of a hegemonic and dominating group that can conduct ethnic discriminatory actions against the 'Others.' Members of the inferiorized groups can equally discriminate members of their own or other ethnic groups. The reasons for this are manifold but can be that some persons with minority or ethnic background need to distance and disassociate themselves from the 'Others' and reinforce established prejudices in order to get advantages from majority society, or simply that they are influenced by these established prejudices about the 'Others' in a society (Du Bois, 1996; Kamali, 2002; De Los Reyes & Mulinari, 2005).

Institutional discrimination takes place because of established institutional policies, routines, norms, and functions, as well as those individuals with power and influence who control institutions. These individuals are called the 'gatekeepers' in an institution. Institutional discrimination can be intentional or unintentional. It can be based on institutional policy and praxis that intentionally have differentiating and negative effects on inferiorized groups (Pincus, 1994). However, there is no consensus among researchers about intentionality as an inherent property of institutional discrimination. Therefore, it is methodologically relevant to consider both intentionality and unintentionality as possible properties for institutional discrimination in order to produce fruitful and reliable knowledge about institutional discrimination from a comparative perspective.

Structural discrimination is about the institutional order, arrangements, and organisations of a society that often indirectly and unintentionally discriminate against individuals and groups with ethnic backgrounds different to those of the majority society. Structural discrimination legitimizes and normalizes indirect forms of negative treatment of the 'Others' and makes it a part of everyday normal life of a society. It is based on established ideologies, patterns of behaviour, and procedures that may not aim to discriminate against any group but practically excludes some groups from having access to jobs and other opportunities. Some forms of organisation of a society can lead to structural discrimination. For instance, research from the United States shows that some kinds of socioeconomic structures lead to segregation and apartheid (see, amongst others, Myrdal, 1944; Massey & Denton, 1996). The role of structures in the discrimination of the 'Others'—who can be black people, the poor, or migrant groups—has been discussed by other researchers too (Pincus, 1994; Bauman, 1995). Structural discrimination is mainly based on policies and laws which are 'race' and gender neutral and practically harm ethnic minorities and women (Pincus, 1996). Structural discrimination through the established institutions of society creates a socioeconomic order in which discrimination becomes a systematic and daily experience of many inferiorized and 'Otherized' people. In this sense, both structural and institutional discrimination provide the ground for the reproduction of an established ethnified inferiority. Accordingly, the power structure of society and its privileges, privileged groups, and its ethnic order is produced through the normal functions of socioeconomic institutions.

However, the theoretical differentiation between structural and institutional discrimination is not clear and creates many methodological problems for studies of routinized and systematic discrimination in society. Therefore, some researchers choose to combine the terms and do not make any distinction between them (Winant, 2000). Therefore, the term 'institutional discrimination,' which is used in this work, includes also the structural aspects of discrimination. Notwithstanding, some degree of differentiation between different levels of institutional discrimination can be of importance when it comes to suggestions for change. The research about institutional discrimination must consider the following spheres:

1. institutional norms and routines; and
2. the institutional arrangement of a society.

Institutions are formed to structure human interaction. They are made of formal structures (laws, rules, policies), informal structures (norms of behaviour, routines, conventions), codes of behaviour, and constraints that shape human interaction (North, 1990). Institutions are the rules of the game in a society and structure incentives in human exchange, whether political, social, or economic (North, 1990). Institutions have also been defined as amalgamation of rules and norms used by a group to organize frequent activities and guarantee its continuation. The sociological definition of institution is mainly related to routinized, normative, and cognitive aspects that influence individual actions. Institutions are also cognitive, normative, and regulating structures and activities that create stability and give meaning to social behaviour (Scott, 1995). Institutions can be openly discriminatory and racist against the 'Others.' Institutional racism is often embedded in routines and organisations' normal functions (Wieviorka, 1995). This means that institutions can exclude the 'Others' from access to adequate services and insult them. Accordingly, institutions' formal neutrality and objectivity can lead to differential treatment of the 'Others' and people from majority society.

Institutions are not isolated islands, but embedded in a range of webs that provide the very bedrock of a society. Schools, for instance, are important social institutions that function in connection with other institutions—such as labour market institutions, institutions of higher education, the political system, the judicial system, and so on—that form the institutional arrangements of society, which, in turn, reproduces established power relations as well as ethnic inequalities.

Discrimination and exclusion are certainly not new, but may take new forms. For instance, some immigrants may be (unintentionally) 'blocked' from information technology, because of their language limitations or lack of appropriate education. Alexander (2001), drawing on Bourdieu (1996), identifies a form of institutionalised racism based on language competence, and the role of the elites and institutions of higher education in establishing this competence as a criterion for discrimination and exclusion. Those social strata and individuals who obtain a high degree of competence in the dominant language, whether through 'inheritance' or through specialised training in institutions of higher education, may impose it as the only legitimate one in formal markets (the administrative, political, educational, and fashion markets) and in most of the linguistic interactions in which they are involved (see also Alexander, 1990).

> The position which the educational system gives to the different languages (or the different cultural contents) is such an important issue only because this institution has the monopoly in the large-scale production

of producers/consumers and therefore in the reproduction of the market
without which the social value of the linguistic competence, its capacity
to function as linguistic capital, would cease to exist. (Bourdieu, 1992,
pp. 56–57)

Those who lack command of this legitimate competence will be de facto
excluded from the social domains in which this competence is defined as
necessary, or are condemned to silence.

Discrimination is also inherent in category systems, laws and regulations, and institutional policies and practices. This is observable with the
police, schools, social welfare offices, markets, private enterprises, and
political parties. In this sense, the problem is not simply a way of perceiving
or categorizing human beings, but also the way in which those categories
serve as a basis for action and the exercise of power that results in discrimination, exclusion, and disadvantage.

Institutionalised discrimination practiced by public authorities and private
enterprises often finds informal support in the dominant community or group.
Institutions embody power and have real consequences. For instance, government may be used through law and the exercise of administrative power in
such a way as to normalize discriminatory or exclusionary practices, in some
cases unintended, affecting the life chances of immigrants. Institutionalised
'racial' discrimination and exclusion involve labour market agents, school
authorities and teachers, public agencies, police, courts, and other institutions. In such settings, discriminatory judgments are made, resources are
allocated, opportunities given or denied, individuals included or excluded.
There are category systems, models defining 'Others' habits and established
practices. Among our questions are the following: Who is being discriminated
against and excluded, where, through what mechanisms, and with what consequences? Due to particular categorisations and labels, groups and populations may be disadvantaged or even denied key resources on the basis of their
ethnicity, skin colour, religion, and so on. As Van Dijk (2000) stresses:

Even if prejudice and discrimination occur at all levels of dominant
group structure, unequal treatment by some members has more impact than when it is practised by others. Ordinary people, for example,
may discriminate against their Turkish, West-Indian or North-African
neighbour in many overt and subtle ways; they will generally be unable
seriously to affect the socio-economic position of these neighbours.
(pp. 15–16)

On the other hand, if influential elite groups engage in discrimination
against immigrants or minorities, the consequences are considerable for the
discriminated: The 'Other' will not be allowed into the country in the first
place, or they will not get a job for which they are qualified, or they will not
be promoted in their job, or will not get decent housing, or the mass media

or textbooks will spread negative stereotypes about them, and so on. In other words, the role of leading agents of society, corporate managers and supervisors, teachers, scholars, politicians, journalists, judges, and police officers, amongst others, is crucial for the (un)equal access to material or symbolic resources in society. It is safe to say that prejudice, discrimination and racism would be significantly less influential if it were limited to popular feelings of resentment against the newcomers (Van Dijk, 2000).

Paradigms of 'Otherism' may be backed by power and systematically institutionalised. This was apparent in the case of South Africa's apartheid system promoting and maintaining white ascendancy, and with the 'Jim Crow' institutions in the southern states of the United States assuring white supremacy. Yet, even less extreme cases than these reveal the problems of institutionalised discrimination. As will be shown in this book, the existing literature suggests that there is considerable discrimination and exclusion in labour markets, in workplaces, and in educational systems.

In summary, the discourses of ethnicity, religion, gender, and 'race' are part of what one can refer to as the representation of the 'Other' relating to specific modes of inferiorization, discrimination, subordination and/or exclusion that manifest themselves differently in different social and historical projects.[2] Ethnic, racial, gender, or religious discrimination refers to any distinction, exclusion, restriction, or preference shown which has the purpose—or the effect—of nullifying or impairing the recognition, enjoyment, or exercise of human rights and fundamental freedoms or participation in the political, economic, social, cultural, and religious life. Equal treatment means that there should be no discrimination—direct or indirect—with respect to profession, work, health and welfare, education, housing, provision of goods, facilities and services, participation in political, economic, social, cultural, religious, or any other public field. In the construction of boundaries involving modes of inferiorization, discrimination and exclusion, collective traits of religion, ethnicity, colour of skin, or gender are the particular bases of constituting the boundary whereby a given category is separated out in a human population.

'Otherism,' including racism, in its institutional forms entails systematic discrimination and exclusion directed at one or more categories of population, whether on the basis of ethnicity, gender, religion, political belief, or class. Such sociopolitical categories of population help make 'immigrants' an *object,* a defined social fact or reality, that can be 'objectively' used for political and/or administrative purposes. The analysis of how categories are constructed and applied, their cognitive basis, and their role in identity (and distinctions between identities) is central to our analysis.

The empirical material of this book is mainly based on a European research project in which researchers and research institutes from eight European countries (Austria, Cyprus, England, France, Germany, Italy, Poland, and Sweden) have participated. The author of the book has been scientific director of the project.

BACKGROUND AND OBJECTIVES OF
THE RESEARCH PROJECT

The project has worked to identify, and map out on a comparative basis, key practices related to racism, xenophobia, and 'racial' discrimination in the eight European countries, and to articulate policy implications and strategies to deal with such practices. In particular, we have focused on: (a) taken-for-granted, institutionalised forms of racism and xenophobia that result in discrimination against, and exclusion of, immigrants; (b) the political, manifest forms of racism and xenophobia and the emergence of sociopolitical movements and parties with xenophobic messages and proposals for discriminatory policies; and (c) the impact of (b) upon (a).

The research entails a multidisciplinary, multifaceted approach to identifying and analyzing the variety of practices that make up the complex phenomena of racism and xenophobia. A diversity of methods has also been employed to 'get at' these phenomena: institutional analysis based on elite interviews; collection of documents and available statistics on institutional practices; focus group methods; discourse analysis; and historical analysis. Our research has entailed the collection of a substantial body of original data, including immigrant focus group studies, expert interviews, and selections for discourse analysis from party programmes and party press, from the public statements of politicians, and from the mainstream press. The project has also carried out secondary analyses using existing statistical data, reports, studies, and other documents in the project countries. In general, we found here excellent bodies of research already carried out on discrimination and xenophobia in the specific context of these countries. What has typically been lacking is a coherent overview that is able to systematically relate these materials to one another. In some instances, earlier research results have been reanalyzed and reinterpreted from a multidisciplinary perspective, also putting national data into a comparative European perspective.

The project began with the following basic questions for comparative research:

- Why do many institutional forms of racism remain commonplace in all European countries, in spite of political elite expressions of opposition to racism and xenophobia, and the existence of laws and programs proscribing it at both the national and European Union levels? What are key factors supporting the persistence of forms of discrimination?
- What are the dominant/significant forms and specific practices of discrimination and exclusion in areas, such as labour markets and educational systems? To what extent do these forms and practices vary in the different European countries—that is, in the substantially different political, institutional, and cultural settings of the countries making up this study?

- Why are forms of xenophobia and racist (often coded) expressions commonplace in arenas of democratic politics, in spite of the norms of democracy, antiracist laws and policies, and expressions of opposition to racism and xenophobia by many political elites?
- How can we clarify the emergence and success in several European countries of xenophobic parties? Why has the xenophobic populist party (XPP) emerged as a political phenomenon in countries such as France, Italy, and Austria—effectively putting immigration and nationalism on the political agenda—but not in other countries?
- What impact are such parties having on policies and behaviour? In particular, how does the emergence of a XPP party (of significant size) affect the extent, depth, and salience of institutionalised xenophobia in a society?
- Do countries without XPPs of significant size (namely, Cyprus, England, and Sweden) have other mechanisms for expressions of xenophobia and the politicisation of immigration/immigrants? If so, what are these and how do they impact on policies and practices?
- What role do preexisting patterns of institutionalised racism and xenophobia play in the emergence and electoral success of XPPs? How do XPPs draw upon and amplify preexisting xenophobic ideologies and institutional conceptions and practices?
- To what extent is xenophobia and racism the same for all countries? Is there a unique European model or framework of xenophobic ideologies, stereotypes, and practices spread over all of Europe? Or are the forms and patterns unique for each society?
- What would be the policy and strategic implications of the project's empirical and theoretical results? What potentially new legal and/or governance measures would provide greater leverage in addressing contemporary problems of xenophobia and racial discrimination in Europe?

Because of the role of taken-for-granted (and often unexamined) institutional practices and the exploitation by xenophobic and racist oriented groups of democratic political arrangements, racism and xenophobia pervade most modern societies and are a major obstacle to genuine democracy and to the effective participation of people with immigrant background in the sociopolitical and cultural life of Europe. In systematically investigating and analyzing these problems, the project has sought to contribute to a deeper understanding of the forces underlying xenophobia and racism and to generate more effective antiracialist and integrative policy making.

AN INSTITUTIONAL APPROACH TO DISCRIMINATION

In an institutional approach to ethnic, racial, national, or religious discrimination, there is a stress on societal wide, enduring structures and trends.

While the personal prejudices and everyday actions of the common person toward people of immigrant background is a problem, a deplorable aggravation, the focus in our study and analyses are structural conditions and, in particular, institutional arrangements and their everyday mechanisms. The main forms of discrimination investigated in this approach are *not* an aggregation of individual acts (embodying personal prejudices and other negative attitudes) between members of different groups. Also, the members of out-groups such as immigrants may be just as prejudiced and prone to 'discriminate' against other immigrants and minorities as members of majority society; typically, however, they do not occupy positions of power, and the major institutions of society have not been created and maintained by them. The stress is *not* on the 'Others' (e.g., immigrant groups and their characteristics) *per se* but on the *relations* between in-groups and out-groups (or majority society and immigrant groups).

Institutional discrimination and racism is often implanted in routine practices and the functioning of organisations (Wieviorka, 1995). In the institutional perspective, discrimination, stigmatisation, inferiorization, and exclusion operate not only in particular interpersonal encounters but also in and through institutions and other complex systems of social relationships. There is often a politically supported narrow definition of racial discrimination that limits the concept's scope by including only actions *intended* to restrict a group's life chances. Thus, *intentionality* becomes the touchstone with which to determine if an action can be categorised as racial discrimination or not. The discussions on intentionality or unintentionality concerning racial discrimination are not appropriate for research on institutional discrimination. Irrespective of individuals' or institutions' intentions, discriminatory practices produce and reproduce differential access to resources, positions, careers, and so on.

Institutional discrimination operates (a) through operative norms, laws, regulations and procedures, as well as in the form of defined positions that determine access to resources and the exercise of fate control, and (b) through interinstitutional 'Otherization' based on widely shared systems of categorisation, stereotypes, inferiorization, and 'Us–Them' paradigms. Institutions and interinstitutional 'Otherization' may operate in discriminatory ways irrespective of the intentions, personal attitudes, or beliefs of the individuals involved. For example, the degree of socially defined 'Otherness' plays a role. This includes established stereotypes of the 'Others,' for instance, about 'Roma people,' Muslims, and Somalians. Up until the end of WWII, categorisation and stigmatisation of the 'Other' was given a 'natural scientific basis' (theories of 'the races' and their biological foundations). Later, after such theories became socially and politically bankrupt, there emerged theories based on essentialised 'cultural differences.' In this perspective, culture is not treated as open, negotiated, and changing, but as *fixed* and unchangeable boxes (Kamali, 2002). For instance, "people of Muslim background will never fit into our tolerant, democratic, and egalitarian society." Culturalisation of individuals with immigrant background has become one of the main public discourses about the 'Others' that in many ways legitimize racism and discrimination against 'Them.' Culturalisation has been institutionalised and created a 'multicultural industry' that involves many institutions, authorities, and 'culturally expert groups' who are highly engaged in 'Otherization' of migrants and minorities (Kamali, 2002; see also Kamali, 2006b). These actions may operate in ways that are not obviously discriminatory. The discrimination and exclusion here need not be reflections of overt racism, but more a concrete judgment of hierarchical 'differences,' 'misfit' or 'contradiction' between established norms and the behaviour (or the potential behaviour) of 'deviants' who 'normally' happen to be individuals with immigrant background.

Among the contributions of an institutional approach are the following: (a) It treats 'discrimination,' racism and 'Otherism' as features of social institutions, hegemonic cultural formations, and societal arrangements, and (b) it breaks the tendency to view discrimination and racism largely in terms of individual psychology, or attitude and simple intentionality. That is why surveys of racist attitudes and prejudices of decontextualised individuals are not an appropriate method to study structural forms of systematic discrimination and exclusion. In particular, an intentionality perspective reduces the problem to one of psychology or social psychology and deflects attention away from institutional arrangements that constrain, select, and discriminate (Pettigrew & Taylor, 1992). Structural discrimination may operate in large part independently of persons' attitudes and awareness. Hence, models based primarily on individual prejudice or 'rationality,' whether psychological or economic, will uniformly understate and oversimplify the phenomenon of discrimination and racism (Pettigrew & Taylor, 1992). In order to determine whether structural discrimination is operating, one must examine the ways in which particular arrangements operate and their discriminatory and exclusionary consequences.

Ethnicity and other objects of 'Otherism' such as 'race,' 'nationality,' and religion may be included here not as a matter of shared traits or cultural markers, although these play a role also, but rather as the social practices of classification and categorisation (Barth, 1969); Barth includes here both self-classification and the classification of others (see also Brubaker, 2004, p. 32). Race has increasingly come to be seen as a manner of dividing and ranking human beings with reference to selected *embodied properties* (real or imputed) so as to subordinate, exclude, and exploit them (Wacquant, 1997, 2003, 2004).

Thus, it is possible for any individual occupying a position of decision making relating to advancement in school, business, office, or government to be unprejudiced but nevertheless discriminating. Similarly, he or she may be prejudiced and nondiscriminating because in his or her position, there is monitoring and strict controls making it difficult to readily apply personal prejudices and stereotypes—for instance, effective antidiscrimination laws and policies.

In sum, many of the major forms of discrimination are institutional in character: markets, government agencies, education, the health system, political parties, associations, and NGOs. In any given institution, there are established organizing principles, rules and regulations, procedures, role definitions, and relationships that may discriminate against individuals and groups that are not considered to belong to majority society, or are marginal to it. Also, there are cultural elements shared in the majority society such as established and legitimised category systems, concepts, stereotypes, judgement principles, generalised strategies, and societal norms that cut across institutions and discriminate against those with immigrant backgrounds. They are 'societal in character,' that is, they are carried and reproduced by particular institutions, professional groups and networks.

THE EUROPEAN DILEMMA

Gunnar Myrdal's classical work, *An American Dilemma,* was used by the civil rights movement in the United States to illustrate the North American society's racist dilemma and its apartheid systems. According to Myrdal, there existed a big discrepancy between the American creed and declarations about equal rights for all, and existing racism and the apartheid system that haunted American society. Myrdal meant that in order to solve the American Dilemma the government should abolish the 'race laws' and the apartheid system. Many European politicians and even researchers have considered the gap between politically correct declarations and existing institutional discrimination against the 'Others' as an American exception; therefore, European racism and discrimination has received less attention than it should.

Racism and discrimination have been an integrated part of European modern history. Modernity that is presented in scientific and other public contexts as the ultimate goal of human history (to use Hegel's term), has, according to Philip Lawrence (1997), three related properties: 'Otherism,' racism, and narcissism. The creation of the 'Other' has been a part of the discursive construction of 'Us' where the 'Other' becomes its mirror image and is formed not only as a different group, different people, and different nation, but also as an inferiorized collectivity. This has been a part of modern racism, both the biological and the cultural, whereby the inferiority of the 'Others' transfers to an ideology with a 'scientific' embeddedness. 'Otherism' and racism lead to a narcissist imagination of 'Us.' The modern history of Europe and extended Europe has created a dichotomy of "the West and the rest" that helps to reinforce racism and discrimination against the 'Others' and preserve, in turn, the dichotomy of 'Us' and 'Them.'

There is also a European Dilemma that is based on the paradoxical declaration of universalism, human rights, democracy, and so forth, on the one hand, and the existence of institutional discrimination on the other. This is the main reason behind the failure of integration in Europe and it creates a major obstacle to promoting social cohesion. Although the acceptance of the existence of institutional discrimination in Europe is an important step forward, understanding the mechanisms of the reproduction of discrimination is much more accurate. This book can be a substantial contribution.

1 Modernization, Social Theory, and the Duality of 'Us-and-Them'

INTRODUCTION

The term 'modern' is one of the most discussed concepts in the social sciences. Modern, modernity, and modernization are interrelated concepts by which social scientists have tried to refer to an epochal change in human history. Despite some disagreements about the origins and the starting point of the 'modern time,' it seems that there is a common understanding of the European origin of modernity. In almost all cases, the modern is coupled with the emergence and development of the capitalist system that changed the history of human beings (Marx, 1954, 1956). The rapid spread of the modern capitalist system all over the world, has drawn together all regions and countries within a world capitalist system (Wallerstein, 1974).

Modernity is, however, not considered as a merely economic transformation, but also as a revolutionary process that has changed societies and cultures in a global arena (Beck, 2000; Giddens, 1990; Eisenstadt, 1966; Featherstone, 1995). The transformation process from premodern societies to modern ones that came to be called modernization, also entailed disruptions in established social institutions, the disintegration of society, wars over nation borders, internal and external migration, and social movements and revolutions. The chaotic situation in many European countries forced the elites to take action in newly organising their national societies. Although modernization created new problems, it also had the capacity to generate solutions to modern problems (Eisenstadt, 1987a, 1999). The modern disintegration of societies generated new ideas about how to create new forms of integration.

Social scientists tried to provide theoretically rigorous models for understanding the new revolutionary system, *the* modernity. Among these were the classics, such as Spencer, Hegel, Marx, Weber, and Durkheim, who developed 'meta narratives' for understanding *the* modern society in order to launch new ideas about the reorganization of new societies. Social scientists situated the modern society in a contradictory relation to premodern ones. The *modern* stood in contrast to the *traditional*. All over the world, social theory came to be dominated by a systematic dualism between contrary poles. Theoretical divisions such as *traditional/modern, mechanical/organic, gemeinschaft/gesellschaft,* and *Occident/Orient* held sway over classical sociology for a very long time (Kamali, 2006c). Many metanarratives, or to use Agnes Heller's comprehensive concept, 'master narratives,' were attempts to theoretically bring order to a world mostly characterized by a constant move towards disorder.[1]

Social theory and its founding fathers did not enjoy an 'objective' existence in a value-free 'scientific world,' but were part of a changing process where the European powers were engaged in colonial wars and occupations. These wars and occupations were legitimized by a systematic inferiorization of colonized people. This was coupled with the presentation of 'Us' as superiors to 'them.' It was not only political and economic elites that saw themselves as superior to 'them,' but also social scientists who considered Europe to be unique in the world and 'the pearl of the globe,' in the words of Paul Valery:

> This Europe, will it become what it is in reality, i.e., a little cap of the Asiatic continent, or will this Europe remain rather what it seems, i.e., the priceless part of the whole earth, the pearl of the globe, the brain of a vast body? (Kingston-Mann, 1999, p. 3)

Such perspectives on history and the place of 'Europe' and 'European civilization' in it are strongly shaped by 19th century views. "This was the formative period of disciplines such as archaeology, art history, philology, sociology and anthropology, as well as the gestation period of European narcissism and imperialism" (Pieterse, 1994, p. 129). Social theory came to be dominated by efforts to explain the *uniqueness* of the 'west.'

THE UNIQUENESS OF THE 'WEST' (US)

Uniqueness theory was formulated by Max Weber who tried to generate a theory for the economic development of Europe. He believed that the modern capitalist system could develop only in western Europe. Christian and Protestant Europe had the cultural and religious ground for the development of capitalism as a victorious and modern system that gave European powers their superiority and victories in the world (see Weber, 1978, 1992).

Weber claims that Christianity through Reformation could create favourable conditions for the development of capitalism in the 'west' in contrast to (amongst others) Islam. He means that: "The character of the Calvinist church differs from that of all other churches, Catholic, Lutheran, and Islamic" (1978, p. 1198). Firstly, Weber makes a fundamental mistake when he states that there are 'churches' in Islam. Islamic mosques cannot be called churches; there are decisive differences. The mosques have no hierarchical organizations such as those of churches. Secondly, Islam is not a homogenous religion that can be compared with different Christian churches and sects. Islam, as with many other religions, has different branches such Shi'ism and Sunnism, not to mention various branches of the two mentioned major branches and Sufism. Thirdly, Islam, as an urban and bazari religion, has always been very positively orientated towards capitalist production and market rules.

Weber claims that it is only in Christianity (Calvinism) that making profits were a sign that "God's blessing rests on the enterprise:

> And since the success of work is the surest symptom that it pleases God, capitalist profit is one of the most important criteria for establishing that God's blessing rests on the enterprise. It is clear that this style of life is very closely related to the self justification that is customary for bourgeois acquisition: Profit and property appears not as ends in themselves but as indications of personal ability. Here has been attained the union of religious postulate and bourgeois style of life that promotes capitalism. (Weber, 1978, p. 1200)

This indicates that Weber, in his theoretical constructions of a 'western explanation' of capitalist development in Europe, ignores the fact that the same definition of religious belief and capitalist activities could also be valid for bazari merchants and craftsmen in Islamic cities (Kamali, 1998; Arjomand, 1984; Algar, 1969). The wealth of bazaris was a sign of the merchant's sincere businesses, which is prized by God.

Weber's discussion of Islam is not scientific nor is it based on fact, but rather is a result of his aim to theorize 'differences' between 'western Christianity' and Islam as an eastern religion. He calls Islam "a religion of warriors" (see Turner, 1974).

Weber, in coordination with the established Orientalist discourse of the 19th and early 20th centuries, created the concept of 'Sultanism' as an Islamic state formation that was a hindrance for democratic development in the 'east.' Weber wrote about the Ottoman Empire without real knowledge and research of the Ottoman governance. He claimed that no independent institution or organ could develop in the Empire because of the absolute power of the sultan. This proved to be a wrong assumption, even during the lifetime of Weber. The researcher who had adequate knowledge about the Ottoman Empire and its governance at the early 20th century was Albert Lybyer who wrote his classical work, *The Governance of the Ottoman Empire* in 1913. He illustrated that although the sultan had a relatively substantial influence over the Ottoman Empire, the exaggeration of this power is misleading. Several sultans have been removed from the throne by other governmental and even civil institutions. This means that the Weberian and Orientalist concept of absolutism cannot be used fairly for governance in Muslim countries, such as the Ottoman and Persian empires. I have also shown elsewhere that the sultan, as the sovereign exerted power, in many cases did make the important decisions in matters significant for the continuation of the Empire's existence; but the sultan's freedom in making such decisions was limited by other influential groups of the ruling strata and groups in civil society (Kamali, 2006c).

Weber's discussions on Islam and Christianity can be counted among those social scientists' efforts that, consciously or unconsciously, 'otherize' non-European countries and people. This is clear in many of his generalizations about the 'Orient' and the 'Oriental church,' in comparison to his writings on the 'Occidental church' and 'Occidental culture' that are considered unique in the world. He means that the 'rationalization of hierocratic domination' is very 'western' and has to do with a 'western tradition' originating from 'ancient Roman traditions' that helped develop capitalism:

> The more favourable constellation for capitalist development that Occidental Catholicism offered (in comparison with oriental religions) was primarily due to the rationalization of hierocratic domination undertaken in continuation of ancient Roman traditions. This refers especially to the manner in which science and jurisprudence were developed. (Weber, 1978, p. 1192)

This is a fallacy that occurs in Weber's work and in many other classical sociological texts. As is now known, science and jurisprudence were much more developed in Islamic empires than in Europe during the medieval period (Saliba, 2007; Huff, 2003; Turner, 1997; Sardar, 1984).

Even in matters of political thought and political science, Islamic scholars were engaged in much more developed discussions and research concerning governance than in Europe (Corne, 2004; Hoexter, Eisenstadt, & Levtzion, 2002; Kamali, 2001, 1998). Social sciences in Islamic empire in the medieval period had more favourable circumstances to flourish than in Christian Europe. The sociological works of Ibn Khaldun is just one example.

The recent research on the Islamic history of Muslim empires and countries shows that even Weber's assumption of relation between hierocracy and state in Muslim countries and Europe is another example of constructing discursive differences between Europe and Islamic countries. He claims that:

> Occidental hierocracy lived in a state of tension with the political power and constituted its major restraint; this contrasted with the purely caesaropapist or purely theocratic structures of Antiquity and the Orient. (Weber, 1978, p. 1193)

It is known that after the death of the Prophet in 1632 AD, the matter of government led to internal conflicts and division among Muslims. Some groups of Muslims such as Shi'is were moved to the civic sphere of society and created opposition to the state. The tension between Shi'is and Sunnis was just one tension between the political leaders of the Islamic Arabic empire and other Muslim groups. Since the 11th century, and the creation of many local Caliphs (such as that of Spain, Damascus, and Baghdad), tensions emerged between the political and the religious leader, the ulama. This became even more evident in the Islamic Ottoman Empire and Shi'i Persian Empire since the reign of Safavids (1501–1722). The Islamic civil society has from very early Islamic reign "lived in a state of tension with the political power and constituted its major restraint," to use the words of Weber (Kamali, 1998, 2001, 2006c; Arjomand, 1984). Weber's claim and generalization is a clear example of the otherization of Muslims and indeed many other groups, such as the Chinese and Indians.

Weber's historiography and sociology suffers from a Eurocentric bias, which is common for many social scientists writing in the 19th and early 20th centuries. If any contribution of the 'Others' to the 'European civilization' was acknowledged, it was in relation to European themes, as in 'Judeao-Christian civilization,' or circumscribed and white-washed, as in the 'Aryan model' of history, in which everything paled into significance next to the creativity and drive of the 'Nordic races' (Pieterse, 1994).

Another social scientist who very clearly declared the superiority of Europeans to all other people (who he referred to as "races"), is Herbert Spencer. He writes consequently about "wild and uncultivated races" and "civilized races" (Spencer, 1878). He makes the 'differences' between 'races' appear natural and biological:

> Biological truths and their corollaries, presented under these special forms as bases for sociological conclusions, are introductory to a more general biological truth including them—a general biological truth which underlies all legislation. I refer to the truth that every species of organism, including the human, is always adapting itself, both directly and indirectly, to its conditions of existence. The actions which have produced every variety of man—the actions which have established in the Negro and the Hindu, constitutions that thrive in climates fatal to Europeans, and in the Fuegian a constitution enabling him to bear without clothing an inclemency almost too great for other races well clothed—the actions which have developed in the Tartar-races nomadic habits that are almost insurmountable, while they have given to North American Indians desires and aptitudes which, fitting them for a hunting life, make a civilized life intolerable—the action doing this, are also ever at work moulding citizens into correspondence with their circumstances. (Spencer, 1878, pp. 346–347)

Europeans are considered by Spencer as a biological category, because of the differences in climate and other "circumstances," different from "all other races."

Spencer was highly influenced by a social Darwinist perspective to the 'evolution' of human societies. He, in his work, *A System of Synthetic Philosophy* (1862), constitutes a range of distinctions between 'the civilized' societies (that interchanges often with Europeans) and uncivilized people and societies. The civilized people, in every aspect, are situated at a higher end of the range than are the uncivilized people, according to Spencer. His social Darwinism had no limits, and he went as far as to propagate the use of deadly force in 'civilising' the 'uncivilized' people. Inspired by Charles Darwin's evolution theory, he believed that the 'uncivilized' will either disappear or follow the European example and become civilized. This is evident from his early publications such as *Social Statica* (1851) and *A Theory of Population* (1852) and *Progress: Its Law and Cause* (1857). He believed that modernization, and modernising forces (who he believed were Europeans), will eliminate those sectors of humanity that stands in its way. In other words, all humans and natural hindrances to modernization and civilization will be removed by Europeans (see also Lindqvist, 1992).

Bound with the deterministic understanding of Darwinist evolution theory, Spencer concluded that there are even psychologically determined differences between different 'races' (Richards, 1997). Spencer is considered to be one of the major scientists who provided the theoretical and scientific basis for 'scientific racism' (Richards, 1997). Spencer, like Weber, believed in the uniqueness of Europeans, and upheld a notion of Europe as the sole site of rationality, reason, development, modernity, and civilization. All other people of the world were considered to exist somewhere long 'behind' Europe. They were to subordinate themselves to the European civilization and follow its example in order to adapt themselves to civilization and leave their uncivilized lives.

Many classical social theorists (including Marx, Weber, Spencer, Locke, and Durkheim), believed strongly in the *uniqueness* of the 'west' that makes it 'the pearl of the globe' and a model for all other nations and groups to follow. The 'superiority' of the 'west' was mainly related to the 'inferiority' of the nonwestern countries and societies. This was not only the assumed 'scientific truth' of functionalist or liberal social scientists, but also equally 'true' in critical Marxist theories of the early modernization period. Marx himself legitimised the superiority of the 'west' to the 'inferior' colonized people, in presenting the 'west' as a historical destiny and a development model for entire world. He believed that even the 'Orient's' economical activities differs basically from that of the capitalist 'west.' He created then a theoretical model for understanding and analysing the Orient. He argued that, in contrast to the Occident, there was an 'Asiatic mode of production,' which was geographically significant and which extended from Sahara through Arabia, Persia, India, and Tartaya (Marx & Engels, 1973; see also

Turner, 1978). 'The Asiatic mode' is "characterized by (a) stagnation, (b) an absence of dynamic class struggle, and (c) the domination of a swollen state acting as a sort of universal landlord. The conditions for capitalist development are here absent" (Hall, 1996, p. 222). This interpretation, which reinforced the *uniqueness* arguments of many social scientists, went as far as Marx and Engels defending colonialism as a "progressive" power of change and "the progress of civilization" (Feuer, 1971, p. 489; see also Turner, 1978). Legitimization of colonialism was, according to Marx and Engels, based on the assumption that the social formations of the Oriental world are stagnant and that capitalism has a historical role to play in smashing the precapitalist modes of production (Turner, 1978; see also Kamali, 2006c).

Emile Durkheim is another social scientist who, together with many others before and after him, was engaged in 'making difference' with the 'Others' (or with the otherization of people) in order to create a universal scientific model for understanding the 'differences' between different people and societies in the world. In his central theoretical discourse on modernity and traditionalism, he divides societies into two categories, the modern and the traditional, with completely different integration models and mechanisms. The modern societies are the western European societies that, as a consequence of modernization and the division of labour in society, have an 'organic solidarity.' The traditional societies are nonwestern countries that are still bound by religious and traditional ties that give ground for a primitive 'organic solidarity' among members of the society. Societies other than western modern ones are more or less primitive. The western modern 'organic solidarity' is therefore *unique*, a fixed model for other societies. In his major work, *The Division of Labour in Society* (1987), he draws the following conclusion: "Thus it is a law of history that mechanical solidarity, which at first is isolated, or almost so, should progressively lose ground, and organic solidarity gradually become preponderant" (p. 126).

He believed in the linearity of history and an evolutionary westcentric development. Durkheim believes in and propagates the superiority of a 'western world' that since, and through, the Greek civilization became clearly 'conscious of itself' and its 'logical thinking.' He (1984) presents it as the following:

> In our Western World, it was with the great thinkers of Greece that it first became clearly conscious of itself and of the consequences which it implies; when the discovery was made, it caused an amazement which Plato has translated into magnificent language. (pp. 484–485)

The Eurocentric understanding of the world has dominated the social sciences since their emergence. Friedrich Hegel (1770–1831), for instance, argues almost along the lines of 'natural selection.' In his famous writings known as *Lectures on the Philosophy of World History* (1822–1828/1975),

Hegel argues that non-European peoples—such as American Indians, Africans, and Asians—are less human than Europeans because of their geographical conditions. According to Hegel, extreme climatic conditions, which are "terroid" or "cold," cannot provide the basis for human freedom or world historical nations. This basis can only be found in Europe, because of its geographical location in the "temperate zone," and which must furnish the theatre of world history (see also Eze, 1997). This understanding of naturalised history was a very established discourse in 19th century social sciences and has its roots in the Enlightenment and earlier philosophers' and historians' understanding of the world. The Swedish natural scientist Carl von Linné (1707–1778) was among one of the first scientists to distinguish between different people and continents, categorising them into four 'races' (Europeans, Americans, Asians, and Africans) and ascribing them distinguished, hierarchical properties. Europe, according to the Enlightenment's philosophers and social scientists of 18th and 19th centuries, was a *unique* place of science, salvation, and civilization.

The influence of climate as a central 'natural' point in the essentialisation of European civilization has been theoretically and methodologically developed by other social scientists, such as Charles de Secondat baron de Montesquieu (1689–1755). In his celebrated book, *The Spirit of the Law* (1989), which was first published in 1748, he put forward the ideas of the influence of climate upon 'the temper of the mind' and the 'passions of the heart.' He wrote:

> You will find in the northern climates people who have few vices, enough virtues, and much sincerity and frankness. As you move towards the countries of the south, you will believe you have moved away from morality itself: the liveliest passions will increase crime; each will seek to take from others all the advantages that can favour these same passions. (p. 234)

Montesquieu and other social scientists make geographical factors the main reason for developments in Europe and the 'backwardness' of non-Europeans. However, the geographical differences were only one side of the development of the idea of the uniqueness of Europe and the inferiority of the 'Others.' The concept of 'race' and biological differences came to complete both the cultural and geographical differences between Europeans and non-Europeans.

SCIENTIFIC RACISM AND THE SUPERIORITY OF 'US' OVER 'THEM'

The historical constructions of the image of the superiority of Europe or the 'west' over the inferior non-Europeans or non-westerners went hand in hand with the construction of an 'us-and-them' division. Such a division is aimed at preserving the privileges of 'Us' and the inferiorization and otherization of non-Europeans. This is, of course, nothing new in human history and has been a part of the construction of 'Us' against the 'Others' from early antiquity onwards. The idea of the 'Others' as inferior to, and the mirror image of, 'Us' has been an integrated part of the Enlightenment's philosophy and science (Eze, 1997; Hannaford, 1996).

Otherization and inferiorization have been constitutive of Europeanness and the European/western identity. Although Europe has never been a continent or socioeconomic or cultural entity 'in itself' as the theory of the uniqueness of Europe tries to constitute, the 'Europeanization of Europe' during the modern time has been a process of narcissism and of inferiorization of the 'Others.'

Inferiorization of other people has a long history and can be observed even in antiquity. 'White Europeans' have encountered Africans and categorized them as blacks or 'Ethiopians' but not with the reference to their 'race' (Snowden, 1970; Thompson, 1989). The differences between Europeans and Africans were rather geographical or based on attributes other than race (Snowden, 1970; Thompson, 1989; Hannaford, 1996; Richards, 1997). As Thompson (1989) concludes, Roman attitudes towards Ethiopians had nothing to do with modern understandings of 'race' and racism, but a very different kind of differentiating between whites and blacks. There was a remarkable *absence* of race as an organising idea during the Greco-Roman period; indeed, the preconditions for generating the subsequently dominant idea of 'race' based on biology and genetics were formed during the thirteenth to the 16th centuries (Hannaford, 1996).

The Spanish Inquisition was among the first precondition for the development of the idea of the existence of biological differences between people based on "clean blood" or "unclean blood." Muslims and Jews were considered as having "unclean blood" in comparison to Christians who endowed "clean blood" (Loomba, 1998). Even those Muslims and Jews who had been forced to convert to Christianity were not considered equal with Christians who enjoyed "clean blood." The development of such ideas resulted in the establishment of an assumption of the existence of different biological 'races' with different properties.

The concept of 'race' and the racialisation of 'different' peoples along biological lines were an integrated part of the philosophy and science of the Enlightenment. The Swedish botanist Carl von Linné was among the first natural scientists to divide people into four different races: Europeans, Americans, Asians, and Africans. While whites were the superior 'race' because of their mental capacity, Asians and in particular Blacks were inferior because of their 'natural' inclinations and biological attributes (Linné, 1735/1964). According to Linné, this division was based on a 'natural system' that he subsequently developed in his book *Systema Naturae* (1735/1964). Others, such as the German anthropologist Johan Friedrich

Blumenbach (1752–1840) and the French anthropologist and historian, Francois Bernier (1625–1688), had also contributed to the idea of the superiority of Europe and Europeans over the 'Others' based on the natural division of people into different 'races' and geographical locations.

As mentioned earlier, one of the important social scientists who contributed to the development of the idea of 'human races' was Montesquieu (1689–1755). He demonized Africans as nonhuman and legitimized slavery. He wrote in his classical work *The Spirit of the Law* (1989) that:

> Those concerned are black from head to toe, and they have such flat noses that it is almost impossible to feel sorry for them. One cannot get into one's mind that god, who is a very wise being, should have put a soul, above all a good soul, in a body that was entirely black. . . . It is impossible for us to assume that these people are men because if we assume they were men one would begin to believe that we ourselves were Christian. (p. 250)

Montesquieu claimed that the 'natural' differences of 'races' is the reason for different systems of governance. The natural inferiority of blacks and other 'races' comparative to Europeans makes them and their social and political systems culturally inferior.

Others, such as the Scottish philosopher David Hume (1711–1776), contested the direct effect of 'natural' reason on differences amongst human beings and amongst human societies. Hume believed that geographical differences exist but that there are rather moral differences that are the reason for 'national characters.' In his famous work *Of Natural Characters,* he claims that geographical differences create different moral conditions that mean people who live in the South indolent, for instance, are inferior to the rest of the species, and are incapable of higher attainments of the human mind.

The works of Hume and other social scientists (such as Montesquieu, Locke, Blumenbach, Bernier, and Herder) established the idea of 'race' and natural and moral differences between human 'races,' and laid the ground for the further development of ideas of the superiority of the 'west' over all other folks and nations. Many other social scientists tried to distinguish the European nations and 'races,' which started to be used interchangeably, from non-European nations and 'races' during the 19th century. From 1815 to 1870, social scientists made fundamental contributions to the development of the idea of 'race.' They introduced the popular notion that the origins of state and nation were rooted in the past of Franks and Gauls, Anglo-Saxons, and Celts (Hannaford, 1996). Among these are the German historian Berthold Niebuhr, the English John Mitchell Kemble, the French Hippolyte Adolphe Taine and Jules Michelet, and Count Arthur de Gobineau, who all justified a 'scientific' view of the interplay of the superiority of 'race' and 'nation' of Europeans over all other folks and nations. Various arguments from 'natural' and 'racial' properties, to social, political, religious, and cultural factors were used to justify the superiority of Europeans over 'other nations.' Hume, in his famous footnote to *Of National Characters,* characterizes the 'superiority of whites' to blacks and all other 'spices of men':

> I am apt to suspect the negroes and in general all other species of men (for there are four or five different kinds) to be naturally inferior to the whites. There never was a civilized nation of any other complexion than white, nor even any individual eminent either in action or speculation. No ingenuous manufactures amongst them, no arts, no sciences. On the other hand, the most rude and barbarous of the whites, such as the ancient Germans, the present Tartars, have still something eminent about them, in their valour, form of government, or some other particular. Such a uniform and constant difference could not happen, in so many countries and ages if nature had not made an original distinction between these breed of men. Not to mention our colonies, there are negroe slaves dispersed all over Europe, of whom none ever discovered any symptoms of ingenuity; though low people without education will start up amongst us and distinguish themselves in every profession. In Jamaica, indeed, they talk of one negroe as a man of parts and learning; but it is likely he is admired for slender accomplishments, like a parrot who speaks a few words plainly. (in Hannford, 1996, p. 238)

Hume combined 'national characters' with individual characteristics to explain the superiority of 'whites' over 'nonwhites.' This kind of thinking was dominant among Enlightenment philosophers and thinkers (Hannaford, 1996; Eze, 1997). The imperative of nature and 'race' determined the destiny of individuals and nations, since for Hume a nation is nothing but a collection of individuals.

Ideas of the 'superiority' of whites to nonwhites (or all other 'races') was not only limited to natural or 'racial' arguments, but the moral, religious, and cultural 'superiority' of white Europeans supported the racial argument and continued to be a dominating argument for colonialism and the imperial dominance of European powers.

CULTURAL DIFFERENCES

Essentialisation of 'differences' between Europeans and non-Europeans was an important part of the construction of the European identity, and of uniqueness, in the social sciences. Some of the 'scientific inventions' of the social sciences in the 18th and 19th centuries are still an inseparable part of the established 'scientific' assumptions of today. One of those assumptions is the 'myth of renaissance individualism' that many philosophers and thinkers of the Enlightenment used to create and essentialise differences between 'white' European colonial powers and the rest of human societies. Much of the contemporary literature in the social sciences is similarly based in discourses created during this period. For instance, the problems of integration of non-Europeans in Europe are mainly related to their 'cultural differences.' One of these essential cultural differences is non-European immigrants' 'collectivist' culture which is contrasted with European 'individualist culture' (see, e.g., Cohen, Howard & Nussbaum, 1999; Okin, 1999). European individualism is often constructed as a European invention with its roots in the Renaissance. One of the most famous social scientists that contributed to the myth of Renaissance individualism was the Swiss historian Jacob Burckhardt, who, in his celebrated book *Civilization of the Renaissance in Italy* (1860/2001), celebrated the birth of European identity and individualism in Italy. He claimed that in the Middle Ages, "man was conscious of himself only as a member of a race, people, party, family, or corporation" but that "it was only in Italy" that "man became a spiritual individual (*geistiges Individuum*), and recognized himself as such" (Martin, 2004, pp. 4–5).

Although the idea of the *uniqueness* of Europeans and the myth of European individualism and self is now increasingly challenged (Taylor, 1989; Martin, 2004), it is still one of the most enduring myths used as a means for differentiating between Europeans and non-Europeans (particularly non-European migrants who live in Europe).

The discourse of *difference* has been a very powerful means of inferiorization, otherization, and colonization of the 'Others' in European history. The 'differences' were not supposed to be solely cultural or biological, but a combination of the both. For example, Muslims and Jews were 'otherised' as 'racially,' religiously, and culturally inferior to Christians for a long time. The history of the racialisation of Africans and indigenous peoples are not separated from that of Muslims and Jews. Although the ideology and philosophy of the Enlightenment was very much engaged in the discussions on the 'racial' differences between white Europeans and nonwhite and non-European peoples, the biological differences was always escorted with arguments of moral, religious, and cultural differences. As mentioned earlier, Hume was very much concerned about the moral differences between European and non-Europeans. All other philosophers and thinkers of the Enlightenment concluded many moral and cultural differences based on nonwhites' and non-Europeans' 'racial' characteristics. One of the most known philosophers of the Enlightenment, Hegel argued (1997, pp. 114–115) the case as to why some "inferior" non-European cultures disappeared in confrontation with the "superior" European cultures:

> We do have information concerning America and its culture, especially as it had developed in Mexico and Peru, but only to the effect that it was a purely natural culture which had to perish as soon as the spirit approached it. America has always shown itself physically and spiritually

impotent, and it does so to this day. For after the Europeans had landed there, the natives were gradually destroyed by the breath of European activity. Even the animals have shown the same inferiority as the human beings. The fauna of America includes lions, tigers, and crocodiles, but although they are otherwise similar to their equivalents in the Old World, they are in every respect smaller, weaker, and less powerful. We are even assured that the animals are not as nourishing as the food which the Old World provides. And although America has huge herds of cattle, European beef is still regarded as delicacy. As for the human population, few descendants of the original inhabitants survive, for nearly seven million people have been wiped out. The natives of the West Indian islands have died out altogether. Indeed, the whole North American World has been destroyed and suppressed by the Europeans. The tribes of North America have in part disappeared, and in part withdrawn from contact with the Europeans. Their degeneration indicates that they do not have the strength to join the independent North American states. Culturally inferior nations such as these are gradually eroded through contact with more advanced nations which have gone through a more intensive cultural development. For the citizens of the independent states of North America are all of European descent and the original inhabitants were unable to amalgamate with them.

The assumption of cultural superiority of European over non-Europeans has a long tradition and has its roots in the crusades and the assumptions of the superiority of Christians to Muslims and Jews. The discourse of the Spanish and European Christians' 'clean blood' compared to Muslims' and Jews' blood, which was dominant in the Spanish inquisition, was not only a sign of cultural differences, but 'racial' differences. For instance, the term Moors at first referred to Arab Muslims, but over time Moors came overwhelmingly to be associated with blackness, as is evident from the 'blackmoors.' Religious and cultural prejudices against both blackness and Islam, each of which was seen to be the handiwork of the Devil, intensified the connection between them (Loomba, 1998).

Cultural inferiorization has been an effective means for the legitimisation of slavery and colonialism that still is in effect in various ways. One of the most enduring manifestations of cultural inferiorization is the discursive and 'scientific' construction of Orientalism.

THE LEGACY OF ORIENTALISM

Marking a distinction between a modern and rational 'west' in cultural contrast to a traditional, irrational, passionate, and exotic 'Orient' has been an important part of European historiography and sociology. This is not only deep rooted in Europe's intellectual traditions, discourses, and self-perception, but also has been institutionalised in many European countries, playing an influence at the level of daily life. The tradition of Orientalism is a very good illustration of the kind of cultural essentialism that dominates the western social sciences. As Peter van der Veer (1993) puts it, the Orientalist discourse that dominates, to an important extent, theories in the social sciences "reifies culture as an unchanging system of ideas and values that is not historically produced but that simply exist out there" (p. 25). Therefore, the established field of sociological research has mainly neglected to conduct research on the complexity, heterogeneity, and major socioeconomic and political transformations of what was called 'the Orient.' For instance, concepts such as an Islamic civil society, Islamic political ideologies, modern Islam, and democracy have been controversial and rejected by many classic and contemporary scholars of the social sciences. The Orient could not have its own existence. As Edward Said (1978) argues, the Orient was a product of the west and therefore it existed according to the wishes of the west.

The Orient has traditionally been considered to be the 'mirror image' of the 'west': western economy (capitalism), 'western values,' western social and political systems, western culture, western traditions, etc. The tradition of Orientalism could not be so established in Europe if there were no intercourses and relations between power centres and knowledge. As Foucault (1977) states: "Power and knowledge directly imply one another, that there is no power relation without the correlative constitution of a field of knowledge, nor any knowledge that does not presuppose and constitute at the same time power relations" (p. 27). Accordingly, power and knowledge have a relationship of mutual dependency. Therefore, the triumph of reason is the triumph of the alliance of power and knowledge. This alliance created whatever would be called the 'Others.' It could be the "insane," the "criminal," the "deviant" or the "Orient" (Turner, 1994, p. 21). Following this line of discussion, one can say that the western image of itself, the Occident, was directly and necessarily connected to the discursive construction of 'the inferior other,' the Orient. The creation of the paradigms of Orient and Occident is a manifestation of western dominance and colonial intentions and politics. Orientalism is a discourse constituted of a network of categories, tables, and concepts by which the Orient is simultaneously defined and controlled.

The role of colonialists and imperial politics has been especially decisive in the constitution of the western image of Islam and an analysis of 'Oriental societies' (Said, 1978; Norman, 1960; Southern, 1962).[2] As mentioned earlier, the interplay of knowledge production and the political and economic interests of colonial powers played a central role in the otherization of non-Europeans in the context of a project where Europe would aim to distinguish itself from the rest of the world. The 'difference' between 'Us' and 'them' was the focal point of the scientific and political discourses which acted as parts of the Europeanization process since the 17th and

18th centuries. Beside the biological thinking and the belief in the existence of 'different races,' the modern history of Europe witnesses the construction of one of the most lasting 'distinctions' between Europeans and the 'Others,' namely the dualism of Occident and Orient. The geographical thinking of the Enlightenment philosophy and science was the focal part of such a dualism. The Occident, as the place 'of us,' received geographical proportions in order to physically distinguish 'Us' from 'them.' One of the most effective distinctions, with deep historical roots, was the religious 'dualism' between Christianity and Islam. Although Orientalism came during the Middle Ages to include even the non-Muslim countries, such as China, it always has related to what was territorially called the 'Muslim World' and religiously Islam: The Occident was Christian and the Occident Muslim. Europe was supposed to begin at Greece's border against the Muslim Orient. Although Greece was for several centuries a part of the Muslim Ottoman Empire, a discursive geographical line was constructed with great sociocultural and political consequences for the whole world. All properties that came to identify Europe or the 'west,' such as science, philosophy, and democracy, were presented as having their roots in ancient Greece. The influences of nonwestern civilizations were intentionally ignored (Said, 1978; Bernal, 1991; King, 1999) in order to purify 'unique' Europe from the rest of the world. As King (1999) puts it:

> Histories of Western philosophy invariably begin with the Greeks and avoid the issue of African and Oriental influences upon ancient Greek thought. What is of particular interest is the absence of reference to the role played by Egyptian and Oriental 'mystery tradition' in the formulation of Greek philosophical ideas and approaches. (p. 29)

The universal was nothing more than the particular experiences of the western European understanding, and socioculturally embedded construction, of a European 'Us' against the 'Others.' As Grace Jantzen (1998) argues, the idea of a neutral, objective, and universal stance is a fiction. By this she means that there have never existed neutral views or beliefs separated from a particular place, because there are no views from nowhere and there are no views from everywhere. There are only views from somewhere, and the particular place will have an inescapable effect on what can be seen. If one assumes the contrary, then what is happening is that one is falsely universalising a particular perspective.

The foundation of Orientalism was laid by John of Damascus (d. 748), a Christian scholar who was a great friend of the Ummayad Caliph, Yazid. His declarations—that Islam was a pagan cult, the Ka'ba in Makkah an idol, and the prophet Muhammad an irreligious and licentious man—became the classical source of all Christian writings on Islam (Sardar, 1999). Christian western attitudes towards Muslim countries have historically been very negative and full of prejudices. Such a negative attitude formed one of the very crucial bases in mobilising European peasants for crusades. The crusades had, in turn, reinforced the dogmatic Orient/Occident categorization. Anti-Islamic attitudes and understandings have consequently become very much a part of western colonialism and self-perception.

The categorization of the two seemingly completely separated 'worlds'—namely, the modern Occidental world and the 'backward' and 'dangerous' 'Islamic world'—was an established understanding of many European politicians and 'even eminent scholars' of the field of Orientalism. An example of this is a history which is told by the Lebanese historian Marwan Buheiry about a symposium that took place in the early 20th century. The symposium was conducted in the fortnightly review *Questions diplomatiques et colonials* (May 15, 1901) to consider the prospects of Islam in the coming century. Speaking for many of the western scholars represented was the eminent Orientalist Baron Carra de Vaux, who wrote that the prospects for progressive change among Muslims were minimal. He wrote that Islam is today vanquished and its political decadence inevitable (Gordon, 1989). He concluded that to destroy any threat from Pan-Islamism one need only play Muslims against one another by encouraging Muslim heresies and the Sufi Orders against the mainstream, and to use nationalism to divide the various Muslim ethnic groups from one another (Gordon, 1989).

Such as Eurocentric understandings of 'progress' and modernity were established in the polity of Europe and even among scientific scholars. The west was the model and the Orient was, and is, reduced to 'the mirror image of the west' and so is defined and disfigured (al-Azmeh, 1981). The discursive construction of the 'Muslim world' as the 'mirror image of the west,' which encapsulates huge number of people, groups and nations under a homogenising umbrella, ignored the complexity of, and differences between, different Muslim countries. Orientalism as an ideology and social scientific legacy is not only homogenising a huge part of the world as 'the Orient' but also is homogenising the Occident, the west, as the counterpart and the mirror image of the 'Orient' or the 'Muslim world.' The two categories are interdependent and need each other for their existence, as do the two discursive categories of 'west and the rest.'

In their mainstream traditions, mainstream 'western' social sciences are Eurocentric and, in many cases, they have reinforced the structural/institutional discrimination against the 'Others' in Europe and elsewhere. Such discrimination still seems to exist in a mutual relationship between the academic, political, and economic powers structures of many 'western' countries. The legacies of colonialism and imperialism that have created what is called a postcolonial order are still influencing social sciences and their privilege of formulating 'scientific questions' and providing 'scientific answers.' In other words, mainstream social sciences that are functioning in close connection to other power centres are a part of the otherization of nonwestern people, groups and nations. This is not only a matter of the European history of the past.

Contemporary scholars, such as Anthony Giddens, Ralf Dahrendorf, Samuel Huntington, and Bernard Lewis, continues in the same foot steps of Orientalists and reinforces the otherization of Muslims both in the world generally and in European and extended European countries specifically. Such scholars, who are the inheritors of the mainstream social sciences, have gained many privileges because of their close connection with the 'western' political powers, their engagement in the otherization of Muslims and other immigrant groups, and, consequently, in the legitimization of 'western' powers' antiimmigrant and anti-Muslim actions in 'western' countries and elsewhere in the world.

Giddens, as a prominent social scientist and an ideologist of the English Labour Party, has been highly engaged in legitimising and even launching the government's policies of being 'tough on immigration' and establishing new discriminatory 'antiterrorist laws.' He wrote in 2002 that:

> Tony Blair's celebrated intention to be tough on crime and tough on the causes of crime was a major element of New Labour's rise to prominence. It recognises that people's anxieties about crime are real and must be responded to. It focuses on concerns that were previously an open field for the right. Social democrats elsewhere need to do likewise if they are to sustain or recover wide public support. Much the same applies to the issue of immigration, perhaps the most testing of all for left-of-centre parties. It is no use merely proclaiming that EU countries need immigrants (although they do). Policies have to be developed which are "tough on immigration, but tough on the causes of hostility to immigrants. (*Guardian*, May 3, 2002)

By relating criminality to immigrants, Giddens recommended social democrats in Europe enter a political field that was previously open for the right. This means that Giddens believes that if the English Labour government (and social democrats in other European countries) adopt the right's policies in "getting tough on immigration," they will manage to "rise to prominence" (*Guardian*, 2002). Elsewhere, he continues to be an important ally of the English government, and to otherize immigrants and in particular Muslims. He recently supported the Prime Minister Gordon Brown's anti-terrorist laws because of the risk that terrorism creates and he wants to have "Liberty in balance" (*Guardian*, July 26, 2007).

Dahrendorf, who is a member of the British parliament, follows the same line as Giddens and wants to be tougher on terrorism and defend 'our western values.' Huntington continues to provide arguments for the existence of two major civilizations, namely the 'western' and the 'Islamic' ones, and claims there is a 'clash' between the two civilizations. Similarly, Lewis claims essential differences between Muslims and the 'west.' He means that something in Muslim countries (except Turkey) 'went wrong' in their modernization process that gave place to Islamists and 'fundamentalists' (Lewis, 2002) Lewis' prophetical claim came before the recent Turkish election that saw the Islamist party of Prime Minister Receb Erdogan rise to power; this election also paved the way for the presidency of another Islamist, Abdullah Gul, in a republic prised by Lewis as secular and non-Islamist.

THE MODERN 'WE' AND THE TRADITIONAL 'THEM'

Social theory has a long tradition of the otherization of non-European, non western groups and nations. The otherization tradition of European modernism created the tradition of dualisms, such as modern/traditional, Occident/Orient, and west and the rest. Both the classics of the social sciences since the 17th century and their post-WWII inheritors have created a theory and understanding of modernization as a straightforward line of development from 'primitive' to modern societies. However, modernization theory had internal inconsistencies. The established Weberian tradition of the *uniqueness* of European modernization within European social theory did not leave any place for different modernization processes. The modern was considered as a single development which could only take place in Europe. European experience was theoretically formulated by social scientists to be the only valid modernization based on prerequisites, such as renaissance, industrialism, and the Enlightenment. Even Christianity was presented as a religion completely separate to other religions (e.g., Islam and Hinduism) and one of the major reasons for the development of capitalism and reason in Europe.[3]

Even Marxist social theory did not free itself from the Eurocentric understanding of modernization and believed in a single, European modernity as universal. Marx and his companion Engels (1973) saw the European bourgeoisie as the source for development in the world and wrote:

> The bourgeoisie, by rapid improvement of all instruments of production, by the immensely facilitated means of communication, draws all, even the most barbarian nations into civilization. The cheap prices of its commodities are the heavy artillery with which it batters down all Chinese walls, with which it forces the barbarians' intensely obstinate hatred of foreigners to capitulate. It compels all nations, on pain of extinction, to adopt the bourgeois mode of production; it compels them to introduce what it calls civilization into their midst, i.e., to become bourgeois themselves. In one word it creates a word after its own image. (p. 71)

The brutality of the capitalist system for cosmopolitan expansion lies, according to Marx, in the "cheap prices of its commodities" which "draws all, even the most barbarian nations into civilization" (Marx & Engels, 1973, p. 71). What he did not mention is the military colonization of what he called "barbarian nations," in which was forced on them an unjust sys-tem of dependency, making them a backyard of western development.

Marx and Marxists have also helped to spread and establish the Euro-centric vision of the linear evolution of all societies, through which the 'primitive' and 'less developed' models—such as the 'Asiatic production model' or feudalism—must leave the scene for the more developed mod-ern capitalist system. The history of the modernization of many nonwest-ern countries, however, particularly in Muslim countries, followed neither Marx's 'structural transformation' model nor Hegel's 'historical reason.' In other words, neither the army of cheap commodities nor the coloniza-tion of such countries helped to create modern societies in accordance with modern western blueprints. It rather helped to create highly disintegrated and segmented societies with huge socioeconomic, cultural, and political problems and controversies (Kamali, 2006). This interpretation, which reinforced the *uniqueness* arguments of many social scientists, went so far that Marx and Engels, as well as many other European social scientists, defended colonialism as a 'progressive' power of change and 'the progress of civilization' (Feuer, 1971; Turner, 1974, 1978).

Not only the critical theory of Marxism, but also other less revolutionary theories, such as those of Durkheim and Weber, have influenced our judge-ment of other 'less developed' or 'traditional' societies. The European model of development, if there is such a homogenous model, was conceived to be the universal model for development. Durkheim, in his classical work *The Division of Labor in Society,* wrote that "it is a law of history that mechani-cal solidarity, which at first is isolated, or almost so, should progressively lose ground, and organic solidarity gradually become preponderant" (1984, p. 126). The belief in evolutionary transformations from 'lower' to 'higher' societies, from 'primitive' and less developed to developed societies, is one of the most enduring 'meta narratives' of social theory. It is generally held by many social scientists, such as Giddens, Dahrandorf, Beck, and Haber-mas, that modernity as a socioeconomic and cultural project has been a European, and later a western, undertaking. This territorial and geographic thinking, which is a legacy of the Enlightenment, is highly Eurocentric and witnesses the ignorance of the multiple modern transformations in the world. Modernity has been purified from its non-European influences and given a European essence. The fact that modernity has no single master process (Hall, Held, & McGrew, 1992) has no place in a theoretical project in which even the economic superiority of Europe, namely the capitalist system, has been related to the "religious superiority" of Europeans (p. 2). Bernard Yack (1997) calls this understanding of modernity, as a coherent and integrated whole, "fetishism of modernity" (p. 7).

The hegemonic understanding that modernity is a singular universal process that started in Europe and later spread all over the world is limited and Eurocentric. The 'genesis-thinking', which has been widespread in the field of historical sociology, is one of the main reasons behind this understanding of modernity as homogenous and purely European. Paradoxically, such a tradition ignores the history of modernity in its global context and in particular sociocultural conditions. It denies that modernity is plural and has emerged in numerous sociocultural forms (see Kaya, 2004; Taylor, 1999; Eisenstadt, 2003; Kamali; 2006).

The idea of modernity as a single phenomenon and the idealization of modernity have been, and still are, a part of the creation of established theoretical dualisms in the social sciences. An example of this is the modern/traditional dualism, based on Durkheimian structural differentiation theory, in which transformations are conceptualised as a single movement from, for instance, simple to complex, tradition to modern, community to society, sacred to secular, and folk/rural to urban (Kamali, 2006). In addition, modernity is presented as a peaceful process of rationality, renewal and development. However, in the face of modern history, many social scientists (even modernity's sincere defenders such as Giddens) accepted recently that modernization or Europeanization/westernization of the world have had a brutal history. Presenting modernity as a peaceful development has been a part of Europeans' self perception as good and human 'Vi,' in contrast to a nonmodern, backward, and traditional 'Them.' The fact is that colonial, national, and World Wars, have been an inseparable part of modernity. Giddens stresses the industrialization of military power as one of the four most important properties of modernity (Giddens, 1990). He writes in one of his earlier works, *The Nation-State and Violence,* that the peace of Westphalia which came about between European powers as a result of the pair of treaties, the Treaty of Münster and the Treaty of Osnabrük (signed on October 24 and May 15 of 1648), as well as the Treaty of the Pyrenees (signed in 1659 between France and Spain), ended the 30 Years' War and the 80 Years' War between warfare countries such as the Holy Roman Empire, Habsburg, Germany, Spain, France, and Sweden.

This was the beginning of the major European colonial expansion in the world that resulted in the expansion of European wealth, and backwardness and many other catastrophes for other parts of the world. As McNeill (1983) puts it:

> [T]he result was systematic expansion—whether in India, Siberia, or the Americas. Frontier expansion in turn sustained an expanding trade network, enhanced taxable wealth in Europe, and made support of the armed establishments less onerous than would otherwise have been the case. Europe, in short, launched itself on a self-reinforcing cycle in which its military organisation sustained, and was sustained by, economic and political expansion at the expense of other peoples and politics of the earth. (p. 143)

The European imperialist expansion was at the same time, "catastrophic to Asians, Africans, and the peoples of Oceania" (McNeill, 1983, p. 143). The colonial wars and occupations were the major source of military expansions and innovations (c.f., Giddens, 1987, p. 223). The British colonial armies, for example, were involved in 50 major colonial wars between 1803 and 1901 (Giddens, 1987). Any resistance to colonialism was considered by the major European colonial powers as an act of enmity to the civilized European nation state. Industrialization of mass killing or industrialization of warfare was both the means and consequence of the expansion of European capitalism. Hans Joas reasonably argues that "wars and civil wars have shaped modernity as we know it in its innermost core" (Joas, 1999, p. 466).

In the colonial wars the already existing European scientific racism legitimized colonial exploitation, slavery, and other forms of racism in the colonies. Both wars and racism are inseparable from modernity. Inferiorization and marginalization of 'western' modernity's 'Others' are constitutive parts of the construction of 'western' identities (Rattansi, 1994).

2 Institutional Otherization, Migration, and Racism in Europe

INTRODUCTION

Recent attitude surveys show that European societies—notwithstanding the increasing attention of the European Union to antiracist issues—exhibit high levels of xenophobia and racism, a desire to limit immigration, and a readiness to exclude foreigners from certain social arenas of European societies (e.g., EUMC, 2001; Hargreaves & Leaman, 1995; Wrench & Solomos, 1993). Furthermore, there is a persistent threat that xenophobic sociopolitical movements will arise and establish themselves, introducing a 'racist agenda,' pressuring established parties to shift their position, and blocking or reversing institutional realignment designed to favour pluralism, equality, and justice. Discrimination on the basis of ethnic, religious, or immigrant status is a persistent and serious human rights violation affecting all of Europe. However, to admit that discrimination is a widespread and serious problem has been, and seems to continue to be, difficult for most European member states; attempts at addressing discrimination have been largely 'symbolic' and rhetorical.

Europe based its antiracist, antidiscrimination policies to a large extent on antinazi legislation adopted after WWII, and in the public condemnation of racism in other parts of the world such as South Africa (between 1948 and 1991) and the United States. There are also many official proclamations and demonstrations concerning openly 'racist' attacks within Europe. The European Council in Tampere, on October 15 and 16, 1999, invited the Commission to come forward as soon as possible with proposals implementing Article 13 of the EC Treaty with regard to the fight against racism and xenophobia. The Employment Guidelines 2000 agreed by the European Council in Helsinki, December 1999, stress the need to foster conditions for a socially inclusive labour market by formulating policies aimed at combating discrimination against, for instance, ethnic minorities. Following the indications of article 13a, community action program was approved in November 2000 to combat discrimination (Council Decision, 2000/750/EC). With antiracist legislation, the European Union seeks to halt "public incitement to discrimination, violence or racial hatred in respect of a group of persons or a member of such a group defined by reference to colour, race, religion or national or ethnic origin" (See 96/443/ JHA: Joint Action adopted by the Council on the basis of Article K.3 of the Treaty on European Union, concerning action to combat racism and xenophobia [July 15, 1996]).

Antidiscrimination legislation was, however, adopted more to fulfill the requirements of international conventions rather than to meet a recognised need within member states. Even the relatively modern antidiscrimination laws of the Netherlands and Sweden were not adopted until the 1990s and as a result of foreign pressures. Racism and discrimination is still mainly addressed by many European member states as a matter of individual attitudes and prejudices. Many groups of ethnicity other than 'white' and of religions other than Christianity are still subjected to discriminatory and racist treatment in many arenas of European societies. Discrimination and racism have been all the more 'acceptable' since mainstream society has done little or nothing about discrimination as a *structural and institutional* problem of Europe. The realisation that the person discriminated against is not 'the problem,' but the discriminator and his or her actions, as well as the 'normal' functions of many established institutions, has been ignored. Therefore, misguided 'integration' programs were many times introduced that ironically provided some of the fuel for xenophobic tendencies and reinforced discrimination and racism. Immigrants have been considered to be the focus of such integration policies and thus the 'object' of change. The structural and institutional properties of European societies, and their role in discriminating against immigrants and minorities and in hindering them from becoming equal citizens, have not received enough attention.

Numerous scientific studies and reports suggest the pervasiveness of the discrimination problem, the different expressions and forms it takes, and the harm it brings to many groups and individuals, from citizens of European member states to immigrants with irregular status in relation to deportation. Although there are different forms of discrimination and racism, there are some common characteristics. These are based on real or imagined 'differences' of the 'Others' from 'Us,' such as their colour of skin, their nationality, their religion, or their culture. The perpetrators seem to come from a wide range of backgrounds, not simply from the extreme political fringes of Europe, and include those in established positions with institutionalised power and influence—in some cases, those trusted to administer justice fairly and equally and to protect citizens from inhuman and discriminatory treatment.

The general failure to recognize 'racism' and discrimination as a broader European problem with structural and institutional dimensions is one of the most important factors behind the pervasive nature of racism and discrimination in Europe. The focus on racism as an American phenomenon fostered the idea that racism and discrimination were not 'real' European problems. In Europe, the problem was at worst limited to a few xenophobic, right wing extremists. The European focus has been mainly on a minority of 'skinheads' and 'thugs' rather than on institutional racism and the racism of elites (Van Dijk, 2000). This is to ignore the historical significance of racism against the 'Others' and the role of scientific and institutional 'Otherization' and inferiorization of non-European people. As discussed in Chapter 1 of this book, xenophobia and racism are integral parts of European history and society. The most extreme and violent racist thinking of Europe reached its culmination in Nazi Germany, but this was not isolated in time or space to Hitler's rise and fall. Anti-Muslims and anti-Semite attitudes and actions, for example, have both deep and broad European roots. This can be traced back to European religious self-identification as Christian white Europeans against Muslims and Jews, starting with the Crusades and culminating in the Spanish Inquisition in the late 15th century.

The colonial history of Europe has reinforced 'racial thinking' in Europe. For a couple of hundred years, an attitude of 'racial,' intellectual, and cultural superiority (subtle and not so subtle) developed in Europe concerning the rest of the world. While the colonies were more or less lost after WWII, the attitude of superiority seems to have remained to some extent as part of the national psyche in many countries. The postcolonial world did not free itself from 'racial thinking' and ethnic/racial inequalities. The postcolonial order of the world includes the superiority of the European (and extended European nations) to non-Europeans from former European colonies. Europe has avoided seriously looking at its own racist, xenophobic and often brutal histories. One of the most important consequences of such ignorance is the reproduction of racism and discrimination against European citizens with immigrant or minority background, as well as immigrants and refugees. The question should not be focused on whether or not there is 'racial' discrimination in Europe, because there is a substantial body of research confirming the existence of racism and discrimination in Europe. Research programs should rather concentrate on the *reproduction mechanisms* of racism and discrimination. In this respect, the role of institutionalised power and domination in each society in the reproduction of 'racial' discrimination is an important research area that should be properly addressed.

POWER AND INSTITUTIONALISED RACISM AND DISCRIMINATION

As has been argued already, the social sciences have a long tradition in the 'Otherization' of non-European peoples. This tradition has influenced not only individual attitudes about the 'Others' but also has become an inseparable part of European societies' structural and institutional arrangements. It also created a 'racialised discourse' by which non-Europeans are referred to as 'a problem,' 'criminal,' 'antiwestern,' and so forth As Goldberg (1993) puts it:

> The underlying point here is that racialised discourse does not consist simply in descriptive representations of others. It includes a set of hypothetical premises about human kinds (e.g., the 'great chain of being,' classificatory hierarchies, etc.) and about the differences between them (both mental and physical). It involves a class of ethical choices (e.g., domination and subjugation, entitlement and restriction, disrespect and abuse). And incorporates a set of institutional regulations, directions, and pedagogic models (e.g., apartheid, separate development, educational institutions, choice of educational and bureaucratic language, etc.). (p. 47)

In much of the literature on the inferiorization of the 'Others,' colonialism and imperialism have played central roles (Mannoni, 1964; Memmi, 1969; Solomos & Back, 1996). War has been an integrated and constitutive part of European modernization and development. Spencer writes that already in 1878: "Unquestionably, that integration of societies effected by war, has been a needful preliminary to industrial development, and consequently to developments of other kinds—Science, the Fine Arts, &etc." (p. 196)

As a gentle defender of European modernism, Spencer does not recognize the importance of colonial wars and occupations, as well as the role of slavery, for modern capitalist development in Europe. Eric Williams in his classical work, *Capitalism and Slavery* (1944), examines the role of the slave trade for the huge accumulation of capital which was used in further investments and capitalist developments in Britain and France. Others, such as Smith (2006), show that from the mid-17th century to the 1830s, upper class families in England successfully created an extensive business empire based on slavery in the West Indies. The new capitalist class created a powerful network of the slave trade in England, North America, Africa, and Europe. Smith examines how slavery formed this British Atlantic World and the role of Yorkshire aristocratic families. He shows how the plantation-owning Lascelles used slavery to create a commercial and cultural empire. Smith argues that it was not only slave traders in the New World who made a fortune out of the system of slave trade, but also English families (such as the Lescelles, raising themselves first to supermerchant status and then to aristocratic preeminence), who did the same. Slavery and colonial wars have been inseparable parts of capitalist developments in the 'west' (Loomba, 1998; Mohanty, 2003; Wilson, 1996; Cooper, 1977, 1996; Wallerstein, 2006; Miles, 1987, 1989).

Colonialism, slavery and racism can not be properly addressed and analyzed without including the theoretical and empirical aspects of power and domination (Gilroy, 1987; Balibar & Wallerstein, 1991; Fredrickson, 2000; La Blance, 2003; Bhattacharyya, 2001; Wilson, 1973; De Los Reyes & Kamali, 2005; Kamali, 2005). A scientific racism could hardly dominate the social sciences of the 18th and 19th centuries without colonialist and imperialist wars and occupations. Racial and cultural 'Otherization' were necessary elements in the creation of a new world system which favoured capitalist and modern European development. Power and domination, then, plays a central role in the reproduction of racism as an important instrument in preserving powerful, and often 'white,' peoples' privileges; it is not only a question of the prejudices and behavioural problems of some individuals, but the structural and institutional properties of modern 'western' countries. Europe's modern history cannot remain ignorant of the role that 'racial' discrimination played, and still plays, in the reproduction of the superordination of 'whites' over the 'Others' and the preservation of their privileges. (Racial discrimination is the unequal treatment of 'Otherised' and inferiorised individuals or groups on the basis of some, usually categorical, attributes, such as 'race,' ethnicity, culture, or religion.)

It is not unusual to relate racial discrimination to individual attitudes and prejudices. Racial discrimination is, however, a result of power relations and structural and institutional arrangements in a society. Although prejudices against the 'Others' arise in the form of individual attitudes, when their holders get access to power and gain sources of influence, they become discriminatory. They are also a part of established racialised discourses (Van Dijk, 1997, 1993; Goldberg, 1993). Importantly, racial discrimination is based on racism that is more than just prejudice and discrimination together. Racism is socially constructed reality crystallised in a society's structural and institutional arrangements. It is a part of the reproduction of powerful groups' privileges by means of objective, differential and unequal treatment of inferiorised groups. It also results in an ideology of supremacy which justifies inequalities between 'Us' and 'Them' by ascribing inferior and negative meanings to the perceived biological or cultural differences of the 'Others.' Racism in this sense is not 'deviant' behaviour, or reflective of the psychological 'abnormalities' of some individuals or groups. Racism is 'rational' and a property of structural and institutional arrangements of a society. It goes beyond prejudices and personal biases, and structures—politically, economically, and culturally—the power positions and privileges of 'majority society' groups (see below for a discussion of the term 'majority society').

In the wake of the European colonial wars and occupations which have restructured the world in accordance with the needs and privileges of colonial powers, European 'white superiority' has become an inseparable part of the reproduction of privileges. Differences between the powerful 'Us' and powerless 'Them,' based on skin and hair colour and other physical features, language, religion, ethnicity, or accent, have become important means of exclusion and discrimination. The 'differences' of the 'Others' are given negative values and meanings that then legitimize the treatment of them as inferior to oneself or ones group. Structural/institutional discrimination cannot be reproduced without the discriminatory groups' frequent access to institutionalised power and influence.

The concept of *domination* is central for the definition of structural/institutional discrimination. The term *dominant* refers to groups who have most of the power and control the reproduction of the power structure in a society. Therefore, some scholars, such as Mills (1997, 1998), suggest the term 'white supremacy' be taken as a theoretical object in its own right, as it points to how racism is an integral part of global domination and national power structures.

The dominance and supremacy of the majority society cannot be understood without reference to the power structure of the society. The term 'majority society' is not only related to the numbers of a dominant group, but also, and in some cases only, to the *supreme position* of a dominant group in the power structure of a society. This is not more complicated than to recall a simple sociological and political truth—not exactly unknown to the western sociopolitical tradition—that power relations can survive the formal dismantling of their more overt supports (Mills, 2003). For instance, whites in South Africa were mathematically in the minority position but substantially controlled almost all power structures of the society and therefore could be called 'majority society.' The centrality of the power relations in a society constitutes the basis for what used to be called 'race relations,' in which there is a majority society which uses its control over power structures and reproduces a differentiated system of domination of one or many ethnic group/s over 'the Other.' This creates an inferiorization process in which 'Others' are sociopolitically produced and reproduced In such a process the dominant group's power position relies also on its ability to *define* 'the Other' as inferior. This is what Memmi (2002) calls the majority group's 'act of definition' that becomes the legitimation of the dominance relation.

INDIVIDUAL VERSUS INSTITUTIONAL DISCRIMINATION

Although the intentionality of acts of discrimination has been a criterion of separation between individual and institutional discrimination (intentional) on the one hand, and structural discrimination (unintentional) on the other, there are many difficulties engaged in such a theoretical approach. Marxist theory, for instance, maintains that even the structural discrimination engaged in class society is intentional and based on a conscious organisation of capitalism. This is also the case with the appearance of xenophobic populist parties on the political scene of many European countries. These parties are engaged in the institutionalisation of discrimination and are intentionally reinforcing discriminatory structures—such as laws—against Muslims and other immigrants and minorities.

Accordingly, the interwoven relationship between structural and institutional discrimination makes the separation of the two forms of discrimination from each other almost impossible. That is why some scholars do not make any substantial differentiations between structural and institutional discrimination (see, e.g., Winant, 2000). We can therefore define structural and institutional discrimination as systemic acts of inferiorization and the 'Otherization' of some ethnic, religious, and/or immigrant groups by the majority society institutions. This kind of discrimination has a history and is institutionalised in the everyday life of a society, helping to maintain the superior position and privileges of the majority society.

The laws, norms, and routines of societies, irrespective of intent, discriminate the 'Others' in many European countries today. To be engaged in discussion of intentionality is essentially meaningless, and, in many cases, counterproductive, in research on structural/institutional discrimination. In a recent European study, individuals from a majority society frequently said that "we have no intention of discriminating against people because of their religion, ethnicity, or skin colour." These are people in positions of power who are, in many cases, the agents of the reproduction of the institutions and the actors of systemic discrimination in society. In other words, their discriminatory behaviours are embedded in important social organisations and institutions, such as companies and schools.

The actual social values and enduring political and economic structures continue to reflect the history of white domination (Crenshaw, 1998). The reproduction of the power and privilege of the majority group is not limited to legal codes and organisational arrangements. It is, as Frances Lee Ansley (1989) suggests, through:

> a political, economic, and cultural system in which whites overwhelmingly control power and material resources, conscious and unconscious ideas of white superiority and entitlement are widespread, and relations of white dominance and nonwhite subordination are daily reenacted across a broad array of institutions and social settings. (p. 1024)

The European roots of modern racism, which go back to the colonial subordination of many non-European nonwhite groups of the world, laid the most important foundation for white European supremacy. Insofar as the modern world has been foundationally shaped by European colonialism, white supremacy could be seen as transnational and global, the historic domination of white Europe over nonwhite non-Europe, and of white settlers over nonwhite slaves and indigenous peoples, making Europeans 'the lords of human kind' (Kiernan, 1981; Cocker, 1998). Europeans thought of themselves as the supreme race of the world as late as the first half of the 20th century. And these were not only German Nazis or Italian Fascists who believed in such a theory, but also the 'civilised free nations' such as the colonial powers, England and France. An illustration of the fact is that a Japanese proposal to include "the equality of races" in the League of Nations' Covenant at the Versailles Peace Conference in 1919 was formally defeated (Furedi, 1998, pp. 42–45). Goldberg (1993) calls this the 'racist culture' of Europe.

Although racism has global characteristics, we are witnessing the development of what one can call a 'European Racism' that is likely to have a major impact on the political and social configuration of European societies over the next decades (Balibar, 1991). The recent developments in the European Union, and the organised attempts to create a European identity, have been one of the reasons for the systemic revitalisation of 'Otherization' in the European Union. The construction of a 'European identity' inevitably involves a pattern of the exclusion of the 'Other,' whether they be 'immigrants, 'foreigners' or 'blacks' (Miles, 1993; Bovenkerk et al., 1990; Wrench & Solomos, 1993). Racism and discrimination of immigrants as the 'Other' takes different forms in the new European environment. The political success of new right wing racist parties, their impact on the established parties' political programs (as well as on the public debate), and the complexity of the covert structural/institutional discrimination forces us, as Robert Miles suggests, to move beyond descriptive accounts of racism to an *explanation* of the forms that racism actually takes in contemporary European societies (Miles, 1993).

The colonial history of many European countries, directly or indirectly, influences their current immigration policies and the established sociocognitive imaginations of the 'Others.' In other words, the majority societies' perceptions of the 'Other' are highly influenced by their colonial past that find its counterpart in the current internal colonialism in the metropolis cities of many European countries. The establishment of segregated areas creates 'racial spaces' (Pred, 2000) that can be observed in the major cities of Europe, such as London, Rome, Paris, Berlin, Vienna, Amsterdam, and Stockholm. It seems that the former colonies have moved into the centres. This entails an established 'pollution' perspective in many European cities on the segregated and poor areas where many immigrants live (Goldberg, 1993). The people living in those areas nowadays have an immigrant background and are poor. This makes them vulnerable to the established structural/institutional arrangements of society.

'XENO-OTHERISM' AND INSTITUTIONAL DISCRIMINATION

Human history is dominated by descriptions of wars and confrontations. The existence and the threat of the enemies of 'Us' has been an inseparable and constitutive part of the social construction of 'Us.' The family, the clan, the group, the empire, and the nation to which we have developed a sense of belonging and identification has contributed to the construction of different levels of a sociopolitical 'Us.' However, the intensity of the levels of identity formation and conceptualisations of 'Us' has varied in various historical socioeconomic and political formations. For instance, although the sense of belonging to an empire or a civilisation was more or less shared by people living within the boundaries of those empires and civilisations, the sense of belonging to a *nation* was much more developed during the formation of modern national states. The nation states' political programs of nation-building or 'nationalisation of the nation' laid the ground for the development of national sentiments which gradually was institutionalised within the political borders of *a country*.

The assumption of the homogeneity of modernity, and the belief in a singular modern project, has dominated modern social theory for more than two centuries. Although the later theory of multiple modernities rejects the validity of the tradition of a singular modernity in the social sciences, one cannot simply deny some common features of multiple modernities (Eisenstadt, 2002; Kamali, 2006). One of these features is the homogenisation of the nation as *a* political and *a* cultural entity, recognizable from other nations and other socioeconomic, cultural, and political formations. The family, the clan, and other primordial groupings were transformed to 'the nation' and the home to 'the homeland.' These sociopolitical and cultural projects of different types of modernities created a cultural stream, called by some researchers, such as Philip Lawrence (1997), 'the modern culture.' Lawrence points out that the modern culture is, at its very basis, constituted by 'Otherism,' racism, and narcissism. Lawrence's assumption does not reveal anything new, but explicitly interrelates seemingly different parts of the same process.

Thus, we can say that the definition and constitution of the nation is always related to the creation of 'Others.' This may be one of the first findings of those social sciences dealing with the uprising of modern institutions and modern changes. 'Otherism' has several dimensions (such as racism, sexism, and homophobia, amongst others), but for the purpose of this book, the form of 'Otherism' related to racist and exclusionary practices against immigrants and minority groups is of central importance. The concept of 'Xeno-otherism' may be legitimate in this context. 'Xeno-otherism' entails negative stereotyping, stigmatising, discriminating, and exclusionary practices with respect to immigrant and minority groups, who are differentiated and categorised based on collective traits such as those of religion, ethnicity, and colour of skin or hair. 'Xeno-otherism' is a concept which can avoid the problems of the dualism of 'institutional' and 'attitudinal,' or individual, racism. While the concept of 'attitudinal' racism relates discriminatory practices of the 'Others' to individual attitudes, 'institutional' racism risks ignoring the intended consequences of institutionally sanctioned individual acts, such as those of 'gatekeepers.' To maintain that structural or/and institutional racism is truly unintentional and does not involve individual attitudes would undermine the conception of racism as an ideological construction and make it synonymous with the statistical inequality and apparent social inefficiency of any group with a sense of racial or ethnic identity, whatever the actual causes of its situation might be (Fredrickson, 2000, p. 80). The concept of 'Xeno-otherism' takes us beyond the duality of intended/unintended or conscious/unconscious discriminatory action. As Fredrickson (2002, p. 82) puts it: "We must be careful to avoid giving credence to the view that racism is an essential or primordial human response to diversity, something that inevitably takes place when groups that we would define as racially different come into contact." He argues that negative stereotyping of the 'Other,' or the alien, may be an inescapable component of identity and boundary maintenance for a group. But *who* the outsiders are, and how much or in what ways they are despised and mistreated, is the product of history, not basic human instincts (Fredrickson, 2002).

'Xeno-otherism' must be understood also in terms of (a) sociocognitive structures (classification schemes, stereotypes, prejudices, beliefs, and so on), (b) institutional arrangements and power structures, and (c) interaction processes in which inequalities among groups are related to biological and cultural factors attributed to those who are defined as a different 'ethnicity,' 'culture,' 'race,' or nation (cf., Essed, 1991, pp. 43–44). The sociocognitive dimension refers to the shared social cognitions of groups, and involves the opinions, attitudes, ideologies, norms and values that constitute racist stereotypes and prejudices, and that underlie racist social practices, including discourses (Van Dijk, 2000). Such an approach tries to investigate stereotypes about, and prejudices against, immigrants or minorities. These are the basis of judgements and actions that discriminate against the 'Other.'

But the sociocognitive approach to racism and xenophobia must not be reduced to the psychological sources of stereotypes and prejudices of the 'Others' but should be put in a broader context of social institutions and the structural properties of a society in a given time. The sociocognitive structure is not static but both influences the institutional arrangements of a society and is itself influenced and reproduced by them. In other words, the normal and daily actions of influential individuals in various institutions and organisations (such as schools, courts, police, and companies), coupled with established norms, patterns, rules, and laws, reproduces the 'otherness' of the 'Other.'

'Xeno-otherism' must also be considered in relation to the power structures of a society and its institutional arrangements, and should be analyzed and understood in terms of power relations and domination. The fact that the dominant group, or more precisely its elite, has access to, or control over, scarce resources—such as residence, nationality, jobs, housing, education, knowledge, health, and capital—must be considered (Van Dijk, 2000). 'Xeno-otherism' is therefore an inseparable part of the social structure, based on a system of inequality that perpetuates the domination of the dominant majority society (typically white Europeans) over others (non-Europeans, especially from economically poorer countries). The social structure of 'Xeno-otherism' comprises a society's institutions, organisations, groups and individuals. This means that the study of 'Xeno-otherism' must include civil society, state, and the polity of a society, as well as the social actors and individuals acting in a society and within the boundaries of its institutions and dominant discourses.

'Xeno-otherism' is also institutionalised in social institutions, such as the labour market, educational system, judiciary, and housing. However, Xeno-otherism takes different forms and has various degrees of intensity in different countries and in different historical moments. It is bound by each country's historical developments, institutional arrangements, and political traditions. This influences the different ways in which discrimination appears and how the mechanisms of discrimination work in each country, although there are many common properties.

The following model is an attempt to illustrate the sociopolitical actors and agencies engaged in the reproduction of inferior 'Others' and, simultaneously, the reproduction of a superior 'Us.'

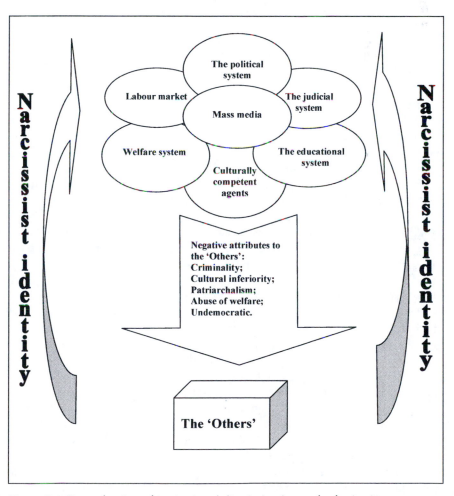

Figure 2.1 Reproduction of institutional discrimination and otherisation

The political system in almost all nation states is influenced by historical challenges and political struggles over the form and nature of state organisation and its area of influence. Nation states not only control a territory, but also have developed very effective means of surveillance (Giddens, 1990). One of the major tasks of nation states concerns the nationalisation of the nation as a homogeneous group separated from other nations. As Balibar (2002, p. 220) puts it: "a social formation only reproduces itself as a nation to the extent that, through a network of apparatus and daily practices, the individual is instituted as *homo nationalis* from cradle to grave." There has been a tendency in the social sciences to consider 'belonging to a nation' as pertaining to individuals' primordial properties, as well as providing a solid ground for collective identity. Among the 'classics,' Max Weber, is probably the most clear about the distinction between the nation and the state. For him the nation is concerned with the realm of *Kultur,* while the state is concerned with the realm of power (Beetham, 1985). The nation was therefore considered as a natural entity that has *a* culture and *a* history. Other social scientists claimed that nations are "natural entities ordained by God," and that state formations which contain more than one nation run the risk of losing identity and of being doomed to decay (Kedourie, 1993, p. 52). Although nationalism is a relatively new phenomenon in human history, many social scientists, in collaboration with the political powers, have presented it as a common denominator for all human communities. The nation state has its very basis in the collective identity generated in the process of the creation of a homogenous nation. As Smith (1991, p. 74) puts it, "nationalism is a political ideology that has a cultural doctrine at its centre with a great potential for the political mobilisation of a population."

Although some scholars, such as Smith (1991), make a distinction between territorial nationalism and ethnic nationalism, the very basis of nationalism remains the same. Smith considers territorial nationalism as 'open' and based on legal rights, while ethnic nationalism is 'closed' and based on a common origin in time and space. Furthermore, he presents territorial nationalism as civic and rational, and ethnic nationalism as 'natural.' Although there are some analytical values in the comparative study of Europe and the United States, Smith's account of the two kinds of nationalism does not hold in the face of the history of nation states. The history of the 20th century witnesses that distinctions between these two kinds of nationalisms are very theoretical. The history of countries such as Sweden, France, Italy, and even Germany, witness the interchangeability of the 'rational' and the 'natural' as a basis for the nation. The political projects of political parties and groups have influenced the basis of collective and national identities. The metaphor of 'family,' which is one of the most important properties of ethnic nationalist mobilisation, is not exclusive to ethnic nations, but was also used by other nations, such as in Sweden. The social democratic project for the homogenisation of the nation, which started in Sweden in early 1930s, was legitimised by the notion of *'Folkhemmet'* ('the people's home'). 'The people' were presented as a family constituted of Swedes with a common origin 'in time and space.'

However, this national exclusiveness was not only a specific characteristic of modern nation states and political parties, but also an integral part of the creation of a nation against the 'Others.' The national projects of all countries, either territorial or ethnic nationalism, have normally entailed a process of self-construction against the 'Others.' In other words, the construction of the 'Us-ness' of the nation goes hand in hand with the construction of the 'Others,' both as other nations and as internal minorities. This modern 'Otherism,' which has been part and parcel of the nationalisation of a community, can be divided into three categories accordingly: (a) ethnic 'Otherism,' (b) nationalist 'Otherism,' and (c) 'Xeno-otherism.' These are parallel processes by which a group (often a majority group), through controlling the sites and means of power, categorize and inferiorize another group based on their ethnicity, nationality, and/or immigrant status. One of the most enduring and problematic 'Otherisms' is ethnic 'Otherism,' where a self-defined ethnic group—again often a majority group—dominates the powerful institutions of a country. Ethno-national categorisation is a powerful mechanism that does not leave any real possibility for the inclusion of the 'Others' in the mainstream category of 'Us.' The ethno-nationalism of Germany and Turkey are just two cases in this respect. The process of ethno-nationalism is sometimes reinforced by some 'Otherised' ethnic groups who, as a reaction to the mainstream ethno-nationalism, develop their own ethno-political nationalist projects. Some Kurdish or Assyrian ethno-political groups who construct a belief in a primordial ethnicity and act accordingly belong to this category.

Nationalist 'Otherism' is mainly based on a process of the creation of a nation within certain geographical boundaries. The nation becomes the major body of identification for, and categorisation of, 'Us.' Language, history, 'race,' and religion have been the most powerful denominators used for belonging. In the case of national formation, Balibar (2002, p. 221) mentions a kind of national belonging which makes a people a "people"; this is, then, a community which recognizes itself in advance of the institution of the state. No modern nation possesses a given 'ethnic' basis, and that is why it is key that the state 'make people' who are invested in seeing themselves as nationals and as part of a national community. Belonging to a 'nation' that has its own state requires, then, identification with other nations which also have their own 'Other states.' The process of nationalisation entails the 'Otherization' of 'Other nations.' This 'Otherism' is one of the main political forces behind the wars and conflicts between various nation states which have formed the modern history of the 'Dark Continent.' [1]

Meanwhile, while nationalist 'Otherism' is normally (but not exclusively) a process of external exclusion of the 'Other nations,' 'Xeno-otherism' should be considered mainly as a process of internal exclusion.

Although this process is not entirely internal, and is a kind of 'spill-over' of the exclusion and inferiorization of the 'Others' that had occurred during the European powers' colonial and imperialist wars and expansions, it is increasingly taking place within the national boundaries of such countries. Immigration, on the one hand, and the success of radical right parties in many European countries, on the other, have recently accelerated 'Xeno-otherism' and created a situation in which *internal* barriers and borders are increasingly becoming more important than external ones. 'Xeno-otherism' has become a part of many 'Otherised' groups' everyday life. Although, the process of 'Otherization' makes use of 'differences,' real or imaginary, between 'Us' (the categorising groups) and 'Them' (the catego-rised 'Others'), in the (re)construction of exclusionary and discriminatory attitudes and practices against the 'Others,' it does not provide a convinc-ing ground for a definition of racism and 'Xeno-otherism.' Oppression and aggression against the 'Others' for a "particular end," as Memmi (2000, p. 102) considers as necessary elements in the definition of racism, are equally valid for defining 'Xeno-otherism.'[2] Furthermore, the process of 'Other-ization' entails unequal power relations between the 'Otherising' and the 'Otherised' groups that make the oppression of, and aggression towards, the 'Others' take form through both symbolic and physical practices.

The categorisation and 'Otherization' of a group of people is not neces-sarily based on intentional actions and practices of another group. It can be an unintended consequence of the actions of a majority society in pro-ducing itself as 'Us.' The Weberian theory of action, namely concerning the unintended consequences of human action, provides proper theoretical means for understanding the widespread institutionalised 'Xeno-otherism' of today. This makes for the very basis of the institutional discrimination of the 'Others.' For instance, in all modern nation states, in particular in western Europe, the educational system plays a central role in the nation-alisation of 'the nation' and, in the Durkheimian paradigm, for the cre-ation of a sense of 'Us-ness' and of belonging to 'a nation,' with 'a common history,' 'a common language,' 'a common culture,' and sometimes even 'a common religion.'[3]

Education

Discrimination in educational institutions continues to be one of the most important reasons for the lower degree of educational achievement among students with a nonmainstream background in all countries studied in our project. This is a fact that finds support in much of the literature concern-ing institutional discrimination in the educational system of many Euro-pean countries.

Recent studies in England, France, and Germany show the signifi-cance of ethnic discrimination in those countries' educational systems (Fitzgerald, Finch, & Nove, 2000; Osler & Morrison, 2000; Derrington

& Kendall, 2004; Pye, Lee, & Bhabra, 2000; Judge, 2004; Gogolin et al., 1998; Reuter, 1999, 2001; Schewe, 2000).

Education has been considered by many sociologists as one of the most important institutions for creating cohesion in the modern fragmented society (Durkheim, 1984). The educational system has also been used by all nation states to create homogenous citizens. The recent studies mentioned above confirm that the 'education norms' of many European countries are still ethnocentric and highly 'majority society'-oriented. This continues to reproduce the structural/institutional discrimination of the 'Others,' often those with immigrant backgrounds, in many European countries.

The majority society's perceptions of students from 'different' backgrounds—such as black people and immigrants—as 'problem students' have been discussed by many researchers (Glasgow, 1980; Wilson, 1987; Anderson, 1990). This has, in many cases, led to the 'drop-out' from mainstream schools of black students and/or those of immigrant background. As Janelle Dance (2004, p. 5) argues, "push-out" mechanisms are more conceivable than is "drop-out" in explaining why students from nonmainstream backgrounds leave school without achieving a high school diploma.[4]

In the European countries, schools produce and reproduce dichotomies of a superior 'Us' against an inferior 'Them.' For instance, the seemingly secular and 'objective' Swedish schools' educational materials (such as history books and books used for educating pupils about religion), are highly selective, nation-centric, and Christian. History books discussing European history, for instance, ignore six hundred years of the Ottoman Empire's European history and reduce it to a half page under the title 'Turks,' who are simultaneously presented as the 'Others.' This inferiorization of the 'Others' goes hand in hand with a sense of narcissism on the part of the majority society. This is evident when Europe's modern history is purified of its 'downside' and presented as an ideal type of progress and humanism.[5] European history starts with the title 'The Birth of Europe,' which is framed by the Renaissance, revolutions, and democracy. Devastating wars, colonialism, slavery, and genocide are basically absent in such story telling. This is a selective history that suits the overall purpose of being a part of Europe and 'a good nation' with a common, 'good' heritage; this forms the basis of belonging to the fair and progressive 'Us' against the inferior 'Them.'

There is the same 'scientific' bias in the schoolbooks on religion. Christianity is sanitised of its negative history, such as its role in missionary colonialism; it is considered the religion of 'Us,' while Islam, Judaism, and Hinduism are the religions of the 'Others.' Christianity is presented as 'a good religion' and the only religion with 'ethical' codes of conduct. There is no single address to religious ethics other than those of Christianity.

Others, such as Batelaan and Van Hoof (1996), Cohen and Lotan (1997), and Runfors (2003), discuss the categorising principles that students from the majority society both learn in school and take with them to school, and which the students then apply to students from the nonmajority society. Many students in schools are subjected to the same status-hierarchy that exists in the larger society (McLaren, 1993; Willis, 1991). Therefore, an understanding of the totality of discrimination and an intersectional perspective is necessary in studies about discrimination; different social sections then become illustrations of the mechanisms of discrimination.

The problem of the 'drop-out' of many black and immigrant pupils from the school system has been argued to in terms of family background, personality traits, and social group characteristics (Natriello, McDill, & Pallas, 1990; Fine, 1991). Fine (1991), Natriello, McDill and Pallas (1990), and Katz (1999) criticize the 'deficit thinking' by which the reasons for the 'drop-out' of minority children are sought in the immigrant community itself. As argued by Richard Valencia, those who engage in such thinking have failed to examine the external causes of school failure that exist beyond the control of the individual students who 'drop-out.' Dance (2004) and Katz (1999) argue that discrimination is central to understanding 'push-out' of the students of colour in the US schools.

Differences between students' results in schools have, by the majority society and researchers with majority privileges, often been related to immigrants' cultural background and not to the school system or discrimination in schools. Ålund (1997) and Ålund and Schierup (1991, 1992) argue that the 'cultural background' of immigrants is used by the majority society to ignore the real class divisions between students. Although there is some truth to this argument, this perspective does not bring much clarity to the question of ethnic discrimination in schools. Ann Runfors (2003, p. 221), in her study of Swedish schools, rejects such arguments and says that in Swedish schools "class dimensions were rather used to explain inequalities and to hide the power-aspect in the evaluation of structures in the dominant perspectives in the schools." As will be shown later in this book, this is a fact that is also confirmed in our study concerning the educational systems in other European countries. Many 'gatekeepers' in schools claim that the problem of children in segregated areas is mainly to do with their economic status or class. This is one of the mechanisms that denies structural discrimination because of the pupils' ethnic background.

However, it should be mentioned that 'class' continues to play a significant role in explaining some problems in the educational systems of European countries. For instance, worse health care for parents and children, poor housing and living conditions, and lack of access to meaningful leisure activities are class-based factors that negatively affect poor and immigrant children's school success. The question is, however, why many immigrant children with high levels of education and of middle class background (in their country of origin) are degraded in their new European countries and became poor and segregated. The growing ethnification of poverty, or what is known as 'ethnoclass' (Gurr, 1993), in Europe is alarming and cannot be discussed without taking into consideration the current structural/institutional discrimination of immigrants in those countries. Accordingly, this is another example of 'spill-over' discrimination, namely, how economic poverty reinforces the 'push out' mechanisms and how educational failure reinforces poverty.

The results of our research project's exploration of the existing research on discrimination in the eight member countries shows that there is widespread 'racial' discrimination against individuals and groups with immigrant background and minorities in all these countries. Concerning the educational system, there are several institutional and structural problems addressed by our research partners. The following are a few examples drawn from the results of the existing research on discrimination in partner countries:

- In Austria, two types of institutional discrimination within the Austrian school system can be distinguished: (a) *Direct institutional discrimination,* which is the unequal application of educational norms to pupils even though equal conditions exist. Deliberate unequal treatment of foreign pupils with a supportive intention is also regarded as discrimination. (b) *Indirect institutional discrimination,* which is the equal application of educational norms to pupils even though unequal conditions exist (cf., Gomolla & Radtke, 2002, p. 326ff). The research indicates too that the efforts made by the Austrian Ministry of Education, Science, and Culture to diminish discriminating effects within the school system in favour of an increasing multicultural reality are mainly additive measures which do not question the existing system itself.
- In France, students with an immigrant background are clearly overrepresented among those who do not finish the first cycle of high school and who are oriented towards professional classes. In the second cycle of high school, they are also more likely to attend professional classes than general or technical classes (where they account for 8.8% and 4.7% of the children attending, respectively). The French restrictive secular legal system concerning public education is another structure that discriminates against Muslim students, in particular against Muslim girls who wear a headscarf. In some cases students were forced to leave the public schools. In a few cases, Muslim girls chose to cut their hair in order to be able to participate in public education.
- In Germany, the exclusion of migrant children, and their relegation to special classes or to special schools, is still a widespread and unquestioned practice. However, most people within and outside of schools find it plausible or even necessary to subject migrant children to "special treatment," justifying this with reference to stereotypes held about "other cultures" (cf., Gomolla & Radtke, 2002, pp. 263–264). Existing research also has found that school heads openly

concede that recommendations given by primary school teachers for their pupils' transmission from the primary to a secondary track do not depend on their grades only, but also on the characteristics of a specific pupil's private surroundings that are regarded as achievement prerequisites. The most important of these characteristics is a 'parental home that is willing and able to support the child's educational efforts' (*unterstützendes Elternhaus*) and this is exactly what is often supposed not to exist in the case of migrant children, so that their grades are evaluated with a degree of negativity usually not applied to German children (cf., Gomolla & Radtke, 2002, p. 247).

• England has a longer tradition of research in the area of discrimination than do other European countries. However, despite a substantial body of research on discrimination and relatively strong antidiscrimination laws, discrimination is still a significant social problem. Recent research into school exclusion and ethnic background has highlighted the disproportionate levels of exclusion amongst children from certain communities (Osler & Hill, 1999). In their work *Examining School Exclusion and the Race Factor,* Appiah and Chunilal conclude that the government currently adopts a "colour-blind" approach to reducing exclusion, which means that even with less exclusion overall, certain groups are still overrepresented in the figures (1999, p. 3). In 2000–2001, black pupils were more likely to be permanently excluded from schools in England than children from any other ethnic group. The highest permanent exclusion rates were among children belonging to the 'Other Black' group (40 in every 10,000 pupils) and Black Caribbean pupils (38 in every 10,000). This compared with 13 in every 10,000 white children.

Labour market

Institutional discrimination in the labour market is relatively well documented. Recent studies conducted by ILO convinced even the most sceptical scholars of the widespread existence of systemic discrimination of immigrants in the European labour market. The Swedish case in very much illustrative of this concern. Sweden has been considered a good example of integration through a general welfare system and an institutionalised humanism. During the last three decades, Swedish immigration policy has largely focused on the integration of immigrants in the Swedish society. There has also been an explicit understanding in Swedish integration policy that labour market integration is the most crucial way of being integrated. At the same time, Swedish integration policy has been based on an implicit understanding that the Swedish labour market is not discriminatory against immigrants. In 1975, the Swedish Parliament stated that the goals of equality, cooperation, and freedom of choice should govern immigration policy (Kamali, 1997).

However, although there has been an antidiscriminatory law since 1989, it has not helped one single case to be brought to court. It was, however, reinforced in 1999 in order to protect foreigners against direct, as well as indirect, discrimination, and against ethnic harassment in the workplace (Lindgren, 2002; Neergaard, 2006; Behtoui, 2006). Yet, despite these legal documents and policy programs, the Swedish labour market is *not* characterised by equal conditions for immigrants and native Swedes, and there are many studies suggesting that discrimination against immigrants—in particular against non-European immigrants—is rather extensive in Sweden. The problems concerning the discrimination of immigrants in the Swedish labour market is summarised by De Los Reyes (2001) as follows:

- low employment rate, high unemployment rate, and long periods of unemployment;
- high proportion of time-limited employment;
- higher proportion of work-related health problems, and worse physical and psychosocial working environments than for 'native' Swedes;
- less chance of finding jobs that match their working experience and/or level of education, something that affects not least highly educated immigrants; and
- lower wage-increases and smaller chances of doing careers.

A usual way of denying discrimination in Sweden occurs through what can be called the 'objectification of description' model. Through this, some researchers try to find 'alternative' explanations for the higher rate of immigrants' unemployment and for their inferior situation in the labour market. The aforementioned characteristics have sometimes been defined as the result of immigrants' 'lack of knowledge about the Swedish codes,' 'applying for jobs for which they are either underqualified or overqualified,' 'lack of language competence.' The existing literature on discrimination in the Swedish labour market shows that discrimination is a very important factor explaining the unemployment of immigrants in Sweden (Kamali, 2005). Another recent nationwide study of the Swedish labour market approves the picture, and, after controlling for other factors (such as the level of education and language competence), points out that discrimination is one of the most important factors that can explain the higher level of unemployment among immigrants in Sweden (Integrationsverket, *Rapport integration*, 2003).

Our project's first research report about the discriminatory landscape in all the countries studied found that the situation is the same in the other seven countries. The exploration of existing research in all countries shows the following common features in the labour market:

- immigrants are often forced to do jobs on a short- and long-term basis, which do not correspond to their education in any way;

- there are substantial differences in the level of salary between immigrants and employees with nonimmigrant and minority background;
- immigrants are mostly employed in low-paying branches;
- the level of unemployment is higher among immigrants than nonimmigrants;
- immigrants' working conditions are not equal with the natives; they work often harder and longer than do the natives, and without a valid working agreement; and
- restrictions on religious cloths and headscarves make it impossible for immigrants to do their jobs without refraining from their religious beliefs.

However, there are some differences between the countries engaged in the project. While the laws are less discriminatory in countries with a long antiracist tradition, such as England, and a tradition of struggle for equal rights, such as Sweden, they are more openly discriminatory in countries such as Germany and Cyprus. In Cyprus, for instance, immigrants cannot work in the public sector. In Germany, the law of the 'right to work' (*Arbeitsberechtigung*) is openly discriminatory against non-Germans. Paragraph 285 SGB III specifies the conditions under which a 'foreigner' can get a work permit, of which the most important are that:

- his or her employment does not have any negative consequences for the German labour market;
- there is no German available for the job (*Vorrangprinzip*); and
- he or she has a residence permit.

However, it is difficult to draw the conclusion that the different legal status of people with an immigrant background under German law means such people are subject to greater discrimination in Germany than they are in Poland, which has more egalitarian legal codes, encapsulated in the constitution of the republic in 1997.

Mass Media

The public sphere is one of the most important social arenas where the struggle for legitimacy takes place. It is not an exaggeration to say that the mass media has become the heart of the public sphere, playing a crucial role in the reproduction of the 'cognition' of society and its legitimate truths. Although the media is a very powerful means in a democratic society for controlling political power, it is not itself independent from the power structure of a society—including its economic and political power centres. Mass media acts in an institutional milieu that reproduces established norms and which has, in many cases, close bonds with powerful political and economic agents. This provides powerful groups from the majority society frequent access to mass media based upon mutual interests. The established power structure and institutions, including mass media, enjoy prominent positions and privileges that they want to reproduce. In this respect, mass media has an interest in the reproduction of established norms, prejudices, and discriminatory structures in society (cf., Van Dijk, 1984, 1991, 1993; Wodak & Van Dijk, 2000).

Established discourses of the 'Others' in society are mainly circulated by mass media and are made to a legitimate public form of representation of 'Us' in contrast to 'Them.' In other words, the negative stereotypes and discourses of 'deviant Others' are necessary components in the reproduction of a 'normal Us.' This makes access to mass media a crucial factor for many groups in their struggle for influencing public opinion and gaining recognition and legitimacy. However, mass media is mainly controlled by the powerful actors of the majority society, and the space available in mass media for minorities and immigrants is very limited (Martinot, 2000). Mass media is rarely independent or 'objective,' as it is often claimed. Their objectivity is what should be called the objective reproduction of the norms of the majority society by which the 'Others' are categorised as inferiors and essentially separated from 'Us.' As Martinot (2000) puts it, the act of the definition of the 'Other' illustrates the power of one group over the other, and, equally proves that the dominant group is dependent on an 'inferior Other' for its own 'superior' social identity (cf., Rattansi, 1994).

The inferiorization of the 'Others,' and the superiorisation of 'Us,' is a complex process with many institutional mechanisms. These mechanisms are often not easy to observe for people lacking the broader knowledge of inferiorization processes. Inferiorization is often understood by many members of majority society as 'normal' and nothing more than the routinized 'objective' actions of different institutions—including the mass media. One of the most interesting cases that was studied within the project's meta-news analysis concerned the reporting of a murder of a girl of Kurdish background by her father in a Swedish city, Uppsala, in January 20, 2001. The mass media did not hesitate to call the murder a case of 'honour-killing' and present it as an integrated part of the non-European, nonwestern, 'immigrant cultures.' The murder was frequently reported and debated. Along with the terrorist attacks of September 11, it became the major news 'hit' of the year and was presented as an example of the criminal actions of the 'Others.' This murder was culturally and essentially differentiated from the murder of Swedish white women by their husbands, fathers, lovers, or sons.

The Swedish case is no exception by any means. There is a strong tendency in the mass media of all the countries engaged in the project to label murder, and indeed any other criminal act in which the perpetrators are immigrants, as a 'cultural case.' It means that these kinds of criminal acts can be done only by people from 'Other cultures.' Consequently, the murder of women by men from the majority society is presented as 'a modern, objective, and noncultural' murder, and the murder of immigrant women by immigrant men, becomes traditional, emotional, and cultural. The study of the exiting literature shows that 'Otherization' of criminality is not a new phenomenon, but has a long history in many European countries. In Sweden, since the 17th century, there has been a tradition of conducting statistics on the criminality of the 'Other,' such as Roma (Svanberg & Tydén, 1992). In England, meanwhile, in 1888 the police issued a cartoon-type caricature of a man alleged to have carried out the murders of six prostitutes in London's East End. The image was clearly meant to establish his Jewish, east European origins. The image worked because it played on precisely those fears and repressed desires of white masculinity (Bhattacharyya, Gabriel, & Small, 2002, p. 18). Stigmatisation of black people and other minority and immigrant groups as criminals and deviants is well documented in the literature on racism and discrimination. One of the criminal acts which have been used frequently in order to inferiorize the 'Others' has been rape. Although rape is a crime which occurs in all societies around the globe, it becomes medially interesting when the perpetrator in such a crime has an immigrant or minority background. This has been a case in many western societies (Ware, 1992). The mass media plays on the prejudices and the 'normal ways of thinking' of the majority, and so makes the act 'culturally' or even 'racially' understandable: 'it is a part of their culture' or 'they are sexually hyper active' (Ware, 1992).

However, it is not only the 'reporting' of criminal acts of immigrants and minorities which is stigmatising and reinforces discrimination and racism by reinforcing the majority society's prejudices and 'normalities,' but also the *debates* following the crimes committed by persons with immigrant backgrounds. In these debates, it is not only the 'experts' of the majority society, but also the cultural 'experts' of immigrant and minority backgrounds, who are highly engaged. Generally, the only 'specialisation' required to be a 'public expert' for this group comes from their immigrant and minority background. For instance, a person who defends the majority society's and media's repertoire of prejudices against, or discourses on, the 'Others,' is in many cases chosen by the authorities and mass media as a 'legitimate' expert on matters of the 'Others.' For instance, some individuals with a Muslim background with strong affiliation with the majority society's established discourses are frequently used by the media and majority society as 'experts' in order to confirm the established discursive prejudiced 'truths' about 'Muslims.' This is based on a tradition of 'Otherization' with the metaassumption that the problems of the 'Others' have different explanations than the problems of 'Us' and cannot be properly understood without help from 'their own experts.' The category of 'immigrant experts' are frequently used by the mass media in order to legitimize culturalisation and essentialisation of the 'Others.' Using the 'culturally competent experts' has become an effective means to normalize and legitimize discrimination of the 'Others' in general and Muslims, as a very well-defined 'Other,' in particular.

Majority society's control of the means of power and influence is one of the most important aspects of what Pierre Bourdieu calls 'symbolic violence.' Although, when Bourdieu (1977, pp. 21–22) introduced the term, he meant positive, status-upgrading practices which obscured the real exploitation and domination in a traditional Kabyl society, "symbolic violence" can also be used to explain the mechanism of reproduction of the domination of majority society over the 'Others' by hiding it behind legitimised discursive presentations. Bourdieu believed that 'symbolic violence' is a compliment to domination in societies that cannot rely on the modern market economy, courts, police or modern politics for the legitimisation of power. Feminist research has redefined 'symbolic violence,' defining it as the mechanism for the denial of the skills and contributions of the 'Others,' that is, women. It draws attention to the 'downgrading' processes by which a male-dominated society denigrates women, leaving their multidimensional and comprehensive contributions virtually invisible, while disqualifying their demands for equal rights and social recognition (Krais, 1993). This theoretical understanding of the term 'symbolic violence' can also be used in the studies concerning discrimination of the 'Others' in European societies. Accordingly, symbolic violence is based on a mechanism of the upgrading of 'Us' and downgrading of 'Them.' However, the relatively widespread use of the 'representatives of the Others,' or 'culturally competent experts,' in the political arenas and debates in European countries, who legitimize majority society's domination, makes it necessary to pay attention also to the upgrading of these 'representatives.' Many individuals with immigrant backgrounds are given space in major mass media to systematically inferiorize the 'Others.' Such individuals do, in many cases, lack journalist education, and possess no merit other than their 'immigrant background' and loyalty to majority society.

Symbolic violence not only legitimizes majority society's dominant power, but also harms 'Otherised' individuals and groups in their daily lives. It is also expressed directly and indirectly through coded expression in the mass media and in everyday life situations. Many persons with immigrant background in Europe express their concern about 'everyday racism' by which they are racialised and 'Otherised' as 'cultural and racial inferiors.'

DISCRIMINATION AND RACISM AGAINST MUSLIMS IN EUROPE

The Crusades to the Middle East and the expansion of the Arab and the Ottoman Islamic empires into Europe created a tradition of confrontations between the Christian parts of Europe and Islamic civilisations. Since the reconquest of Spain and establishment of the Spanish

Inquisition in 1478 by the king Ferdinand and the declaration of war on Muslims and Jews (who were considered non-Europeans), anti-Muslim sentiments and systematic propaganda have been supported by many European states, which considered themselves Christians. The Inquisition was not abolished until 1834, during the reign of Isabel II. However, the formal abolishment of the Inquisition did not mean the end of racism and discrimination against the 'Others,' namely Muslims, Jews, Gipsies, and Africans, among others.

The wars and conflicts between Christian European powers and Muslim civilisations have also been the basis for 'civilisational' and cultural exchanges between the two parties. The religious, philosophical, medical, and other scientific exchanges, including political science, go back to the early establishment of the Islamic reign in Spain (see, e.g., Castro, 1971; Al-Hamawi, 1974; Turner, 1994; Hoexter, Eisenstadt, & Levtzion, 2002). However, the great Muslim influences in Christian Europe have systematically been downgraded and ignored. Notwithstanding the long historical exchange, the 'narcissism of minor differences,' to use Hegel's term, has been one of the reasons behind the 'Otherization' and inferiorization of Muslims.

The established Orientalist assumption about Muslims, and the misconception of the 'Muslim world' as a homogeneous entity and as constituting the other side of reason, modernity and progress, does not just belong to the past, but is very much a real phenomenon of today. The September 11 terrorist attacks on the Word Trade Centre and Pentagon, and the declaration of the 'War on terror' by the USA, not only reinforced prejudices against Muslims, but also deteriorated the positions of Muslims in many 'western' countries. Muslims who were seen as a threat became the focal target of the new racism.[6]

The existing structural/institutional discrimination in European and extended European countries (which includes Canada, Australia, New Zealand, and the United States) have come to harm Muslims more than other immigrant groups. The increasing racism and discrimination against Muslims after September 11 is well documented. The International Helsinki Federation of Human Rights Report, *Intolerance and Discrimination against Muslims in the EU: Are Muslims "An Enemy Within"?*, for instance, concludes the increasing racism and discrimination against Muslims in all European Union countries. The report indicates that in the aftermath of September 11, there is a tendency in the media to write about issues relating to Muslims with a stereotypical approach, resulting in stories which reinforce public misconceptions. The report criticizes the homogenised negative image of Islam published by media that overlooks the internal diversity of Islam. Islam is represented as a 'monolithic and one-dimensional religion that is fundamentalist and threatens western democratic values.' The report concludes that the media portrays Muslims as 'alien' to European Union societies, 'an enemy within,' and as a 'fifth column.' This has influenced public opinion about Islam. For instance, in Germany more than 80% of those surveyed in 2004 associated the word 'Islam' with 'terrorism' and 'oppression of women.'

The report says that Muslims of immigrant background have a higher unemployment rate and a comparatively lower standard of housing than members of the majority population. They are reportedly subjected to discrimination in employment, at schools and universities, and when seeking access to service in places such as town halls, hospitals, shops and banks. In Sweden, studies have shown that up to every fifth job is closed for people with Arabic-sounding names because of discriminatory hiring practices. In the US, reports claim that Muslims have the lowest employment rate of any religious group, and their unemployment rate is three times the national average and twice the level of other religious minorities.

The Helsinki report also presents the facts around the restriction to freedom of religion for Muslims and even of the personal abuse of individual Muslims. In several cities, plans to construct mosques have met with strong protest, and citizens' movements have been established to oppose the realisation of such plans. According to reports from the United Kingdom, Spain, Greece, and other countries, Muslims have been further subjected to arbitrary identity checks and arrests by police since September 11. The French Organisation against Islamophobia (CCIF) said that during the period from October 2003 to August 2004, 26 cases of verbal and physical assaults on Muslims, 28 cases of vandalism and attempted arson targeting mosques, and 11 cases of desecration of Muslim graves have been registered. Because of the discriminatory treatment often faced by veiled Muslim women, public employment offices reportedly consider the use of the headscarf a 'disability' in the job search process.

The International Helsinki Federation for Human Rights' executive director concludes that these developments threaten to undermine positive efforts at integration and further increase the vulnerability of Muslims to human rights violations and marginalisation.

DISCRIMINATION AS AN INTERINSTITUTIONAL PHENOMENON

As Figure 2.1 suggests, racism and discrimination in the labour market, in the educational system, and in the mass media should not be considered institutionally isolated forms. Discrimination is a complex phenomenon that takes place within and across many different institutions. Since institutions are not isolated from each other, discrimination in an institution has many 'spill-over' consequences for other institutions and spheres of lives. As Glasgow (1980) points out, black males from low-income urban communities tend to be rejected and labelled as 'social problems' by the police, the school, employment and welfare agencies; they are the victims of the new camouflaged racism. "Racism cannot be explained in abstraction from other social relations, even if alternatively one cannot reduce it to those social relations" (Hall, 2002, p. 57).

One of the most effective ways of reproducing the status quo of European societies through which many influential and powerful groups reproduce their dominance in society is a strategy of *denial* of racism and discrimination. As Miles (1993) puts it, what is novel about contemporary forms of racism is not the proliferation of racist social movements, but an intensification of ideological and political struggle around the expression of a racism that often claims not to be racism (see also Miles, 1989). The strategy of denial is well established among the gatekeepers of many institutions of the majority society, such as the educational system, the political system, and the judicial system. It is fruitless to discuss discriminators' *intentions* concerning reinforcing discrimination and racism in society; it is rather the *consequences* of the individual or institutional actions that should be studied and considered to be discriminatory or not. In our interviews with employees and school authorities, which will be presented later in this book, many claimed that discrimination in *their fields* have to do with the 'real consequences' of processes occurring in *other areas*. School authorities for instance claimed that the housing situation of pupils with immigrant backgrounds influences their chances negatively in schools. Employees claimed also that discrimination in the labour market is often a result of bad education. The fact is, however, that discrimination takes place in many different institutions with 'spill-over' effects for other institutions. The interviewees are probably right when they talk about these spill-over effects of problems in other institutions. However, what they often use as a clarification for problems in their own institutions is arguably not correct and is, in many cases, a means of self-defence. However, it is important to systematically explore the interinstitutional relations that provide the ground for institutional/structural discrimination.

3 The Uprising of Xenophobic Populist Parties and the Reinforcement of Institutional Discrimination

INTRODUCTION

The uprising of the Xenophobic Populist Party (XPP) since the 1980s has been a new phenomenon in post-World War II European liberal democracies that has increasingly engaged many social scientists in debate concerning the reasons for the uprising of such parties. There are several scientific approaches to why these parties have emerged as a 'challenge to European democracies.' Some argue that rising unemployment is a reason behind XPPs' success (see Jackman & Volpert, 1996) and others claim the decline in welfare state policies is the main reason (Eatwell & Mudde, 2004; Mudde, 2007; among others).

Although unemployment and decreasing welfare can play a role in the electoral success of XPP, such variables have many shortcomings. There are examples in Europe that show that the success of XPP is not directly related to the increase or decrease in unemployment or welfare regime of the country. In Sweden and Denmark, for instance, we are witnessing the success of established XPPs in a time of increasing employment and a good economy. In Sweden (as we will see later in this chapter), a XPP, Nydemokrati (New Democracy), had electoral success in the early 1990s and arrived in the Swedish parliament when Sweden had not changed its traditional welfare state. Even in the Swedish last parliamentary and local elections (August 2006), a new XPP, Sverigedemokraterna (Swedish Democrats), had substantial electoral success in a time of very low unemployment and good economic growth in the country.

What is not normally discussed in the research and debates on XPPs' electoral success is the relationship between the xenophobic discourses and policies of established parties, mass media, and the political success of XPP. As discussed earlier, 'Xeno-otherism' is institutionalised in European, and extended European, countries and influences many groups' attitudes and preferences—in this case, those of the electorates. In this chapter, the uprising of XPP and the favourable roles of established parties and mass media in its success are discussed.

METHODOLOGY AND RESEARCH DESIGN

The role of discourse in producing and reproducing xenophobia and racism within the field of politics has been discussed by many scholars in recent years (Reisigl & Wodak, 2001; Wodak & Van Dijk, 2000; Wodak & Pelinka, 2002; among others). However, there is no systematic study, apart from that of Wodak and Van Dijk (2000), which uses a comparative, qualitative, and discourse-analytic perspective in cross-national research to identify the discursive mechanisms of xenophobia and racism. It would be highly desirable to observe in a scrutinized, discourse-analytical way how various groups from the entire political spectra of the countries in question construct and recontextualise various arguments in favour of racist and xenophobic actions. For this purpose, it would be very interesting to observe how racist and discriminatory views 'circulate' within the entire national public spheres, including the media, and how, within the political realm alone, both new xenophobic and mainstream political parties and groupings 'use' anti-immigration and 'Otherising' arguments to strengthen their political role. The discourse analysis in this part of the research allows us to focus on the ways in which XPP is assisting in the creation and social-wide dissemination of racism and discrimination through their discourses.

In looking at speeches and public statements of politicians, as well as at the party programmes and programmatic documents of XPP, we are interested in identifying the form of these political discourses which might have influences on the development of racist, xenophobic and discriminatory views in each of the eight countries engaged in this study. It is only the combined and mutually-influential analysis of the 'typical' genres of XPP that will help us to identify those discursive practices which are set to discriminate in an open and direct way. The main focus of analysis is on the creation of effective discursive tools and mechanisms for exclusion of the 'Others' (immigrants and minorities) from a collective European and national identity, which serve to reproduce an exclusive 'Us.' This is proceeded by investigating the arenas where politics are performed, such as parliamentary discourse, election campaigns, public speeches, and media reporting. In these cases, we study discourses *about* the 'Others,' as well as the positive self-presentation of politicians which manifests itself *inter alia* in disclaimers and even in the denial of racism.

Critical research in the field of language, politics and discrimination has expanded enormously in recent years (e.g., Wodak & Chilton, 2005; Chilton & Schäffner, 2002; Van Dijk, 2005). According to the underlying specific theoretical approach, the notion of 'discourse' is frequently defined in many different ways. For example, in British research, the term 'discourse' is used frequently synonymously with 'text,' that is, meaning authentic, everyday linguistic communication. The French 'discourse,' however, focuses more on the connection between language and thought, for example, meaning the "creation and societal maintenance of complex knowledge systems" (Ehlich, 2000, p. 162). In German pragmatics, 'Diskurs' denotes 'structured sets of speech acts.' In the analysis of discourse and politics, the meaning of the notion of discourse is therefore closely linked to the respective research context and theoretical approach. We endorse in this research Lemke's (1995) definition, which distinguishes between 'text' and 'discourse' in the following way:

> When I speak about discourse in general, I will usually mean the social activity of making meanings with language and other symbolic systems in some particular kind of situation or setting. . . . On each occasion when the particular meanings, characteristic of these discourses are being made, a specific text is produced. Discourses, as social actions more or less governed by social habits, produce texts that will in some ways be alike in their meanings. . . . When we want to focus on the specifics of an event or occasion, we speak of the text; when we want to look at patterns, commonality, relationships that embrace different texts and occasions, we can speak of discourses. (p. 7ff)

The most salient feature of the definition of a 'discourse' is the macro-topic, like 'language policies.' Interdiscursivity can be detected when, for example, an argument (taken from the discourse on immigration restrictions) is used while arguing for other policies to combat unemployment. Each macrotopic allows for many subtopics: 'unemployment' thus covers subtopics like 'market,' 'trade unions,' 'social welfare,' 'global market,' and 'hire and fire policies.' Discourses are not closed systems at all; rather, they are open and hybrid. New subtopics can be created, and intertextuality and interdiscursivity allow for new fields of action and new genres. Discourses are realised in both genres and texts and every discourse is socially and historically embedded and has repercussions for other (current and future) discourses. Since discourse is a part of social reality and plays an important role for the reproduction of power relationships and, in so doing, are engaged in construction of social context for action, racist discourse must be studied in the context of established institutions, political agents, and other public actors. As Van Dijk (2000) puts it:

> Especially because of their often subtle and symbolic nature, many forms of the new racism are discursive: they are expressed, enacted and confirmed by text and talk, such as everyday conversations, board meetings, job interviews, policies, laws, parliamentary debates, political propaganda, textbooks, scholarly articles, movies, TV programmes and news reports in the press, among hundreds of other genres. (p. 34)

The *new racism* denies that it is racism, because it "wants to be democratic and respectable. Real Racism, in this framework of thought, exists only among the Extreme Right. In the New Racism, minorities are not biologically inferior, but different" (Van Dijk, 2000). An embedded discourse analysis is able to provide insights into the discursive mechanisms of the role of public discourse in the reproduction of institutionalised racial discrimination.

The notion of 'politics' is also defined in many different ways depending on the respective theoretical framework: Definitions range from a wide extension of the concept according to which every social utterance or practice of the human as a 'zoon politikon' is 'political,' to a notion of politics referring only to the use of language used by politicians (both in the context of political institutions and across various settings). As Chilton (2004) puts it:

> On the one hand, politics is viewed as a struggle for power, between those who seek to assert their power and those, who seek to resist it. On the other hand, politics is viewed as cooperation, as the practices and institutions that a society has for resolving clashes of interest over money, influence, liberty, and the like. (p. 3)

Chilton (2004) embraces an interactive view of politics, which cuts through both dimensions mentioned above. This is also the perspective endorsed in this part of the research.

The method of analysis used in this chapter is also inspired by the Critical Discourse Analysis (CDA) discussed by Fairclough and Wodak (1997), viewing "language as social practice" and considering the *context* of language use to be crucial. Moreover, CDA takes a particular interest in the relation between language and power. This research specifically considers institutional, political, gender, and media discourses (in the broadest sense) that testify to more or less overt relations of struggle and conflict. CDA may be defined as fundamentally interested in analysing opaque, as well as transparent, structural relationships of dominance, discrimination, power, and control, as manifested in language. For CDA, language is not powerful on its own, but it gains power by the use powerful people make of it. Thus, CDA focuses on processes of 'inclusion' and 'exclusion,' of 'access' to relevant domains of our societies.

One of the main roles of discourse is the reproduction of social representations, such as knowledge, attitudes, ideologies, norms, and values. This means that discourse constitutes the main interface between the social, emotional, and cognitive dimensions of racism (Van Dijk, 1993). On the one hand, it may itself be a discriminatory social practice, and on the other, it expresses and helps reproduce the negative social representations (prejudices, etc.) that are socially shared. However, not all types of discourse are equally influential in the reproduction of society and of systems of domination such as racism. Obviously, public discourses are more influential throughout society than are private discourses, such as everyday conversations in the family, among neighbours or friends.

Those groups who are in control of most influential public discourses, that is *symbolic elites* such as politicians, journalists, scholars, teachers, and writers, thus play a special role in the reproduction of dominant knowledge and ideologies in society (Van Dijk, 2005). Since prejudices are not innate, but socially acquired, and since such acquisition is predominantly discursive, the public discourses of the symbolic elites are the primary source of shared ethnic prejudices and ideologies (Van Dijk, 1993). Popular racism, and its practices and discourse, are often based on, exacerbated, or legitimated by such elite discourse and racism. It is unlikely that popular discourses have the widespread influence of public discourses such as parliamentary debates, news, TV programmes, novels, movies, or textbooks. Even when the media or politicians may 'give voice' to popular racism, it is still the media and political elites who are responsible for this publication and reproduction in the public sphere. That is, the elites at least preformulate, legitimate, or condone popular racism.

The definition of the term 'racism' includes many theoretical controversies whenever one intends to provide a final definition of the term. The term racism in this study considers at least two levels: the level of *ideology* and *beliefs* about the 'Others,' and the level of *social practices* of *inclusion* of 'Us' and *exclusion* of the 'Others.' Moreover, it is important to stress that the term 'racism' means different things in different languages. In English, there is a tendency to label any discrimination as 'racist' whereas due to the semantic history of the term in Germany (i.e., in National-Socialism), only biologically constructed inferiority is accounted for by the term '*rassistisch*' or '*Rasse*.' Clearly not all discrimination experienced by migrants, for example, is racist in a sense that is universally acceptable.

In order to capture the multidimensional nature of racism, the concept of *syncretic racism* is useful in encompassing everyday racism, xeno-racism, and other concepts of racism (such as racialisation and 'Otherism'). By *syncretic racism* we mean the construction of 'differences,' which serve ideological, political, and/or practical discrimination at all levels of society. Old and new stereotypes form a mixed bag of exclusionary practices, used whenever seen to be politically expedient, such as in gaining votes. It is a 'racism without races' in which the discourse of racism has become dereferrentialised, that is removed from any direct relation with a specific constructed racial subject (Muslims, Jews, Blacks, Roma), and has become a 'floating discourse' (almost an 'empty signifier,' in the view of Ernesto Laclau and Chantal Mouffe) in which xenophobic attitudes are combined with racist stereotypes.

What this finally draws attention to is the discursive nature of racism. Racism exists without concrete or observable 'races'; it is bound up in language and proliferates in our societies at all levels and in many subtle ways. Differences between various social groups take on a negative character. It is not the fact of difference that produces discrimination or racism, but the generalisation of such difference into negative categories, and attribution of these categories to whole groups, which constitutes the public imagination as against the 'Others.' Within the system of racism, this means that just like other discriminatory practices, discourse may be used to problematise, marginalize, exclude, or otherwise limit the human rights of those who are categorized as the 'Others.'

The discursive construction of 'Us' and 'Them' is, thus, the foundation of prejudiced and racist perceptions and discourses. This discursive construction starts with the labelling of social actors, proceeds to the generalisation of negative attributions, and then elaborates arguments to justify the exclusion of many and the inclusion of some. The discursive realisations can be more or less intensified or mitigated, and more or less implicit or explicit, due to historical conventions, public levels of tolerance, 'political correctness,' context, and the public sphere.

In this chapter, the discourses of XPP in eight countries (Austria, Cyprus, England, France, Germany, Italy, Poland, and Sweden) are investigated in the broad time-scope of the last 25 years ranging between 1980 and 2005. This time span is divided in three periods, which help us scrutinize the research in order to systematize our empirical findings in a diachronic way. The three periods in question are: (a) Period I: between 1980 and 1989, (b) Period II: between 1989 and 1999, and (c) Period III: between 2000 and 2004.

Comparing the discursive patterns identified in the periods I, II, and III allows us to identify processes of change. While the study includes the period I (1980s), emphasis must be given to periods II and III (1990s and the early years of the new millennium) for the following reasons:

- throughout the 1990s many of the (western-)European XPPs (re)gained social-wide acceptance and appeal (this has been proven by the electoral success of many XPPs);
- elements of XPP discourses penetrated into public discourses and, by the same token, racist and discriminatory elements became widely represented in public debates;
- Many racist, discriminatory, and xenophobic elements were 'normalised' and accepted in the public discourses of many European countries; and
- since the mid-1990s, European Union enlargement has been on the agenda.

However, there are some differences between the eight countries engaged in this research. Cyprus and Poland, for instance, were both countries without membership to the European Union when the research started in 2002, and both had a tradition of emigration to the 'west.' This makes their 1980s' history in particular incompatible with other 'western' European countries. There are also historically specific events and reasons behind the varieties of political formations of each the eight countries that provides diversity to the analysis. However, the main aim of the research has been to compare those countries and identify both similarities and differences in 'Otherization,' discrimination, and racism against immigrants and minorities.

The analysis has been focused on the impact of XPP on the mainstream political parties and politics of the eight countries. The following documents and material have been used in this respect:

- XPPs' and mainstream parties' party programmes, electoral documents, and party press;
- XPP leaders' political speeches, statements, and declarations;
- parliamentary debates concerning immigration and minority related events, such as changing national laws and asylum rights; and
- mainstream mass media articles concerning 'critical events' of international and national scale, such as the attacks of September 11, 2001 on the World Trade Center and the Pentagon in the United States, and the success of a XPP in national elections in each country.

The results of the country-specific analyzes are presented for each country, and a summary of the comparison between the eight countries engaged in this research concludes the chapter.

THE CASE OF AUSTRIA

The Political Context of Xenophobia in Austria

When World War II draws slowly towards its end, Austria, which spent WWII aside its NS German ally (with many Austrians becoming one of the key perpetrators of the Holocaust and the NS era), is being reinstituted as an independent state according to the agreements which crystallised the new East–West divisions of Europe (e.g., Yalta or Potsdam). The latter leave Austria more or less 'in the middle' of the new divide, yet clearly prompt the development of the Western-like economy in the country. After 1945, Austria is occupied by the allied forces of the United States, the United Kingdom, France, and the Soviet Union (forming respective 'zones'). The aforementioned '*Staatsvertrag*' of May 15, 1955, marks the end of the occupation of Austria by the 'allied forces' and the institution of the Austrian military neutrality. The implementation of the 'Swedish model' of the economy soon puts Austria on the way to economic prosperity and political stability.

The beginning of the postwar era is mainly characterised by the rising balance of power between the two Austrian 'mainstream' parties: the Social-Democratic Party of Austria (SPÖ) and the Austrian People's Party (ÖVP). In the meantime, the VdU (and later The Freiheitliche Partei Österreichs [FPÖ]) develops to become the 'third' party. In 1966, the ÖVP forms a majority government, yet, soon after the 1968 occurrences (similar to those of the majority of the Western-European countries) the SPÖ comes into power and continues to form consecutive Austrian governments throughout the period between 1970 and 1999 (under

Bruno Kreisky between 1970 and 1983, Fred Sinowatz between 1983 and 1986, Franz Vranitzky between 1986 and 1997, and Viktor Klima between 1997 and 1999). The 'notorious' elections of 1999 take place in December that year, allowing the winning party (ÖVP under Wolfgang Schüssel) to form the government with the FPÖ led by Jörg Haider. After the elections of 2002 (caused by the Knittelfeld coup in the FPÖ initiated by Haider) the same coalition forms the second government, again under Schüssel.

It is not possible to give monocausal explanations for the voters' attitudes because the arguments which are decisive for giving a vote are complex bundles of reasons. Topics and current issues of an election campaign generally reflect traditional party commitments. The voters interpret these issues against the background of traditional power and competence. Therefore, despite traditional reasons also the actual party's performance is always a divisive factor (cf. Falter, 2003, p. 18f).

The following data and analyses cover the Austrian National Parliamentary Elections (NPEs) from 1986 until 2004 with consideration of the two mainstream parties ÖVP and SPÖ as well as the xenophobic populist party FPÖ. In order to present the voters' attitudes towards immigration issues over time, the results are not presented on a one-year basis but according to the relevant NPEs which took place within the given time frame. For the NPEs between 1986 and 1994, two conditions had a significant impact on the voters' decisions: first, the landscape of social and political topics which have been discussed during electoral campaigns, and second, the constellation of government that is the change of power of political parties and their strategic impact as being the party in power or not.

The election of 1986 was characterised by a breakdown of the social-liberal coalition of the SPÖ/FPÖ and the reorganisation of smaller parties like the Greens (*Die Grünen*) and the FPÖ. Jörg Haider was designated as the new chairman of the FPÖ which had to redefine itself as a nongovernment party. Despite the intensive medial self-production and representation of the ÖVP, the coalition between SPÖ and ÖVP continued.

Generally, the NPEs between 1986 and 1995 were influenced by several 'scandalous' topics whereas the voters' reasons to decide pro SPÖ actually stayed the same over four election periods: Traditional reasons and the representation of social interests as well as the party's image as being the party of workers and 'small' people were dominant. Also the personnel aspect (Prime Minister Franz Vranitzky) influenced the voters' decision. Specific issues, such as immigration, did not play a crucial role in the decision making process of voters pro-SPÖ in the years 1986 to 1994. The same is true for ÖVP voters: Traditional issues as well as the image of representing economy and farming have been in the foreground of decision making, whereas personnel reasons (Mock, Riegler, Busek) were secondary (cf. Plasser & Ulram, 1996, pp. 37–38).

Concerning the FPÖ, the situation was totally different. The FPÖ under Jörg Haider as a new party leader presented itself—in comparison to the 'old' and 'immobile' mainstream parties—as a new, innovative, and dynamic political power in Austria. The voters' reasons were first of all the hope of change within the Austrian political landscape which was grounded on several protest-oriented negative topics. In the context of turning into a xenophobic populist party within these years, the immigration issue became more central within the party's programmatic discourse and also crucial for the voters' decisions. (cf. Plasser & Ulram, 1996, p. 39). After the referendum on the 'Austria First' Petition in January 1993 (initiated by the FPÖ) the issue of immigration was more present within the Austrian society than it has been in the decades before. This referendum also influenced the voters' supposition of the parties' competences concerning the question: How to get the 'problem of immigration' under control? According to Fessel+GfK statistics in 1994–1995, FPÖ was the party that could controll the 'problem of immigration' more than the mainstream parties.

According to IFES statistics as well as to the exit poll of Fessel+GfK, the high mobility of voters of the NPE 1995 on a national as well as on a regional level was very significant: About every eighth voter changed his or her party allegiance. Further, the mobilisation of former nonvoters was outstanding. Most floating voters changed from mainstream parties to the FPÖ.

The topic which was predominant in the SPÖ's election campaign in1995 was the question of guilt of the breakdown of the former SPÖ/ÖVP coalition as well as warnings of a forthcoming ÖVP/FPÖ coalition. Central issues of domestic politics were tax- and social-policy, especially the discussion about the reduction of the budget deficit. The ÖVP slogan '*Sparen*' ('*Save your money*') was central in the party's election campaign. Further, they put great effort on recruiting 'Haider voters' by taking up traditional issues of the right populist discourse, for example, the abuse of the welfare state and the proposal of a reform of the Act on Foreigners (*Ausländergesetz*). The ÖVP also tried to introduce a more moderate language to talk about these issues of social abuse. Wolfgang Schüssel, for instance, called himself '*der gute Haider*' ('*the good Haider*') whose language and behaviour are not as radical and negative.

The NPE 1999 was one of the most dramatic elections in the history of the Second Republic of Austria. It was characterized by harsh confrontation between the two mainstream parties on different political issues. The result was a rather defused atmosphere among voters which was of advantage for the FPÖ. The issue of immigration came in the forth position by the FPÖ voters as the reasons for voting to FPÖ.

In January 2000, the negotiations on the proceeding of the coalition of ÖVP and SPÖ failed. As a result, the ÖVP and FPÖ agreed on a common government which was not only tremendously criticised within Austria but also on an international level. Fourteen European Union member states set up sanctions against Austria which were also supported by other countries (Norway, Czech Republic).

Generally speaking, during the election campaign of 2002 the ÖVP and SPÖ were 'neck to neck' right to the very end. According to SORA analyses[1] there are several reasons why the ÖVP finally made it: They got gains from former FPÖ voters (+602,000) and managed to use the FPÖ crisis about chairmanship to their own advantage. FPÖ Vice-Chancellor Susanne Riess-Passer and the Minister of Finance Karl-Heinz Grasser were praised for their efforts in the former coalition period whereas at the same time they distanced themselves strongly from Jörg Haider and the partakers of the 'Knittelfeld Coup' (cf. Hofinger, Ogris, & Thalhammer, 2003, p. 163). The ÖVP made profit from typical FPÖ issues like asylum policy and warnings of a SPÖ/Grüne coalition. Finally, they were also able to mobilise about 122,000 actual nonvoters. (cf. Plasser, Ulram, & Seeber, 2003, pp. 138–141).

As the analyses shows, only two out of 14 topics are immigration related issues. The analysis of voting reasons which were central to NPE 2002 shows that the reasons concerning immigration issues only occur in the context of FPÖ voters. Here, the reasons concerning immigration issues only occur in the context of FPÖ voters. Fifty three percent judge the fact of standing up against immigrants and against the EU-enlargement as decisive factors for voting FPÖ. For voters of ÖVP and SPÖ, other nonimmigration related reasons are predominant. These results are confirmed by other polls which also show that the issue of immigration mainly occurs among FPÖ voters (cf. SORA/IFES December 2002, January 2003, 2005[2]; cf. Hofinger & Ogris, 1996, pp. 330–335).

The analyses of the NPE from 1986 until 2002 show that the issue of immigration has never been central to any election campaign of the mainstream parties and therefore has not been a decisive factor for their voters. Only for FPÖ voters, immigration issues were important—but not as much as one would have expected. Additionally, immigration issues were first raised in the 1994/1995 elections with an increasing tendency until today. The Eurobarometer surveys (1997, 2000, 2003) shows that the antiimmigrant sentiments and attitudes has been in constant increase during the last decades in Austria.

Increasingly, the FPÖ succeeded in introducing the issue of immigration into public discourse. The party's aim was to profit from already existing xenophobic attitudes among Austrian voters. The highlight of 'racial' policy making by the FPÖ was the referendum Austria First in 1993. Its intention was to mobilise and create xenophobic potential and climate in Austria what should be of benefit for forthcoming national elections (cf. Bailer-Galander, 1995, pp. 140–148).

Discursive Reconstruction of 'Us' vs. 'Them'

After being defeated tremendously in the 1964/1965 election (5, 35%), the FPÖ was engaged in forcing the issue of a 'German' community of one people and one culture (*Kultur- und Volksgemeinshaft*) more into the background. This issue was no longer a political slogan or instrument (cf.

speech of Friedrich Peters at the FPÖs national party conference in Bad Ischl, 1968). Thus, a new party programme was released in 1968. The FPÖ stood up for a united Europe in any respect. The idea of a 'German' community only came up in the context of education and culture. The following data have been used and analysed:

- the FPÖ's party programmes: Burgenland Resolution, 1986; Lorenzener Resolution, 1989; Parteiprogramm der FPÖ, 1993; and ‚10-Punkte Programm der FPÖ: Österreich ist kein Einwanderungsland (10 theses of the FPÖ: ‚Austria is not an immigration country);
- the FPÖ party press: FPÖ-AULA (Die Aula, 1983–2004) and FPÖ PD (Der Freiheitliche Pressedienst, 1993–2004); and
- the FPÖ leaders,' Jörg Hider and Ewald Stadler, speeches between 1996–2002.

The selected speeches are: Jorg Haider, 1996/1 (Wahlrede am 10. Oktober 1996); Jörg Haider. 1996/2 (Rede vor dem Nationalrat am 18. Juni 1996); Jörg Haider, 1998 (Rede vor dem Nationalrat am 27. November 1998); Jörg Haider, 2001 (Rede am Aschermittwoch in Ried am 28. February 2001); Ewald Stadler (2002 Sonnwendrede in Seebarn am 21. Juni 2002).

Until 1986, the merits of the FPÖ were predominated by the issue of freedom. The issues of folklore and home often appeared in various colours. Multicultural societies were disapproved at all. Thus, the confession to the 'German' community was permanently stressed. Concerning the FPÖ family policy, the so-called smallest 'cell' of society—the family—still was most important for a healthy society. Culture and art were regarded as being free as long as they did not violate manners and customs. Again, central was the idea of a community of one people and one culture, which the Austrian XPP always clearly defines as being 'German.' Class struggle, generation conflicts or conflicts between different professions were rejected. Rather, they wanted the individuals' rights and duties against the community to be well-balanced.

The foreign policy of the FPÖ was dominated by questions of joining the European Union. Other principles of the FPÖ foreign policy were a general European orientation and the fact of being part of the 'German' community which resulted in an obligation against German minorities living in countries of the former Habsburg Monarchy.

Moreover, until 1986 the issue of immigration was increasingly given special emphasis. For instance, a programmatic resolution concerning the question of immigrants was formulated by the *'Burgenland'* according to which FPÖ took a firm stand against improvement of the immigrant status. After Jörg Haider was designated to be the new chairman of the FPÖ in 1986, the so-called 'Lorenzener Circle' was established. They saw themselves as the party's conscience and formulated the ideological basics of the Haider-FPÖ. Twelve theses concerning the FPÖ's political revival were published in 1989 which was called the 'Lorenzener Resolution.' In the introduction they clearly take stand against a pluralist or heterogeneous society. The theses clearly display the party's attitude against foreigners in the context of integration status, welfare state, pluralism, and criminality which was related to immigrants.

The propagated concept of an immigrant as being an 'enemy' mainly confers to economically and socially weak people from Eastern and South East Europe. People from Western (European) countries are hardly associated with this concept except for people with a different skin colour.

The following frames have been chosen to analyse the role of XPP, mass media, and mainstream parties for reinforcement of the 'Us' and 'Them' asymmetric categories in the Austrian public debate: Collective Identity, Employment Issues, Welfare Issues, Law & Order Issues, Antiestablishment.

From the Austrian XPP perspective, immigrants function as 'scapegoats' mainly in two respects: first, for social and economic grievance like unemployment, housing storage, criminality, etc., and second, for 'racial reasons,' which means that immigrants are not regarded as a part of the 'German' community which is defined on an organic basis. Therefore, immigrants are labelled as 'a danger' to Austrian society and have to be excluded. This is reflected in the FPÖ's agitation and language: They present themselves as being the friends of 'natives' (cf. slogan: '*Ein Herz für Inländer*') and against immigration that they see as a major problem for Austrian society: 'Immigrants destabilize the country. Immigrants create chaos. Immigrants are responsible for the problems with Neo-Nazis.'

The analysis shows that the frames of 'collecitve identity,' 'criminality,' and 'employment and welfare' are the most used frames by FPÖ.

Collective Identity

FPÖ have since its early days of establishment propagated for a united Europe and the defence of German and Western culture. It said in its party programme of 1968 that: "A special task of the cultural policy is to maintain and develop the German culture and all aspects of western cultural values." As mentioned earlier, FPÖ have during its existence in the Austrian political scene also stressed the homogenous culture and people of Austria. Therefore, a belief in and propaganda of the German origin and exclusive ethnicity of 'true Austrians' have been an inseparable part of the party's political agenda.

FPÖ have strongly opposed 'pluralism' as a danger to Australian people and society. The party declares in the party programme of 1989 that:

> Individual freedom has its limits, when ethnic fundamental values, the collective freedom of the people, community interests and the like are concerned. These are absolute truths. An ideological pluralism is therefore limited by cultural and patriotic traditions, customs and, above all, by objective truths. (FPÖ party programme, 1989, p. 1)

This is even a main theme in the debate and discourses used in the party press of FPÖ:

> Instead of pompous conferences on the Multikulti-Spuk and discussions on the concept, should Vranitzky [the leader of SPÖ] finally take the concerns of the Austrians seriously and not the foreigners, in accordance to the policy of 'Austria first' act. (PD, 1993, No. 10)

Jörg Haider and Ewald Stadler have been very aware of the dualism of the categories of 'Us' against 'Them' in the political curriculum of Austria. The following is just one illustration of many speeches of the party leaders of FPÖ: "I do this but, knowing how necessary it is that we preserve our folk by healthy, strong and large families organize themselves, and not by immigration experiments" (Ewald Sadler, 2002). The government policies, such as the family policy and the policy of labour force immigration have also been attacked as degrading of 'our Western culture'. This is clearly stated in party programmes:

> The family policy has also to do with the preservation of our nation, our Western culture, and our traditions. We therefore reject the compensation of our birth deficit through the naturalization of foreigners, mostly still a cultural underclass with huge disabilities. (Party programme, 1989, p. 4)

Employment and Welfare

The frame of employment and welfare has been one of the most important issues in FPÖ's party programmes, party press, and the leaders' speeches. Immigrants have presented as a danger to the Austrian people's welfare and jobs. FPÖ has been very successful to put this issue in the political scene of the country and even influence other parities and political actors to in one way or another mention and debate this perspective.

In the party programmes and party press the FPÖ immigrants are taken responsible for unemployment and shortages in the welfare subsidies for 'natives.' It is clearly declared in the party programmes that 'native' Austrians should be protected against unemployment and immigrants' who are a burden on the welfare system (e.g., FPÖ party programmes of 1986, 1989, and 1993). The PD writes in 1996 that: "There are 300.000 unemployed and 300.000 immigrants in Austria" (May 1996).

> The welfare state Austria has such generosity, that we have to cut the money to our women and mothers, because we have no more money, that we have to halve the pocket money to the disabled, because we have no more money, but we have money for each asylum seeker, here in the country, 30.000 S and more is available for an asylum seeker, even if he is delinquent. (Jörg Haider, 1998)

The shortage of housing is also related by the XPP and its press to the existence of immigrants and asylum seekers in Austria. The other party organ, AULA, writes:

> As long as we have 11,000 residents who are seeking for social housing, these houses must be reserved for these people. It is not acceptable that an immigrant entering Austria also automatically receive a community housing. (AULA, October 2000)

The understanding and propaganda that jobs must go to 'Austrians first' is a constitutive part of the party's propaganda. It was stated already in the FPÖ's party programme in 1986: "Austrian jobs will be filled by Austrians" (Party programme, 1986, p. 1). FPÖ presented immigrants as lazy people coming to Austria for holiday and not willing to work: "With an asylum application should automatically follow the work obligation. It would also stop the comfortable asylum holiday in Austria" (Party programme, 1986, p. 1). This is a contradictory position held by FPÖ. The party propagate that immigrants are not willing to work, on the one hand, and that the positions in the labour market must be fulfilled by Austrians on the other.

Law and Order

This frame is also very common and used as a marker for the separation of the category of 'Us,' who follow the laws and regulations, and 'immigrants,' the 'others,' who have no respect for 'our' laws and are presented in many cases as criminals. Such categorization and inferiorization of 'immigrants' are not often overt or straight forward. The FPÖ tries many times to distance itself from the accusation of being racist or xenophobic when presenting immigrants as criminals. The following is an illustration of this when the leader of FPÖ, Jörg Haider presents Turkish youths as criminals:

> And we need in this community in Vienna also say that everything is not allowed, that this has nothing to do with xenophobia. But if it has gone so far that our children in some districts no longer can go to the playground because their Turkish youth gangs demand protection money, then it is time that we take appropriate actions, ladies and gentlemen, because this is our city and here are our democratic laws! (Jörg Haider, 1996)

The FPÖ's party press have also in several articles stigmatized 'black Africans,' Turks, and other immigrant groups as 'drug dealers' and engaged in other criminal acts. For instance, in an article about immigrants in the party organ AULA (September, 2002) it is concluded that: "In Vienna and Graz hundreds of drug dealer black Africans are driven around." Two years later the party organ AULA declared:

Particularly acute is the security problem in those areas where the current flow of asylum seekers has turned the whole villages to "crisis regions." . . . Above all, the African drug mafia targets Vienna. Drug trafficking is going on almost uninhibitedly on the open street. (AULA, November 2004)

Presenting asylum-seekers and immigrants as a problem for Austria has been of central importance for FPÖ which is presenting itself as a party for the Austrian people whose rights, 'way of life,' and security are endangered by the 'others.' The discussions and debates on law and order are highly connected to the existence of immigrants in the country.

Antiestablishment

The antiestablishment issues have been used by FPÖ more frequently before their success of gaining political power in 1990s. However, they continued to accuse the mainstream parties, Social-Democratic Party of Austria (SPÖ) and in a lesser extent the Austrian People's Party (ÖVP). The mainstream parties and politicians are taken responsible for increasing immigration, as well as increasing immigrants' political influence. They opposed any national and municipal franchise right to immigrants. The mainstream parties are also accused for increasing criminality, unemployment, and decreasing social welfare subsidies for 'true Austrians' (Party programmes, 1986, 1989, 1993, 2002; Jörg Haider, 1998; party press, AULA, October 2000, among others).

The party leaders and party press make it clear that when they get ride of the establishment and succeeded to defeat the mainstream parties, they will stop immigration and compensate for the establishment's mistakes:

> FPÖ wants that Vienna regain its identity as a Central City. Finally it will be a real immigration stop, criminal aliens and illegal immigrants actually deported, which means about 100,000 persons. In addition, those foreigners who only recently arrived in the country and have no chance of getting a job, will return to their homes. (AULA, March 1999)

In order to portray itself as the only truly antiimmigrant party, the FPÖ criticises frequently the establishment, namely government in general and SPÖ in particular.

The Dichotomy of 'Us' against the Muslim 'Others'

Although Islam was officially recognized in Austria in 1912 during the reign of Czar Franz Joseph as the second religion in the country after Catholicism, the xenophobic propaganda against Muslims is a part of the country's public debate. FPÖ has consequently used the discourses against Muslims as the 'others' and as the counter side of the Austrian German and

Western culture in order to mobilize support. In the Austrian sociopolitical context the concept and category of 'Turks' is representing 'Muslims' who are mainly considered culturally as one of the most different groups of 'foreigners' from 'Us.'

The European Commission Against Racism and Intolerance (ECRI) *Third Report on Austria* (2004, p. 29) confirms the racist discursive and even physical attacks on migrants in general and on Muslims in particular.[3] The report states that FPÖ and its antiimmigrants and anti-Muslim political propagandas played a central role for the increase of xenophobic and anti-Muslim sentiments in Austria. The anti-Muslim rhetoric and discourses used by the FPÖ have encouraged hostility towards Muslims in Austria. Party programmes, the party press, and party leaders speeches, especially after September 11, 2001, show drastically increased anti-Muslim discourses in addressing immigrant groups in Austria. The questions of *Hijab* and *halal* staughter have been frequently used to 'otherize' Muslims and legitimize discrimination against these groups. In the elections campaign in 2002, the FPÖ opposed the right of foreigners, who were portrayed as Muslims, to vote in local elections. In the party's election material Muslim women who wear the headscarf was presented as a symbol of the 'enemy within.' For example, in FPÖ brochures, pictures of veiled Muslim women were combined with the provocative question: "The mayor of my district is from Turkey, what about yours?"

There are many 'warnings' for the 'Muslim threat' in the FPÖ's party press and the party leaders' speeches. This was also criticized by Muslim and antiracist organizations in Austria. In 2004, Carla Amina Baghajati, spokeswoman of the Islamic Community in Austria, warns for the increasing anti-Muslim propaganda, not only from FPÖ but even from mainstream press's prejudiced presentations of Muslims.

Assessing Impacts of the XPP

Since FPÖ enters the Austrian government in the early 2000, its influence on political 'acting' against migration and migrants (rather than just 'talking' about it) becomes ever more visible. It must be noted that it is during the both 'Schüssel' governments (of FPÖ and ÖVP) in power since 2000 that many crucial antiimmigration laws are passed and implemented: with the most controversial 2002 Integration Agreement at the fore, followed by the 2004 Act on Asylum, and, more recently, the currently debated 2005 Act on Foreigners. These are among the FPÖ's direct impact on the Austrian society and the reinforcement of structural/institutional discrimination of the 'others' in Austria.

To illustrate the direct impact of the FPÖ, the introduction of the controversial law which was called 'Integration Agreement' (IA) will be shortly discusses below. The government declared that it had an intention to improve integration in order to guarantee 'peaceful coexistence' of different ethnic groups in Austria. They declared that the target groups of the IA are:

- new migrants who come to Austria as so-called key employees (*Schlüsselkräfte*) together with their families;
- unemployed nationals of non-European Union member states who are qualified by the Labour Market Service (*Arbeitsmarktservice AMS*); and
- people who do not yet hold a residence permit in the sense of the Aliens Act (*Fremdengesetz*).

EEC-citizens, infants, and school-age children are excluded from the Integration Agreement. Foreigners whose circumstances of living are crucial in some way—for example, pregnant women or mothers with babies, etc.—are temporary released from the contract as long as they can prove a certain command of the German language (§ 10a of the 1985 Nationality Act—*StbG—Staatsbürgerschaftsgesetz*).

The law stipulates that within the first 4 years of residence in Austria, 100 instructional units of 45 minutes each of a German language course are compulsory for:

1. Foreigners who belong to one of the above mentioned target groups. Again, foreigners or key workers who can show evidence according to § 10 StbG are excluded. The courses are organised by the Federal Government and offered by authorised professional organisations of the adult education sector. The curriculum for these courses— German language classes and classes on nationality (*Staatsbürgerschaftskunde*)—are provided by the Austrian Ministry of Education, Science, and Culture which also verifies examinations occasionally. The course participants have to prove their successful participation. Fifty percent of the costs are covered by the federal government.
2. Key employees who intend to stay for more than 24 months in Austria (again with the exception of those people who come under § 10 StbG). At that point, language courses are organised by the employers, but again carried out by authorised professional organisations. The course participants have to prove their successful participation. Fifty percent of the costs are then covered by the employer.

If people do not start the language classes within the first two years of stay in Austria they will be fined 100 to 200 Euros. If they have not completed the language course after four years, the following sanctions come into force:

- resetting of an extension to bring forward a proof of completion of the required course hours;

- cut or loss of the governmental grants for language courses;
- denial of issuing a permit of settlement;
- relative fine for denying integration; and
- expiring of the residence permit.

Officially, the intentions of the Integration Agreement are defined as follows: The creation of the Integration Agreement extends the supply of language acquisition within the educational sector and supports the social and cultural living together of natives and nonnatives in a positive way, for example, improvement of the situation in the labour market. Additionally, prejudices could gradually be overcome and social abuse can be contained. However, the Integration Agreement was criticised on several dimensions by scholars in 'German as a Second Language' and by linguists specialised in Language Policies and Foreign Language Teaching (e.g., Conference 'Language and Integration: the Integration Agreement in Comparison' organised in February 2002 by the Viennese Integration House; Austrian Association of Applied Linguistics 'Verbal'; Austrian Association for German as a Foreign Language 'ÖdaF'; Association of Viennese People's Education 'VWV'; and the Minorities Redaction of the Austrian Public Broadcaster ORF; cf. also Krumm, 2002): Experts were not involved into the construction of the curricula; 100 lessons are by far not enough to acquire the necessary competence in German (The Netherlands and Germany provide about 900 lessons paid by the state); the compulsory dimension is quite unique in Europe (sanctions if the test is not passed, see above); the name 'Integration Agreement' is misleading: Neither is there any 'Agreement' (nobody was asked to agree), nor is the present policy adequate for any level of 'integration.'

Critiques concerning the coercive attendance of German classes emphasise mainly the expense factor. The institutions providing these courses are hardly able to comply with the cost regulations that may not exceed more than 364 Euros per language course participant. Instead, they bargain for at least 450 to 500 Euros per person per course. Although 50% of the expenses are covered by the government or the employers at that time, language course participants still have to pay up to a maximum of 182 Euro (cf. Kurier, March 16, 2003, p. 11). The FPÖ is one of the XPP in Europe that have direct impact on Austrian society and succeeded to reinforce the existing structural/institutional discrimination in the country.

The indirect impact of the FPÖ on the mainstream parties and politics of Austria has been studied by analyzing the change in the party programmes of the mainstream parties, namley SPÖ and ÖVP. The following party programmes of the two mainstream parties have been selected:

- SPÖ-1978 Das neue Parteiprogramm der SPÖ, May 20, 1978 (The New Party Program);
- SPÖ-PS Das Grundsatzprogramm der SPÖ ('Policy Statments of the SPÖ');

- SPÖ-1998 SPÖ Parteiprogramm (Party Programme of the SPÖ);
- SPÖ-2002 Wahlprogramm: Projekt 19, (Election Programme: Project 19);
- SPÖ-2003/1 Argumente 9': Integration ist kein Thema, 2003 (Argument 9: Integration is not an issue);
- SPÖ-2003/2 Argumente 15: Aktive Integrationspolitik, 2003 (Argument 15: Active Integration Politics);
- ÖVP-72/95 Salzburger Programm, 1972/1995 (Salzburg Program);
- ÖVP-1985 Das Zukunftsmanifest der ÖVP: Österreich hat Zukunft (The Future Manifesto of the ÖVP: Austria has a Future);
- ÖVP-1995 Grundsatzprogramm neu (New Party Program);
- ÖVP-1999 Der bessere Weg. Programm der ÖVP am Beginn des 21. Jahrhunderts, 1999 (The Better Way. ÖVP Program at the Beginning of the 21st Century);
- ÖVP-2002 Das Österreich-Programm der Volkspartei (The Austria-Programme of the ÖVP); and
- ÖVP-2003 Regierungs programm (Government Programme).

The party programme of 1978 stressed the four principles of freedom, equality, justice, and solidarity. Central to the SPÖ's philosophy was the guarantee of freedom from fear, hunger, exploitation, and unemployment for all Austrians. They claimed that the freedom to pursue wealth had to be balanced by the government's guarantee of equal opportunity and social justice.

In the parliamentary election of 1983, the SPÖ lost its absolute majority, and Kreisky decided to retire from politics rather than preside over a coalition government. Fred Sinowatz was selected chancellor in a coalition government with the FPÖ. The Sinowatz era, from 1983 until 1986, proved to be a short interregnum and was not distinguished by any great achievements.

Franz Vranitzky became chancellor in June 1986 when Sinowatz resigned after the SPÖ lost the presidential election to Kurt Waldheim. Under Vranitzky the SPÖ moved to restore its image among rank-and-file members by improving its methods of intraparty communication. The SPÖ stressed that limits on state activity were necessary, although he noted that health care and education were sectors where market forces had to be regulated. Vranitzky displayed an open attitude toward the question of privatizing government industries and embraced the principle that privatization should be pursued if it would lead to greater operational efficiency.

Party organization remained centralized as of the early 1990s.

Collective Identity

For traditional reasons, the representation of social interests as well as the party's image as being the party of workers and 'small' people were dominant. Issues on immigration did always play a marginal role in the programmatic development of the SPÖ. The party declared in its party programme in 2002 that: "The right to a homeland of all Austrians and the right to integrate the migrants who come to Austria legally belong together" (Party programme, 2002). Although the both parties make a categorical differentiation between 'Austrian people' and 'immigrants,' the concept of an exclusive 'Austiran collective identity' is not much elaborated in the both mainstream party programmes.

Meanwhile the SPÖ had a more proimmigrant agenda, the ÖVP seemed to be more affected by the discourses and the frame of the FPÖ. This is also affected by the governmental coalition between ÖVP and FPÖ. The ÖVP stressed that: "Unlimited immigration at the expense of the Austrian people is not possible. Not every foreigner will finally get the permission to stay in Austria" (ÖVP, 1995, p. 1). The ÖVP concluded then that "not every foreigner have a right to stay in our homeland" (ÖVP party programme, 1995).

After analysing the selected ÖVP programs, it is obvious that the party make a distinction between 'the Austrian people' and immigrants. However the immigration issue is marginal within the ÖVP's programmatic discourse. It is also striking that this issue is often placed within the concluding chapters of the ÖVP party programmes.

Employment and Welfare

This frame is not used by the mainstream parties extensively. However meanwhile SPÖ tries to show a more human and positive image of immigration, the ÖVP indicates more concern about the number of immigrants and the capacity of the Austrian society for accepting the newcomers. They declare in their party programme in 1995 that: "The number of foreigners should not exceed the absorption capacity of the Austrian labor market, the school, and the regional housing market" (ÖVP party programme, 1995).

The ÖVP is very concerned about patterns of the legal immigrations status, that is mainly a differentiation between migrants and asylum seekers. They stress that the Austrian labour market needs immigrant labour force, which they concequently call 'foreign worker': "The Austrian economy needs foreign workers. . . . The goal should be the better integration of foreigners and their family members by increasing their access to the labour market" (ÖVP party programme, 1999). The party programmes of ÖVP shows an increasing concern about immigration and their status in the Austrian labour market. This can be said to be an effect of ÖVP's cooperation and alliance with FPÖ and the change in the public debate where immigrants came to be increasingly presented as problem.

Law and Order

This frame had not have a central role in discourses concerning immigration dring the 1980s. The fall of Berlin wall and the increasing immigration from Balkan, as well as, the increasing support for the FPÖ during the

1990s changed the debate and put the immigration on the political agenda of both the FPÖ and the mainstream parties. The attacks of September 11, 2001 on World Trade Center in New York and the Pentagon in Washington, DC, related the debate on immigration to national security. The threat of terrorism came a central discourse for the FPÖ in its discourses on asylum seekers who are coming here to 'abuse our system' and plan terrorist attacks. This forced the SPÖ and VPÖ to debate on the issue of law and order and present themselves as strong parties in fighting terrorism and guranteeing the Austrian people's security. The protection of Austrian borders to hinder illegal immigration and the 'abuse of the asylum law' has been a part of the mainstream parties' election manifestos.

Mass Media and the 'Others'

In the analysis of frames used by the mainstream press, the material from the following nationwide, daily Austrian newspapers have been analysed:

- *Der Standard* (ST), liberal daily;
- *Die Presse* (PR), conservative daily; and
- *Neue Kronen Zeitung* (KR), daily tabloid.

In our analyses, we have gathered and analysed the material surrounding the following events:

- The fall of the Berlin Wall November 9th 1989 and the Crisis of 'Romanian Orphans' (December 1989/January 1990);
- FPÖ's Austria First Petition (January/February 1993);
- 1997 Act on Foreigners (June/ August 1997);
- The Marcus Omafuma Case (May/June 1999);
- Attack on the World Trade Center in New York on September 11, 2001; and
- Asylum-Camps Debate and the 2004 Act on Asylum (October 2004).

The Fall of the Communism (in Romania) and the Crisis of 'Romanian Orphans' (December 1989/January 1990)

Reporting on the fall of Communism and on the end of the communist rule in Romania was rather extensive. In the aftermath, reporting on the refugee crisis which broke out in Austria following the arrival of several thousand Romanian children orphaned during the bloody riots in Romania.

Very typical for the reporting of the fall of the communism and the refugee/immigration as its aftermath, the reporting on the Romanian fall of the communism and the following refugee crisis (in all three newspapers in question, i.e., ST, PR, and KR) does not include any negative references to the issue of migration as a 'problem' (viz. this tendency starts in the Austrian media/politics only afterwards) and therefore contains almost no application of the frames in question. Migration and the intake of refugees are portrayed as positive (although not actually given prominence unlike, e.g., the Austrian help and charity to Romanians in Austria and in their homeland). If spoken at, migrants/refugees are not portrayed as a 'threat' and are limited to a set of numbers and statistics. Since the reporting concerns (mostly) Austria-external occurrences, no agents apart from the newspapers themselves are 'given voice'; if any party-specific behaviour is mentioned it is described in a positive way (e.g., as supporting charity- and aid-actions).

FPÖ's Austria First Petition (January/February 1993)

This event caused a rather extensive reporting on national referendum on the FPÖ's Austria First Petition (launched in December 1992 and put under the national referendum in January 1993) which was proposing general changes in several legal acts regulating immigration and asylum seeking in Austria as well as other acts 'defining' principles of the Austrian socio-political system. FPÖ was proposing, *inter alia*, writing into the federal constitution a statement that "Austria is not a land of immigration." The FPÖ which authored and initiated the petition out of a clearly political will, namely to become the main party 'dealing' with migration in 'a proper way,' was willing to collect approximately 800,000 signatures in the referendum, that is, the number of votes for the FPÖ scored in the previous NPE. Although only approximately 400,000 Austrians backed the petition, yet the fact that the petition passed the threshold of 100,000 signatures allowed the FPÖ to make it an official act-proposal in the parliament (it was taken under debate in the parliament in April 1993). Although highly unsuccessful in immediate political terms, the 'Austria First' must be considered a 'milestone' and the starting point for: (a) making immigration a highly political and voter-sensitive topic for all political parties in the years to come, and (b) changing the mainstream political language into a more 'negative' and 'discriminatory' discourse when speaking about immigration, asylum seeking, etc.[4]

Der Standard (ST) portrays the referendum mainly as a tactical–political move which should secure the FPÖ the place of the only party which cares for Austrians and their 'right to fatherland' (one of the main arguments in the referendum). ST takes the very critical stance towards the FPÖ itself in general, and its referendum in particular, yet the paper very rarely does the criticising itself. In the opposition to the latter, key politicians of the FPÖ and proponents of the referendum as well as some 'allies' of the FPÖ are also given voice (e.g., the very conservative wing of the Catholic Church) and are juxtaposed with FPÖ's 'enemies.'

Unlike the *Standard*, the *Neue Kronen Zeitung* (KR) takes up a semi-latent pro-FPÖ stance. KR is also less prone to quote and is therefore using its own voice of its editors and journalists to utter several voices against immigration and for the FPÖ's referendum. In a typical manner for the newspaper, very populist buzzwords and very frequently strong antiimmigrant claims are used to speak against the immigration. Such discriminatory discourse is hidden in typically KR language of Austrian traditionalism, nationalism and interests. KR generally opposes the establishment, mainly the SPÖ government as the main enemy of the FPÖ, but also the ÖVP is strongly criticised, as well as, all those who are seemingly 'undemocratic' and not really taking care of the Austrian 'Volk.' These 'undemocratic' agents, according to FPÖ, are trade unions and other social partners in general, and their 'non-democratically' elected leaders in particular. Several articles in KR are clearly in favour of the petition; one of them even includes an appeal starting with a title "one can sign it easily with a clear conscience" (KR, January 1993, No. 14) listing the arguments proreferendum (resembling the leaflets sent by post by the FPÖ in favour of the referendum). In order to reinforce antiimmigrant sentiments, KR writes many articles quoting the "layman" and "everymen" on the street saying: "we say no to economic-asylum-seekers, fake-asylum seekers and criminals who are now present in several parts of Austria" (KR, February 1993, No. 1).

Finally, *Die Presse* (PR), as the main conservative and ÖVP-friendly newspaper, is also against the FPÖ and its referendum. Unlike the other two newspapers, PR goes much more into details and attempts at portraying all parties' attitudes towards migration rather than focusing on the ways in which FPÖ on the one hand, and SPÖ and ÖVP on the other, are trying to construct the conflict between them 'about' the referendum. Thus, unlike ST and KR, *Die Presse* is trying to deconstruct the actual reasons for the FPÖ's initiation of the anti foreigner petition. Throughout the reporting, PR is trying to deconstruct whether there are indeed any widespread fears against foreigners/asylum-seekers within the Austrian society. Arriving very frequently at the conclusions that the foreigner hatred is not actually very strong in the Austrian society in general, PR argues that the most of the antiforeigner moods are actually heated up by the FPÖ out of tactical–political reasons.

1997 Act on Foreigners (June/August 1997)

This analysis of media reporting is based on the debates on and passing of the 1997 Act on Foreigners and Act on Asylum, the main legal acts regulating immigration- and asylum-related issues Although traditionally supporting the SPÖ, the ST seems to be very much distanced from the new 'anti-foreigner' laws of that party as far as reporting on debates and passing of the 1997 'Integrationspaket' is concerned. Instead, ST gives some voice to parties of a strongly proimmigrant attitudes (Greens, LIF) as the ones opposing the new legislation and portrays the SPÖ in the 'neutral' form and only resorts to quoting the SPÖ officials without actually assessing their stance; as if not willing to criticise the party on the one hand, but also not willing to back the antiimmigration laws on the other. The ÖVP (in coalition with the SPÖ and backing the 'Integrationspaket') remains not mentioned.

KR seems to overlook the very heated debate on the new immigration laws in its reporting. It seems to not willing to back the SPÖ as the party which now embarks on typically FPÖ-specific field of political action. KR does not seem to be very much concerned with the new 'Integrationspaket' and instead is reporting extensively on the KR-exclusive interview with the Minister of the Interior (SPÖ) who claimed that the large percentage of asylum-seekers coming into Austria are actually criminals.

Die Presse (PR) presents a very 'dry' reporting on the new legislative package. However, PR reports on several 'voices' against the new legislative package (by quoting the main 'criticisers' such as Greens, Catholic Church, other religious organisations, and NGOs) as well as presents one article criticising the package by a renowned intellectual. The interview with the Minister of the Interior (SPÖ) does not seem to include much of critique and instead focuses on the 'rational' arguments prolegislation presented by the interviewee.

The Marcus Omafuma Case (May/June 1999)

The analysis concerns the press debate after the death of Marcus Omafuma. Omafuma, a former Nigerian asylum applicant in Austria who was found dead during his deportation trip on the Bulgarian Airlines flight after his asylum application was rejected by Austria (he was being deported to Bulgaria, the country from which he arrived to Austria). It was supposed that he suffocated after his mouth was taped by the escorting Austrian policemen. The incident was followed by numerous references to asylum-seeking and its role/status in Austria in general, and to a general debate on the frequent breaches of human rights in the asylum procedures in Austria in particular.

Der Standard (ST) focuses very extensively on the case of Omafuma's death. In particular, ST presents several arguments against the current system of asylum denial and deportation. The main 'target' of the ST is the Minister of the Interior Karl Schlögl, who is called to resign by several of his political opponents (including Greens, LIF, and several NGOs and religious organisations). Schlögl is also being accused of having received hints about very aggressive behaviour of migrant police during several deportations in the past and for not having reacted properly to those hints and allegations.

Unlike ST, *Die Neue Kronen Zeitung* (KR) is itself becoming an 'agent' which is very frequently constructing racist and discriminatory opinions against migrants in its reporting (cf. below). Also unlike ST, KR fully backs

Minister Schlögl and portrays him as the man who shows a strong hand against illegal immigration (viz. Omafuma was not an illegal migrant) and as a victim of a campaign initiated by the media and by his political opponents *Die Presse* (PR) offers seemingly the most comprehensive reporting of the case Omafuma and attempts ate presenting all the possible arguments for and against the case. PR reporting seems somewhat deeper than that of the ST, as the former attempts to show several inconsistencies in deportation procedures and presents several arguments showing that aggressive behaviour of the police assisting the deported asylum-seekers was frequently the case. Unlike the ST, PR tries not to attack the Minister of the Interior but to present him as one of the key people in the case (and not as the 'main perpetrator' who is defending a human-rights-violating system of deportations). Several views against the Minister are also portrayed (including, e.g., the arguments by Amnesty International). In a very unusual tone for the PR (viz. the newspaper was usually presenting very reliable and well proven pieces of information) the reporting on the Omafuma case ends up in a rather discriminatory article stating that he was 'possibly' living in Germany under a false name/citizenship before and that he was allegedly a drug dealer.

Attack on the World Trade Center in the United States on September 11, 2001

The attacks on the World Trade Center in New York carried out a huge immigration related debate in Austria. The reporting of 9/11 in ST focuses on presenting some general facts about the attacks as well as about the possible organisers of the attacks (Bin Laden, Al-Qa'ida, radical Islamist groups, etc.). The majority of the ST reporting focuses on the problem of possible extension of the stereotypes against radical terrorist groups "recognising themselves as belonging to Islam" onto the entire social and international images of Islam. In particular, several opinions and warnings by the Catholic Church (including Pope John Paul II) about the increasing anti-Muslim sentiments are being frequently quoted. The party–political interchange of views (typical for the issues in question) does not occur in the reporting.

Similarly to ST, KR focuses on the explanation of possible reasons for the terrorist attacks and their possible organisers. In its typically semiofficial tone (i.e., populist-like) the newspaper presents several organisers of the attacks. KR uses very frequently various stereotypes and prejudices against Islam, Muslims, and Arabs. Headings like "where did the fundamentalists get their money from" are frequently used. KR resorts to several even stronger racist and discriminatory arguments against Islam, Muslims, and 'wave of asylum-seekers' following the 9/11 attacks. Almost no Austrian political actors are quoted/mentioned in the reporting. Headlines and subheadlines are particularly crucial here in a typically tabloid-like manner.

Die Presse, similar to ST, focuses on the very broad and general explanation of the reasons for 9/11 attacks in the United States. It is frequently interpreting them as a logical aftermath of U.S.'s Middle East politics, while also trying to point to organisers of the attacks. Unlike the ST and quite typically for the new 'slightly-populist' trend acquired by PR already in the Omafuma reporting, the PR is frequently not enough cautious and utters several racist and discriminatory and stereotypical views on several occasions although in an interesting, nonmainstream location in the headlines/subheadlines. It writes for instance: (without any explanation or introduction): "72 virgins are waiting for the Islamic suicide-terrorists who gave their life for the widespread of Islam or for the defence of the Islamic territory" (PR, September 14, 2001).

Asylum-Camps Debate and the 2004 Act on Asylum (October 2004)

The analysis concerns the press debate on the Government's proposal of a new act on asylum (replacing the 1997 Asylum Act). The act was supposed to be one of the flagship antiimmigrant projects of the second ÖVP-FPÖ 'Schüssel' government. The government project, as well as the nationwide debate on asylum within which it was initiated, were triggered by the alleged 'overflow' of the Austrian refugee camps and the 'burden' caused to the Austrian state system by the allegedly increasing number of asylum-seekers.

In a highly politicised manner, ST focuses on the critique of the government (ÖVP-FPÖ) and its irresponsible asylum policy and its misleading projects of the new asylum laws. Traditionally, the political actors are being positioned as those 'pro' government (ÖVP, partially FPÖ) and those 'against' (SPÖ, Greens, NGOs). The position of the FPÖ seems to be ambivalent, with, on the one hand, clear progovernment stance and, on the other hand, the critique of the government as far 'too soft' in the asylum issues.

KR focuses on the 'asylum crisis' much more than on the new legislative project of harshening the asylum laws. The reporting of the newspaper is kept in the mood of a crisis and creates 'social fear' of the alleged waves of asylum-seekers flowing into Austria and endangering peace and tranquillity of everyday lives of many Austrians. Like in ST, the debate is highly politicised, yet clearly the FPÖ politicians are given far more space for expressing their views and opinions, against both the asylum problem as such and against the 'far too soft' policies of their coalition partner ÖVP. As usual, racist and discriminatory arguments are used, very frequently in combination with the visual data (e.g., large numbers of 'black' people walking down streets of Austria in the night). As usually, the power of messages distributed by the Krone is on headlines, notably almost all headlines of articles on asylum issues are with exclamation marks (meaning 'important/problem').

In a fairly populist tone, PR focuses on 'voices of Austrian everymen' and their fears of increased numbers of asylum-seekers. Interestingly, PR is the only mainstream newspaper to emphasise that the costs of asylum-seeking in Austria are not solely funded from Austrian budgetary means, but that also the European Union is supporting Austria with its asylum funds. Elements of typical party political exchanges and debates are also reported yet not put into the foreground, like in ST and KR.

Conclusion

The study shows that despite political propaganda of the FPÖ and in some cases even from of the mainstream parties and press, the economic situation, and the 'global changes' (frequently invoked when arguing against immigration to Austria) are not the real reasons for the very rapid change of negative attitudes towards migration. On the contrary, it must be noted that Austrian economy is still in a relatively very good shape. It also seems that demographic and other changes in the Austrian society, such as rapidly decreasing birthrates among the 'natives' and the increasing need for external labour force make the recent 'negative' attitudes towards migration even more ungrounded.

Thus, the only plausible answer to the question why the social attitudes towards migrants have changed so dramatically in Austria in the late 20th century and in the wake of the new millennium is actually the political use of immigration and increasing electoral importance of otherization. As it seems, it is the immense eagerness of Austrian politicians to take up negative stance towards migration throughout the last fifteen years which has, by now, 'rooted' and 'imprinted' the public image of migration as a 'problem.' Thus it is 'the political' strongly influencing 'the social' and learning well how to use the 'fears' of the latter for their political advantages. The politicians have, in almost 15 years now, made migrants the main scapegoats of the problems which have recently appeared in Austrian economy and society.

Unlike in many other European countries, where the radical right and populist parties constitute a new political occurrence, the 'populist' tradition is very old in Austria. The Freedom Party of Austria (FPÖ) is, by now, almost 50 years old while it is also anchored in the pan-Germanic ideologies and movements dating back to 19th century. Hence, one may conclude that the 'creeping smoke' of the xenophobic populism has always been 'out there' in the Austrian politics. The widespread racist Nazi ideology in the 1930s and 1940s is also another contributing factor behind the increasing xenophobia in the country. Thus, it was not at all surprising that the FPÖ effectively put 'immigration' at the centre of the political and public discourse in Austria. Although not always very effective in immediate political terms, many actions of the FPÖ (such as, e.g., the 1992/1993 'Austria First' petition, cf. above) put the 'immigration' topic onto the agenda of the Austrian political scene thus allowing the party to become the main 'articulator' of the rather established and old social fears of 'the other' in general, and of migrants as 'default scapegoats' in particular. It is through actions and words of the FPÖ that migration changes its public meaning (into a negative, unwanted, and, at its best, uneasy public term) in the new geopolitical situation in Europe after the fall of the iron curtain and the demise of the Soviet empire. All in all, the "poisoning of the political language in Austria" (a term used by the late Austrian President Thomas Klestil) in general, and with regard to migration in particular must and should be ascribed to the Freedom Party.

Since FPÖ enters the Austrian government in the early 2000, its influence on political 'acting' against migration, rather than just 'talking' about it, becomes ever more visible. The FPÖ could exert direct impact on the reinforcement of structural/institutional discrimination in Austria. It must be noted that it is during the both 'Schüssel' governments (of FPÖ and ÖVP) in power since 2000 that many crucial antiimmigration laws are passed and implemented: with the most controversial 2002 Integration Agreement at the fore (cf. above), followed by the 2004 Act on Asylum (cf. above for press debate surrounding this project), and, more recently, the currently debated 2005 Act on Foreigners.

The fact that FPÖ is the main 'articulator' of the antiimmigrant stance in the Austrian politics does not make other mainstream parties 'immaculate' as far as the issue of immigration is concerned. On the contrary, while the FPÖ was still only 'talking' about migration as a problem and scapegoating migrants as the main reason for Austrian social problems (e.g., during the 1993 'Austria First' petition) the mainstream 'red' and 'black' parties (viz. SPÖ and ÖVP) quickly recognised that getting harsher on immigration might be the key to winning large parts of the Austrian electorate. Thus, it was SPÖ/ÖVP governments which introduce and implement the first and foremost radical changes in the Austrian migration policies (e.g., the 1997 Act on Foreigners and the 1997 Act on Asylum). As the migration-related opportunism cuts both ways, it seems that while embarking on the antiimmigration ship proved detrimental for the SPÖ which in 1999 moved into opposition after 29 years in power, the ÖVP actually gained in electoral support and could finally become the 'main government party' in the early 2000.

The Austrian mainstream 'red' and 'black' parties have also been responsible for legitimization of the FPÖ and allowing it into mainstream politics. While the government coalitions with the FPÖ have been the case throughout the most of the postwar era (dating back to the minority government created by the SPÖ and FPÖ under Bruno Kreisky in 1970), in a similar vein, the recent accommodation of antiimmigration views in the Austrian politics must also be ascribed to the fact that the ÖVP accepted the FPÖ as a coalition partner in 2000. Our study of the change of mainstream political discourses in the last fifteen years shows that both of the Austrian mainstream parties, SPÖ and ÖVP, must actually be located at the core of political xenophobic 'right' as far as migration-related issues are concerned. Obviously, the recent rise of the FPÖ must be seen as both cause and effect of that 'right-bound' tendency in which the normalisation and accommodation of strong antiimmigrant views in mainstream political discourses has become the everyday practice.

It must also be concluded that it is not only the political parties that have been moving to a more xenophobic populist 'right' position during the last 15 years, but also the media discourses concerning the 'others.' As politics are traditionally of utmost importance on the national public spheres, in a similar vein, the contents of the media have been changing in the last 15 years in Austria in accordance with the aforementioned 'move to the right' of the almost entire Austrian political spectrum.

THE CASE OF BRITAIN

The Political Context of Xenophobia in Britain

'Immigrant' has highly racialised connotations within the United Kingdom, which make its unqualified use problematic in a British context. The term 'immigrant' is frequently used in anti-immigration, racist discourses in the U.K. media, and as such is a strongly normative term that many suggest should be avoided. In the United Kingdom, the vast majority of people from Asian and Afro-Caribbean communities are not, and are not regarded as, 'immigrants,' although they are often referred to as such in other parts of Europe, where being 'Black' is widely treated as a mark of immigrant status (Moore, 2000)[5] and a matter of 'Otherization.' Ludi Simpson has recently suggested that, in the contemporary British context, both 'race' and 'ethnic group' have become synonyms for immigration, further confusing an already highly contested area. He says that to talk of "immigrant populations" or "a permanent foreign population" is to fall back on meaningless terms, given the fact that all people have mixed and migratory origins. He argues that "foreign is also a pernicious term to use for the Black and Asian citizens of the UK, carrying a sense of permanent limitation of rights and settlement, which is contrary to the law of the land" (Simpson, 2002, p. 3).

Given these qualifications, the migrant population can be defined as those people who are born in a country other than, but who are residents in, the United Kingdom. Using this definition there are 4.8 million migrants in total in the United Kingdom, which means migrants make up 8% of the total U.K. population and 10% of the working age population (16–59 for women and 16–64 for men). Forty seven percent of these 'migrants' have acquired British citizenship. However, it is important to bear in mind when looking at such statistics that migrants should not be considered a coherent, homogenous group. Notwithstanding, the category of 'immigrants' recalls non-Britons and 'foreign' elements among 'Us.'

The ECRI (2001) found that the U.K. population demonstrated high levels of 'xenophobic intolerance.' These attitudes were reflected not only in the media, but also "in the tone of the discourse resorted to by politicians in support of the adoption and enforcement of increasingly restrictive asylum and immigration laws" (ECRI, 2001). This conclusion seems to imply the state in the proliferation of racist/xenophobic tendencies, with the report indicating the damaging effect of the increasingly coercive nature of immigration and asylum policies on public opinion towards migrant groups. The report was particularly scathing about politicians who use "charged racist language in the hope of gaining mass appeal for their own political agenda . . . politicians have contributed to, or not adequately prevented, public debate taking an increasingly intolerant line with racist and xenophobic overtones" (ECRI, 2001). The report explicitly criticized the Immigration and Asylum Act (1999) for withdrawing benefits from the majority of asylum seekers by introducing "degrading and stigmatising" food vouchers and the dispersal scheme as a means of "sharing the burden" of asylum seekers among local communities.

Another survey carried out by the European Monitoring Centre on Racism and Xenophobia (EMCRX) found that more and more Britons want established immigrants to be sent home; 23% of British citizens polled think that even legally accepted political refugees should be sent back to their country of origin. Nearly 39% of Britons surveyed said that legal immigrants who became unemployed should be forcibly repatriated (EMCRX). In a comparable research project drawing on data from the British Social Attitudes survey (BSA), Dustmann and Preston (2002) found that two-thirds of the public are opposed to any further migration into the United Kingdom by ethnic minorities. They concluded that this hostility was closely linked to racist views about ethnic minorities. They also found that opposition to further immigration is heavily correlated to racist attitudes, as revealed by the BSA questions about ethnic minorities. Significantly, they discovered that worries about immigrants taking jobs or welfare benefits—traditionally a 'competition for resources' argument—are a less important factor. Low-skilled workers, who might be thought to worry about competition for jobs, are in fact more likely than more highly skilled workers to be hostile to immigrants because of racist views, according to the report. Sixty six percent of the sample stated that they would want less immigration from the West Indies, while 70% wanted fewer migrants from Asian countries. The fact that only a minority oppose immigration from ethnically similar countries such as Australia and New Zealand is further proof of entrenched public hostility towards people of Asian or Afro-Caribbean origin. The research concluded that racism explained these variations towards immigration of ethnically different populations (Dustmann & Preston, 2002).

The interesting point in Dustmann and Preston's research is that they argue that European countries are going to have to change their approaches to immigration because they are running out of workers. To keep a stable working population stable between now and 2050, the European Union as a whole needs to import 1.4 million immigrants a year (2002). This is influenced by an instrumental approach by which 'immigrants' are seen as a solution to Europe's falling working population. That is why although the government has recognized the need for immigration to attract skilled workers in some sectors and has changed work permit rules to allow in a limited number of migrants, they are still considered by many to be 'anti-immigration' (Alibhai-Brown, 2002; Sivanandan, 2001; Fekete, 2001).

The United Kingdom part of our research is conducted in such a context. The idea is to study the role of XPP in the reinforcement of antiimmigrant and xenophobic ideas and sentiments in the United Kingdom. The role of mass media (namely, the major newspapers of the country) is also studied for the same reason. In the first part, XPPs' party programmes (1982–2005) and party press, as well as the speeches of the party leaders, have been analyzed.

Discursive Reconstruction of 'Us' vs. 'Them'

Politicisation of immigrant issues has to do with the increasing awareness of political agents—including political parties—of the political potentiality of the dualism of 'Us' against 'Them.' The institutional 'Otherization' creates solid grounds for the demonisation of 'Them' and the mobilisation of 'Britons' in a process of creating a sense of 'white Weness.' Such a 'We' is not only based on the real category of immigrants, but rather on 'Otherised' groups with immigrant background who 'differ' from the category of 'Us' based on colour of skin, hair, religion, or other attributes.

In this section, the results of the following studies and analysis will be presented:

- selected British National Party (BNP) party programmes (or manifestos) have been selected from the period 1982–2005: BNP (1987) *BNP Manifesto,* BNP (1997) *BNP Manifesto,* BNP (2001) *People Just like You Striving for a Better Britain,* and BNP (2005) *Rebuilding British Democracy;*
- the BNP party press papers (*British Nationalist* and *Identity*), published between 1992 (when the papers started) and 2004;
- the leaders' speeches between 1985 and 2001; and
- parliamentary debates between 2001 and 2005.

While BNP have always been a strongly antiimmigration party, the way in which they have 'framed' this issue has changed markedly over time. The

1997 BNP manifesto put forward a two-strand policy for immigration: to halt future nonwhite immigration, and the repatriation or relocation of nonwhites living in Britain. It claimed that this would succeed in 'returning' the country to its white 'status.' BNP candidates in the 1997 General Election had nominal success. Three deposits were saved, two in East London and one in West Yorkshire, but elsewhere its vote was negligible. The 2001 BNP manifesto changed the party's immigration policy. It altered from total repatriation to voluntary repatriation with financial backing. However, BNP made it clear that housing and jobs would be prioritized for 'native' white Britons.

The following frames have been chosen in all eight countries engaged in this research, including the United Kingdom, to analyze the role of XPP, the mass media, and mainstream parties in the reinforcement of the 'Us' and 'Them' asymmetric categories in public debate: (a) Collective Identity; (b) Employment Issues; (c) Welfare Issues; (d) Law and Order Issues; (e) Liberal Values; (f) Antiestablishment; (g) Immigrant Status; and (h) Legitimisation of Racism.

The results show that the most frequent frames used in the United Kingdom context in order to reinforce 'Otherization' of immigrants, and in turning this to political and electoral advantage, are those of 'Collective Identity,' 'Law and Order Issues,' 'Employment and Welfare Issues,' and 'Antiestablishment.' The frames of 'Employment Issues' and 'Welfare Issues' proved to be interrelated and in many cases difficult to separate from each other; therefore, they are presented as one frame, namely 'Employment and Welfare Issues.' There are other frames, such as 'Liberal Values' and 'Immigrant Status,' which are also used in this respect but to a lesser extent than the aforementioned frames. Here the most frequent frames are illustrated.

Collective Identity

This frame is the most frequent one used in the BNP party programmes, party press, and speeches. Immigrants are seen as a threat to the British collective identity that should be controlled and expelled from the country. After the introduction, which referred to Britain's "glorious imperial past," the Party stated that immigration is "a crisis without parallel" and that "Britain's very existence today is threatened by immigrants" (2005, p. 13). The Party provided a 'disastrous' demographic picture of what is happening and how 'threatened' the 'native English people' are as an 'ethnic group':

> On current demographic trends we, the native British people, will be an ethnic minority in our own country within sixty years. By 2020, an extra 5–7 million immigrants will have entered Britain, whilst immigrant communities already resident here are having more children than the indigenous British people. (2005, p. 14)

The Party claim then that the 'threat' to the British nation must be addressed by stopping immigration: "To ensure that we do not become a minority in our own homeland, and that the native British peoples of our islands retain their culture and identity, we call for an immediate halt to all further immigration" (2005, p. 18).

Several established and institutionalised discourses are used to 'Otherize' and inferiorise the 'Others,' as well as represent 'Us' Britons as the supreme category and a group that deserve protection and defence. The discourses engaged in the process of British 'collective identity' reconstruction in the party programmes are, for instance, the discourses of culture, religion and democracy. The party states that:

> We demand the right to preserve our culture, heritage, and identity. Our national character and native institutions are a precious inheritance, for which our ancestors have paid a high price over the centuries. . . . We will ensure that appropriate areas of public life, including school assemblies, are based on a commitment to the values of traditional Westernised Christianity. Levels of religiosity have always fluctuated in Britain, and while our great inheritance of cathedrals, churches and liturgies has less resonance with the broad mass of the population at present, the wheel of faith will one day turn again and they will be fully valued once more. (2005, p. 21–22)

The party wants to reinforce British culture and identity by, for instance, establishing traditional British national and cultural symbols such as the annual celebration of St. George's (Patron Saint of England) Day festival (2001, p. 7).

The party extend its notion of British 'collective identity' to include even 'limited numbers of peoples of European descent,' who are supposed to guarantee the existence of 'British democracy.' In 1987, the party declared that:

> In order to guarantee the continued existence of our British democracy, we also intend to take long-term steps to guarantee the continued existence, as the clearly dominant ethnic, cultural and political group, of the native peoples of these islands—the English, Scots, Irish and Welsh—together with the limited numbers of peoples of European descent, who arrived as refugees or economic immigrants. (1987, p. 21)

The party propagated in the party press that 'blacks' do not really want to be in Britain because they have no future, and they are not British: "Blacks desperate to Go Home! Black People, given the incentive, would go back home tomorrow. They don't want to go for the sea, sand and surf, but to escape the no-hope future of Britain's blacks" (September, 1996, p. 1).

In another article, of April 2004, the Party declared that they will even help 'blacks' and other immigrant groups to go back to "a more suitable country": "The BNP will financially assist those immigrants, who feel that they can't adapt to our British way of life and Christian values, to go to a more suitable country" (April 2004, p. 1). The article claims that many immigrants of Muslim or other religious and 'cultural' background cannot adapt to the British way of life and its 'Christian values.' Immigrants are supposedly completely different from British people, and disturb the British collective identity.

The famous leader of BNP, Tyndall, has on many occasions used the frame of 'Collective Identity' to define the borders between 'Us' and 'Them' and to make immigrants non-British elements amongst 'Us.' In the following speech he uses both 'culture' and 'race' as two threats to British identity:

> Popular anger at mass immigration and its consequences naturally finds its initial flash-point at the level of culture, where totally foreign customs and folkways irrupt into a previously settled and determinate community whose members are both culturally and in a high degree physically and biologically, kindred. (Tyndall, 2004)

He continues then to alarm the British and Europeans for degrading of their identity by claiming that "there are in reality two levels at which the British and European identity is being threatened: that of culture and that of physical or biological race" (Tyndall, 2004).

In an article from 1995 published in Rune Magazine, Nick Griffin, the other leader of BNP, propagates for unity among the superior 'race' in order to avoid disappearance. He said that:

> Mass alien immigration and suicidally low birth-rate mean that the White Race is poised on the brink of a precipice of rapid and irreversible decline. If we do not step back now, we face political and then physical extinction. A stark choice: UNITE OR DIE! (BBC, 2001)

The frame of 'Collective Identity' is very much equal with a concept of a superior 'Us' against an inferior 'Them,' the latter of who are threatening 'our culture,' 'our race,' and 'our religion.'

Law and Order Issues

This has emerged as the second most used frame of BNP in framing 'immigrants as problem' for British society. In the party programme of 2005, the BNP claims that British society will deteriorate if immigrants are allowed to continue to arrive in the country:

To take just one example, it is a hard fact that, according to official figures, 15% of the UK's male prison population is black, despite black people accounting for only 2% of the total population. Victim-reported figures concerning the race of criminals give the lie to the leftist argument that this is due to discriminatory prosecution. It is an inescapable statistical fact that immigration into Britain increases the crime rate. Figures for unemployment, welfare dependency, educational failure, and other social pathologies tell a similar story for most other foreign ethnic groups. There is simply no escaping the fact that choosing to admit such persons into the country in significant numbers means choosing to become a poorer, more violent, more dependent and worse-educated society. (2005, p. 13)

The Party not only claims that "whites make up the majority of victims" of crimes committed by immigrants, but also that these crimes are "racist hate crimes" against "whites" (2001, p. 7). The same frame is used in the party press: "The Tories [then in government] have allowed [drug pushers] to swarm into Britain under their policy of unrestricted third world immigration" (1993, p. 4). The party leader Nick Griffin uses the same frame in order to present immigrants as a security problem and a threat to 'whites':

We do not treat anybody differently. . . . Fundamentally the people treating people differently because of the colour of their skins are the Asian thugs who for some years now in places like Burnley have been winding this up by attacking innocent white people. (Nick Griffin, BBC Radio 4, *Today*, June 30, 2001)

The concept of 'Asians' is frequently used by BNP to stigmatize Muslims in the first place. The party often appeals to the established prejudices against Muslim Pakistanis.

Employment and Welfare Issues

The issues of employment and welfare have been the third and fourth most used frames by which immigration and immigrants were represented as problems for Britain's employment and welfare system. The party programmes declare both 'immigration' and the 'threat' of 'globalisation' as urgent concerns of Britain. The following are illustrations of the frames: "Britain is full up and the government of Britain has as its first responsibility the welfare, security and long-term preservation of the native people of Britain" (2005, p. 4); "Globalisation, with its export of jobs to the Third World, is bringing unemployment to British industries and the communities that depend upon them" (2001, p. 2).

The party press in 1993 writes that there is an "unemployment time-bomb" that is a result of "mass immigration" and threatens "British workers" (September, 1993, p. 2) and continues: Only the BNP is prepared to stand up to big business for the benefit of the native British. It is the only party whose policy is to stop immigration, start repatriation and reserve British jobs for British people (September, 1993).

Stopping immigration to prevent "zero unemployment" and in defence of "whites" (March, 1994, p. 1) has been a continued slogan of BNP, frequently used in its press and by the leaders in their speeches.

Antiestablishment

This is the fifth most used frame by BNP. The political elite of the country are held responsible for increasing 'immigration-related problems.' The Party presents itself as a 'true democrat' that defends the democratic rights of people:

> The British people invented modern parliamentary democracy. Yet in recent years the British people have been denied their democratic right. On issue after issue the views of the majority of British people have been ignored and overridden by a politically correct 'elite' who thinks it knows best. (2001, p. 4)

The responsibility for the aggravation of democracy, and the preservation of the British people's democratic rights, lies with the mainstream parties and political elite, according to BNP:

> On immigration, on the surrender of British sovereignty to the EU and in numerous other areas democracy has been absent as Labour, Tories [Conservative] and the Lib-Dems all conspire in election after election to offer the British people no choice. (Party program, 1997, p. 4–5)

In the party press we are witnessing the same antiestablishment propaganda aimed at putting the 'blame' for increasing immigration (and other, framed 'problems') on the mainstream political parties: "Time and again the party has stood up for the rights of white people, where the three old parties [Conservative, Labour, and Liberal] have deserted them in favour of chasing the immigrant vote" (March 1994, p. 1). In April of the same year, BNP writes:

> Labour's record on immigration is a disgrace, but the Tory record is even worse. Despite Margaret Thatcher saying she was aware of the British peoples' fears of being 'swamped,' more immigrants came to Britain under the Conservatives than any other Government. (April 2004, p. 1)

Antiestablishment propaganda is a useful means to mobilise those groups who are disappointed with the mainstream political parties and politicians. Mainstream parties are blamed for not acting against the 'threat' of immigration and the 'degradation' of the nation. The frames, mentioned above, are the most frequent frames used in party programmes, the party press, and in the leaders' speeches, for reinforcing 'Otherization,' for demonisation of the 'Others,' and for gaining political advantage. However, other, less common, frames have been used too.

The Dichotomy of 'Us' against the Muslim 'Others'

Frames such as 'Liberal Values,' the 'Immigrant Status,' and 'Legitimisation of Racism' have been used in order to reinforce the 'Otherization' and polarisation of the categories of 'Us' against 'Them.' The main political strategy of the XPP is to present itself as the only 'true' representative of 'our people' who are threatened by immigrants coming 'in' from completely different 'cultures' and 'ethnic backgrounds.' Cultural differences are essentialised and, in many cases, interchanged with the concept of 'race.' BNP has often openly defended racism as 'a part of human nature.' They wrote in their party programme of 2005 that: "Racism, in other words, is not a consequence of 'false consciousness,' economics, imperialism or the work of evil agitators, it is part of human nature" (2005, p. 18).

Paradoxically, the XPP, with its violent and racist background, propagates against the 'Others' by representing 'Them' as antiliberal, lacking a tradition of democracy and liberalism. BNP's party programmes, party press, and leaders' speeches contain frequent defence of "our natural born democrats" (2005, p. 17) from the antiliberal and nondemocratic 'Them.' In many cases, Orientalist fallacies and anti-Muslim sentiments are used in order to reinforce XPPs' 'Islamophobic' and antiimmigrant propaganda.

Immigrants are frequently 'scapegoats' for a wide range of perceived social ills and economic grievances, such as, but not limited to, unemployment, housing, education, healthcare shortages, criminality, and so on. Whether BNP explains these social outcomes as a result of an incompatibility of cultures, a scarcity of resources, or due to other reasons, the commonality in these conclusions is that migrants are constructed as somehow 'outside' British society: a threat from within. In presenting both *diagnostic* and *prognostic* frames, BNP situate themselves and their ideology as the 'solution' to the 'problem' of immigration. Doubtless many of BNP's ideologies genuinely help in associating the British socioeconomic problems with migration and migrants, and so profit from existing xenophobic attitudes among U.K. voters. However, they have to be more xenophobic than mainstream parties, such as Tory and Labour, who are operating on almost the same political terrain.

Muslims are the most stigmatized and 'Otherised' of any group of immigrants in the United Kingdom today. The attacks on the World Trade Center in New York and on the Pentagon in Washington, D.C. have reinforced old Orientalism and anti-Muslim sentiments in the United Kingdom. BNP has used such attitudes, and 'Islamphobia,' to demonise Muslims and mobilise political support among voters. Griffin, the leader of BNP, propagated in 2001 that: "You've got to stand up and do something for the British National Party because otherwise they [Muslims] will do for someone in your family. That is the truth."

The new opinion polls and studies show that the attitudes and hate crimes against Muslims is increasing and that XPPs, and in some cases even the mainstream parties, are gaining political advantages of demonising Muslims.

Assessing Impacts of XPP

BNP has not yet succeeded in entering British parliament. This limited political power makes it almost inconceivable that they would have the potential to directly impact on discourses surrounding major acts of parliament. However, the key frames that were used by BNP *have* influenced the debate on immigration. For instance, the Nationality, Immigration, and Asylum Act of 2002 made applicants for British citizenship sit a language test to demonstrate that they have 'sufficient' language skills in English, Welsh, or Scottish Gaelic. Exactly what level of competence is needed to pass such a test has been a matter of some debate. According to Home Office minister, Beverley Hughes, "sufficient" pertains to enough linguistic ability to "sustain unskilled employment" (*Guardian*, December 12, 2002). This new language requirement is part of other measures in this act that have become widely referred to as the 'Britishness test,' whereby applicants for citizenship are also required to be familiar with other aspects of 'British culture.'

The indirect political impacts of BNP on mainstream parties are studied by analysing the frames used by the Conservative Party and the Labour Party in their party programmes of 1983 to 2005. The following Conservative party programmes were analyzed:

 1983—The Challenge of Our Times;
 1987—The Next Moves Forward;
 1992—The Best Future for Britain;
 1997—You Can Only be Sure With the Conservatives;
 2001—Time for Common Sense; and
 2005—Are You Thinking What We're Thinking?

It is interesting to note that the Conservative manifestos, released when the party was in government (1979–1997) have far fewer references to immigration policy than do those published since 1997, yet this was precisely the period (especially when Thatcher was in power [1979–1990]) that the Conservative Party took an incredibly coercive approach to U.K. borders. As an opposition party, the issue of immigration has been given much greater coverage in the party's programmes. The extent to which migration is 'on the political agenda' is clearly crucial here, and this is illustrated by the fact that, in terms of a simple content analysis, the 1997 manifesto makes two mentions of the term 'immigration,' while the word is missing entirely from the 2001 programme. The 2005 manifesto has 12 citations and a dedicated chapter on the issue.

The following Labour party programmes are also used and analyzed:

1983—Labour Manifesto;
1987—Britain Will Win with Labour;
1992—It's Time to Get Britain Working Again;
1997—New Labour Because Britain Deserves Better;
2001—Ambitions for Britain; and
2005—Britain Forward Not Back.

The frames that were used by BNP also appear in the party programmes of both the Conservative Party and the Labour Party.

Collective Identity

During the time that the dominant discussion was about the concern for 'British borders,' the Conservatives declared that: "How to defend Britain's traditional liberties and distinctive way of life is the most vital decision that faces the people at this election" (The Challenge of Our Time, 1983, p. 1). Labour's party programmes also contain many addresses to 'Britishness,' in the sense that Britain is viewed as the home of liberty, welfare, and equal rights. "The distinctive way of life" of Britons, as "tolerant" and democratic people, is frequently explored in these programmes. In the 1980s and 1990s, the prise of the collective national identity of the United Kingdom was used to legitimise the British act of "race relation": "Tolerance, civility and respect have always been hallmarks of our nation. It is thanks to them that we have an excellent record in race relations" (Conservative Party Programme, 1997, p. 3). However, these discourses have been used as the exclusive properties of the British people and government.

The victory of Margaret Thatcher, and the subsequent Conservative reign during the 1980s, reinforced nationalist, xenophobic, and antiimmigrant sentiments in Britain. Immigrants were increasingly portrayed as a group that either creates problems *or* solves them. They were addressed as the opposite of 'Britishness.' For example, they could work and raise the welfare of the 'British people,' but they should be examined and tested in order to be a citizen of the United Kingdom. The Labour Manifesto of 1983 confirms it thus:

> We will repeal the 1971 Immigration Act and the 1981 British Nation-
> ality Act and replace them with a citizenship law. . . . The Act will en-
> able other Commonwealth and foreign nationals to acquire citizenship
> if they qualify by objective tests. (1983, p. 26)

However, during 1980s and 1990s, the party programmes show that the
debates of BNP do have not much influence on either the Conservatives or
Labour. The parties continue more or less their traditional policies concerning migration. As was mentioned earlier, BNP's 'Antiestablishment'
frame includes both the Conservative and the Labour parties, claiming that
the Conservatives could do more to control immigration but have failed to
do so. They criticize the Labour Party for being proimmigration and promulticultural society.

Employment and Welfare Issues

Issues concerning the role of immigrants for the British labour market and
welfare system are raised by both Labour and the Conservatives. Meanwhile,
the two parties defend a limited immigration to the United Kingdom, arguing
that they will impose effective control on levels of immigration. Although the
issue of immigration was not a central electoral question in the early 1980s, it
came gradually to be an important question for mainstream parties. This can
be counted as part of the indirect influence of BNP on mainstream politics.
The Conservatives write in their party program of 1997:

> Britain has benefited from immigration. We all gain from the social
> diversity, economic vibrancy and cultural richness that immigration
> brings. But if those benefits are to continue to flow we need to ensure
> that immigration is effectively managed, in the interests of all Britons,
> old and new.

Therefore, they declare: "We will introduce a points-based system for work
permits similar to the one used in Australia. This will give priority to people with the skills Britain needs" (1997). The Conservatives continue to
be a party that will convince the voters of its concern about the control of
immigration and the preservation of the contribution of immigrants to the
welfare of the British people.

The Labour Party has more or less argued the same position: Immigration is defended, but it also requires effective control. They declare that:
"For centuries Britain has been a home for people from the rest of the
world. Immigration has been good for Britain. We want to keep it that
way" (Party programme, 2005). Therefore they outline in 2005 the party's
simple philosophy of immigration: "Our philosophy is simple: if you are
ready to work hard and there is work for you to do, then you are welcome
here" (Party programme, 2005).[6]

Law and Order Issues

This frame is not used frequently by either Conservative or Labour politicians and their press. However, the higher level of criminality among immigrants and minorities is a discourse used by both parties. One major change in party programmes, party leaders' speeches, and party press articles are discourses on 'terrorism,' 'Muslim fundamentalism,' and 'Muslim terrorism.' The discourse of 'national security' has become a dominating political discourse in the propaganda of mainstream parties. The topic of 'control of immigration' and 'interior security' is highly related to the fear of terrorism.

Mass Media and the 'Others'

Mass media is an important agent within the democratic societies of Europe. The increasing role of mass media for 'Otherization' of those who have either immigrated to the United Kingdom or who belong to minority groups has been studied over the last few decades. The intention of the present research project has been to study the role of mass media in reinforcing 'Xeno-otherism' by assessing the impact of XPP on the public debate in the United Kingdom. In this respect, the mass media articles have been selected in relation to 'critical events.' The following are the critical events that have been used in the analysis:

1. the fall of the Berlin Wall, November 9, 1989;
2. the attacks on the World Trade Center and the Pentagon in United States, September 11, 2001;
3. the enlargement of the European Union, May 1, 2004;
4. riots in the English mill towns, April 28, 2001; and
5. the BNP winning council seats in Burnley, May 3, 2002.

The mass media that has been used for the analysis consisted of two major newspapers, namely, *The Guardian* and *The Telegraph,* and a tabloid paper, *The Sun.*

The Fall of the Berlin Wall, November 9, 1989

The fall of the Berlin Wall was not frequently used by the mass media to warn against increasing immigration. Rather, the fall was used as a sign of the victory of 'Us' against 'Them.' The articles mostly deal with a kind of western narcissism in which the fall of the Wall and subsequent migration to the west are presented as proof of 'our superiority.' As part of this assessment, *The Guardian,* the left-wing broadsheet, did note that:

> [The fall of the Wall] was accompanied by wider hosannas for the proof this migration offers of the superiority of the western system. In

the popular triumph of liberal democratic values, it is fashionable to say in some quarters, lies the end of history: and we in Britain, under the leader who has done so much to preach these values, take our own little bow of self-congratulation—pausing only briefly to note that, after 1992, these eastern refugees will be free to make their way to this country whenever they choose. (November 9, 1989)

In these cases migrants were portrayed not as a 'threat' but as the victims of a political rule, although there was heavy weighting given to the stories of individuals who could potentially be displaced by the events.

The Attacks on the World Trade Center and Pentagon in the United States, September 11, 2001

Press debates carried out after the series of terrorist attacks on New York City's World Trade Center and the Pentagon were very different in the three papers. *The Sun* had 29 pages of blanket coverage on the 12th of September, the majority of which was sensational accounts of eye witnesses (e.g., "I watched as bodies rained from the sky"). In their editorial of the same date, *The Sun* called for all the world to "unite to defeat these evil cowards"—of course at this stage there was no clue as to who the perpetrators were. However, interestingly, *The Sun* in general avoids the 'Islamic angle' on all these reports, preferring to emphasize the sensationalist nature/images of the attack. *The Guardian*'s reporting of 9/11 is more oriented to an explanation of the reasons for 9/11, frequently linking the events to United States' Middle East politics. Invoking the inevitable images of World War II, the paper says that "the horrors of September 11, 2001 will go down in the annals of infamy, like the unprovoked Japanese attack on Pearl Harbour." The reporting of 9/11 in both *The Guardian* and *The Telegraph* presented some 'objective' discussion about the extent of the loss of life but, especially in the time after 9/11, presented some analysis concerning those thought to be responsible for the acts, the broader political context, and so on (e.g., Bin Laden, Al-Qa'ida, radical Islamist groups). BNP were absent in all the reports in the assessed period. However, the threat from the 'outer world' or from the 'Others' was elaborated in the articles.

The Enlargement of the European Union, May 1, 2004

During the assessed period, another single-issue XPP called the United Kingdom Independence Party (UKIP) dominated media coverage. The combination of a clear anti-European Union/European stance and the high profile of one of its candidates—Robert Kilroy-Silk, a former Labour MP and a well-known talk show host—meant that UKIP was uniquely well-placed to take advantage of media interest in discussions around European Union accession. Indeed, UKIP's exaggerated anti-EU stance, which stressed United Kingdom sovereignty—anti-Euro, anti-CAP—and the 'media-friendly' nature of its star candidate Kilroy-Silk, guaranteed UKIP a profile that BNP could not match. As would perhaps be expected, given the accuracy of the frames assessed above in the context of BNP, UKIP mobilized antiestablishment frames common to XPP (Kilroy-Silk said: "We [UKIP] are the only party throughout the election that had a very clear, straightforward policy. We are the only party that talked about Europe and didn't actually tell any lies" [BBC, 2005]). To some extent this was reflected in the results. Although BNP failed to gain an MEP, 808,200 people voted for the party in the European elections, meaning that the party now has 21 councillors, which has been interpreted by some as an indicator of the mood of the British electorate. The BNP has also stated that it believed it could win "between one and three seats" in the 2003 European election. (However, although their share of the vote increased to 4.9%, they did not win any seats.) UKIP polled 16% of the 2003 vote.

Riots in the English Mill Towns

Oldham includes the third poorest council ward in the United Kingdom. Oldham's population of 219,000 includes around 24,600 of Asian ethnic origin—14,000 Pakistani; 9,000 Bangladeshi; and 1,600 Indians. The town is divided up into mainly 'white,' Pakistani and Bangladeshi areas (Marsden, 2001). Fighting occurred in the summer of 2001 between Asian and 'white' youths and the police in Oldham, near Manchester (around 500 young Asians and hundreds of 'white' youths were involved). Trouble flared after Asians fought with 'white' youth outside a fast food outlet. A group of racist 'white' youths gathered together in response, and then attacked a number of shops (also throwing a brick through the window of a house where a pregnant Asian woman lived) in the Glodwick area where many Asian immigrants have settled (Marsden, 2001). The rioting came after provocation by BNP, with violent members of NF following BNP's provocative presence in the area. NF intended to hold two marches in Oldham in May, but then Home Secretary Jack Straw banned all political marches in the area for 3 months (hundreds of fascists nevertheless descended upon Oldham; Marsden, 2001). Other catalysts were long-term unemployment and the associated poverty and social deprivation experienced by many and linked to the collapse of the textile and manufacturing industries that had provided employment for local people:

> Most Asian immigrants came to Britain to work as nightshift labour in the textile mills and in other poorly paid occupations. They were usually the first to be laid off when the mills closed. As a result of the urban deprivation that afflicts the area, along with continuing racial discrimination, unemployment is as high as 25 percent amongst Bangladeshis and 16 percent among Pakistanis. For young Asians it is even worse, with unemployment rates of 40 percent. (Marsden, 2001, p. 1)

The press joined in to back up the Conservative Party's staunch rejection of any connection between their anti-asylum seeker political rhetoric and the disturbances in Oldham. The main Conservative-supporting broadsheet, *The Telegraph,* insisted on discussing the "many tens of thousands of people slipping into this country under false pretences" even though this was nothing to do with illegal migration. They also claimed that: "There is no evidence . . . that Saturday's unrest was significantly different from the yobbery that disfigures so many British towns at weekends," which would seem to downplay the crucial role of XPP in whipping up animosity between communities. (Former Conservative Party chairman Lord Tebbitt made explicit the racism underlying the Conservative's attacks on migration and asylum when he said the lesson he drew from the Oldham riots was that "separate and distinct societies living in the same territory are always at risk of clashing . . . they have not got enough binding them together to avoid them creating themselves into tribal factions.")

BNP Winning Council Seats in Burnley

The council by-elections in May 2003 caused a great deal of controversy and were the focus of media, political, and popular discourses, as they witnessed BNP become the official opposition party in Burnley (a former mill town in Lancashire, in the north of England). The party took their total seats on the council to seven amidst stand-offs between BNP and Anti-Nazi league supporters. Trevor Phillips, chair of the Campaign for Racial Equality, identified a set of "special circumstances" that allowed BNP to poll so many votes: "In their town the particular conditions of especial disillusionment with the local council and the collapse of the Conservative vote gave the BNP a unique chance to creep in" (BBC, 2003).

So, in the council elections of May 2003, BNP increased its Burnley total by five seats, thus briefly becoming the second-largest party and official opposition on that council, a position it narrowly lost soon afterwards to the Liberal Democrats, who beat BNP by a margin of just 0.4% in a by-election. The five new Burnley seats were formerly held by a combination of all three mainstream political parties, suggesting that BNP was winning votes from across the political spectrum. The party contested a record 221 seats nationwide (just under 4% of the total available).

By definition, BNP do appear in this media reporting, the vast majority of which situates BNP as the antithesis of Britain's liberal, multicultural, and tolerant value system. Their rise to power prompted a special report entitled "The British Far Right" in *The Guardian,* which gave the most in-depth coverage. Initially this tended to be relatively objective in nature—for example: "Labour's grassroots supporters stayed away in their droves in a sign of dissatisfaction with Mr Blair's progress. And there were fears that the low turnout could let the racist BNP gain a toehold in Lancashire towns like Burnley and Oldham, hit by riots last year."

Reporting in *The Sun* was of an altogether more sensationalist nature, with opinion often linking BNP's power in Burnley with further disturbances. For example, headings such as "BNP seats could lead to more riots: Police Fear" were frequently used. Even when employing the 'Liberal Values' frame, *The Sun* had sensational headings, such as "Democracy means you get vermin like the BNP elected," without any in-depth analysis.

The Telegraph, along with *The Guardian,* initially focused primarily on the results of the election. It wrote, for instance:

> The biggest shock of the night was in Burnley, where the far-Right British National Party won two seats on the council and was involved in a recount in another ward. Success for David Edwards and Carol Hughes was a symbolic victory for the BNP—and a setback for Labour, which had appealed to Burnley's voters to reject extremists.

The Telegraph and *The Guardian* subsequently assessed the implications of the result for the local population and the broader political system: "Their success aroused the fears of local Asians, whose leaders said Burnley would now have a reputation as the 'racist capital of Britain.'" BNP's success in the Lancashire town was seen as a symbolic victory for the far-Right and a setback for Labour, which had appealed to the town to reject extremists.

Conclusion

The immigration issues have risen from a marginal question in the political sphere of the United Kingdom in the early 1980s, to being a central issue for the two major parties to an unprecedented degree in 2005. There are many reasons to believe that the question of 'Xeno-otherism' is going to be one of the central political matters even in the near future. The political discourses of the both mainstream parties and BNP have been framed explicitly in 'Xeno-otherising' terms. While the politicisation of the immigration issue is, of course, nothing new, the centrality of the issue in a general election campaign is. The construction of the migrant 'Other' in these discourses—not to mention the conflation of all forms of 'immigration,' including refuges, asylum seekers, migrants, and so on—is a main component of the discourses analyzed in this study. However, the role of BNP in influencing the discursive 'Otherization' of immigrants and minorities by mainstream political parties is more complex.

As is demonstrated by the frame analysis above, it is clear that BNP did not have a direct role in the shift in political discourse. It is also clear that they did not benefit from the main parties' focus on immigration in electoral terms, with their performance not being a significantly improved one from previous national elections. British political history has taught us that mainstream parties dominating right-wing, antiimmigration discursive spaces can disadvantage XPP in a counterintuitive way. This was certainly the case when the fascist National Front found themselves marginalised by Thatcher's brand of conservatism, which captured votes on 'traditional' XPP territory of a coercive stanch on law and order, free market capitalism, and, of course, antiimmigration. The presence of a right-wing frame of political discourse can actually serve to exclude XPP from such debates and to deny them votes. This was most clearly the case in the 1979 election when the fascist National Front found themselves marginalised by the Thatcherist brand of conservatism, which captured votes on 'traditional' XPP territory of a coercive stanch on law and order, free market capitalism, and, of course, antiimmigration.

Resultantly interesting parallels exist between the electoral performance of BNP and NF in the periods when the government have adopted 'tough on immigration' stances. Certainly, as the U.K. government actively seeks to reduce access to asylum, there is a marked tendency to 'play a numbers game,' with mainstream political parties—both Conservative and New Labour—competing to cut down numbers of asylum seekers and get 'tougher' on asylum claimants. That this focus is often on the numbers of asylum applications, rather than the small number of individuals who are actually granted refugee status, is perhaps one reason why the BNP are often perceived to have more of an 'impact' than their electoral achievements would actually suggest.

While the main two parties have couched their antiimmigration and xenophobic discourses in 'pragmatic' discussion of the economy and welfare implications, BNP's open hostility to further migration from 'non-European' countries belies their claims to not be a racist party. As is typical of an XPP, their antiimmigration discourses are inherently linked with a whole range of other discriminatory and other exclusive ideologies, such as homophobia and sexism—frequently wrapped up in a paradoxical deference for traditional institutions such as the monarchy and the Church that it ostensibly at odds with the strong antiestablishment frames expressed throughout the BNP party press, manifestos, and speeches assessed above. Conservative suggestions that immigrants should be checked for HIV and TB served, in the time-honoured strategy of the right, to associate migrants with disease. This has been a form of XPP propaganda that was adopted by mainstream parties as an electoral issue. Although it is difficult to prove certain causality in this matter, there is no doubt that the political debate was *influenced* by the BNP and the NF in a time of revitalisation of British nationalism by both the Conservatives and the Labour Party. It is clear that Conservative and Labour politicians compete in being 'tough' on immigration in order to stop voters supporting the BNP. In practice, such discourse only legitimate the racism inherent in BNP policy and encourages a further shift to the right, both in the BNP's and the Conservative and the Labour parties' language and conduct.

There are both notable continuities and shifts within the BNP party press. New frames situating the party as tolerant and open to a range of distinct—but crucially 'separate'—cultures have emerged in the post-2001 context. This is a 'new' type of racism that is not only directed at 'nonwhite' groups and individuals (as older, more biologically-based discrimination was), but is a "xenophobia that bears all the marks of the old racism, except that it is not colour-coded" (Sivanandan, 2001, p. 2). The new framework of xeno-racism developed by Fekete (2001) is particularly useful for interpreting the growing racism directed towards people seeking asylum and refugees in both popular media and political discourses.

The newspaper analysis indicated that the BNP had little or no profile in any of the discussion of major international events (9/11, the fall of the Berlin Wall, and European Union Accession). Where the BNP were more prominent were in regionally specific discussions such as the Mill Town disturbances in Summer 2001. Indeed, the presence of the BNP in these areas was a *catalyst* for the violence, and served to attract the attention and approbation of both the national media and the mainstream political parties, who all spoke out against their pernicious influence. For instance, as is illustrated above, Michael Howard, the Conservative leader, dedicated a whole high profile speech to disavowing the BNP's ideology and attempting to minimize their influence in these towns.

In short, we can see a marked shift in the BNP's political discourse: frames drawing explicitly on the concept of 'race' have been replaced with more xeno-racism and culture. This is illustrated by the electoral/ideological terms the BNP currently uses to appeal to those members of the population who consider immigration to be a threat to their jobs, a cause of rising crime, and a basis for cultural decline. Although they are increasingly speaking of culture, we should be clear that the BNP is still a party founded on deeply racist perspectives towards immigration.

THE CASE OF GERMANY

The Political Context of Xenophobia in Germany

The most extensive and regular survey on xenophobic attitudes in Germany is the biannual German General Survey (*Allgemeine Bevölkerungsumfrage der Sozialwissenschaften*), the ALLBUS. It provides systematic data on attitudes towards immigrants and foreigners living in Germany. Attitudes towards different groups of immigrants (namely German resettlers, asylum seekers, employees from European Union, and employees from outside the European Union) are surveyed for the years 1990 (West-Germans only), 1991, 1992, 1996, and 2000. In assessing the data, it is important to notice that, in 1996, the entire ALLBUS focused on the topic 'foreigners.' The results of this year differ consistently from those produced by surveys in other years. Supposedly this is due to a 'context effect.'

The results from the German General Social Surveys, which were accumulated in respect of the period 1980–2002, shows that in all years a majority of the respondents (from the smallest at 53% to the largest at 79%, with an average of 64%) think that there should be restrictions placed on the inflow of immigrants to Germany, no matter what type of immigrants are concerned. Secondly, the percentages of the population demanding restrictions have become higher by 2000 than was originally the case in 1990 and 1991, even for East Germans whose attitudes have been rather stable, or for subgroups whose attitudes fluctuated a lot. The number of those demanding restriction on immigration has been raising consistently (apart from deviating percentages in 1996), although with some exceptions: in 2000, less East Germans than in 1992 wanted restrictions on immigration of employees from outside the European Union, while the group wanting the complete stop of their immigration grew. In 1992, in West and East Germany[7] the number of people wanting restrictions on immigration of asylum seekers decreased, while more people wanted a complete stop to their immigration. It might be worth mentioning here that this was the time (1992) of a series of violent attacks on the housing of asylum seekers, as well as of the debate about the asylum law in which the discourse about restrictions on immigration by the new asylum law played a very important role.

Another general result is that immigrants are, very obviously, rejected more in East Germany than in West Germany (with a 'more' of 0.8 up to 25.6 percentage points), again with one exception: the rejection of asylum seekers. This group of immigrants was disliked less in East Germany until 1996 (and welcomed more until 1992); also, the percentage of people wanting restrictions on their inflow was more in East Germany until 1996, but from then onwards the attitudes that were expressed were more of dislike and less of welcoming. Thus, until the mid-1990s, attitudes towards asylum seekers were less hostile towards asylum seekers in East Germany than those in West Germany, the trend reversing later on.

West Germans tend to avoid extreme positions, such as 'Migration should be possible without restrictions' and 'Migration should be stopped completely.' However, they still hold a rather disapproving attitude, largely supporting the idea that 'Migration should be restricted.' This is to be observed with regard to all four groups of immigrants. In East Germany, meanwhile, this is only the case concerning the approving attitude towards asylum seekers and German resettlers. In the case of employees from the European Union, the general attitude in East Germany is developing towards being more approving but wanting restrictions on their inflow, while the number of those who disapprove is decreasing. Approving attitudes towards non-European Union members the approval, meanwhile, is decreasing, with increasing numbers wanting restrictions or the stop of inflow, though here the attitudes only vary a little over time.

In general, the employees from the non-European Union countries are the most disliked group of immigrants across all Germans. In 2000, 21.3% of West Germans and 38,6% of East Germans wanted to stop immigration completely. Discrimination against immigrants, who are considered 'foreigners living in Germany' can be captured with the German General Survey (ALL-BUS) by means of four items that measure respondents' readiness to exclude foreigners from the labour market and cut down on their freedom in the fields of political activity, choice of marriage partner, and overall lifestyle. These items were included in ALLBUS in 1980, 1984, 1988, 1990, 1994, 1996, 2000, and 2002. The results show that there is a substantial share of respondents who expressed discriminatory attitudes towards immigrants. Across all years, a clear majority of West Germans agree that foreigners should do more to adapt to the German way of life, and this is also true for East Germans in 1996 and 2000. In East Germany, the years 1996 and 2000 show a sharp increase in 'intolerance' regarding this issue. Overall, Germans are most 'intolerant' where life style is concerned. Looking at the years 1994, 1996, and 2000, one can see that almost one out of three respondents in both parts of Germany agree that foreigners should be prohibited from taking part in any kind of political activity, thus showing their willingness to deprive immigrants of a basic human right. Since 1994, 24% of West Germans and 33% of East Germans agree that foreigners should be sent home.

Overall, the differences between East Germans and West Germans are not as big as one might have expected considering that unemployment rates are very high in East Germany compared to West Germany (19.9% on the average, in some regions 40% or more). The adaptation to German lifestyle/habits (*Sitten*) is a major demand of 70% of all Germans, and this is on the rise. This has been used by three main XPPs in Germany to gain political advantages and entrance to local political organs and parliaments. There are three extreme right-wing parties in Germany that have a more or less regular presence on the political stage in both national and regional elections. The first one is the National-Democratic Party of Germany (NPD) (*Nationaldemokratische Partei Deutschlands*). It was founded on November 28, 1964 in Hanover by members of the former German Reich-Party (*Deutsche Reichspartei*).

The Republicans, or REP (*Die Republikaner*), were established on November 26, 1983 in Munich by the former members of the Christian Social Union (CSU), the Bavarian representation of the conservative Christian Democratic Union (CDU).

The third right-wing party, the Union of the German People (DVU; *Deutsche Volksunion*), was also established in Munich but on January 18, 1971, initially as a citizens' initiative. Apart from its founder and president Gerhard Frey, who is still in duty, the founders were former members of NPD and CDU/CSU as well as the ranks of Old Nazis (Altnazis). The citizens' initiative turned into a political party in 1987. Its first name was German Peoples Union–List D (*Deutsche Volksunion–Liste D*). Its name was changed into the Union of the German People-DVU) (*Deutsche Volksunion-DVU*) in 1991.

On a national level, a XPP has never, to date, managed to enter the *Bundestag*, failing to get over the 5% hurdle required for entry. XPPs have been successful only on the local and regional level in Germany. These parties are REP (Republicans), DVU (German People's Union), and NPD (National Democratic Party of Germany). In contrast to other small and locally bounded nationalist parties (i.e., the so-called Schill-Party in Hamburg), these three parties managed to enter regional parliaments at different times. REP was successful in the late 1980s and in the beginning of the 1990s. At its peak, REP stayed for two legislative periods in the regional parliament of Baden-Wuerttemberg between 1992 and 2001. During this time the REP faction in Baden-Wuerttemberg presented itself as moderate and less nationalistic than most REP factions in local parliaments (e.g., in Dortmund or Cologne). Similarly to the local REP factions, DVU and NPD each portrays itself as nationalistic and relies on antipolitical establishment populism.

Both parties, DVU and NPD, are still present in regional parliaments. DVU is found in different regional parliaments, whereas NPD is only present in Saxony since 2004. Particularly interesting is that the alliances between XPPs seem to be the main reason for their electoral successes. Thus, REP had agreed to forego its election campaign in Bremen and Brandenburg in 1999. It supported DVU which, therefore, could enter both regional parliaments. A similar arrangement was made between DVU and NPD for the elections in 2004. Both parties were running their election campaigns in separate federal states but agreed early in the campaign to back just one of the two parties in each federal state. As a result, DVU was reelected to the regional parliament of Brandenburg and NPD entered the regional parliament of Saxony. This success brought them back into regional parliaments in two *Bundesländer* for the first time after more than 30 years.

In addition to seats in regional parliaments, XPPs are also present in several local parliaments. In some municipalities they have even received more than 20% of all votes (e.g., NPD in Königstein achieved 21.1% in 2004, compared to 11.8% in 1999). They are accepted and they cooperate with other interest groups and parties at this level. This is mainly based on the media reports of XPP electoral and local policies because there are very few scientific analyses or observations in this respect. An exception is the book *Rechtsextremisten in Parlamenten* (1997) by Christoph Butterwegge et al. who say that there are only reports about certain events (i.e., violent offences) associated with right-wing extremism but there are no long term studies of extreme right-wing parties. Therefore, the contributors present case studies about the appearance and the presence of REP in local and regional parliaments.

REP won 7.4% (or 28,641 voters) of all votes in Cologne. One should note that Cologne is a city of different ethnic groups. In this multicultural context, REP won the election with their nationalistic campaign. Their main requests and proposals circled around migrants and criminality (Griese & Niermann, 1997). Later, REP in Cologne broke up into three factions due to inner conflicts which also caused withdrawals from the party. Mainstream parties declined cooperation or alliance with Cologne REP.

Similar developments occurred in Dortmund. REP won 6.3% of all votes but broke up one year later. Before its collapse it handed in requests and proposals concerning migrants, asylum seekers and criminality. Particularly interesting is that their political work in parliament was only done by single persons. They wrote the proposals and presented them in meetings. SPD and the Greens' strategy was to appoint REP to all commissions but its representatives never showed up for the meetings. Thus, it was possible to show that REP did nothing to promote local interests. Along with SPD and the Greens, CDU accepted that REP was elected to the local parliament but, at the same time, they refused to ally with it.

In contrast to Dortmund and Cologne, REP in Hamm had different topics on their parliamentary agenda. They presented themselves as close to the citizens [Bürgernah] and they were active in parliamentary work concerning housing, infrastructure, and traffic issues. Its representatives took up xenophobic and racial themes only *outside* of parliament. However, mainstream parties also refused to ally or to cooperate with REP in Hamm.

REP received 10.9% of all votes during regional elections on April 5, 1992. It even became the strongest opposition party in parliament due to the coalition between SPD and CDU in Baden-Wuerttemberg. Apart from proposals concerning migrants, asylum seekers, and criminality, REP led a defamation campaign against all parties in parliament. But their chair, Rolf Schlierer, also tried to reverse their antidemocratic and antiparliamentary image. His objective was to cooperate with CDU. Although this cooperation never materialised, conservative politicians supported REP on the issue of banning two members of SPD from parliament on the grounds that they were members of the Associations of the Persecuted during the NS-Regime/Association of the Anti-Fascists (*Vereinigung der Verfolgten des Naziregimes/Bund der Antifaschisten* [VVN-BdA]).

XPP has been successful on the regional and on the local level. On the local level, XPP is well-established in some places and cooperates with other interest groups and parties. Unfortunately, there are only few scientific analyses on this level of extreme right-wing political participation. According to the book by Butterwegge et al. (1997), XPP is ignored by most mainstream parties. SPD and the Greens in Dortmund developed counterstrategies to reveal the inability of XPP to do parliamentary work. In contrast, the conservative politicians in Baden-Wuerttemberg accepted and supported XPP.

Thus, one can assume that cooperation between XPP and other parties can possibly occur on the local level but it is almost impossible on the regional and federal levels in Germany. An important reason is that most XPPs have no tradition as political parties. It often causes conflicts and frictions within their parties as soon as they are elected to a parliament.

There are, however, reasons to assume that NPD's recent electoral success, most notably in Saxony, could represent the starting point for a long-term presence of NPD in German parliaments. This apprehension is based on the observation that a broad coalition is forming across the extreme right spectrum, since a 2004 declaration by the NPD party board ("Popular Front instead of Group Egoism") spoke for cooperation between NPD and other extreme right parties (such as DVU) as well as so-called Free Fraternities (*Freie Kameradschaften*).[8] The explicit call for cooperation with potentially violent neo-Nazis marks the culmination of a development that began in the early 1990s when the NPD youth organisation Young National Democrats (*Junge Nationaldemokraten* [JN]) first incorporated neo-Nazis. Since the late 1990s, NPD's collaboration with neo-Nazis has manifested itself predominantly in large-scale demonstrations. As for NPD's "three pillar strategy" (*Drei-Säulen-Konzept,* declared in 1997) consisting of "the war of the heads," "war of the streets" and "war of the parliaments," violent neo-Nazis are seen as responsible for "the war of the streets" in order to create neo-Nazi-controlled no-go-areas for migrants (*national befreite Zonen*). Furthermore, an extreme right subculture—including fanzines, music, fashion, and symbols—has developed over the past 15 years. This subculture has become increasingly popular with youths and is close to achieving cultural hegemony especially in provincial areas of East Germany such as 'Saxon Switzerland' (*Sächsische Schweiz*) in eastern Saxony. The fact that NPD courts Free Fraternities and their local associates is likely to strengthen the latter's support of the party, which might result in long-term electoral success.

Discursive Reconstruction of 'Us' vs. 'Them'

Despite the Nazi political history of Germany, the country has had a long tradition of displaying liberal attitudes towards immigrants and minorities (Mazower, 1998). However, the modern history of Germany shares the same properties as many other European nation-states. 'Otherization' has also been a part of the country's political system and, in many cases, its institutional arrangements. Politicisation of the immigration issue is also a part of German democracy today. There is a widespread awareness of the political and electoral utility of the migration issue.

In this part, the role of the three German xenophobic populist parties (REP, NPD, and DVU) in the change of xenophobic discourse, and their possible influences on the mainstream parties, are discussed.

The following frames have been chosen to analyze the role of XPP, mass media, and mainstream parties in the reinforcement of the 'Us' and 'Them' asymmetric categories in the public debate in Germany: (a) Collective Identity; (b) Employment Issues; (c) Welfare Issues; (d) Law and Order Issues; (e) Liberal Values; (f) Antiestablishment; (g) Immigrant Status; and (h) Legitimisation of Racism. The results show that the frames most frequently used in Germany in the discursive 'Otherization' of immigrants in the political scene of the country are 'Collective Identity,' 'Law and Order Issues,' 'Employment and Welfare Issues,' and

'Antiestablishment.' There are other frames, such as 'Liberal Values' and 'Immigrant Status' which are also used in this respect. Here the most frequent frames are illustrated.

Collective Identity

This frame encapsulates the discourses which are used in XPPs' party programmes, party press, and by the leaders of the parties in their political speeches. In more than 32 years of the postwar history of XPP in Germany, the importance of immigrant-related issues in XPPs' political propaganda has substantially increased. The 1973 NPD party programme, which was in effect until 1985, is characterized by a biological notion of the German nation, although rarely referring to the immigration issue. At this time, the NPD programme was dominated by a deep fear of the undesirable effects of Communism, Marxism, Socialism, and Materialism, which were considered as leading to social disintegration. Moreover, this programme points to falling birth rates as a key aspect affecting the prospects of the German people. Negative effects of immigration were highlighted only in connection to employment issues. This frame was detected in three sentences. Even the slogan "Germany for the Germans!" (1973, p. 25) was related to the presence of the allied forces in Germany rather than immigration, while the future buzzword "over-foreignisation" (1973, p. 10) referred to the possible effects of cultural and educational policy measures on German culture and language. Consequently, the respective sentences have not been interpreted as concerning immigration. Apart from 'Employment Issues,' the frames concerning reasons for migration and collective identity were contained in one sentence each.

However, in the German context the concept of collective identity is of great importance. This is mainly due to the experience of Nazism and the disastrous World War II. XPP use the concept of German collective identity as an exclusive property of a folk to distinguish themselves from 'alien elements' who are believed to be immigrants, and even those of German descent immigrating from the former Soviet block.

The 1985 party programme pays more attention to immigration, as 1 out of 10 chapters is dedicated to immigration related issues. Seven different types of frames are lumped together in this chapter titled "Internal peace is threatened by mass immigration of foreigners!" Without a doubt the most important frame is 'Collective Identity,' which is represented in 8 out of 13 sentences and constitutes the nexus of this chapter, while the other immigration related issue frames—such as 'Employment Issues,' 'Welfare Issues,' 'Law and Order Issues,' and 'Antiestablishment'—are among the most common. Other frames, such as 'Immigrant Status' and 'Liberal Values,' are used too, but not as frequently as the above mentioned frames. However, these frames together form a dense summary of NPD's attitude towards migrants and immigration, which is based on the assumption that ethnic homogeneity is to be retained in order to avoid conflicts, and which thus results in the call for repatriation.

A relatively high proportion of immigration related frames can be found in the 1997 NPD party programme. Immigration is referred to in the introduction, as well as in 6 out of 15 chapters. Frames were found in chapters on (a) 'the people'; (b) 'the family'; (c) 'social policy'; (d) 'Germany's German identity'; (e) 'Germany's sovereignty in the European context'; and (f) the legal system. Even a chapter from the 1985 party programme was included (with small amendments) in a chapter titled 'Once again.' The majority of sentences referring to immigration (22 out of 36) contain the 'Collective Identity' frame, followed by 'Law and Order Issues' (six sentences), 'Welfare Issues' (five sentences), and 'Antiestablishment' (three sentences). 'Employment Issues, 'Immigrant Status,' and 'Racism' were found only once. Thus, 'Law and Order Issues' and, especially, 'Welfare Issues' have gained greater importance than they held in the 1985 programme. Furthermore, the 'biological' notion—that is, that the social order in Europe is based on the principle of ethnic/racial descent (*Volksabstammung*)—is made explicit only in 1997. Even the call for the support of potential migrants in their native countries, which was a part of earlier party programmes, is missing in the 1997 programme.

At the party congress in October 2004, 6 weeks after the party's great electoral success in Saxony, NPD leader Udo Voigt gave a speech (entitled "Work, Family, Fatherland") in which he rejected any existence of a "multicultural society." (Deutsche Stimme, 2004, no. 10) In defence of an ethnically homogenous state, Voigt highlights the right of every people (*Volk*) to preserve its collective cultural identity in a defined territory:

> We love, for example, the Chinese in China and the Turks in Turkey . . . we want to send them back to their countries of origin. . . . When speaking of our people we do not mean the resident population of the FRG, but the German people.

The most important finding of the analyses of the speeches of NPD party leader, Udo Voigt, is that he adheres to a biological notion of 'people' (*Volk*). This ethnic nationalist model of collective identity has also been promoted in the party press, *Deutsche Stimme* (DS), throughout the entire period of the study (1980–2005). Most crucial aspects of this frame unfolded as early as 1980/1981. The party declares in DS (1980) that: "The NPD stands up for the preservation of the national identity and the cultural tradition of every people; of course, in their respective homelands" (No. 3, p. 1).

This very notion of nationally and culturally homogeneous societies is fundamental to DS coverage to date. In its view, "mass immigration leads to separation and ghettoisation" (1980, No. 9, p. 8). Consequently, NPD argues in favour of repatriation of migrants, stopping immigration, restrictions on naturalisation, and opposing alien suffrage. One has to keep in mind, though, that the NPD concept of ethnic nationalism cannot be separated from biological racism. Although avoiding explicit inferiorization of other groups, NPD often frames the German people (*das deutsche Volk*) as a biological and/or cultural entity threatened with extinction through falling birth rates as well as immigration, and it writes: "Our people is dying. Bereft of its national identity, its culture and history . . . it tumbles into ruin" (*DS*, 1981, No. 3, p. 4).

Employment and Welfare Issues

The frame of 'Employment Issues' is closely linked to the frame of 'Welfare Issues,' as both address the economic dimensions of immigration. They are frequently combined in *DS*, since wage-earners with alien status are defined as the major 'takers' of unemployment, welfare, and educational benefits:

> Whoever tackles unemployment cannot ignore the army of foreign workers and the burden of billions swallowed by unemployment benefits, child benefit, educational costs and additional expenditures (*DS*, 1981, No. 9, p. 1).

Over the years, asylum seekers have been continuously targeted by *DS* as living a life of luxury at the expense of Germans. Since the mid-1980s, asylum seekers were accused of "abuse of the right to asylum" (*DS*, 1985, No. 3, p. 1; 1986, No. 9, p. 1; 1988, No. 9, p. 9; 1990, No. 9, p. 1; 1991, No. 9, p. 2). Germany was considered to be the "welfare office of the world" (1990, No. 9, p. 1) and seeking asylum in Germany was equated with holidays: "Asylum-holidays have never been as cheap as they are today!" (1991, No. 9, p. 14). As a consequence, *DS* demanded the amendment of the Asylum Law in Article 16a of the Basic Law, which defines Germany as open to asylum seekers, and instead called for the expulsion of people which *DS* perceived as criminal and as pseudo asylum seekers (1989, No. 3, p. 1; 1993, No. 3, p. 4).

The leader of NPD, Udo Voigt, argues in favour of job priority for native Germans to be based on a Job Protection Act and repatriation of foreign labour. He also proposes the exclusion of persons regarded as foreigners from the insurance system, as well as the repatriation of migrants who have been unemployed for more than 3 months.

Employment and welfare issues have been an effective frame to mobilise the fear of unemployment and social insecurity based on cuts in the welfare subsidies.

Law and Order Issues

Another frame identified as being of major importance right from the start concerned law and order issues. Already in 1980 migrants were conceptualised by the XPP party press as a destabilising factor for German society:

"Social peace is threatened by a multitude of foreigners. . . . A dangerous time bomb is ticking in the country" (DS, 1980, No. 9, p. 8). Blaming the victim, DS predicted a horror scenario including "hatred of foreigners (*Fremdenhaß*), race riots (*Rassenkrawalle*), Turkish ghettos (*Türken-Ghettos*), and right-wing terrorism (*Rechtsterrorismus*)" (DS, 1981, No. 3, p. 2). Migrants have generally been associated with crime. For example, DS (1980, No. 2) reported that "90% of drug traffic is in the hands of foreign bandits." In addition, asylum seekers were presented not only as a threat to the German welfare system but also as criminals. A front page caption of DS from 1986 constitutes a prototypical example of the aggressive demonisation of asylum seekers: "They overrun our country. They loot and rape. They destroy our youth with drugs. But they call themselves 'asylum seekers' (*Asylanten*)" (1986, No. 9, p. 1).

Not surprisingly, reference was frequently made to supposedly criminal asylum seekers for the decade to follow (DS, 1986, No. 9, p. 9; 1989, No. 3, p. 1, 1993, No. 3, p. 7; 1994, No. 3, p. B). The direct association of immigration with crime—as encapsulated in the equation "multi-cultural=multi-criminal" (*multi-kulturell=multi-kriminell*) (DS, 1992, No. 9, p. 2)—has gained popularity in DS since the early 1990s. Accordingly, migrants, and asylum seekers in particular, are seen as having criminal tendencies. This has become a politically mobilising issue as part of XPP propaganda. In 2004 issues of DS, crime was presented as an intrinsic quality of multicultural societies: "Violence, criminality and drugs belong to a multicultural society as fleas to a dog" (2004, No. 4, p. 4). A qualitative dichotomy of people living in Germany, that is, Germans *and* migrants—provides the central themes of the articles in DS.

Migrants are generally associated with violence, crime and 'welfare cheating' in DS, and Germans portrayed as their innocent victims who are deprived of due protection by the police, the authorities and the political parties. The notion of innocent German victims of crime was also expressed in one of the selected DS of 1995 (No. 9, p. 2), where NPD leader, Günter Deckert, complains in an entire page about how slowly police reacted to his emergency calls in which he asked for help while 'exotics' threw eggs and dented his car tyres. His key comment was: "My wish to have a police car positioned in front of my house . . . does not become fulfilled—[since] I am not a Turk nor a 'Normal Jew' nor even Ignatz/Michel."[9]

Criminality is one of the most effective discourses that has been used by XPP press and party leaders to legitimise their arguments for the restriction and repatriation of immigrants and so to mobilise political support among the voters.

Antiestablishment

Established parties are portrayed as champions of 'the multicultural society' aiming to exclude NPD from the political arena due to its being the only party strongly opposed to multiculturalism and globalisation. In the party programme of 1997, NDP declared:

> The multicultural society is increasingly seen as the only key to the solution, which is to keep the ruling classes [*tragende Schichten*] in power by replacing the people. In contrast, the National Democratic Party of Germany strives for a replacement of those in power in order to give the German people a future within the European family of peoples [*europäische Völkerfamilie*].

The party press, *DS*, has been highly engaged in blaming the established political parties as a problem for Germany. Since 'the establishment' (*die Etablierten*) has been held responsible for the promotion of immigration, *DS* coverage has always been characterized by a palpable antiestablishment element. As opposed to the uniform bloc of established parliamentary parties—that is, CDU/CSU, SPD, FDP, and the Greens (often metonymically replaced by 'Bonn' or, since the late 1990s, 'Berlin,' as the respective seats of the German government)—the National Democrats present themselves as true democrats who represent the popular will expressed in opinion polls (1981, No.3, p. 4; 1982, No. 9, p. 1; 1984, No. 4, p. 1; 1986, No. 9, p. 9; 1989, No. 3, p. 1; 1992, No. 9, p. 1; 2000, No. 9, p. 5). At times, the mass media are also included in what *DS* regards as the establishment. Antiimmigrant attitudes are presented as resulting from political failure to satisfy the needs of the German people. While rejecting violence as a political tool, the National Democrats attributed the responsibility for the 1992 arsons of asylum homes (East Germany) and houses inhabited exclusively by Turks (West Germany) to the political establishment:

> The established Bonn parties bear the blame for these assaults, as they ignore the worries of their own people, continually acting scandalously, hostile towards autochthonous people. . . . Assaults on foreigners only happen because Bonn does not react to our country being increasingly threatened with over-foreignisation. (*DS*, 1992; No. 9, p. 1)

The most ferocious of polemics against the establishment accused "Bonn political criminals" of "genocide of their own people" due to having turned Germany into "some kind of multiethnic state" (1999, No. 3, p. 2). In contrast, the National Democrats defined themselves as the "stigmatized opposition" (2001, No. 9, p. 4). According to *DS*, the solution lies in voting for NPD in order to remove the corrupted established parties and politicians, and to make possible policy measures intended to serve the interests of the German people (1985, No. 3, p. 1; 1986, No. 9, p. 1; 1986, No. 3, p. 10; 2002, No. 9, p. 2).

The Dichotomy of 'Us' against the Muslim 'Others'

Although the frame of 'Liberal Values' has been not used by NPD (probably due to National Democrats themselves being far from the promotion of liberalism and of considering themselves liberals), immigrants cultures and traditions have been presented as 'alien' to and dangerous for German collective identity, culture, and society. They consider Muslim immigrants as potential allies in their authoritarian quest for ethnic and religious homogeneity:

> Also, devout Muslims think much less of multicultural kindergartens and school classes than do dogmatic pluralistic foreigner-ombudsmen (*Ausländerbeauftragte*) and integration fanatics. It is good that way. Neither should Muslim children be integrated into the Western system of values (*Wertewelt*) nor Europeans into the Islamic. (*DS*, 2003, No. 9, p. 7)

The debate after the 2004 murder of a Dutch filmmaker, Theo van Gogh, in Holland by a young man of Muslim background also illustrates how old response patterns condition the present. Demonising of Muslims as essentially different from 'our' society and 'our' culture' is a part of the daily political actions of XPP, and in some cases even a part of mainstream parties political agenda and the mass media. A high-pitched discussion about the German and Muslim 'parallel societies' was launched by XPP but supported by the mainstream parties and even some leftists. The XPP leaders and press in Germany argued for forbidding migrant languages in the Mosques, substituting Muslim specialists on Islam by providing German-supervised instruction in Islam to school children, and, finally, the authorities used the opportunity to deport a Muslim religious leader from Köln who was known to the police for fundamentalist agitation. Furthermore, they have aimed to forbid many Muslim organisations accused of being fundamentalists. The 'German-ness' is considered to be alien to Islam and Muslims.

Since the late 1990s, crime becomes more and more associated with Islam and Muslim groups in Germany. These groups appeared to the conservative politicians as more threatening to German culture than the right- or left-wing radicals. The discussion heated up after the terrorist attacks in the United States in September 2001. The old prejudices and racist categorisations of Muslims as the 'enemy from the east,' as well as the 'inferior Others,' are today a very common feature in German public debate. It is not only XPP, but also the mainstream parties and mass media which are highly engaged in the 'Otherization' and demonisation of Muslims.

Assessing Impacts of XPP

The study of frames used by the mainstream parties (CDU/CSU and SPD) on the one side, and the extreme right-wing party NPD on the other, conducted in the time period 1980 to 2005, suggests that the frames of XPP have not exerted much direct influence on the mainstream parties. The material indicates that the direct impact of XPP was measurable in just one case, namely that of support for development aid.

Firstly, we have to notice that XPP never could gain seats in the German parliament (*Bundestag*). There is only one exception. Dr. Rudolf K. Krause, who was previously in CDU, moved to the *Republikaner* (REP) in May 1993. He became a free parliamentarian since he was elected to the *Bundestag* without REP's presence in it. In the debate about the right of asylum which took place on May 26, 1993, he was arguing that Germany has only a limited ability to absorb migration. But this perspective was also put forward by CDU- and the CSU-representatives. It is unlikely that Krause had any particular influence over the outcome of this particular debate because conservative politicians often evoke similar negative images about migrants and speak of the absorption, viability or endurance limit being surpassed. Probably, the presence of Krause in the parliament encouraged a more aggressive debate on immigration in the parliament.

Secondly, it is also important to note that the mainstream parties never allied with XPP at the national or the regional level. Thus, XPP was unable to impose constraints on a coalition partner. Therefore, there is no doubt that its direct impact on the mainstream parties is very limited.

However, the *indirect* impact of XPP on the mainstream parties and the mass media has not been as limited as the direct effect. All party programmes and election manifestos of the following major mainstream parties, namely Social Democratic Party of Germany or SPD (*Sozialdemokratische Partei Deutschlands*) and Christian Democratic Party or CDU (*Christlich Demokratische Union*) in the years 1982 to 2004 have been selected and analyzed. The antiimmigrant frames of 'Collective Identity,' 'Employment and Welfare Issues,' and 'Law and Order Issues' are frequently used by the both parties.

Collective Identity

This frame is used by SPD for the first time in their 1983 party programme, where they claim that the foreign population must not increase: "It [integration] can only be successful, if the foreign population does not increase more. For this reason the recruitment stop [*Anwerbestopp*] is to be retained" (SPD election manifesto, 1983). Discourses on 'German-ness' as a positive property of the German society, in relation to immigration as a threat, are frequently used by the two mainstream parties. The discourse of restrictions on immigration has been also used in many cases to preserve the positive properties of the German society. One can see from the party programmes of SPD and CDU that the parties express their fears of increasing immigration; they even argue that multiculturalism is endangering the inner peace of society. CDU illustrates its fear for multiculturalism as follows: "Living in community with people from other culture areas also implicates problems and fears which can lead to xenophobia and antialien feelings" (CDU party programme, 1994).

Presenting immigrants as "people from other cultures" indicates very much the 'differences' between 'Germans and non-Germans' that are used in party leaders' and 'mass media' debates of the mainstream parties. There is a common understanding that Germans and immigrants can be categorized as two completely different people with externally different, but internally homogenous, cultures. The concept of 'different cultures' at many times comes very near to the concept of 'different races.'

This problem of 'Otherization' is very common in both parties' party programmes. Even the immigrants from European Union and non-European Union countries are divided into two groups, since European Union migrants are considered a part of 'Us.' For instance, CDU distinguishes, in its party programme of 1994, between various groups of immigrants, namely the welcomed and the unwelcomed immigrants. Thus, they prefer late resettles, as well as European Union citizens, to other groups of immigrants. They declare that: "The freedom of movement of the EU citizens and the rights of German Resettles laid down in the Basic Laws must have priority" (CDU party programme, 1994). Other groups of immigrants, who mainly come from non-EU countries, are distinguished from those coming from the European Union and addressed as "foreign employees living here": "We want to make it possible for the foreign employees living here and their relatives to appropriately participate in our economic, social, and cultural life" (CDU election manifesto, 1987).

This is even a focal point in the mainstream parties' party press. The party presses that have been studied and analyzed in the project were the party press of the Social Democratic Party of Germany (SPD), and of the Christian Social Union (CSU). CSU has, for decades, formed a strong alliance with the Christian Democratic Union (CDU), and we selected its party press because CDU has no 'party press' (*Parteiorgan;* or at least none with much presence or continuity). CSU's party newspaper is called the Bavarian Currier (*Bayernkurier*) and is edited by Franz Josef Strauß, a former leader of CSU. *Bayernkurier* is a weekly party organ. The SPD party paper is called *Forward* (*Vorwärts*). It was founded by Wilhelm Hasenclever and Wilhelm Liebknecht in 1876.

For each party paper, the first issue of March and September of every year was selected because the most elections in federal states are held at these times. The debates in the party press are almost the same as the declarations in the party programmes of SDP and CDU/CSU. The two categories of 'Germans' and 'immigrants' are taken as two different categories that either should live together in a multicultural society (as discussed by SDP press, *Vorwärts*, September 2000) or becoming assimilated with or rejected from the German society (as claimed by CDU/CSU press, *Bayernkurier*, September 2002).

Immigrants are considered by both parties to be 'foreign elements' in German society by both SDP and CDU. The latter declared the nonimmigration 'essence' of the German country: "Germany is not a migration country" (CDU party manifesto, 1994). Furthermore, the party portrays immigrants as a danger to German society:

> Numerous, mainly young foreigners having insufficient knowledge of language, lacking prospects at the labour market and the difference of education between German and foreign young persons are only some visible forerunners of a threatening social explosive in Germany. (CDU election manifesto, 2002)

Employment and Welfare Issues

Employment and welfare issues have been used by the both mainstream parties in an instrumental way. Their arguments revolve around the positive and the negative contributions of immigrants to German society. The main question is if 'they' are good for 'Us.' The following is an illustration of SDP's position on this matter:

> A reasonable work-migration thus limits the immigration to what is economically reasonable and is necessary in employment without being too much for the country's capability of integration. (SPD election manifesto, 2002)

Here we find an argumentation which welcomes those needed at the German labour market, but not those who are not considered to be 'useful.'

The same theme is frequently addressed in the speeches of the mainstream parties' leader. For instance, the CDU/CSU leader, Stoiber, in his electoral speech (March 7, 1998) argues against illegal asylum seekers because illegal immigration would increase the income taxes and welfare payments for lower class people. Attacks against the government (the SPD/Greens) are frequent; the state, according to Stoiber, prevents integration and facilitates abuse of the German welfare state through its policy. The solution should be more restrictive national regulations that stop immigration and welfare abuse. Later, on March 3, 2002, the new CDU/CSU leader, Angela Merkel, proposes to limit immigration to well-educated people and foreign students in order to prevent burdens and 'dangers' to the welfare system.

The frame of migrants as 'illegal competitors' was applied in CDU/CSU's party press, *Bayernkurier*, when speaking of high unemployment rates. After the change of government in 1998, conservative parties, now in opposition, argued against policies which eased access to the domestic labour market for migrants because "there are many unemployed Germans." *Bayernkurier* argued:

> Taking foreign experts is only possible as a temporary solution but it cannot be a general rule for migration. . . . According to the government, there were 31000 unemployed IT-specialists [*Fachinformatiker*] in Germany in the end of last year. Therefore it is necessary to provide massive skill up-grading measures [for Germans]. (2000, No. 9, p. 2)

Such frames were used again in 2001 and 2002 election discussions. *Bayernkurier* frequently reported about threats to the German welfare system by migrants throughout the years. Beginning in 1982, there is an article about asylum seekers who refused to clean up streets. It was said that they would earn 1.25 Deutsche mark per hour. *Bayernkurier* wrote:

> If one considers that asylum seekers also receive social benefits from Berlin they earn around 20 German marks per hour—it's nothing but a hypocrisy to talk of starvation wages in that case. . . . After WWII Germans cleaned up wreckage for less money. (1982, No. 10, p. 5)

Such statements about migrants living at the expense of German taxpayers and municipalities were published over and over again. In texts, common terms for asylum seekers were "pseudo asylum seekers" (*Scheinasylanten*) (Bayernkurier, 1992, No. 10, p. 1) or "economic refugees" (*Wirtschaftsflüchtlinge*) (Bayernkurier, 1990, No. 9, p. 1). In many cases the notion of "big waves of economic refugees" as a tsunami was used as a warning for the "threat of immigration" to Germans. In the SDP party press, *Vorwärts*, migrants are often presented as making a contribution to "Us" (e.g., in 2000, No. 9, p. 6). Although publishing articles against illegal immigration and the need for effective migration control, *Vorwärts* wrote several times that migrants contribute positively to the German welfare system; they spend more money than they receive (2000, No. 9).

A general topic is the 'misuse' of the right of asylum. As Germany has the laws encouraging political refugees to seek asylum, migrants can apply for asylum and their application is individually reviewed. While asylum seekers are waiting for the decision, they are entitled to social benefits. According to *Bayernkurier*, this opportunity is misused by most refugees who have economic instead of political reasons for migration. But the image of migrants is not only created by the notion of misuse. In *Bayernkurier*, migrants are further considered as cheating and dirty: "the same people hand in several applications for social benefits using different names—which sometimes are very preposterous" (1992, No. 10, p. 1) or "asylum seekers—most of them are illegal—camp in gardens, pile up tremendous rubbish in there, thefts are rising, and they are beg-gars" (1992, No. 36, pp. 1, 8).

Law and Order Issues

This is one of the three most common frames used by the German CDU/CSU, its press, and its party leaders. Large scale, organized, and frequent indi-vidual criminality committed by migrants and foreigners is often used as an 'Otherising' frame. It is said that with migration to Germany, conflicts and criminality are brought to the German society. According to CDU/CSU's party press, *Bayernkurier,* criminality and extremism are rising in accordance with the increasing number of migrants. Even "international terrorism is creeping into Germany" together with immigrants (1995, No. 9, p. 2) or:

> Organized criminality (OC) becomes more and more a threat to the so-ciety . . . over 76 percent of all cases shows international connections. Over 62 percent are migrants. Therefore one can say that OC has in fact an external origin. (1999, No. 35, p. 4)

Since 2001, extremism has been strongly connected with "Islamic terror" (2002, No. 36, p. 6; 2004, No. 36, p. 4). One response to that problem offered by *Bayernkurier* is deportation and repatriation of foreign crimi-nals. The conservative party press, the party leaders of CDU/CSU, and their party programmes have been extensively engaged in cultivating an image of immigrants as 'foreign criminals' and as a 'threat to Us' and the Germans' interior security. Waigel, as party leader of CDU/CSU prior to Stoiber, in 1998 connects inner security and criminality in Germany with migrants. Stoiber then proceeds to relate the question of migrants from Eastern Europe and of asylum seekers with criminality, illegal activities, and trafficking. Germany is depicted as the country that has to deal with more than half of the asylum seekers that come to Europe. Even more, asylum seekers in general are connected with the rise of XPP and criminal acts against asylum seekers. Waigel claims that the left-wing politicians who argue against restrictions for asylum seekers are responsible for the accession of XPP. The solution to this problem, according to the leaders of CDU/CSU, is more repressive measures against criminality in general, deportation of migrant criminals, and stronger controls on the eastern and southern borders.

Although SDP's party press, *Vorwärts,* did not use the frame of 'Law and Order Issues' as frequently as CDU/CSU, neither did they develop a counterdiscourse to the discourse on criminal migrants, which is typical for the conservative parties; they did not write about the issues, either to offer their own interpretations or to challenge existing ones. However, SPD parliamentarians used the frame of 'Law and Order Issues' and the topic of "increasing criminality by increasing immigration" in a debate on May 26, 1993, when they, together with CDU/CSU, voted for a more restricted right to asylum. According to them, asylum seekers burden the social system, particularly German taxpayers and municipalities.

In the years after 2001, we are witnessing a rise in negative discourses about Muslims and 'Islamic terrorism,' both in the SDP's party press and the speech of its leaders. It seems that the concept of 'foreigners' and the 'foreign threat' is mostly applied to Muslims.

Mass Media and the 'Others'

The role of mass media in influencing public opinion has been extensively researched and debated. The intention of the present research project has been to study the role of mass media in reinforcing 'Xeno-otherism' by assessing the impact of XPP on the public debate in Germany. In this respect, the mass media articles have been selected in relation to 'critical events.' The following are critical events that have been used in the analysis:

1. the asylum debate, September 1986;
2. the fall of the Berlin Wall, November 9, 1989;
3. the attacks on the World Trade Center and Pentagon in the United States, September 11, 2001;
4. the change of citizenship law, May 7, 1999; and
5. the enlargement of the European Union, May 1, 2004.

Three national newspapers with the highest circulation figures are selected for analysis. The *Süddeutsche Zeitung* (SZ) is chosen as the serious, liberal newspaper, while the *Frankfurter Allgemeine Zeitung* (FAZ) was chosen as the conservative daily newspaper—as we were assured by different publications on the subject of German media (i.e., Schönbach, 1977; Hömberg & Schlemmer, 1995). The third newspaper is a tabloid, *Bild* (BILD), which according to some scholars (Jäger, 1993, p. 12), has a right-wing populist position that "try to bring (at least in part) radical right-wing ideology into the heart of society."

The results are based on the analysis of a total of 930 texts on migrants or migration policy selected from the three newspapers. In terms of timeframes for the reporting of given events, stories from 2 weeks before, and 2 weeks after event dates were reviewed, along with the stories published during an event. (An exception was made for the terrorist attacks in September 2001 for which there was no prior reporting. Instead, samples were taken 1 week before and 3 weeks after this event.) Similarities to XPP frames were looked for in articles, interviews, and commentary columns of the selected newspapers. Letters to the editors were excluded, as it is said in the newspapers that editors are not responsible for the content of readers' letters and their opinions may differ from the editors' position.

The Asylum Debate, September 1986

The asylum debate raised in 1986, when a relatively high number of refugees entered West Germany by passing through East Germany, provoked a discussion about restricting the right to asylum. There is no change over time when it comes to framing migrants as a threat to the German labour market. In 1986, restrictions on the number of asylum seekers were demanded for the first time. *FAZ* wrote: "80 percent [of voters] stand for restrictions [for asylum seekers] whereas only 20 percent are against it. Therefore voters say: yes to asylum but a controlled one. This way of thinking is in fact very rational" (*FAZ*, September 15, 1986). From 1986 to 2004, one finds articles in all selected newspapers which are concerned about the rising numbers of migrants in times of high unemployment. It has to be noted that unemployment has been very high in Germany since 1982 (10%). In 1990, it was 8.4%, and, in 1997, it was almost 13%. In this time period there were comments in *BILD* and *FAZ* demanding restrictions on immigration. *FAZ* warned that: "The number of foreigners which dropped between 1983 and 1984 was again by 100.000 higher than in 1985 [when it reached] 4.34 millions at the end of June [1986]. This progress is alarming to the labour market experts" (September 20, 1986). All three papers were in favour of a restriction to immigration as a result of the rising numbers of immigrants coming to Germany in 1986. The question of employment and welfare were of central importance for the media debate.

The Fall of the Berlin Wall, November 9, 1989

The fall of the Berlin Wall was of great importance to Germans. It created a difficult situation even for the media. It created a frame in the public debate that can be called the 'resource drain' frame, which means that immigrants drain the country of resources that could have been used for the benefits of 'native' Germans. It was difficult to apply this for refugees from the German Democratic Republic (GDR). On the one hand, shortly before the reunification East Germans were perceived as competitors for housing and work. On the other hand, conservative and extreme right-wing ideologies distinguish between 'ethnic Germans' and 'foreigners.' In their view, all 'ethnic Germans' are welcome and it is 'our' duty to help them. 'Foreigners,' however, have no similar a priori right to help. A comment in *FAZ* in this context blamed leftists for their resentments against 'ethnic Germans' and for their demand to restrict immigration of 'ethnic Germans' (November 1, 1989).

The differentiation between immigrants from East Germany and non-European immigrants was very common in the debate of the reunion in 1989. An article in *BILD* in 1989, where a CDU politician was cited, blaming asylum seekers instead of East German refugees for problems on the housing market, is illustrative. In this article, the author used the notion *'Asylantenwelle,'* which means the wave of asylum seekers, a word evoking a threat to the German nation.

The Attacks on the World Trade Center and Pentagon in the United States, September 11, 2001

The attacks on the World Trade Center in New York and the Pentagon in Washington, D.C. was one of the most critical events used by the mass media in 'Otherising' immigrants as 'criminals,' and in particular Muslims, as 'terrorists,' 'anti-German,' and 'antidemocratic.' In 2001, it was reported that Germany hosted terrorists (*FAZ*, September 21, 2002): "The example of three students, who in Hamburg prepared themselves for several years for the suicidal attack in the United States, show that Germany does not longer serve as just a retreat, but also as a passage or preparation country." The reporting on the WTC terrorists in *BILD* is more emotional and detailed. In this context, *BILD* labels terrorists as foreigners by using their names as markers (also see Jäger et al., 1998). Thus, it was written: "They lived among us in Harburgs, Marien- and Wilhelm street. The assassins Mohamed Atta (33) and Marwan Alshehhi (23) were sleepers—agents of terror" (September 14, 2001). This report was followed by a general presumption about more 'sleepers' in Germany. As usual, *BILD* produced a climate of fear: "There are 100 so-called sleepers in Germany. Men who were trained by Talibans in Afghanistan, ready to attack at any time" (September 21, 2001).

According to the total number of articles, *FAZ* and *BILD* wrote most reports about migrants—in particular Muslims—as criminals or extremists. Usually these articles were written as factual reports. Comments on this subject were rare. In their coverage about migrants as criminals or extremists, *FAZ* and *BILD* produced and reproduced a discourse on 'foreigner-criminality.'

The Change of Citizenship Law, May 7, 1999

The united Germany changed the right to citizenship for young migrants and legalised double citizenship on May 7, 1999. A negative debate dominated all three newspapers about the law of double citizenship for young migrants. On May 21, 1999, Berthold Kohler wrote: "More than half a century after its delusional excesses, is the national in Germany still negated, tabooed and demonized." The debates were generally negative about double citizenship which was considered as problematic for Germany as a nation.

The Enlargement of the European Union, May 1, 2004

Conservative politicians were generally negative about the enlargement of the European Union and the inclusion of new member states from Eastern

Europe. The fear about 'mass migration' from the new member states was presented in the newspapers. In 2004, *BILD* published an article by a CSU member who said that immigration from Eastern Europe would cause worse pay in Germany: "Certain economic areas ask for high numbers of immigrants from Eastern Europe as more employees continually help to reduce payment" (April 16, 2004).

XPP media were also engaged in the debates on each of the aforementioned critical events in Germany. Their positions in respect of different questions have been also mentioned and discussed in mainstream media. All three selected newspapers report more or less about right-wing parties and their prominent members. There are periods of ups and downs concerning the reporting on rights. These observations can be made in all papers. But *FAZ* and *SZ* differ from *BILD* in their number of entries. Rights are always less mentioned in *BILD* than in the serious newspapers. It can be explained by the fact that the serious newspapers generally have a broader and more comprehensive coverage. Thus, *FAZ* and *SZ* easily reach a higher number of entries than does *BILD*.

All selected newspapers show an increased reporting on XPP around parliamentary elections or court procedures concerning XPP and its members. High entries particularly occurred in *FAZ* and *SZ* when XPP won elections or when the government tried to ban NPD between 2001 and 2002. Notably, the reporting on the Neonazi-movement and its leaders displays a stronger focus on right-wing extremism by *SZ* than do conservative newspapers. Finally, one can say that *SZ* mentions right-wing activities and members more frequently. It means that they are more aware of right-wing extremism than are *FAZ* or *BILD*. Similar conclusions were derived from a comparative analysis of different newspapers by Kirwel (1996).

Conclusion

In general one can say that the impact of extreme right-wing parties on national politics and policies is very small for the time period between 1980 and 2005. On the German national level it is even possible to assert that these parties have no direct influence at all. In electoral terms, they are successful only at the regional and local level. REP is has greater presence in the south, whereas DVU can be found in the north and the east of Germany. NPD is slightly overrepresented in the east but can also be found in other places. Often the former XPP disappeared after a short period of time. It was usually caused by conflicts and friction within the parties themselves, whereas recent XPPs, such as the NPD and the DVU, seem to have become more organized and coordinated. Thus, they were able to maintain themselves in the regional parliaments of Bremen, Brandenburg, and Saxony, although in Saxony (at the time of writing), a split between 'Wessis' and 'Ossis' within NPD is leading to major conflicts. NPD produces and reproduces negative frames concerning asylum seekers and immigrants. Until the mid-1990s most themes were about asylum seekers or criminal migrants. Since the end of the 1990s, repatriation issues became more frequent. Of course, NPD does not display liberal orientation. Probably for the same reason, it has not accused the migrants of undermining liberal values. According to its paper, *DS,* liberalism weakens the uniqueness of every culture, so it is rejected as a value.

Finally, definition and frequency of the 'biological racism' frame can be said to have been in constant change between 1982 and 2005. Particularly in the 1980s biological racism was quite popular in the right-wing discourse. At the end of the 1990s this argument appeared again in a new shape. One may speak of a 'differentiating racism.' Nations are equated with cultures which, in turn, exist as part of an overall biological-ecological design which has to be kept in balance by preserving the uniqueness of each culture and by keeping the cultures separate from each other. To insure the survival of the German nation, for example, any new migration should be stopped, and existing migrants should be repatriated and 'development aid' channelled to them where they now live.

However, the open debates and frames of XPP seem to have exercised some *indirect* influence. They constantly reproduce a discourse about immigration and its negative consequences. In the 1980s, one could see the frame 'tackle reason for migration' in the party media of NPD. Later, this frame can be found in the parliamentary debates about asylum rights and in other mainstream discourses, whereas it disappears in the extreme right-wing discourse.

Since Germany has a long record of employing seasonal/guest workers and of putting homogenising-disciplining pressures on its migrants and minorities, it is difficult to know who influenced who on the German political scene. However, in some cases, such as the 'criminality' issues, both CDU/CSU and SDP have had 'a move to the right,' which is a position nearer XPP, in the public debate. This is, of course, not only because of the influence of XPP frames, but also the influence of critical events, such as the fall of the Berlin Wall and the attacks on the Word Trade Center in New York. However, it can be said that some of the discourses which were used by XPP are now established discourses of the mainstream parties, as well as the mainstream mass media.

The indirect impact of XPP can be also related to the change in their strategies. From being small extremist groups, they are adjusting themselves to the democratic system and to presenting themselves as 'normal' political parties that can reform and change the society by democratic means.

THE CASE OF FRANCE

The Political Context of Xenophobia in France

Immigrants from non-EU and non-'western' countries are the main victims of racial violence in France. Voting surveys and opinion polls show a growing tendency for racist and discriminatory attitudes towards immigrants. The surveys confirm the role of the 'French's' conception of themselves as superior to the inferior 'Others.' The 'Others,' mainly immigrants, are considered socially and culturally inferior to 'Us,' and thus must be controlled and ruled, as they cannot be easily integrated in French society. Immigrants from Africa, the West Indies, and the Middle East suffer particularly from stereotypes about French former colonies.

However, the topic of the ethnic or religious background of those living in France is an officially illegitimate concept and research agenda. Therefore, the people who are suffering from racist actions are portrayed as *individuals* and not *groups*. Alongside this, the French conception of racism has long been limited to intentional racism, and not to contextual, institutional or symbolic racism. Yet, because of the dominance of the republican model, civil servants do not take racial discrimination of any description into account. As a matter of fact, they too often consider that immigrants are simply insufficiently integrated, when public services are proved to be discriminatory. This means putting the blame on the victims and making them responsible for their own discrimination. Since the beginning of the economic crisis in the 1980s, immigrants became the scapegoats of unemployment in France. For instance the famous phrase: "Three million immigrants in France, three million unemployed people," which frequently was used by the extreme right groups, meant that "if there were no immigrants everyone in France could have a job." Immigrants were also held responsible for the heavy burden on the French welfare system.

While, as a result of increasing European Union influence, the concept of 'racial discrimination' has been part of the French public discourse for almost a decade, celebration of diversity is still banned in France. Diversity is considered as giving rise to 'multiculturalism' and sectarianism, these often portrayed by the French media as ethnic 'ghettos.' Anglo-Saxon countries are presented as negative examples of diversity and multiculturalism. Despite recurrent opinion polls, the extent of racist and xenophobic attitudes among the French voters is not well-known. However, there is an increasing negative attitude against Muslims among French voters. In respect of this, the National Front's anti-Arabic and anti-Muslim propaganda can be counted as one of the major influences.

Discursive Reconstruction of 'Us' vs. 'Them'

The discursive reconstruction of the dualism of Us' against 'Them' is rather old in France. However, the politicisation of immigration and immigrants as a domestic problem is relatively new. The historical denial of 'differences' between people living in France, by addressing them as 'citizens of the republic,' has entailed a denial of racism and discrimination in French society. The emergence of Front National (The National Front) on the political scene of France created a new political arena in which parts of the 'citizens of the republic' were officially addressed as 'non-French,' 'deviant,' 'criminal' and thus 'unwanted.' 'Otherization' achieved a new political dimension in France.

The history of XPP in France is relatively short. The Front National (FN) was founded in 1972 out of the ashes of previous right-wing populist (*Poujadism*) and nationalist (*Algérie Française*) parties. It remained a marginal party until the early 1980s, when it experienced its first victories at local elections. The history of these victories has been very well documented (Perrineau & Mayer, 1996): among the reasons cited to explain them has been local militant work, along with a famous topic—the creation of an electoral basis for FN. Previous research indicates that this basis was partly created by FN through aggregating unregistered voters and people abstaining from voting, before the appeal of the party attracted voters from other popular parties.

Until its electoral breakthrough, and even for some time after, FN was a party close to its movement roots: methods and themes reflected the prominence of neonazis within the structure. During its electoral ascension, FN aggregated several extreme-right trends which actually have little in common: neonazis and defenders of colonialism, Catholic fundamentalists and neo-pagans, all merged within a single celebration of the populist leader, Jean-Marie Le Pen. This diversity made it difficult to establish a single discourse: It can be hypothesized that immigration is one of the themes which allow some political unity within FN.

In this part, the analysis of the Front National's (FN) party programmes, party press, and the leaders' speeches will be presented. FN's party programmes were not available prior to 1998. We have supplemented the shortage of party programmes by studying internal documentation, namely, party books (written mainly by the leaders) that are more a kind of 'declaration of intent' than a party programme *per se*. However, they do function as a way of being able to view the party's declared policies and electoral programmes. These books were obtained by conducting fieldwork at FN.

Three following party programmes are analyzed: (a) a regional programme from 1998, for the regional elections in Ile-de-France (i.e., Paris and its suburbs). The programme was mainly influenced by the ideas of Jean-Yves Le Gallou, a prominent member of FN, who is a specialist in immigration matters and belongs to the New Right. He also works in close connection with the Club de l'Horloge, which is very active in promoting the ideas of the New Right. The programme is shorter than the two programmes from 2002 and 2004, but very similar in its thematic orientations, even if the style is more openly xenophobic. The programme of 2002 (b) is the presidential program, which was written, as a FN leader told us in an interview, because FN was frequently accused of "having no programme." It is very detailed. The programme of 2004 (c) is composed of two parts: the first part is a general comment on the philosophy of the party; the second part is the program *per se,* and it is the same as the 2002 party programme.

Besides the party programmes, the party press of NF, *Français d'abord* (FDA), and four speeches of Jean-Marie Le Pen, the leader of FN, were analyzed. They cover the years 1997 to 2004, which was an important period for FN with respect to its impact on French politics. The frames used in the analysis of the party programs, party press, and the leaders' speeches were the following: (a) Collective Identity; (b) Employment Issues; (c) Welfare Issues; (d) Law and Order Issues; (e) Liberal Values; (f) Antiestablishment; (g) Immigrant Status; and (h) Legitimisation of Racism. The analysis shows that the following frames were the most frequent frames used in French political context.

Collective Identity

FN puts the focus of its antiimmigrant propaganda on an 'Otherising' discourse, stressing the fact that different civilisations had incompatible sociocultural models. FN discusses the integration of ethnic, national, religious, and cultural groups originating from countries they describe as 'barbarian.' The party programme of 1998 declares that differences between the native French and the 'Others' are rooted in deep cultural values, 'civilisation against barbarians.' Here, the neo-colonial theme of the French culture capable of civilising the 'Others' is strong. The main object of such propaganda is to please an electoral base inherited from the 'French Algeria' movements of the 1960s (Mayer & Perrineau, 1989). It is equally present in the regional as well as the national programmes.

Concretely, this theme ends up in proposals aimed at rejecting any visibility of cultural differences in the public sphere. This is hidden under the cover of a principle of strict laicisation. FN declares that it will apply the principles of the French public law and national sovereignty and forbid any anti-French propaganda (FN party programme, 2002). The party programmes of 2002 and 2004 frequently portray Islam and Muslims as a danger to French sovereignty and security. It will forbid 'family reunion' (which is related to 'polygamy'), animal killing according to Islamic tradition, and impose restrictions on the generous social welfare subsidies to immigrants. Muslims as a group are considered noncivilized and anti-French, and they should be taken under control (FN party programmes, 2002, 2004). FN presents immigrants, in particular Muslims, not only as fundamentally different from the 'native' French, but also as those who are plotting to invade and rule France. Islam is presented as a suitable tool for this conspiracy.

FN takes a very simplistic nationalist stance against all 'Others' who are living in France. It propagates that French interests must come first and all policies that "undermine the national sovereignty and rips out the wallet of the wallet of the taxpayer must be stopped" (FN party programme, 2004). The slogan serves here as an introduction and an ideological basis to an antiglobalisation and anti-Europeanization discourse, by linking a global process of anti-French activism to such different facts as globalisation and immigration.

The frame of 'collective identity' has also been used by the FN leader, Le Pen, in his speeches by categorising people in terms of those who 'love France' and those who 'do not.' He says in 2001, for instance, that:

> There are many patriotic French women and men that are isolated but good-willing. They should not wait for Joan of Arc, because there was only one. But they should recognize those who defend her patriotic ideal in the spirit of Joan of Arc. They should unite and join us. They will not be asked of their political or social origin, nor their religion, nor their race, but only if they love France and want to fight for her when there still is time, but the time is getting short.

Employment and Welfare Issues

The notion of immigrants as a burden to French society and how much they cost to the French state has become fundamental to FN discourse on migration since the 1990s. The success of this theme can be linked to the 'research work' done inside the party by such members as Pierre Milloz—who wrote numerous 'reports' about 'the costs of immigration'—that are cited in the party programmes. The argument here is to show that the balance of public accountability could be reached by cutting down the 'costs of immigration.' Therefore, by curbing the number of immigrants, savings can be made—which is here linked to an antitax argument, traditional in populist discourse. FN says that the cost of immigration in the regional budget is 1 billion a year and that if we stop immigration we are going to save this same amount each year: "The state should not support, with the money of the taxpayers, the immigrant criminals and the 'peace of the barbarians' in our suburbs, that have been transformed to free zones for criminals and places outside the law" (FN party programme, 1998). The theme of the costs of migration serves to portray migrants as law-breakers who come to France in order to receive welfare subsidies. The party declares later that: "Illegal migrants will no more receive these aids [social welfare] which will be given only to French citizens" (FN party programme, 2004).

FN propagates for the institutionalisation of a 'French first' credo in the labour market. The party programme of 1998 claims that 'native' French must be given priority over immigrants concerning the allocation of scarce resources, whether in terms of welfare or jobs: "In the case of hiring, a just law will apply the national preference and will give priority to the French in the field of employment. Similarly, in the case of layoffs in companies, the French employees, when equally competent, will have priority in keeping their jobs" (FN party programme, 1998). Significantly, FN can accept immigrants only as part of the 'work force' and claim that every immigrant who loses their jobs should also lose their residence permit:

Legal migrants are supposed to stay in France in order to work here. If they do not have a job anymore, it is logical that they leave the country. The foreign unemployed who reach the end of their unemployment subsidies will lose their residence permit. They will be, at that time, asked to return to their country of origin. (FN party programme, 2002)

FN concludes in all of its party programmes that immigrants should be sent back to their countries of origin. When such goal has been attained, FN promises to solve all social problems, including the housing problem. It says that the 'ethnic ghettos' will be 'dismantled': "The ethnic ghettos in the suburbs will be dismantled. This will take the rehabilitation of social housing and their hand over to the French" (FN party programme, 1998). In the last excerpt, we see that the FN reuses themes that are frequently present in media discourses, such as 'ethnic ghettos.' When discussing immigrants' bad housing conditions and spatial segregation, FN takes immigrants as being responsible for these problems.

Le Pen has, in almost every speech, used the threat of immigrant ghettos and their anti-French position. He has accused them of abusing the generous French welfare system, and of participating in anti-French activities.

From an economic point of view, the social benefits that the immigrants receive automatically when they arrive in France actually make an attraction and pulling drive for the Third World populations. All of this has a cost that the French economy is bearing. Maurice Allais, the winner of Nobel price in economy, estimates that each immigrant costs in collective infrastructures four years of his salary and twenty if he comes with his wife and kids. The difference between what they receive and what they pay in taxes is amounting to as much as 300 billion francs. As Jacques Dupâquier states it: "If Europe welcomes too many unqualified foreign people, it will become an underdeveloped continent." (Le Pen, convention on immigration, 2002)

FN's party organ, FDA, propagated consequently that immigrants, the French state, and European institutions have a plot against French people by favouring immigrants and giving them uncontrolled welfare assistance.

Law and Order Issues

This frame has been frequently used by FN and its leaders in presenting immigrants as criminals and a problem for France. There is a very clear victim/perpetrator dualism that dominates FN's political propaganda on 'criminality and immigrants.' 'Native' French are presented as victims of the violent and criminal immigrants' acts. FN legitimates its position on crimes in a rather military language in which criminality is given a place, the suburb, which is located almost out of the control of the French state.

Delinquency and insecurity have been major themes during the presidential election campaign of 2002, which saw the FN leader, Jean-Marie Le Pen, facing Jacques Chirac, the leader of UMP, for the second row. Many analysts at that time pointed to this increase in the media coverage of criminality in order to explain the election results. This theme has become more prominent in the past years. It is actually composed of different subthemes, which converge towards this description of migrants as criminals. The party wants 'immigrant criminals' to be sent back to their countries of origin:

> After their time in prison, foreign delinquents and criminals will systematically expelled back to their countries of origin. . . . The police will do multiple identity checks in order to arrest and send back criminal immigrants and delinquents residing in our country. (FN party programme, 2002)

The FN discourse on migrants and delinquency serves different objectives: The first one is to portrait migrants as deviants; it is attained by focusing on such topics as prison, how the police should deal with them, and so on, and pertains to thematic orientation. Such expressions as 'immigrant delinquents' are understood here as pleonasms. The second one is to reinforce the populist argument on the costs of immigration, and to present 'criminal immigrants' as very costly for the French society. The third one is to construct a populist 'image of threat' by which the 'native' French are threatened by organized foreign powers and groups who are determined to 'wipe out' both France and the French identity. Immigrant Arabs and Africans in general, and Muslims in particular, are the target of FN's anti-Muslim and antiimmigrant attacks. The party argues for prohibition on Muslim worship and religious activities as these are supposed to be anti-French:

> Forbid all subversive behaviour under the cover of Islamism. In application of the principle of international law, the building of mosques financed by foreign states that do not accept Christianity and punish those who leave the Muslim religion with the death penalty will not be authorized. (FN party program, 2002)

The discourses of migrants and criminality are frequently used and adopt a pseudolegal style in order to back the party's antiimmigrant and anti-Muslim claims. FN's party leader, Le Pen, frequently refers in his speeches to the 'criminal immigrants.' He puts the blame for the marginalisation of immigrants in the suburbs upon immigrants themselves. The party organ, FDA, does the same and attaches immigrants to criminality and portrays them as a threat to the security of the French and to the European territory.

Antiestablishment

In their antiimmigrant stance, FN has been consequently accusing established parties and politicians of being responsible for many socioeconomic problems supposedly related to immigration, such as high taxes and criminality. They propagate for the removal of the corrupted establishment by voting for FN. This is a well-established theme in every one of their party programmes. The image of being the 'real opposition' to the establishment, and the plot of the latter to stop FN from 'telling the truth,' is widely propagated. The party leader, Le Pen, illustrates this in his speech from 2004:

> Despite a severe boycott from the media and a devilish description based on lies and calumnies, the Front National appears more and more to the French people to be the only alternative for change. Their trust is increasing when they see its political lucidity and courage in such various fields as immigration, insecurity, AIDS, mad cow disease, drugs, and political corruption. (Le Pen, 2004)

Le Pen (2004) presents FN as the only party that cares about French people and criticizes both the "lazy right and crazy left." The antiestablishment arguments and propaganda also appear in the party organ, FDA, which often connects the critics of the 'corrupted politicians' with a critique of European institutions.

The Dichotomy of 'Us' against the Muslim 'Others'

FN, its leaders, and the party organ, FDA, disseminate severely anti-Muslim attitudes and propaganda. Both before the attacks of September 11 and after that critical event, Muslims are portrayed by FN as anti-French, as criminals, and as welfare abusers. Jean Marie Le Pen has almost in every political speech and interview accused Muslims (who he has often called 'Arabs') of being the main problem of the French society. He goes so far as to argue for a revitalisation of a law from 1939 in order to hinder Muslims' 'anti-French activities':

> Today terrorism and subversive or fundamentalist activism requires the maximum attention of the state. To apply the norm according to which a previous authorisation should be granted for foreign publications to be circulated in France. Coming from the decree-law of May 6th 1939, this norm will allow the limiting of the diffusion of terrorist, subversive or anti-French propaganda. (Le Pen, convention on immigration, 2002)

The call towards more security is here, at the same time, a way to convey the idea that Muslims share and spread 'anti-French' ideologies.

Although FN criticizes the strong secularism of the French state concerning the rights of Catholics in France, when it comes to Muslims it claims the application of French secular laws. It propagates for forbidding Islamic culture and traditions, religious freedom, building of new mosques, the Muslim girls' right to wear headscarves in schools, and so on. When criticising Muslims, based on French secular tradition, Le Pen does not hesitate in making clear references to Catholic symbols such as Joan of Arc.

Considering and presenting Islam as a totally foreign religion, and a tool for foreign states to intervene in French society and destroy the French state, is a powerful means of propaganda and of reinforcing the imagined categories of 'Us' (in this case, Christians and secularists) against 'Them' (Muslims). It is interesting that the concept and tradition of laicity is applied selectively in the case of Christians and Muslims by both FN and by other mainstream parties. FN's ambivalent position on secularism/Christianity more generally is also found in the mainstream parties. For instance, the leader of the mainstream party UMP, Alain Juppé, argues against his own party colleagues when discussing whether the European so-called 'Christian inheritance' should be mentioned in the Constitutional Treaty in 2004. But his argument still refers to Christianity as 'part of our inheritance' and describes Muslims as potential threat:

> To deny that the Christian values are part of our inheritance would boil down to denying that it is daytime at noon. The European convention has found a compromise that makes a reference to the "spiritual, religious and humanist" values of Europe. It would be wise to stick to that. Those who absolutely want to inscribe this reference to Christianity in the fundamental European texts are preoccupied by a concern I cannot share: they want to somehow put laicity into question. This, for me, is not negotiable. Laicity is also a debate that we have with fundamentalist Islam, since it mixes up temporal and spiritual matters. (Alain Juppé, interview with *Lé Figaro,* June 2004)

There is a common feature of the conflation of Islam with fundamentalism in contemporary French politics. FN's and other mainstream parties' programmes, debates, press and speeches are fuelling the feeling that there is a 'Muslim problem'—frighteningly similar to the 1930s 'Jewish problem'—in France today.

Assessing Impacts of XPP

Jean-Marie Le Pen's Front National and Bruno Megret's Mouvement National Republican (the latter of which was formed by a separatist group in FN after 1999 European elections) do not benefit from a good political status in France. Despite their electoral successes and gaining regularly between 15% and 20% of the total votes, they have no seat in the French Parliament due to the first-past-the-post system, implemented by General De Gaulle in the 1958 Constitution to prevent extremist parties from coming to power. For the Senate, the explanation is also due to indirect suffrage, which means that senators are elected by local elected people. Most of them are 'leading citizens,' who used to be deputies or mayors, and who have been on the political scene for decades. In such conditions, the radical right has very little chance of getting seats in the Senate.

Exceptionally, the legislative elections of 1986 were a proportional representation, on a decision of President Mitterrand who wished to weaken the republican right. He helped the Front National to obtain seats at the National Assembly. It got 33 deputies and prevented the liberal right, Chirac's Rassemblement pour la Republique (RPR), which won the legislative election, from governing as it wished, because Chirac (who is a Gaullist) always refused to make an alliance with FN and other XPPs. Paradoxically, the Mitterrand move provided FN the opportunity to make a direct impact on French politics. The first direct impact was on the politicisation of 'immigration' and presenting immigrants as a 'problem.' This has influenced the mainstream parties in their discussions about, and the measures they have taken against, so-called illegal immigrants, for instance, and Muslims.

However, the study of the *indirect* impact of FN on French politics and other political parties is of much more importance. The indirect impact is much more enduring since they become a part of the mainstream parties and politicians' 'own' political agenda. Influenced by the FN debate and electoral antiimmigrant concepts, the right-wing prime ministers of Mitterrand—namely, Jacque Chirac in 1986 and Edouard Balladur in 1993—took a harsher position on immigration. The two right-wing governments chose Charles Pasqua as the Minister of Interior, who restricted migration law and changed the conditions to obtain French nationality and asylum in France. He also gave more power to the police. The rising popularity of FN in France forced mainstream right-wing parties to take a tougher stance on immigration. After the victory of the right-wing parties in the legislative election of 1996, the new minister of the Interior, Jean-Louis Debré, reinforced antiimmigration actions and demanded that people who knew illegal immigrants report them to the police.

In 2003, Nicolas Sarkozy, another right-wing politician with antiimmigrant attitudes, became the Minister of the Interior and started 'fighting against' illegal immigrants and 'immigrant related criminality.' Sarkozy's tough measures towards illegal immigrants and criminality reinforced a FN-initiated public discourse on immigrants as 'problem' and as 'criminals.' The successive Minister of Interior, Dominique de Villepin, has continued in these footsteps, inviting experts to think about new measures to fight against anti-French activities and illegal workers.

After the presidential election of 2002, which reinstalled Jacques Chirac as the president in a rally for presidency with Jean-Marie Le Pen, a new right-wing party, Union pour un Mouvement Populaire (UMP), rose from the ashes of the Rassemblement pour la République (RPR) (Chirac's party of origin), in cooperation with UDF (a more liberal party than the Gaullist RPR). Therefore, only the 2002 party programme was available for UMP. However, in order to achieve comparability over time, we also studied the unified programme of RPR and UDF, in which, on the eve of the 1997 election, both parties agreed on shared electoral lists. The party programmes of Parti Socialiste (PS) (from the years 1997 and 2002) have been also chosen for the analysis. The following frames that were used by FN and in public debate have been also appearing in the party programs of the mainstream parties:

Collective Identity

The 1997 party programme of RPR/UDF declares the 'republican values' of the French society against Muslim 'fundamentalism.' (Although the "Muslim" pretext was not included, it was clear what the party meant by "fundamentalism.") Even in UMP's party programme of 2002, the 'fight against terrorism' and 'illegal immigration' are the concepts used to declare a will towards the defence of the 'liberal French values.' The French liberal society and historical mission to defend democracy, humanism, and solidarity is confronted with the new threat from terrorism, which is often addressed in close connection with illegal immigration. 'Illegal immigration' is a matter that is much discussed in definitions of French immigration policy. The mainstream parties and FN have the same policy in this concern. It is clear that the mainstream parties, UDF and PS, have adopted the antiimmigration propaganda of FN. For instance, in its party programme of 2002, PS declares a support for the old regulations concerning 'citizenship law' and the '10 years residence permit,' but at the same time writes:

> Foreign residents will be granted again the right to renew their 10 years card. We will develop new means to fight against illegal immigration and we will vigorously sanction the companies that do not follow the law. We will start cooperating with the immigrants' countries of origin in order to regulate and control the flux of immigration.

It should be noted that it was not only in the area of illegal immigration that there exists a consensus between mainstream parties and FN, but also in the way that immigrants as 'foreigners' on the one side, and 'French' as a 'natural integrated' group on the other, are defined in the party programmes. Immigration is considered as a problem for 'Us' and for 'our society'; therefore, both mainstream parties and FN are agreed on the policy of international cooperation as a way to prevent immigration. The major point of consensus between the mainstream parties and FN is that they believe that they have to fight against immigration in order to promote integration. The identification of an 'immigration problem' in France converges clearly with the views and political agenda of FN. This is directly connected to the main essence of the French collective identity, namely 'republican values.' Both sets of parties, UDF and PS on the one side, and FN on the other, emphasize 'republican values' for the legitimisation of their antiimmigration policies. Although arguing the same consequence for French immigration policy in many cases, the interpretations of 'republican values' varied between the mainstream parties and FN.

Law and Order Issues

This is one of the most frequently used frames in the French political debates. Immigrants are considered as a 'security problem' for the French society and must be controlled and in many cases 'fought against.' This applies not to 'illegal immigrants,' but also fundamentalists (Muslims), and, as was mentioned frequently, "immigrant criminals gathered in our suburbs." All parties, both the mainstream and FN, are agreed upon such an understanding and spell it out in their party programmes, press, and speeches:

> The modern state must strengthen its authority everywhere where it cannot be replaced: the fight against drugs, against fundamentalisms, against delinquency, against illegal immigration and clandestine work. (RPR/UDF party programme, 1997)

By listing law and order issues—including immigration, fundamentalism, and clandestine work—it is clearly implied that these problems are caused by immigrants and must be fought against by government.

Although the party programme of the newly formed UMP for the legislative elections in 2002 clearly aimed to challenge FN, and immigration is barely discussed, the frame of 'Law and Order Issues' in direct connection with immigrants is presented. The party declares that: "In order to reinforce European internal security, the fight against illegal immigration and antiterrorist actions is necessary." Even PS takes the discourse on 'security' of the French in its party programme and relates it to immigrants, criminality and terrorism. Although by different means, both mainstream parties and FN consider criminality and immigration as interrelated problems.

Mass Media and the 'Others'

Mass media is a very important actor on the French political scene and plays a crucial role in framing debates and political issues in the country. Since the early 1980s, various issues related to immigration and foreigners have been frequently debated in the mass media and the public sphere. Since the mass media and the established political discourses are very closely linked, it is not always easy to determine if it is the political agendas that influence the media agenda or vice versa. There is no doubt, however, that in many sociopolitical situations, the mass media has the power to frame political debates and influence politicians.

The role of mass media in reinforcing 'Xeno-otherism' by assessing the impact of XPP on the public debate is also studied in France. In this respect the mass media articles have been selected in relation to 'critical events.' The more serious mainstream newspapers, *Le Monde* (centre-left, daily), *Le Figaro* (centre-right, daily), and the tabloid newspaper *Le Canard Enchaîné* (satiric, weekly), have been chosen in the study. The following are the critical events that have been used in the analysis:

> 1987—the first of the 'Muslim veil affairs' in French secondary schools;
> 1989—the fall of the Berlin Wall;
> 2004—debates on the entry of Turkey in the European Union within 15 years; and
> 2005—debates on the enlargement of Europe

The newspapers were gathered and studied in respect of a period of one week before and one week after the aforementioned events.

The First "Muslim Veil Affairs" in French Secondary Schools (1987)

Le Monde was rather in favour of tolerating the veil in French public schools in 1987–1988, but changed its opinion drastically until 2004. In earlier years, *Le Monde* had a supportive stance towards immigrants who it considered as victims of the rightist governments' (through Ministers of Interior, Charles Pasqua's in 1986 and 1993, Debré's in 1995) antiimmigrants measures. It is clear that *Le Monde* adopted a critical attitude towards Muslims and veil. *Le Figaro* is very critical of the veil in schools and presents almost the same argument against Muslim girls' veil as FN. It raises many objections to the veil in schools and takes a very overtly anti-Muslim stand in its articles. It defends the prohibition of the veil and writes about the 'Muslim fundamentalism' being reinforced in French schools. In many cases, *Le Figaro* exhibits the same opinion as FN when it comes to immigrant issues also. The tabloid paper, *Le Canard Enchaîné*, was, in a satiric way, very critical of the veil and of Muslims in general. It often made very stereotypical, and in many cases racist, jokes and satirical comments about immigrants in general and Muslims in particular.

The Fall of the Berlin Wall, November 9, 1989

The fall of the Berlin Wall caused a lively debate in France and all the three newspapers wrote about the values of freedom and democracy on the one side, but also a warning on increasing immigration from the east. *Le Monde,* which had a relatively positive opinion towards immigration and immigrants *contra* FN, became more and more moderate in its articles on the issue of migration. Since the beginning of the 2000s, the issue of immigration from Eastern Europe and its 'threat' to the French workers has been regularly brought to the public debate by *Le Monde.* The other two newspapers exhibit an even more negative attitude in their articles against the 'eastern threat.' The media coverage of 'illegal immigrants' from Eastern Europe, North Africa, and the former Soviet Republics was very wide. *Le Figaro* had a similar position against immigration from the east, and, in its many articles and interviews, it argued for a better control of French borders and more restrictive control of illegal immigrants. *Le Canard Enchaîné* presented its antiimmigrant position and fears of 'eastern immigration' in spectacular warnings, and in a more antiestablishment manner.

The Debates on the Entry of Turkey in the European Union within 15 Years in 2004

Turkey is considered by many French politicians as a non-European country. The rather extensive negative attitude against Muslims in France is also influencing the French politicians' position in the debates concerning the Muslim Middle East. The issue of Turkey's prospective membership in the European Union causes always a lively debate in which the opposition to the membership of Turkey is always more visible in the mass media. All three newspapers showed a united opposition to Turkish membership in the European Union. Specifically, *Le Monde* considered Turkey as a non-secular, nondemocratic, and non-European country, while *Le Figaro* and *Le Canard Enchaîné* overtly showed an anti-Muslim attitude, sometimes in the same line as FN and its leader Le Pen, who wrote about the dangers of the existence of a Muslim country in the, paradoxically, Christian and secular European Union.

The Enlargement of Europe, 2005

Le Monde is in favour of the enlargement of Europe but seems to have been concerned about the loss of French jobs since the fall of the Berlin Wall in 1989. It supports French and European institutions but advocates the creation of a 'social Europe' in order to protect the current French labour market and the welfare system from being overloaded. Contrary to *Le Monde,* the concern of *Le Figaro* regarding the enlargement of the European Union is not the loss of jobs, but problems with European integration, the social costs of the enlargement, and criminality. *Le Canard Enchaîné* is also suspicious of Europe and shows nationalist sentiments. It fears that socioeconomic differences in Europe could lead to higher socioeconomic costs for France.

Conclusion

The role of the Front National has been crucial in framing 'immigrants as problem' in the French public sphere and in making a political advantage of widespread xenophobia (against immigrants in general, and Muslim Africans and Arabs in particular) in France. French colonial history also plays a role in this xenophobia, providing the ground for established perceptions of people from the former colonies who are living in France today.

France is one of those countries in which XPP has had a *direct* impact on the mainstream politics. The decision of President Mitterrand in the legislative elections of 1986 that helped the Front National to obtain seats at the French National Assembly gave FN the best opportunity to directly (and from the seats of the parliament) spread xenophobic propaganda. The major direct impact of FN was on the politicisation of 'immigration' and presenting immigrants as a 'problem.' This has even influenced and, in many cases, forced the mainstream parties to adopt similar attitudes to FN on the matter, such as in making links between 'illegal immigration,' Muslims, and criminality.

However, the *indirect* impact of FN on the mainstream parties and politics in France is much wider than their limited direct impact. The presence of FN in the French parliament, and their raising the issue of immigration as an important political problem, influenced the right-wing prime ministers of Mitterrand to take a harsher position on immigration. The rising popularity of FN in France forced mainstream right wing parties to take a tougher position on immigration. The French right-wing prime ministers since 1986, such as Jean-Louis Debré, Nicolas Sarkozy, and Dominique de Villepin, all reinforced antiimmigrant and anti-Muslim attitudes and sentiments in France. To be tougher on immigrants—framing them as a 'threat' to French national security, jobs, and welfare—has been a political triumph card in the hands of all politicians in France. Even the later leftist governments did not change the restrictive laws against immigration that were passed by the right-wing parties.

Immigration has been a central theme to FN programmes ever since the party tried to systematically use it as a political and electoral strategy. It seems that the electoral success of FN has, on its own, been a powerful motivating factor behind the adaptation of a more antiimmigrant position by the mainstream parties.

THE CASE OF SWEDEN

The Political Context of Xenophobia in Sweden

Sweden has, according to some researchers (Svanberg & Tydén, 1992), been a country of immigration for many centuries. It was not until the

1930s, however, that Swedish immigration became larger than emigration. Immigration increased even more during the post-World War II era. 'Modern immigration' can be divided into two periods: one of predominantly labour immigration (from the 1940s to the early 1970s) and one of refugee immigration and kin reunification immigration (the 1970s and onwards). During the 1940s, mainly as a result of a growing demand for labour, 200,000 individuals immigrated to Sweden. Most of them came from Finland, Norway, Denmark, Poland, Italy, and the Baltic states. During the 1950s, 250,000 individuals immigrated to Sweden, most of them from the Nordic countries (40% of them from Finland). In addition, there were refugee immigrants coming from Hungary after the repressive events of 1956. During the 1960s, labour immigration peaked, and almost 450,000 individuals immigrated to Sweden. Most of them came from Yugoslavia, Turkey, Greece, and the Nordic countries (in particular, from Finland). There were also a growing number of refugees coming because of upheaval events in Vietnam, Greece, Poland, and Czechoslovakia. During these decades, almost 60% of all immigration to Sweden was from the other Nordic countries. However, immigration to Sweden started to change character after the oil crisis of 1973. There was a decreased demand for labour immigration, which, as we will see below, was combined with a stricter immigration policy. At the same time, there was increased refugee immigration.

During the 1970s, many refugees came from Chile, Syria, Turkey, and Lebanon. Yet, non-European immigration only accounted for about 25% during this decade (which nonetheless could be compared with only 10% for the period before 1975). During the 1980s, there was a great increase in non-European immigration, and 50% of all immigration was from outside of Europe (especially Iran and Iraq). During the 1990s, many came from the former Yugoslavia, but there were also numerous immigrant groups coming from Africa and Latin America. In fact, because of the war in former Yugoslavia, 1994 saw the highest number of individuals immigrating to Sweden to date, with 83,000 immigrants (Vilhelmsson, 2002; Ekberg & Gustafsson, 1995). According to the most recent available census (2001) there are today 1,027,974 people born abroad living in Sweden, which is 11.5% of the total population. Of these, 475,986 are still foreign citizens. Finns are the largest immigrant population, with 193,465 people (18.8% of all immigrants), and immigrants from the other Scandinavian countries are numerous as well: 43,414 from Norway and 38,870 from Denmark. Among the other large immigrant groups, we find 73,274 Yugoslavs and 52,198 Bosnians; 55,696 Iraqis; 51,844 Iranians; 40,506 Poles; 32,453 Turks; 27,153 Chileans; and 20,228 Lebanese. Among the new immigrant groups, we find 13,489 from Somalia, and among the older ones we find 14,027 from Hungary (Data from Statistiska centralbyrån, SCB, in Sweden, 2004).

Immigration issues in Sweden have always been a political matter, and therefore subject to management by public authorities. Sweden's current trajectory in policy related to immigration and integration can be traced back to the mid-1970s, when Sweden's policy orientation toward immigrants began a shift away from assimilation and toward integration and multiculturalism. These developments are reflected in a progression of policy changes pertaining to integration of immigrants in Swedish society that represent a long-term process of incremental developments in considering immigrants as 'culturally different' from Swedes. Nevertheless, there remain significant undercurrents of nationalist and xenophobic sentiment that continue to provide a base for extremist organisations to organise and agitate, and to indirectly influence the public debate.

Xenophobic and racist attitudes have a relatively long history in Sweden that can be traced back to the 17th century's biological racist thinking of the Swedish botanist Carl von Linné. His students formed Race Biological Association in Uppsala, which led gradually to the establishment of Race Biological Institute in Uppsala. The institute replaced its leader, Herman Lundborg, in 1936 with Gunnar Dahlberg who focused on 'race hygiene.' The institute changed its name to The Institute of Race Hygiene, which recommended the sterilisation of 'mentally ill' individuals as a way to preserve the 'healthy Swedish race.' The sterilisation policy was in effect until early 1970s.

Discrimination of immigrants in Sweden is well-documented (see, e.g., Wadensjö, 1997; Lange, 1998, 1999; Lange & Hedlund, 1998; Le Grand, 1999; Jonsson & Wallette, 2001; Le Grand & Zulkin, 2002; De Los Reyes & Wingborg, 2002; Lindgren, 2002; Martinsson, 2002). National opinion polls show that antiimmigrant attitudes are relatively widely-spread in Sweden. Taking advantage of negative attitudes among voters, two new xenophobic political parties were formed in 1989 and 1990. The xenophobic and racist party, Sverigedemokraterna (Sweden Democrats), emerged from the xenophobic and racist organisation Keep Sweden Swedish (BSS-Bevara Sverige Svenskt) in 1989, and it received popular support in the late 1990 and 2002 and 2006 municipal elections. Nydemokrati, fitting more properly in XPP category, was subsequently founded in 1990. On a nationalist, anti-immigrant and antitax platform, the fledgling Nydemokrati passed the 4% threshold required to win seats in Parliament with 8% of the popular vote. The entrance of Nydemokrati into the Swedish parliament fuelled already existing antiimmigrant sentiments, helping to make the critique of immigration and Swedish integration policy an established political discourse.

The Swedish census published in two reports (or 'Rapport integration') in 2004 and 2005 showed an increase in antiimmigration ideas in general, and anti-Muslim attitudes in particular, in Sweden.[10] We start our study of Sweden in this political context.

Discursive Reconstruction of 'Us' vs. 'Them'

As has been said, immigration issues in Sweden have always been a political matter. However, during the 1960s and into the mid-1980s, immigrant-related issues were far less overtly political in comparison with recent years. This general lack of politicisation was at least in part the product of having reached a significant measure of consensus on immigration and integration policies among the established parties during the period after World War II up until the end of 1960s, in which workforce integration dominated.

The issue of immigration and integration snared its more dominant position in Swedish mainstream policy since 1970s, when new political refugees came to Sweden. Swedish immigration policy was changed in 1975, shifting from assimilation to integration with a policy of 'multiculturalism' based on 'cultural differences' between immigrants and Swedes. However, the significant shortcomings in Swedish integration politics and widespread discrimination increased segregation and the dualism of 'Us' against 'Them.' The integration policy based on 'multiculturalism' was also responsible for this increased segregation and discrimination. Realising the problem, the Social Democratic government introduced a new policy of integration through centralisation of integration measures and the creation of the Central Board of Integration (Integrationsverket) in 1996. This was not as successful as the government had hoped, and increasing discrimination and segregation led to more politicisation of the issue of immigration that engaged even the mainstream parties.

In the study of the impact of XPP on the mainstream political parities and politics, the following party programmes of Nydemokrati (ND) and Sverigedemokraterna (SD) have been chosen and analyzed: the ND party programmes of 1990, 1993, 1994, and 2002, and the SD party programmes of 1989, 1999 and 2003. ND has no party press. The party leaders' speeches between 1990 and 2002 are used instead in the analysis of the party's influence on mainstream parties and politics in Sweden. SD's party press, *Sverige Kuriren* (*SK*), which has been publishing since 1988, is also used in the analysis of the discursive construction of the duality of 'Us' against 'Them.'

Collective Identity

The declaration of differences between a rather 'homogeneous' folk (namely, 'Swedes') who are confronting new and 'different' groups (namely, immigrants) is the focal point in ND's party programme and its leader's speeches. The party programme of 1990 was published as a political declaration in the mainstream press under the title "This is our programme." The main attacks of the party were directed towards what was called the social state and immigrants. They have severely criticized 'multiculturalism' and argued for the preservation of 'Swedish values.' Many problems, such as unemployment and criminality, were related to increasing immigration. In the party programme of 1994, ND declared that: "The goal of the immigration policy should be assimilation of immigrants/refugees.

This can easily be explained by 'they should be like us' or they should 'take the customs where one comes' *(ta sedern dit man kommer)*." The party declared then that: "The Swedish culture, traditions and values will be protected through working for the refugees' adaptation to our society and our culture" (ND, 1994). . . . The concept of 'cultural distance' and 'difference' is frequently used by ND:

> An immigration from countries far away from the Swedish and European culture and way of living, has, with the capital strong human smugglers assistance, made Sweden to an important place for this alarming growing group of people. These persons are not allowed or do not want to integrate in the Swedish society. (ND party programme, 2002)

They stress the weight of the "language ability in Swedish" for immigrants and will "abolish the home language education" (ND party programme, 1993). ND considers the establishment of a 'multicultural society' as dangerous for Swedish society and declares: "We do not believe that Sweden should strive to be a multicultural society. It leads, as international experiences shows, to rootlessness and in the longer run to criminality" (ND party programme, 1993). The ND party programme of 2002 makes it even clearer:

> We oppose the idea that cultures based on totally different values and norms than the Swedish should take over in our culture. The Swedish culture cannot survive if we let people with other culture and other religions swell up in our country.

SD also declares that the important Swedish identity is endangered by 'mass immigration': "The mass-immigration of the last decades seriously threatens the national identity, through the construction of areas which are occupied by people who will never feel Swedish, or be involved in our culture and in our history" (SD party programme, 1999). The frame of 'Collective Identity' was consequently used by SD in presenting itself as the only defender of the 'Swedish people' who were threatened by immigration. In his speech in 2004, SD leader Björn Söder declared that:

> The Sweden Democrats constitute Sweden's and the Swedish people's last line of defence, and if we give up, so it will most probably mean that all hope of re-establishing Sweden as an independent, well-doing and a great nation, would be eliminated. Therefore we will stop the mad policy of mass immigration and multiculturalism. (Björn Söder, November 20, 2004)

The biological racism is very obvious in the seemingly politically correct propaganda. In its party press, SD writes already in 1988 that: "Sweden is no more a Swedish nation and Sverigedemokraterna is worried about the low nativity of ethnic Swedes, at the same time that the number of immigrants is growing" (*SK*, 1988, No. 2). The high nativity of immigrants is presented as a threat to the reduction in the number of 'biological Swedes.'

Employment and Welfare Issues

This is one of the most important frames that were used by ND to categorise immigrants as a burden for Swedish society. The first party programme of 1991 was full of reference to the immigrants who 'cheated' the state and preferred subsidies and allowances instead of work: "As it is today it is not profitable for an immigrant to work!" The party continued in its later programmes of 1993 and 2002 to use this frame to legitimise its antiimmigrant ideology and policies. ND claims in its party programme of 1993 that more control and restrictions must be put on immigrants and refugees:

> That social and accommodation allowances could be suspended if refugees who are accommodated in a municipality move to other municipality without authorized permission. The refugees' social allowances are connected to their participation in the learning and education of the Swedish language.

The matter of costs of immigrants is another discourse that was frequently used by ND in its party programmes. For example:

> The economic burden of immigrants, such as travel costs, education, medical care, more work for the police and the judicial system, costs of the prisons, is too high for our society. The total sum of the costs is approximately 100 milliard krons per year and will be so many years ahead. The political establishment do not present these costs in an informative and relevant way. The only thing that is said is that immigrants enrich our culture! The costs lead to reductions in the welfare and we get less and less welfare for our tax money. For this more than 100 milliard krons per year we could get rid of all waiting lists in receiving medical care, make all the surgery that is needed, make smaller school classes, get better care for all of the older persons, reduce the total tax burden so that people can live on their incomes and create more real jobs, reduce the working hour, reduce the retirement age etc. (ND party programme, 2002)

Even in the party leaders' speeches there are many addresses to the role of immigrants in the reduction of welfare subsidies for 'Swedes.' Immigrants are presented in the speeches of ND party leaders, Bert Karlsson and Ian Wachtmeister, as the main cause of the Swedish welfare system's problems (that mainly had to do with the economic crises of the early 1990s and the following welfare reforms). This was very effective in the rise of the party's popularity, reinforced by their frequent access to mass media.

SD used also this frame in order to present immigrants as a threat to 'unemployed Swedes' and a problem for Swedish society:

> Today we have big populations of newly immigrated people from "the third world" who are totally alienated from the Swedish society. As Sweden has a high native unemployment, and no possibilities to integrate these people [immigrants], great social tensions have been built up in our society. Therefore, *Sverigedemokraterna* will work for returning of these kinds of immigrants as they do not have any need of protection. (SD party programme, 1999)

SD, in its party press, warns in a dramatical fashion that: "The Swedish economy collapses because of refugees and asylum seekers" (*SK*, 1990, No. 11).

Law and Order Issues

Increased criminality was also a main theme in ND's party programmes and the party leaders' speeches. However, the issues of 'cheating' and 'burdens on the welfare system' were more frequent than 'criminality' when ND presented the 'immigrant problem.' The discourse of the 'addiction to allowance' has been used frequently and in some cases was presented as a reason for increasing criminality. The party programmes of 1993 and 2002 argue that immigrants are gathered in some areas where they use 'social allowances' and other allowances to 'stay out of society,' and that this, in its turn, leads to increasing criminality. Warnings about 'Muslims' and the 'threat of terrorism,' also, have been used by the party leader in 2002. The ND party programme of 2002 declares that:

> The growing suburbs outside of the main cities have become ghettos with criminality and disorder. . . . The level of violence and criminality is much higher among immigrants than among the Swedish population. The Swedish judicial and social systems are unable to handle such an influence of immigration.

The party programme of 1993 makes many references to the 'immigrants' criminality' and states that: "Foreign citizens who are sentenced for committing crimes or committing several crimes and have been imprisoned will be deported from the country. Even those who hide refugees will be punished." The party program continues that the punishment for human smugglers will be even harder.

The party leaders, including Vivianne Franzén (who became the party leader in 1994), have consequently related welfare subsidies to immigrants and their cultures as the main reason for higher rates of criminality among 'Them.'

SD also uses the frame of 'Law and Order Issues' in order to present immigrants as criminals and a danger for Swedish society. It declares in its party programme of 1999 that:

> Through a moral anomie, unrestrained immigration, and minor punishments for criminal activities Sweden has become an arena for international criminal leagues and (war) criminals. Drug syndicates and terrorists have been able to establish themselves here and in many cases the tax-payers have been forced to pay for their living. Sverigedemokraterna believe that immigrants who have committed crime have abused our hospitality and should be returned to their countries of origin.

In the same programme, SD declares that every immigrant who has committed serious crimes should be deported from the country and even pay the costs of the deportation. SD reinforces the antiimmigrant propaganda of ND and presents itself as the defender of the 'Swedes' right' to safety. Its party leader, Söder (November 20, 2005), says that: "We will fight the criminal elements that now are freely active and ruin our country, and we will give the Swedes back the safety."

Antiestablishment

This frame has been used in order to disqualify the established mainstream policies and political parties, and to present a radical populist alternative politics and political agents. ND attacks the established politicians and media for confusing the public and telling lies about the Swedish immigration policy and its consequences:

> The media make us to believe that the immigrant policy is a gift given to us from a higher power. It is not in that way. It has to be questioned, and this is done by the Swedish people and by the Nydemokrati (ND). In Sweden, two of three people want a more restrictive refugee and immigrant policy. Nydemokrati attacks the refugee and immigrant policy for many reasons. It is too expensive, it is controlled by the mass media, it has undesired consequences for our society, and it lacks clear goals. It also results in the antagonism between different ethnic groups that in definitely not good for our country. (ND party programme, 1993)

The interesting point in ND's propaganda is that even the arguments in the 'favour of the sending countries' are used to show that the establishment is making mistakes in their immigration policy and they should be changed. The party writes in the party programme of 1993 that:

> The immigrant policy of Sweden during the past 10 years is deeply unmoral and wrong. It is often the well-educated people, who are needed

for the development of their own countries, who emigrate and when we give them asylum in Sweden we help causing huge problems for the developing countries.

ND accuses politicians of "hiding the facts about the costs of immigration." It writes in its party programme of 2002 that the political establishment lies about the costs of immigration and rejects any attempts at clarification on this matter.

In the party leaders' speeches, too, there are continuous critics of the established politicians and media for defending the country's immigration policies. They are accused of hiding the facts about the "costs of immigration," the "abuses of the welfare system," "the higher rate of criminality among immigrants," and so on.

SD declares clearly that it was founded on the basis of dissatisfaction with established policies:

> The Sweden Democrats was founded in February 6, 1988, first and foremost as an interest party for Swedes. The unifying factor was the opposition towards the official immigration policy, which we regarded as far too detailed, and therefore as a threat against our country, both economically and socially. (SD party programme, 2003)

Using an antiestablishment frame, the party leader, Söder, declared in his speech (October, 2003) that: "This policy [of the established parties] has given rise to a multicultural chaos in the form of social, economic and administrative problems, and to a devastating rise in criminality and ethnic tensions."

They also accuse the establishment of censure and of not allowing those who 'dare' to criticize the established immigration policy to speak: "The lack of freedom of speech has clearly appeared in the hate-campaigns of politicians' and mass-media against all the parties, organisations and individuals who have dared to question the present immigration policy" (SD party programme, 1999).

SD criticizes even the major governmental party, SDP, for being the new upper-class who just think about their own benefits: "The Social Democratic leadership constitutes both metaphorically and literally the new landowners in our country" (Björn Söder, November 20, 2005). The SD concludes then that: "The Social Democrats, with help from the conservative parties, have created a system that in the long run means only that Swedes lose their country" (*SK*, 1990, No. 11).

The Dichotomy of 'Us' against the Muslim 'Others'

ND has always had an antiimmigrant and anti-Muslim agenda. Both the old leaders, Karlsson and Wachtmeister, and the later one, Franzén, have on several occasions 'warned' against the 'Muslim threat.' The party leader Franzén warned in 1993 about the consequences of immigration from Muslim countries. She said that "Muslims will take over our country" if we do not stop immigration in general and immigration from Muslim countries, in particular (Franzén, Party speech, April, 1993). In the same speech she rhetorically asked: "How long does it take before our Swedish children turn their faces towards Mecca?" She added that Muslims are engaged in "ritual murders."

The anti-Muslim propaganda of ND and SD show an increase in their respective party programmes and speeches of 2002. They consider Islam incompatible with democracy and a reason for illiteracy and lack of development. The ND party programme states that: "Many immigrants are formed by their religion and habits that have made their societies poor, unfree, and difficult to live in." These groups of immigrants, namely Muslims, who are equated with 'fundamentalists,' are seen as now endangering Swedish society. The programme continues thus: "Illiteracy and women's oppression has become a part of the everyday Sweden" (ND party programme, 2002). The party attacks the concept of 'tolerance' and writes: "Tolerance means nowadays the will to accept the narrow outlook that characterizes fundamentalist religions which now have immigrated to Sweden" (ND party programme, 2002).

The same discourses about the Muslim threat in the name of 'multiculturalism' (which helps the harbouring 'terrorists' and criminal immigrants in Sweden) is used by SD in its anti-Muslim and antiimmigrants propaganda. Even the construction of mosques has been heavily attacked by SD and became a part of its party programme. The party declares: "No mosques should exist on Swedish ground. Islam is not only a religious belief, but it has social and political ambitions which we regard as undesirable in Sweden. Mosques and minarets are symbols of these undesired views" (SD party programme, 1999).

In its party programme for 2003, SD declares that there are only two solutions to the problem, namely: (a) returning and (b) assimilation. It means those who have immigrated, adopt the majority culture, and in the long run become a part of the nation. There is no room for freedom of religion or the preservation of immigrants' cultures. The party declared in its party press that: "With an all too numerous Moslem population in Sweden we are going to get major problems in the future" (*SK*, 2003, No. 51).

The ND leaders have consequently addressed Islam as an "aggressive" and "oppressive" religion and Muslims as "people" from "foreign cultures and religions" who cannot adapt to "our democratic society." They have also criticized the "established politicians" for being responsible for the deterioration of the "Swedish culture." Demonisation of Muslims and anti-Islam propaganda have been a focal point of ND's and the SD's party programmes, of their articles in the mainstream media, and of the party leaders' speeches.

Assessing Impacts of XPP

The impact of the Swedish XPP can be explored through a consideration of the direct impact of ND through its electoral success in the 1990 parliamentary election that helped it to take its place in the Swedish parliament, and also in terms of both ND's and SD's *indirect* impact upon Swedish politics. The period following the election success of ND was characterized by intense speculation in the national media regarding the likely impact of ND. Not surprisingly, ND leadership boasted that their election victories and position as the swing vote between blocks would grant them substantial influence in the coming period. The ND leader Bert Karlsson stated, for example: "Remember, we could be holding the balance of power in the Parliament. Then the other parties can't make any decisions over your head" (*Dagens Nyheter,* September 11, 1991).

In contrast, numerous seasoned political observers (*Dagens Nyheter,* September 17, 1991; *Aftonbladet,* September 20, 1991) speculated that the nature of ND's politics would and should relegate them to the margins on the extreme right of Swedish politics. In order for ND to use their electoral gains to leverage the Conservative minority government into turning their proposals into policy, ND would have to be willing to vote with the Social Democrats or Left party. This path was seen as problematic by *Dagens Nyheter* because it ran contrary to the new party's own politics and would therefore run the risk of undermining the party in the eyes of its voters (September 17, 1991). This prediction was played out in the forming of a Conservative government under the Moderates. Despite their striking election victory, the Moderates were forced to form a minority government when one of their partners, the Liberals (under party leader Bengt Westerberg), refused to participate in a government that included ND.

Coverage in the mainstream print media tended to be quite critical of Swedish asylum policy, with concrete examples of cases in which individuals whose requests seemed reasonable had been refused and were slated for deportation. In one instance, the decision to deny residence to a suicidal 18-year-old was reversed when some 800 students from his school demonstrated in protest—the first case in which asylum was granted for medical reasons (*Aftonbladet,* September 11, 1991).

However, the direct impact of this XPP has been very limited. ND's success in the parliamentary election lasted only one term, and their concrete impact was severely limited by the refusal of mainstream parties to collaborate with them. A much greater level of success has been achieved at the local level in local elections and in terms of getting media coverage. However, even here the gains have been limited to only a handful of localities, and have been further diminished by ND's inability to establish working alliances with any of the mainstream parties. The unwillingness of mainstream parties to cooperate or even associate themselves with nationalist parties has been one of the main reasons for the limited direct impact of such parties both locally and nationally. Although the direct impact of XPP on the Swedish mainstream politics is arguably weak, its indirect impact can by no means be considered trivial.

In order to assess the impact of the Swedish XPP on the mainstream parties and politics of the country, the party programmes of the two most important Swedish mainstream political parties—namely, the Social Democratic Party (SDP—the largest political party in Sweden) and the Conservative Moderate Party (MP) have been chosen and analyzed. The following party programmes of SDP have been analyzed: 1975 (which was in effect until 1990), 1990, 1993, and 2000. MP's party programmes analyzed in this study concerns those of 1984, 1993, and 2001. The party press of the two parties have been also analyzed in order to assess the impact of XPP on the mainstream parities. These party press have been SDP's party press *Aktuell i politiken* (*AiP*), and MP's party press *Medborgaren* (*M*), both between the years of 1989 and 2005. The time frame of the analysis is chosen due to the emergence of the populist xenophobic parties, ND and SD, on the political scene of the country during this period. In this section, the Swedish mainstream parties' engagement with and contribution to the construction of the most frequent frames used by ND in their populist and xenophobic propaganda are discussed. These frames, as mentioned earlier, are the frames of 'Collective Identity,' 'Employment and Welfare,' and 'Law and Order.'

Collective Identity

Historically, the concept of a nationalist collective identity in Sweden is not a major political issue. 'Swedish-ness' is, at least politically, often related to the belonging to Scandinavia or other Nordic countries. The sense of belonging to a 'Nordic heritage' is used even to define Swedish-ness or Nordic-ness against non-Nordic immigrants. MP, for instance, differentiates between immigrants from non-Nordic countries, and immigrants from Nordic countries: "The historic kinship and heritage as well as the free Nordic labour market, makes it natural to pay special attention to the situation of the Nordic immigrant groups, for instance when it comes to education and cultural exchange" (MP party programme, 1984).

In this concern there is a common understanding between all political parties that there is a difference between 'Nordic' and 'non-Nordic.' The Swedish political debates on immigration had, since the early 20th century, been influenced by a racist understanding of the 'value' of different immigrant groups. The concepts of 'Nordic race of high quality' and 'immigrants of low quality' have dominated political, including parliamentary, debates in Sweden.

However, this does not mean that there is not a sense of Swedish-ness in Swedish political life. Despite the support for 'cultural diversity,' the need for special attention to Swedish 'cultural heritage' is addressed in the SAP party programme of 2001: "The cultural institutions and the culture life must reflect the cultural diversity in today's Sweden, as well as *our cultural heritage* shall be given attention" (italics by author). The study shows that the Swede-ness as the core of the 'Us' against 'Them' is a part of the established political parties rhetoric and discourses. MP in its party press, *Medborgaren,* has frequently addressed the importance of 'immigrants' following the 'common value ground' of 'our society.' In an article criticising the Social Democratic concept of 'equality,' the party press writes:

> But, to achieve this [equality] we have to begin making demands of our citizens because it is important that they and future citizens have the benefit of knowledge of the language, structure of the society, and the common value ground as Sweden is built upon. (*Medborgaren,* 2002, No.1)

The concept of Swedish 'common value ground' has been frequently used by many politicians, including the former Social Democratic ministry of integration, Mona Sahlin, in order to mark the borders between 'Swedes' and immigrants. However, nobody has ever explained what these 'common values' are. Often concepts such as 'equality between sexes,' 'freedom of religion,' and 'respect for the laws and rules,' has been used in the public debate in order to make the distinction between what is considered to be 'Swedish' or 'Swedish culture' in contrast to immigrants. The concept of 'language competence' is also used as a marker. MP and other Conservative alliance parties, and even SDP, use the discourse of "nearly perfect knowledge of Swedish language" (*AiP,* 1988, No. 11) as the only way for immigrants to enter the Swedish labour market.

In the public debate, immigrants are presented either as 'a problem' or 'a resource' to solve 'our problem.' While XPPs, and some political parties in the Conservative coalition of the country (such as the liberal Folkpartiet [The People's Party]), presented immigrants as a 'problem' for Swedish society, other parties on the left, such as SDP, presented 'them as a resource' for 'Us.' An article in the SDP party press (*AiP,* 2003, No. 33) with the title "Sweden needs more working age immigrants in the future" is illustrative.

Employment and Welfare Issues

The Social Democratic party has always had the 'job policy' or 'full employment policy' as its core programme. Everybody, including immigrants, should have a job and help the generous welfare state. However, this started to change in the late 1980s. This can be counted as a result of the increasing critical voices of XPP and other groups against immigration. It is not surprising that the Social Democratic prime minister, Ingvar Carlsson, promises in 1989 (the year of the establishment of ND and SD) that "the government will propose measures that enable immigrants to more quickly begin to work"

(Carlsson, Party speech, October 3, 1989). This is even a focal point in the MP's party programme of 1993: "The strive should be that those who get permanent residence permit and work permit as soon as possible learn Swedish and earn their living." This kind of political rhetoric, which indicates that immigrants are living on social welfare, became a part of the political discourse in Sweden following ND's national success in 1990 and SD's local electoral gains over 1990s. The MP's party leader, Bo Lundgren, writes in the party press:

> For a new non-Socialist government one of the most important tasks is to break the 'outsidership' for immigrants. But of course also for the people born in Sweden who the Socialdemocrates has betrayed. We have to dare to be demanding. Those who can work should not live on contributions. (Lundgren, *Medborgaren,* 2002, No. 5)

He continued in his electoral campaign to present immigrants as those who use subsidies and never work. He declare in his electoral speech (July 27, 2002) that "it has to be an end to let people go in course after course, but never get a chance in the society. We also have to put clear demands on people that have ended up outside society." MP declares that: "One of the most important measures to reduce both the unemployment and the social problems among immigrants is to facilitate their taking their own initiative and start their own business" (*Medborgaren,* 1996, No. 2).

Putting the blame of higher rates of unemployment and dependency on the social welfare system among immigrants *upon* immigrants or upon the policies of SDP is a focal point of MP and other Conservative parties. MP combines an ideological 'do-it-yourself' measure for reducing unemployment among, and the 'welfare costs' of, immigrants by criticising SDP's policies with declarations of "the will of immigrants to cheat" the state (declared by Mauricio Rojas, MP's spokesperson in the questions regarding integration in early 1990s).

Law and Order Issues

This frame was frequently used by the Conservative government between 1991and 1994. The focus on the fight against increasing criminality was presented by the government and its justice minister, Gun Helsvik. Increasing criminality was covertly and overtly related to immigration and was even addressed by the earlier Social Democratic government. In defending a 1988 Social Democratic proposal to tighten immigration requirements, the Immigration Minister makes a statement that "immigrants are overrepresented in certain crime statistics." This is among the first times the 'Law and Order' frame, in which immigrants are labelled as more prone to criminality than 'native' Swedes, is used by a mainstream party. The violence of the Swedish law by immigrants as a political discourse was reinforced after the electoral success of XPP in the early 1990s. The MP party programme of 1993 declared that: "Foreign citizens who have committed serious crimes or have been engaged in repeatedly criminal activities in Sweden should be deported after their punishment in prison. Foreign criminals should be at risk to be denied residence permit."

Even when criticising the existing laws and structures of Swedish society, the mainstream parties covertly indicate the cultural or social problems of immigrants. For instance, the Social Democratic Member of Parliament, Monica Green, criticizes the Swedish legislation that allows arranged child-marriages. She writes: "The reason is that foreign citizens are allowed to marry themselves according to the current laws in their home countries" (*AiP*, 2001, No. 41). MP's press emphasizes the same list of social problems associated with immigrants: "Most visible is the outsidership for immigrants and refugees where there is unemployment, social problems, violence and an increasing ghettoisation" (*Medborgaren*, 1996, No. 4).

Mass Media and the 'Others'

A governmental investigation of power in the late 1980s declared that after the political and the economic power institutions, the Swedish mass media is the third powerful institution in the country. Mass media and its role in 'Otherization' of immigrants in Sweden has been researched and debated in the country over the last decades (see, e.g., Brune 1998, 2004; Camauer & Nohrstedt, 2006; Petterson, 2006).

In this study, three major print media sources were examined. These include *Dagens Nyheter* (*DN*), an independent liberal paper and Sweden's largest and probably most influential paper, *Svenska Dagbladet* (*SvD*), a conservative daily, and *Aftonbladet* (*AB*), an independent tabloid with a generally social democratic orientation. Each of the three papers is Stockholm-based and has national distribution.

Coverage of immigrant and immigrant issues in the mainstream media is examined around a total of six events for this section:

1. the murder of Prime Minister Olof Palme, 1986;
2. the fall of Berlin Wall, November 9, 1989;
3. the election breakthrough of ND, September 1991;
4. the tightening of asylum and immigration laws in the revised Aliens Act, 1996;
5. the attacks on the World Trade Center and Pentagon in the United States, September 11, 2001; and
6. the enlargement of the European Union, May 1, 2004.

Three of these six events coincide roughly with new policy developments on immigration and integration issues, while the other three were major events that gave new intensity to discussions already taking place. The shocking murder of Prime Minister Olof Palme took place during a time in which immigration issues were beginning to enter the public discourse more consistently, and in which other difficulties between 'native' Swedes and immigrants were being increasingly discussed. The fall of Communism in 1989, for example, coincided with the passage of legislation tightening immigration laws under a Social Democratically controlled government and with an upsurge in organising by neo-nazi and racist groups in Sweden that included the founding of the two XPPs, ND and SD. ND surprised most observers by winning seats in the Swedish Parliament in 1991, generating intense speculation and debate. The period examined in the autumn of 1996 focuses once again on the passage of new restrictions and changes in Swedish immigration law. The autumn of 2001 includes the attack against the World Trade Center in New York, but also encompasses a period in which there is a marked upsurge in activity among nationalist groups and political parties. This surge of activity was later reflected in significant electoral breakthroughs by XPPs in 2002. Although neither of the two largest XPPs reached the threshold necessary for winning seats in the Swedish Parliament, gains in a handful of local elections generated a number of challenges for mainstream parties as well as considerable attention. The sixth period examined, the 2004 expansion of the European Union, included discussions of what effect possible immigration from the new member states might have on the Swedish welfare state, as well as ongoing debate about Sweden's immigration and asylum policies.

The Murder of Prime Minister Olof Palme in 1986

An increasingly lively debate about immigration and integration issues was well underway at the time of Olof Palme's murder. This debate took up issues dealing with Sweden's immigration and refugee policies, with the treatment of more established immigrants in Sweden, and with home language education (also known as mother-tongue education) for the children of immigrants. The suspicion of immigrant involvement in Palme's death served as much as anything else in further sharpening those debates.

Media coverage takes up several of the problems connected with immigration and refugee policies that would intensify in the future. "Right now we have 3000 refugees in our camps that the municipalities don't want to accept" (*DN*, February 2, 1986). However, it is not only in the refugee camps and in the initial process of getting resettled that there are problems. Many immigrants face ongoing difficulties getting work commensurate with their education and experience.

> When they came to Sweden they are offered jobs as, for example, dishwashers and cleaners. This is understandable when at first they don't have enough command of the language. But when they have learned to

speak perfect Swedish, then why don't we make use of these resources? (*DN*, March 1, 1986)

The discussion about "putting demand on immigrants" was also in effect in the mass media. An example is the case of Rafeat el Sayed, a highly successful Swede of Egyptian origin, who was found to have fabricated his credentials and who was subsequently deprived of his job and prominent board positions. Björn Gillberg generated strong responses when he expressed his view in a *DN* editorial that "the truth is rather that el Sayed probably succeeded unusually well just because he is an immigrant and we Swedes because of our fear of discriminating often place fewer demands on immigrants than on natives" (February 17, 1986). Several articles also focused on home language education, and in general, whether the use of the parent's native language at home is conducive to the immigrant child's development (e.g., in *SvD*, February 16 and 25, 1986). Immigrants' role in failed integration was also discussed.

These above tensions also play out in the investigations and coverage connected with Olof Palme's murder. An article in *AB*, speculating about Palme's murder suggests, for example, "the pattern corresponds too much with the way terror groups such as Abu Nidal work" (March 2, 1986). The same newspaper reports about immigrants' concern of being accused of the murder of Palme (March 3, 1986).

The Fall of the Berlin Wall on November 9, 1989

The dominant mass media themes at the time of the fall of the Berlin Wall highlight the increasing difficulties in managing effective policies on immigration and integration. Critics tend to assign blame for the problems to a number of different sources that can generally be grouped into four categories: (a) immigrants themselves, (b) the government's effectiveness in carrying out its responsibilities, (c) the government immigration policies themselves, and (d) on external factors beyond Sweden's control. Christian Democrat chair Alf Svensson, for example, leans toward the first in stating that immigrants should be required to adopt the Swedish democratic worldview:

> I believe it is the biggest mistake of the Swedish refugee policy, that we Swedes turn our backs and do not dare to ask questions, and do not dare or want to think what kinds of demands are included with Swedish citizenship. (*DN*, October 26, 1989)

The Social Democratic government, in contrast, tends to emphasize external factors, with reducing the intake of refugees as their strategy for managing ongoing difficulties with refugees and integration generally. It emphasizes its efforts to reduce the flow of immigration of refugees and asylum seekers into the country. Social Democratic Immigration Minister Maj-Lis Lööw announces a decision to tighten certain procedures, making it more difficult to get asylum in Sweden: "An asylum seeker who comes to Sweden without documents runs a bigger risk of being turned back directly at the border" (*DN*, November 3, 1989). This has the dual purpose of demonstrating the government is taking action to remedy certain problems while sending a message to would-be refugees or asylum seekers that Sweden will be tougher in granting permission.

Other articles highlight the image of refugees as more likely to engage in criminal activity. The vice chair of the Parliament's Committee for Social Insurance, Gullan Lindblad (MP), demands an inquiry about the refugee issue because of the increasing number of asylum seekers and because of the "expressly high criminality among immigrants" (*DN*, November 10, 1989). Two days later, an article in *AB* suggests that immigrants are more likely to engage in criminal activity than Swedes. The article further claims that criminality is part of some immigrant groups' culture (*AB*, November 12, 1989). *DN* runs an editorial which shifts attention partially from immigrant failings to policy failures, arguing that Swedish refugee policy makes it difficult for refugees to get jobs and forces them into a dependence on subsidies (November 17, 1989).

Bo Göransson, a Secretary at the Immigration Department, is critical of Swedish refugee policy, arguing that it could lead to increasing xenophobia. He argues for the development of a more "open and humane refugee policy built on a global basis":

> I think the Swedish people have a great commitment to solidarity if everyone knows that we receive people who really are refugees according to the UN's definition. But today there is a widespread understanding that the most are not. We cannot accept this opinion. (*DN*, November 19, 1989)

Even Immigration Minister Maj-Lis Lööw expresses concern over the conditions in the country's refugee facilities. On the other hand, Lööw defends the tightening of immigration policy, arguing among other things that immigrants are "over represented in certain types of criminality" (*SvD*, November 21, 1989).

The Election Breakthrough of ND, September 1991

The period following the election success of the ND was characterized by intense speculation in the national media regarding the likely impact of the ND. During this same period in the early 1990s, numerous news articles noted with concern an increase in the number of Nazi-related organisations in Sweden. Such articles include descriptions of armed groups with Nazi sympathies that are allegedly preparing for a 'holy race war' against immigrants, gay people, and other opponents. Such coverage is especially pronounced in *AB*. For example, one article describes how "the neo-nazis in Sweden found more and more armed small groups. Behind them there is a contact network with organisations where lawyers, service men, and academics are members" (*AB*, September 19, 1991). The same story reveals that:

> the Swedish Security Policy today warn about the neo-nazis in Sweden, "they are well-known perpetrators of violence who equip themselves with weapons," says the Chief of the Swedish Security Police. We take very seriously the risks of a growth in the neo-nazi movement in the country. It is very worrisome. (*AB*, September 19, 1991)

Nevertheless, both immigration policy and the plight of refugees and asylum seekers facing deportation from Sweden were also common topics. Media coverage tended to frame immigrants and immigration as a major problem in society, reflecting the increasing political interest in such questions and the increasingly polarized nature of the issues. Signs of the indirect effect of XPP on the debate were also apparent. For example, a Centre Party politician in the south-central Skåne region argued that established parties must dare to tackle such problems as criminality among immigrants or else risk ceding immigration issues to XPP:

> When an unacceptable number of those who live in a refugee centre in a small community like Vejbystrand commit crimes like shoplifting and theft it is not strange if the local population becomes despondent, indignant, and disappointed. . . . Nothing gets better if we politicians don't say anything about what everybody else knows (*DN*, September 20, 1991)

The Tightening of Asylum and Immigration Laws in the Revised Aliens Act in 1996

MP supports a Social Democratic government proposal to tighten the Aliens Act. This takes place in a time when the problem with the 'immigrant cultures' in general and 'Muslim culture' in particular is highly debated and addressed in the mass media. Two articles suggest problems with immigrant culture—in this case, issues specifically related to Islamic countries. One article suggests that Muslim women's headscarves can be dangerous to women wearing them, suggesting that "the veils lead to lack of vitamin D" (*AB*, December 2, 1996). Headlines for a story describing how two boys with an immigrant background had murdered an immigrant girl from Iraq ran: "Family honour redressed: a disgraced culture" (*DN*, December 19, 1996). While only one of these emphasizes the criminality frame, both reinforce the widely held view that the culture of Islamic countries is oppressive to women that makes a strong and damaging accusation in a country where women's equality has been an increasingly important part of the political discourse (being especially important during the mid-1990s). Both of these stories, together with many other similar stories and reports, portray Muslims' culture as deviating from Swedish societal norms connected with civic virtue and women's place in society.

The debate on the revised Aliens Act reveals different positions in the Swedish media. Some criticize the alliance between SDP and MP on the issue; meanwhile, others address the difficulties concerning the "generous asylum policy" that can make Sweden a free-zoon for those who do not have a "real need" for protection. The mass media addresses also the "eastern mafia" or the "Russian mafia" as an external danger that can come to Sweden if "we do not take accurate measures."

The Attacks on the World Trade Center and Pentagon in the United States, September 11, 2001

The major emphasis during this time frame is on the unsuccessful integration policies and the government being under heavy attack by the opposition on this matter. Simultaneously, images that represent 'Muslim culture' as oppressive to women are frequently present. Even before 9/11, there is much discussion about female genital mutilation of Muslim girls. Imams are viewed as responsible for promoting and perpetuating the practice, and there is a tendency to characterize it as a Muslim tradition.

Following the World Trade Center attack, Swedes express their solidarity with and support for the United States. However, the darker side of this expression of support is that Muslims in Sweden are exposed to violence and racial insults. The government takes exception to such acts of hatred and violence, and as a symbolic gesture, Prime Minister Göran Persson invites Muslims to Rosenbad, the government headquarters.

During the period immediately following the attack, news coverage depicting people from Islamic countries as a potential threat is common. A *DN* article the day after the attack notes that "a 55-year-old Tunisian man with permanent residence in Sweden tried to hijack a passenger plane from Sicily to Berlin on Saturday" (*DN*, September 2, 2001). Reporting on progress being made in US in efforts to identify people who might have been involved in the bombing, the tabloid press, *AB*, headlines noted that: "Five Arabs identified as suspects by USA this morning" (September 12, 2001). *DN* noted that Muslims have been harassed and threatened in Sweden after the terrorist attacks (September 13/14, 2001). Pointing to the same trend, *SvD* notes that hatred against Muslims is increasing in Sweden after the terrorist attacks (September 14, 2001). In the midst of this coverage, the image of the culture of Islamic countries as a pressing threat to women and women's equality remains visible (see *AB*, September 5, 2001, among others).

Increasing anti-Muslim sentiments are reinforced by the mass media openly publishing negative articles and 'expert opinions' on Islam and terrorism. The two largest liberal news papers, *DN* and *SvD*, frequently address Muslims who are portrayed as 'fundamentalists' as dangerous for the security of the country. The duality of 'Us-Christians, Europeans, modern people' against 'nonmodern and fundamentalist Muslims' are frequently addressed in the two major newspapers. In the editorial pages and debate sections of these papers, Muslims are, in many cases, equated with the 'Taliban.' *DN* openly advocates and supports the US plans to attack Afghanistan.

The Enlargement of the European Union, May 1, 2004

The main debate on immigration and immigrants occupied the pages of the mainstream press during the weeks immediately prior to, and following, the May 1, 2004 expansion of the European Union to include 10 more member states. The media is not only focused on positive effects, however, as coverage of refugee policies and immigrant issues highlights specific controversies, struggles, and difficulties. In one instance, Swedish television has, under pressure, reversed its decision not to permit 21-year-old Nadia Jebril from appearing as programme leader while wearing a head scarf (*AB*, April 27, 2004).

A second important set of discourses focus on the treatment of people in Sweden suspected of involvement in terrorism, especially those of Arabic descent. Individual cases are in the news, in which Sweden has cooperated or permitted the arrest of suspects—sometimes in apparent violation of the rights of naturalised Swedish citizens. In one instance, Ahmed Agiza is given over to Egypt (*DN*, May 6, 2004), while in another, the police raid a house in the small town of Växjö on the basis suspicion of individuals there on the part of Spanish police (*AB*, April 21, 2004). Mistrust of some immigrant groups is sufficiently large that one article contends "in Sweden there are many groups very close to Al Qa'ida and other terror organisations" (*AB*, April 21, 2004). In the article, Anders Hellner suggests this is because there is a high degree of political activity among immigrants in Sweden.

A third and dominant set of discourses is directly linked to European Union expansion and the possible effects of increased immigration from the former communist countries. Social Democratic leaders expressed, on numerous occasions, their fear that people coming to Sweden from the new member states would either cause new problems in the labour market (by, for example, pressing down wages), or that they might simply come to Sweden to take advantage of Sweden's generous welfare benefits. Prime Minister Göran Persson spoke with concern of the prospects for such 'social tourism,' suggesting transitional rules of some order might be necessary to prevent such abuse of the system. "Will it be harder on the Swedish labour market? There is risk for that, especially in small companies in the building sector, hotels and restaurants, housing and farms" (*AB*, April 29, 2004). Nor was such talk limited to 'normal people' seeking work or support. In an *AB* article, one person interviewed claimed that "every year thousands of criminals from Eastern Europe are invited to come to Sweden to pick berries or fish. But the invitation is a cover. Many are just admitted to steal, sell drugs, or to become prostitutes" (May 6, 2004).

Conclusion

The impacts of XPP on Swedish mainstream parties and politics have been both direct and indirect. The direct impacts of XPP start with the electoral success of ND and its entrance into the Swedish parliament in 1991. However, the mainstream parties' rejection of cooperation with ND makes the party's possibilities for direct influence over parliamentary decisions limited. The mass media coverage of ND and its populist agenda forced the mainstream parties to more or less 'take over' its antiimmigrant programmes and politics. ND influenced the debate on immigration, and helped to take the debate in a xenophobic direction.

The emergence of ND and SD has been contributive to the politicisation of immigration that made it to a part of every mainstream parties' party programme. This forced the mainstream parties to realise the electoral potential of the immigration and integration issue and use it in their populist electoral propagandas.

Some of the problems that XPP seeks to force onto the political agenda have been taken up and addressed by mainstream parties, but with generally different emphases. One question is whether this has the effect of pulling issues out from under XPPs, thereby weakening them (which is claimed often by mainstream parties), or if it simply legitimizes their claims and contributes to their further development. Undoubtedly, the effect has much to do with the consequences of such policies for the 'Others' and for established institutional discrimination in the country. One clear example of this is the tightening of immigration requirements in which MP and SDP collaborated. A new, sharpened Aliens Act was passed in 1996 and came into effect in January 1997.

A more recent and currently controversial example is the Liberal Party's adoption of numerous demands related to immigrants previously made by ND and currently supported by xenophobic parties such as SD. The Liberals' embrace of these policy proposals was sufficient for one of the former ND leaders, Bert Karlsson, to claim that the Liberals had adopted all of their previous proposals. This represents in many people's eyes a dramatic reversal from the refusal of the Liberals' earlier party leader, Bengt Westerberg, to serve in a government containing ND members, or to even sit in the same room as them! On the other hand, the Liberals' fortunes in the 2002 election shifted from a generally bleak outlook only a couple months prior to the election, to a surprise gain on voting day—a gain attributed largely to the 'get tough on immigrants' stance adopted by the party.

The impacts of XPP have moved Swedish 'political correctness' along more xenophobic paths. However, it is not only XPP, but also the mass media and mainstream parties' adaptation of antiimmigrant, anti-Muslim discourses that have helped increasing racism and discrimination in Sweden. It must also be said that such developments has not been without resistance from some politicians and journalists, who have tried to counteract racist and xenophobic trends in Sweden.

THE CASE OF ITALY

The Political Context of Xenophobia in Italy

The establishment in 1946 of an Italian republic based on liberal democratic values provided the opportunity for a fresh start for the country following the fall of fascism. The final years of the fascist regime represented a particularly ignominious period in Italian history. This included the introduction of 'racial laws' in 1938 following the cementing of the axis with Nazi Germany; and then invasion and surrender to the allies in the south in 1943 (following the dismissal of Mussolini by the king) and the installation of a 'puppet regime' (under a reinstated Mussolini) by the Nazis in the north—namely, the Italian Social Republic (RSI)—which collaborated in the holocaust.

However, one could argue that the political system put in place following the fall of fascism, and the collective memory of the fascist experience, contributed to some of Italy's postwar political problems. The system of checks and balances deliberately built into the postwar republican constitution, in order to prevent a repeat of the fascist abuses of political power, contributed to a political system characterized by weak executive leadership. The electoral law set out in the Italian constitution, based as it was on a pure system of proportional representation, exacerbated the problem of a fragmented party system and thus militated against strong stable government. For much of the postwar period, indeed up until the 1990s, Italy was regarded as having a 'blocked political system' with no proper alternation of government—a situation which fostered stagnation and corruption. The lack of alternation stemmed from the way in which the party-system was organized in order to keep the major party of the left, that is, the Italian Communist party (PCI), out of government. Its exclusion created a serious distortion. Government would revolve around Italy's biggest party, the Christian Democrats (DC), who would be continuously in government until 1994. Italy would become the only major western democracy in which there was no alternation in government. Although the exclusion of the left from government office became the organising principle of the postwar party system, the postwar constitution was nevertheless actually drawn up on the basis of an antifascist consensus. While PCI participated in the drafting of the constitution, the neo-fascist Italian Social Movement (MSI) (the party formed by fascist veterans) was deemed outside of the constitutional arc. However, in the cold war climate of the 1950s, such was the fear of communism that MSI was seriously considered by some DC leaders as a potential coalition partner in order to prevent the left parties from gaining power. Nevertheless, a wave of popular protest in 1960, when DC formed a government with the support of MSI on a vote of confidence, led to MSI being dropped from such considerations and being forced back into a political ghetto, in which it was to remain until the 1990s.

Although continuously in government, the proportional electoral system and fragmented party system required that DC rule in coalition with other, smaller parties. Similar to the practice of *trasformismo* that had been observed prior to fascism, new parties would be co-opted into the system, giving them a share of the spoils of office and binding them into the system. While some parties may have entered the ruling coalition with the intention of reforming the system, they soon ended up behaving like the others. For example, the socialist party (PSI) was originally a radical ally of PCI, but was invited into government in the 1960s, in what was then seen as an opening to the left. However, it soon became absorbed into the system and rivalled DC as skilled practitioners in the clientelistic system. The sharing of spoils was known as *lottizzazione,* with key posts and fiefdoms within Italy's public sector being divided among the ruling parties. Parties colonized the public administration and through an extensive network of state intervention extended their reach into civil society. This was referred to as *partitocrazia*—the rule of the parties. Parties organized their supporters, not on the basis of policy programmes, but through exclusive subcultures in which political loyalty was rewarded through preferment in employment in the bloated state sector, or through the award of lucrative contracts to undertake public works. Often the intervention of party contacts was required in order to make the inefficient public administration function. Policies were bargained upon between the various parties and factions in government, bearing little relation to the policy preferences expressed by electoral demand. Substantive change was frequently prevented by the breadth of the coalition of interests needed to take decisions and hence the likely existence of a veto group within it (Hine, 1993). This paved the way for the emergence of antiestablishment parties.

However, the outbreak of the *tangentopoli* (kick-back city) political corruption scandal in the 1990s led to an astonishing and rapid collapse of the party system and the emergence of the Legas in Northern Italy. The emergence of the various northern Leagues (most notably the Lega Lombarda) at the end of the 1980s—eventually uniting under the Northern League (Lega Nord) in 1991—was key to bringing down the old party system, offering as it did an alternative to voters in the north and northeast disgruntled by the inefficient and corrupt governing system presided over by DC. The Lega employed a radical antiestablishment discourse which denounced the corrupt *partitocrazia* and linked this with a general attack on the nature of the Italian state and the way in which the 'backward south' acted as a drain on the resources of the 'productive north' (calling for autonomy for the northern regions and the decentralisation of government in general). The Lega was aided by the ideological vacuum left behind by those subcultures which, up to the 1980s, dominated the political scene in Italy: communism and Catholicism. (Borcio, 1997; Ruzza & Schmidtke, 1993)

The emergence of XPP coincided with racist and xenophobic attacks on immigrants. For instance, a South African refugee, Jerry Maslo (who had fled apartheid), was murdered in the so called 'Villa Literno ghetto' near Caserta in 1989. The case received a great deal of public and media attention. This was the first major act of violence against the immigrant population to get national attention. Immigrants reacted to the murder with a strike—the first strike in Italy (and in Europe) of immigrant workers—leading to the adoption of a new law on immigrant employment. The incident perhaps marked the emergence of immigration as a salient political issue in Italy, and the law marked a new awareness of the issue and the need for better regulation. The 1990 law, the so-called Martelli law, has been described as a "watershed" (Ambrosini, 2001, p. 22) in terms of the way this phenomenon was perceived in Italy, because it acknowledged the existence of a defined and established group of immigrants in the country.

In this period, Italy was widely perceived as a country free of racism and, in general, it was thought that racist feelings, attitudes or episodes would not develop: this related to the tendency not to attach much value to Italy's fascist and colonial experience, to its race protection policsies and to racial laws against Jews. These episodes were considered as a kind of distant 'folklore' or aberrations not in keeping with Italian traditions. Nevertheless, some authors consider that a more thorough analysis of the abuses of the colonial period could prove that some colonial racism could be traced also in the Italian collective memory.

However, antiimmigrant and xenophobic attitudes were also reflected in the term used for immigrants. For example the term 'vù cumprà' (based on the apparent immigrant mispronunciation of the Italian for 'vuole comprare'—'do you want to buy?') was coined, reflecting the image of immigrants as street vendors. Rivera (2003) underlines that the term *vù cumprà* was a stereotyped word used to laugh at them on the one hand, but at the same time it was a coarse attempt to assimilate the image of the migrant by giving him a name in order to oversimplify a very complex situation. It was because of this complexity that the migrants were classified in an abstract and inaccurate way. Although this phenomenon was much more complex, as time went by, the social perception of immigrants became restricted to the immigrants who had more visibility—like illegal ones and street vendors. Whereas the term 'foreigner' has taken on a juridical and neutral connotation, the term 'immigrant' has turned into a category combining ethnic criteria (geographical origin and cultural distance) and class-related criteria; in other words, the immigrant is associated with a precarious and marginalised social condition.

A rise in the entrance of illegal (clandestine) immigrants and the difficulty the state had in controlling this led to an atmosphere of public alarm, which resulted in a higher demand for security. This crystallized in major fashion in August of 1991, when the cargo boat Viora, carrying thousands of Albanian refugees fleeing the collapsing communist regime, landed on the Puglian coast. The refugees were rounded up and taken to the football stadium in Bari. Poor living conditions within the stadium caused protest and episodes of violence. As a consequence, if at the beginning they were considered as refugees who had fled from a cruel regime, after this episode the portrayal provided by some elements of the media and some political actors transformed them into undesirable guests, thus increasing general apprehension and uneasiness. The authorities gave the impression of being unable to control and manage the situation, and of using heavy-handed law and order measures, signalling the development of a policy environment based on alarmism and closure against immigrants (Dallago, 1999). Italian immigration law was perceived as being ill-designed to cope with such large influxes, and there were subsequent demands from right-wing and populist politicians for the law to be tightened up. This period saw a notable increase in the exploitation of the issue by politicians. Members of LN, but also MSI-AN exponents, employed an exclusionist xenophobic discourse. The metaphor of immigration 'invasion' of Italy, from Albania and elsewhere, was frequently invoked. Calls for vigorous immigration controls were demanded. It was noted in this respect that Italy's geographical features and position made it a favoured landing destination for migrants from the south and east. Moreover, the close link between illegal immigration and human trafficking aroused serious concern. Its contribution to the growth and spreading of criminal organisations, both at the local and international level, was highlighted.

Thus, the hardline approach to clandestine immigration could be justified by surveys such as that of ISPO (2001), which showed that 65% of Italians polled agreed strongly or rather strongly with expelling illegal immigrants even if they have not committed any crime. Support for this is growing (in 1998, 57% of Italians agreed on this position). Furthermore, 3 out of 4 agree on the taking of fingerprints and on the utilisation of armed forces in controlling coastal waters (another feature of the Bossi–Fini law).

At the same time, surveys register a strong consensus around regularisation of foreign workers: 70% agreed on giving a *permesso di soggiorno* (resident permit) to illegal immigrants when they find a regular job. Another opinion poll showed that 8 out of 10 affirm that an immigrant should have a job organized before coming to Italy. Moreover, the public appears to share the centre-right's indifference towards promoting social integration of immigrants. Eurobarometer (2000) registers weak support for implementing specific policies promoting equality of opportunity in social life: 31% of Italians respondents agree that the state should have a role here, revealing the lowest percentage of support in Europe. Moreover, many Italians feel that immigrants abuse social welfare; Eurobarometer surveys in 2000 showed that 42% of Italian people agree with this statement. However, as migration in Italy is a recent phenomenon, scholars estimate that currently very few immigrants are beneficiaries of earnings-related benefits, although their number will potentially arise in the near future.

Discursive Reconstruction of 'Us' vs. 'Them'

Both the Lega Lombarda, out of which the Lega Nord's leadership emerged, and the Lega Nord fit the model of XPP. Various regional leagues, including the Lega Lombarda (LL), unified under the Lega Nord (LN) in 1991. In this study, the party programmes of LL in 1980s and LN's party programmes, party press, and the party leaders' speeches since its establishment in 1991 are analyzed. The following party programmes of the Italian XPPs, namely LL and LN, are analyzed: the LL party programme of 1983, and the LN party programmes of 1994, 1999, 2001, and 2004.

Analysis was also undertaken of interventions in the parliamentary debates during the passage of two recent key laws on immigration in Italy: The Turco–Napolitano law adopted by the centre-left government in 1998, and the Bossi–Fini law adopted by the centre-right government in 2002. This shed further light on the positions of the parties covered by the analysis of party documents, and provided a deeper understanding of differing positions internal to the parties, and of individuals and currents within parties that were not necessarily in accord with official party lines.

LN's party press, *La Padania*, was also analyzed. From its launch in 1997, the immigration issue was central to the editorial line of *La Padania*. Immigration was generally treated as a front page issue, with lead articles. The newspaper also published *Fatto del giorno* (Facts of the Day), where the immigration issue figured highly. The issue heavily permeated the politics section, and was also found in the 'Ideas' section. In the local sections, incidents of crime committed by immigrants are covered on a daily basis. In a sample of 51 articles that were analyzed, the association of immigration and crime was central (17 quotations), as was that between illegal immigrants and crime (13). There was also strong criticism made of 'inefficient governments' (25) and 'a weak left' (20) in relation to the issue. Quite often identity aspects were underlined, with a strong opposition to multiculturalism (12), and nationalistic appeals (11). On the positive side, the importance of helping migrants in their country of origin (5), and the need for more law and order (5), was mentioned.

The following frames were used for the analysis: (a) Collective Identity; (b) Employment Issues; (c) Welfare Issues; (d) Law and Order Issues; (e)

Liberal Values; (f) Antiestablishment; (g) Immigrant Status; and (h) Legitimisation of Racism. The frames that have been most frequently used in Italian political context are now discussed.

Collective Identity

Frame analysis confirms that identity themes are absolutely central in the politics of LN, both generally and with regard to the immigration issue. The need to protect 'national' identity and culture in opposition to non-EU immigration is generally emphasized. For example, the following quotation from a party document emphasizes opposition to immigration as a reasonable consequence of a positive valorisation of one's own culture:

> Quite often people who oppose non-EU immigration are only people who do not despise their own ancestors, their language and cultures, who are proud of their ethnic community, without thinking that it is superior to the others, accept differences and prefer their own people to members of other ethnic communities, but without refusing to cooperate. (LN document, *Ragionare sull'immigrazione*, 2002, p. 21)

However, in emphasising local or national identity, there is often an ambiguity in the Lega's documents and speeches as to what the reference point of this national identity is: Italy or Padania? References to Padanian nationalism are present mainly in the phase of the earlier regional Leagues and in the early phase of the Lega Nord. Among the documents that were analyzed, these can be found, for example, in Umberto Bossi's opening speech at the first party conference of the Lega Nord in 1991. It is interesting to note how here the new non-European Union immigration is compared to the old one (from the south) as a threat to the integrity of the social and communitarian identity of the Padanian communities:

> We were forced to analyse the issue of the collective social identity of our society in order to assess what danger the past and recent immigration from third world countries represented for the integrity of the Lombard social will. (Bossi, *Pieve Emanuele*, 1991)

It should be pointed out here that the Leagues, in their initial stages, sometimes referred to the Italian south as a third world country. Its previously virulent antisouthern rhetoric gradually faded out as the Lega Nord progressed and evolved in the 1990s. References to the Padanian nation, however, remained, and were revived in particularly between 1996 and 1998, when the Lega returned to a strategy of proposing the secession of the north from the rest of Italy. In general, however, the identity to be defended is not always clearly defined, and can refer to Lombardian, Padanian, Italian, European, western, or Christian identity. The Lega appears to be moving increasingly to an emphasis on a general European or western Christian identity, in the face of Islamic immigration. Its anti-Islamic stance has become particularly pronounced since 2001 and the 9/11 attacks (and therefore was not so evident in the analysis of mainly pre-2001 documents discussed here), and it is also linked to its campaign to prevent Turkish accession to the European Union, launched in 2004–2005.

The emphasis on defence of identity (be it Padanian, Italian, or Christian) is connected to the specific theme of ethnopluralism, and the correlation made between the ethnic homogeneity of the community and the integrity of the nation. The immigrant, therefore, represents a threat to this ethnic homogeneity and potentially damages the national fabric, perceived as dependent on the homogeneity of culture that derives from the single ethnic unit. Thus, for example, Bossi, in his speech to the 1991 party conference, suggested that immigration leads to the destruction of ethnic identity and that by "destroying the process of ethnic identity, the multiracial society provokes the decline of morality and therefore of solidarity." These themes are repeated in the party documents and speeches of the 1990s and 2000s. For example, a recent party document on immigration of 2002 includes the following claim:

> When we face the accusation of racism against us, who oppose the destruction of our people, we have to maintain the sacred right of our people to maintain and defend our ethnic-cultural and religious identities and not to become a residual minority. (LN party document, *Ragionare sull'immigrazione*, 2002)

This ethnopluralist message is married to a strong rejection of notions of multiculturalism and a 'multiracial' society. This is used to attack its opponents: "Because what they praise is an imported heterogeneity, created exclusively by the arrival of non-EU population" (*Per una Padania libera e antagonista all'omologazione*, Congressional thesis, 1998). Multiculturalism is also rejected when it is presented as the copresence of parallel societies or as a homogenising force linked to globalisation: "multiculturalism in the form of coexistence of parallel societies does not represent an acceptable model for the future" (LN party programme, 2001).

Employment and Welfare Issues

In relation to the employment issue, and the role of immigrants in the labour market, the frame analysis again illustrated the Lega's propensity to employ the ethno-populist frame whereby immigrants are portrayed as taking jobs from local workers. This is notable on the debate on the Turco–Napolitano law adopted in 1998, which the Lega opposed and went as far as to label 'racist' against Italian workers:

The act is also racist against our own people and workers. Rifondazione comunista believes that with demagogic words you can give something to everyone, but does not realize that, in the end, there will be a war among the poor. Our workers, or at least some of them, will be expelled from the productive world, from the job market in favour of these non-EU workers. I am not against the fact that these workers can, and eventually must, work in our territory, but I believe that we have to protect our workers first and only later, if there are still job opportunities, give them to others. But the bill contains indiscriminate openness, also in favour of the access to the job market for non-EU workers. Rifondazione comunista even boasted the fact that the bill in question, allows non-EU workers to look for jobs. But is obvious that for every place taken by a non-EU worker there will be one less for our workers. And this, in due course, will provoke huge social conflicts and public order problems. And in this war among the poor, in this conflict of the weakest, it will be certainly our people who will lose out. (Rolando Fontan, LN, Turco–Napolitano House of Representatives, November 11, 1997)

LN's representatives frame non-EU workers as a threat to Italian workers who are stealing their jobs: "The economic problems affecting the Italian families are certainly not solved by importing millions of non-EU workers, who, if they find jobs, are stealing them from Italian workers" (Oreste Rossi, LN, Turco–Nap House of Representatives September 30, 1997), and rejects the argument that: "The reported statement that there are jobs Italians refuse is obviously false: we all know of needy people available to do any type of activities" (Oreste Rossi, LN, Turco–Nap House of Representatives September 30, 1997).

Even in LN's party programmes it is stressed that immigration for job purposes represents a threat to Padanian, Italian, and European workers, not only because of the fear that they would take away jobs, but, above all, for the possible effects that this would have on driving down working conditions: "European citizens must oppose every attempt to stop the improvement of working conditions through the use of an unlimited reserve of non-EU labour" (LN party programme for the European elections, 1999).

Furthermore, in the programme for the European elections in 2004 there is a strong opposition to any type of 'affirmative action' which, according to LN, could result from the implementation of the European Union directive 2004/43 "that implements the principle of equal opportunities for anyone independently from race or ethnic origin": "This directive is aimed at opening the job market and public administration to non-EU workers through law enforcement, that means de facto enforcing the system of ethnic quota."

The welfare chauvinist frame again appears in the documents of the Lega, though perhaps with a lower frequency than previous frames. Although it was present in earlier documents—for example, in the general election programme of 1994 ("No to preferential welfare and healthcare services to immigrants, because it is a form of injustice for socially excluded Italians")—it is a theme that has been developed more fully in the most recent documents.

However, the theme cropped up in the parliamentary debate on the Turco–Napolitano law adopted in 1998, in relation to provisions in the law which provided immigrants with access to public housing and other social benefits:

> I can't understand why we cannot raise our pensions, we do not offer health safety, housing etc. to those people who really deserve it, to our people who have worked all their lives and instead we want to give free access to our health system and even housing to non-EU workers, obliging the local councils to offer such services out of their budget. It's a shame! (Rolando Fontan, LN, Turco–Napolitano, Chamber of Deputies, November 19,1997)

Generally, there is a complaint in the Lega's recent documents that discrimination exists in *favour* of immigrants, for example, in housing policy, it is claimed that "any immigrant has higher points than one of our families" (General Election Programme, 2001) or "the health system has privileged ranks for immigration at any cost" (*Ragionando sull'immigrazione*, 2002, p. 10). The Lega has thus called for a welfare system that puts Italian citizens first: "Social policies should favour Italians, not illegal immigrants" (General Election Programme, 2001). It is notable here that this example of welfare chauvinism emphasizes the need for preferential treatment of Italians and not just Padanians. A more notorious example of the Lega using the welfare chauvinist frame was in 2003, when Bossi complained about the 'bingo, bongo' getting priority access to housing over the Milanese in Milan. On this question, the following intervention by a Lega speaker in the parliamentary debate on the Bossi–Fini law can be found:

> We, Lega Nord padana, completely agree on building houses where foreign citizens temporarily working in our country, could live, but we strongly disagree with the use of funds to favour permanent accommodation for foreign families who come here to substitute our own Italian families that are living in difficult times. Foreigners, who come here to bring, more or less through force, their customs, traditions and religions. (Vanzo, LN, Bossi–Fini senate, February 19, 2002)

The theme of welfare finds less space in the articles analyzed in *La Padania*. There are some hints when discussing specific issues, such as the proposal for introducing new rules for citizenship presented by the German government in 1998. Also, in this case it is stressed that there is a tendency to discriminate against Italian (or German) citizens and in favour of immigrants. This is also couched in terms of an attack on the Lega's political opponents (i.e., the left) for being too soft on immigrants and giving them preferential treatment:

> As in Italy the red-greens want first class citizens, the immigrants, with all the rights but no duties, and second class citizens, the residents, with all the duties to support the others but with very few rights, because anyone who would like to have his/her historical rights on his/ her land is immediately accused of racism. ("In difesa dei diritti della gente perbene," *La Padania,* February 9, 1999)

Again there is a continuity here between the Lega Nord's present rhetoric and that used in its earlier phases against southern migrants. Thus, in the following excerpt from *Lombardia Autonomista* there is a complaint made about existing political leaders giving preferential treatment to immigrants, where the immigrants referred to are actually migrants from the south of Italy:

> Certainly they are the wrong political class which has not yet realised that the economic development model based on immigration is finished, and that laws which assigned council homes to immigrants, discriminating local residents, must be changed. (Lo sfrattato vale più di un immigrato, *Lombardia Autonomista,* No. 20, 1986)

Law and Order Issues

The theme of law and order is certainly an important one for the Lega Nord; in quantitative terms, it ranks second only to identity themes. The link between immigration and crime is made very frequently. In particular, the tendency for immigrants to fall into criminal activities is stressed. For example, in the 1994 general election manifesto:

> "Without a job and a house (immigrants) fall into the hands of crime and become part of its workforce as drug traffickers, pimps, or sellers of counterfeited goods" (LN party programme, 1994). Although this quotation could be interpreted as possibly suggesting some sympathy for the poor conditions that immigrants find themselves in and which lead them to a life of crime, other statements from LN are more explicit in scapegoating immigrants for the rise in crime that they supposedly bring: "This rise in crime is explained by both regular immigrants and illegal ones, even though the latter are the main culprit" (LN document, *Ragionare sull'immigrazione,* 2002, p. 9).

The problem of illegal-clandestine immigration is focused on by LN as a major problem to be resolved. However, it is notable that many of its statements do not exempt *legal* immigrants from the blame for crime. Indeed, some statements make no distinction. For example, in its 2002 document: "Immigration and rise of crime in Italy: a true equation" (LN document, *Ragionare sull'immigrazione*, 2002, p. 9). This scapegoating of all immigrants is sometimes backed up with statistics: "The latest data on our area tells that one foreigner out of four has problems with the legal system" (LN document, *Ragionare sull'immigrazione*, 2002, p. 9).

Thus, the Lega Nord, in its documents, calls for a much stricter law on immigration and a better use of the various police forces to implement controls. Such statements are rather frequent. In terms of specific proposals, there are calls for the use of the Carabinieri for the control of immigration, the use of fingerprinting of immigrants, and the possibility of suspending the Schengen agreement on specific occasions. In general, the procedures proposed are restrictive ones: more efficient procedures to regulate the entrance of immigrants and more efficient procedures to speed up expulsions.

More recent documents, post 9/11, also focus on the threat posed by terrorism, linking Muslim immigrants with an increased terrorist threat within Italy and the European Union in general. Thus, for example, in the electoral programme for the 2004 EP elections, this statement is found:

> Thanks to the far-sightedness of false do-gooder politicians, who opened the door to hundreds of thousands of non-EU workers, it was possible for Islamic terrorists to create an invisible (or almost) network of cells ready to bring death and destruction into the western countries.

Traces of such positions can also be found in documents prior to 9/11, for example in LN's European election programme of 1999:

> If one time we saw ourselves exposed to a possible armoured invasion on the threshold of Gorizia, today Padania suffers from a growing insecurity linked to risks of international terrorism and to the pernicious policies of the Italian state towards these immigrant fluxes and to the movements of large criminal organisations.

In LN's newspaper, *La Padania*, the 'Law and Order Issues' frame is the most frequently found, with similar statements to those found in party documents, restating the perceived link between immigration, illegality, crime and terrorism. Local Lega councillors are often portrayed as the only ones taking steps to counteract the supposed immigrant crime invasion. Proposals for tackling the crime allegedly brought by immigrants are also emphasized in *La Padania*. These have included proposals to open fire on boats of traffickers illegally bringing immigrants to Italy's shores:

Against this type of crime, stronger than ever, there is only one way of combating: authorising the law and order forces to open fire against boats once they have released their illegal burden. (Borghezio, *La Padania*, July 25, 2000)

In the summer of 2003, Bossi repeated the suggestion that these boats be fired at, although this time he seemed to imply that this should take place even if still full of migrants.

Antiestablishment

LN has always presented itself as a party different from the other parties and in clear opposition to them. Therefore, a certain animosity in describing its opponents (sometimes also its allies) is a central feature of its message. It emerged as an antiestablishment movement which denounced the corrupt political class of the 'first republic.' However, vicious attacks on the other parties (particularly those of the centre-left but also sometimes its government partners, UDC and AN) have continued into the so-called 'second republic.' Its general antiestablishment discourse is also sometimes combined with an attack on the failings of political leaders with regard to the regulation of the immigration issue. This was particularly the case at the time of the centre-left government between 1996 and 2001, when the Lega made frequent attacks in relation to its perceived soft and inefficient stance. The complaint was that the centre-left had favoured uncontrolled immigration, had irresponsibly made frequent recourse to *sanatoria* (amnesties for illegal immigrants), had wasted international aids funds without producing economic development, had not guaranteed security, and had allowed crime to increase and terrorist bases to be established at the hands of the large numbers of immigrants it had allowed into the country. Both the centre-left and the Catholic centre were attacked for weakness and misplaced 'do-goodism' in their attempts to address the immigration situation. Thus, the legislation on immigration introduced by the centre-left was strongly criticized:

> With these norms (the Turco–Napolitano Law) which replaced (for the worse!!!) the infamous Martelli Law, the Ulivo regime decided to impose a multiracial society in Italy and in Padania, creating chaos and greatly increasing the rate of illegality. (LN document, *Ragionare sull'immigrazione*, 2002, p. 10)

In addition to the accusations that the centre-left government had been too soft, the judicial system was also attacked as an 'accomplice' in facilitating immigration. In more recent documents, the same accusations are also directed at the European Commission: "It is therefore clear that the Commission is opposed to the limitation of non-EU immigration that is considered to be a positive and irreversible fact" (LN European Election Programme, 2004).

In early 1990s, LN presented a theory of conspiracy about an alliance comprising capital, the left and the Catholic Church. Thus, the left sought immigrants as potential electoral supporters, the church sought immigrants as potential priests and to boost falling congregations, and capitalists sought immigrants as a reservoir of cheap labour:

> This is so true that behind immigration of coloured people is not only the disbanded left which is looking for a new under proletarian class to gain votes; it is not only the Catholic Church, closed in the palaces of greed, which has lost all credibility and tries to fill its empty seminaries with religious people that can only be found in the Third World; but there is also the capitalist interest, that through migrations, lets its citizens pay the cost of its development. (Bossi, Conference 1991)

This theory of conspiracy and alliance has also cropped up in more recent documents:

> Non-EU immigration is favoured and supported by different forces that represent it as a spontaneous and irreversible phenomenon to which you cannot oppose; the multiracial society is mainly supported by an alliance of financial globalisation forces and the international left and is based on economic and ideological reasons. (LN document, *Ragionare sull'immigrazione*, 2002, p. 19)

When the Lega attacks the left, it stresses its (the left's) interest in immigration as providing a future reservoir of voters and even suggests that the left intentionally seeks the destruction of European civilisation:

> The Marxist orphans and the proponents of the dictatorship of the proletariat in a 'cattocomunista' sauce, who today converted to globalisation theory, continue (and would like to continue nowadays) their fine work of destroying the European civilisation, by using immigration as a picklock and future element of destabilisation and chaos; but they have met the Lega Nord on their way. (LN document, *Ragionare sull'immigrazione*, 2002, p. 11)

LN's political campaign is always coloured by an antiestablishment position. It attacks other political parties for being part of a conspiracy against Italians—and occasionally against Europeans.

The Dichotomy of 'Us' Against the Muslim 'Others'

The antiimmigrant position and political propaganda of LN have been, in many cases, anti-Islamic. Islam and Muslims are portrayed in the party programmes, in the party press, in party leaders' speeches, and in the parliamentary debates as a threat to the Italian nation. Muslims are considered, and presented as, an 'alien folk,' people from an 'alien culture,' and terrorists. The anti-Islamic position of LN became more obvious after the September 11, 2001 attacks in New York and the Pentagon in Washington, D.C. It was further reinforced in the aftermath of the terrorist attacks in London in 2005. In September 15, 2001, just a few days after the attack in the United States, Silvio Berlusconi made these comments:

> We must be aware of the superiority of our civilisation compared with the developing ones, of which some are still in the Middle Age. Our civilisation gave birth to welfare and respect of human and religious rights, that are still absent in the Islamic countries. We must avoid putting the two civilisations on the same level. Freedom does not belong to Islamic civilisation. Our civilisation must extend to those who are still behind by 1400 years in history the benefits and achievements of the West.

Since the terrorist attacks on London of July 2005, the LN exponents (notably the Minister for Institutional Reform, Roberto Calderoli) have stepped up the anti-Islamic rhetoric, endorsing the 'clash of civilisations' thesis, claiming that there is no moderate side to Islam, and declaring that "all Muslims are potential terrorists."

The anti-Islamic propaganda is also frequent in LN's press, *La Padania*. Among the articles examined, the greatest attention given to the theme can be found in those published in September 2001. However, this theme had also cropped up previously, with LN spokesmen stressing the need to stop 'an Islamic invasion,' protect Christian culture, and give preference to Christian immigrants:

> The Lega, on the contrary, has always stated that immigration is a phenomenon that can and must be governed: firstly, by avoiding an Islamic invasion, which is a great threat to the cultural and religious identity of a country with deep roots in Christianity. (Borghezio, *La Padania*, September 14, 2000)

It was not only the September 11 attacks that evoked anti-Islamic sentiments and propaganda. The Islamic threat to the 'western world' was propagated before these attacks. In the example below, the suggestion was that there was also a connection between fundamentalist groups and drug trafficking:

> Two terminal threats for the western world are uniting in the far steppes of central Asia, in an alliance which will have devastating effects. Islamic fundamentalism and drug trafficking are expanding side by side in the area and find very few obstacles. ("Islam e narcotraffico," *La Padania*, November 5, 2000)

Even the claim of the Pope in 1993 that: "The Catholics have to pay attention to oppose marriages with persons of different faiths" (Pope John Paul II, September 17, 1993) fueled the anti-Muslim propaganda of LN and other centre-right coalition partners, such as AN. Further, in the 'postterrorist' attacks of July, 2005 in London, LN politicians and press used the attacks to reinforce the image of Muslims as terrorists. They made the anti-Islamic debates and references a common part of many political articles and discussions, both in parliament and in mass media.

Assessing Impacts of XPP

Upon initial examination of the development of legislation on the immigration issue in Italy in the 1990s and early 2000s, the argument that the emergence of a radical-right populist or ethno-populist party (the Lega Nord) has significantly shifted the political debate on the issue, and led to the adoption of more severe immigration controls, is a persuasive one. Pressure by the Lega appeared to lead to the adoption of the Dini decree on immigration in 1995. It was notable in this period that the centre-left and Catholic parties had collaborated with the Lega in propping up the Dini caretaker government following the fall of the first Berlusconi government at the end of 1994. LN demanded action on immigration if it were to continue to 'prop up' the government and ensure the passage of other crucial legislation (e.g., the financial and budgetary package for the year). However, although the Dini government did take action, the measures adopted on immigration did not go as far as the more extremist solutions proposed by LN. Following on from this, and against the backdrop of the more hostile (towards immigrants) political climate shaped at least partly by LN, the Turco–Napolitano law was adopted by the centre-left government in 1998 (although the law was vociferously opposed by the Lega). Finally, in 2002, the Bossi–Fini law was adopted by a centre-right government which actually included LN. The leading role played by LN in the law's formulation is reflected in the cosponsoring of the law by its leader, Umberto Bossi.

Nevertheless, further examination of the parliamentary debates that led to the adoption of the 1998 and 2002 immigration laws (together with analysis of documents adopted and speeches made by the main political actors involved, as well as media coverage of the political debate) shows that the range of influences in political discussions and the shifts in opinion that have taken place are rather complicated, and that the nature of alliances that developed in the adoption of this legislation was sometimes rather surprising. Moreover, other factors need to be taken into account such as the influence of EU-level decision making. Indeed, legislation on immigration in Italy was often portrayed by its proponents as necessary to get Italy up to speed with regard to European Union-level agreements (such as the Schengen accord), and as a response to pressure from Italy's European partners to remedy a situation in which Italy was viewed as the soft underbelly of Europe, with a long unprotected coastline vulnerable to clandestine immigrants using Italy as a landing point before taking advantage of the European Union's open borders in order to travel on to northern Europe. It needs to be emphasized in this respect that Italy's immigration controls were virtually nonexistent prior to the 1990s. Thus, when immigrants began to enter the country in large numbers at the end of the 1980s, it was predictable that national legislation to regulate this would be deemed necessary by mainstream political actors, irrespective of the existence of a populist party seeking electoral gain through the adoption of an antiimmigrant platform.

The Turco–Napolitano law could actually be interpreted as a compromise between opposing positions: the centre-left position advocating better guarantees for the social integration and citizenship rights of legal immigrants (e.g., the right to vote), and the right/centre-right position favouring more security controls and more stringent regulations on immigration entry (e.g., the combating of clandestine immigration and the better definition of criteria for regular immigrant entries). The centre-left parties adopted some of the frames of the centre-right, while at the same time shunning xenophobic statements and balancing tougher immigration controls with measures to improve the social integration of immigrants. LN's propaganda on the "fear of mass immigration," claiming that clandestine immigration was out of control and presented a threat to security and the maintenance of law and order, has influenced the mainstream parties even in the centre-left coalition. But, in terms of direct effects, it is in the whipping up of public fears that it is maybe more effective.

The *indirect* impact of LN in increasing xenophobia and racism in Italy is of more importance than its direct legislative impact. In this concern, selecting the appropriate 'mainstream' political actor was more problematic given the transformations that have occurred in Italy since the beginning of the 1990s. Until 1992, Italian politics was dominated by the Christian-Democratic party (DC) which had been present in government (along with a variety of smaller coalition partners) in continuation since the end of the 1940s. It was thus *the* mainstream party in Italian politics until 1992. It presented itself as a party of the centre, though it contained a number of factions some of which were fairly conservative and some of which were of a fairly leftist orientation. The main party of opposition in this period (and the second largest party after DC) was the Italian communist party (PCI). PCI could not however be described as a mainstream party. The party system was organized in such as way as to permanently exclude it from government. Although by the 1980s its political programme resembled that of mainstream centre-left social democratic parties in the rest of the European Union, its association with the Soviet Union prevented other political actors from viewing it as a legitimate governing alternative to DC. However, following the collapse of the Soviet bloc, PCI transformed itself into a more conventional European social democratic party, the Democratic Left party (PDS), and helped to legitimise it as a governing alternative to the DC, which had previously been able to justify its behaviour in terms of its presence as an anticommunist bulwark. These changes, combined with the emergence of LN and other internal and external factors, contributed to the collapse of DC in 1992 and 1993 and the emergence of a new party system in which a new centre-right pole (led by Silvio Berlusconi) was opposed to a new centre-left pole organized around PDS.

For the purposes of this research, the discourse of PCI and its successor PDS (later to become the DS) is analyzed as representing the main centre-left party. On the centre/centre-right, DC is analyzed up until 1994 and Forza Italia thereafter. However, in the case of the latter there is a clear discontinuity. As already mentioned, DC eschewed the 'right-wing' or 'centre-right' label (until the 1990s, the term 'right' was associated with fascism so only the neo-fascist MSI happily took the label). Nevertheless, DC occupied the space on the political spectrum generally occupied by centre-right conservative parties in the rest of Europe, and was backed by conservative forces in society (the church) and the economy (e.g., big business and large landowners). Following the collapse of DC, Forza Italia inherited much of its electorate and the support of conservative interests, though it was much more unashamed about presenting itself as a centre-right party and presented as a very different political animal to DC. The situation is further complicated by the presence in Italy since the mid-1990s of another centre-right party, the National Alliance (AN), now perceived (within Italy at least) as mainstream political actor, yet having its roots in Italian fascism, being the direct successor of the neo-fascist Italian Social Movement (MSI) (the latter being dissolved into the AN in 1995). Given this transformation, along with the alliance between AN and Forza Italia, and AN's current leading role in government, an analysis of the changing discourse of MSI-AN was also deemed highly pertinent and necessary to the research.

In addition to the analysis of the documents of DC, PCI-PDS-DS, Forza Italia, and MSI-AN, analysis was also undertaken of the party newspapers of each of the parties. In the case of PCI-PDS-DS and MSI-AN, the continuity was evident in the sense that the new formations inherited the party newspaper of the old formations (*L'Unita* and *Il Secolo d'Italia,* respectively). *Il Popolo,* the newspaper of DC, actually outlived the defunct party (tending to align itself with the positions of the part of the ex-DC that then aligned itself with the centre-left). Thus, analysis of *Il Popolo* into the 2000s provided an opportunity for further continuity in the research, allowing light to be shed on the views emanating from the Catholic political world long after the demise of the party. In the case of Forza Italia, although the party does not have an official newspaper, it was possible to focus analysis on *Il Giornale,* which happens to be owned (along with Italy's three leading private TV channels) by Forza Italia's leader and founder, Silvio Berlusconi.

Analysis was also undertaken of interventions in parliamentary debates during the passage of the two recent key laws on immigration in Italy: the

Turco–Napolitano law adopted by the centre-left government in 1998, and the Bossi–Fini law adopted by the centre-right government in 2002. Perhaps more interestingly for the research, the analysis of parliamentary debates (together with that of party programmes and of mainstream media) allowed for a tracking of the positions adopted by the various Catholic parties that emerged out of DC, some of which allied themselves with the centre-right (CCD and CDU, later unifying to form the UDC) and some with the centre-left (notably, the Italian Popular Party). The Italian Popular Party (PPI) was the name taken by DC as it sought to purify and reinvent itself in the midst of the *tangetopoli* scandal in 1993, in fact returning to its social Catholic roots, and retaking the name of the Catholic party prior to the fascist regime. This was perceived as a shift to the left, leading to the splitting off of CCD which instead allied itself with Berlusconi in 1994. PPI stood independently of the two poles in 1994, but when its leader, Rocco Buttiglione, sought to later ally it with Berlusconi, another split was created and Buttiglione was forced to create a new party allied with the centre-right, CDU, while the rest of PPI would form part of the centre-left pole in 1996. PPI formed a joint parliamentary grouping after 1996 with the Democrats of Romano Prodi (another former Christian Democrat)—referred to as PopDem in the 1998 parliamentary debate—which then developed into the Margherita (Daisy) formation after 2001.

For the assessment of the impact of XPP on the mainstream parties, the analysis has been structured around the identification of key frames associated with the discourses of XPP and its political actors in Italy.

Collective Identity

This frame is used by mainstream parties in reference to the Italian nation. The centre-right party, AN, expressed in its party documents and debates the negative effects of immigration on Italian cultural and national identity. However, AN is more cautious about stressing its xenophobic and nationalistic propaganda. There is occasional recourse to positive promulticultural frames, suggesting that AN's position on this theme is more balanced. This is mainly due to its attempt to distance itself from its fascist roots and present itself as a moderate and modern party. However, the concept of the 'clash of civilisations' that is frequently used by LN is also presented in AN. It warns that mass migration movements risk bringing a destabilising clash of cultures:

> The quantitative weakening of certain peoples, the incremental explosion of others, the territorial transfers which tend to assume mass character, further to the intense risk of becoming overwhelming and destabilising, presents the theme of the relationship between very different cultures, expressions of ethnic realities which end up finding

themselves in contact with ambience different to those historically habitual. (AN party programme, 1998)

Although AN declaration of the 'cultural clash' comes before the same argument of LN, AN continues its line of the defence of the "sacred rights of Italians": "And let's say that even we do not believe in this type of internationalism: we believe that the sacred and legitimate rights of Italian citizens should come first" (Valditara, AN, Bossi–Fini Senate, February 2, 2002). AN has generally not followed LN's increasing anti-Muslim propaganda, but has used, on many occasions, the same arguments. In the pages of *Il Secolo* for example, an AN deputy, Alfredo Mantovano, suggested that preference be given to Christian immigrants before those from other religions: "There is a need therefore to consider 'the question of integration' orienting the migratory fluxes from zones which present the most cultural homogeneity with our nation" ("La miopia della sinistra contro Biffi," *Il Secolo*, 2000).

Moreover, Mantovano later suggested discouraging marriages and miscegenation between Christians and those from other religions: "marriages between Catholics and non-Christian migrants should be discouraged, above all in light of the education of their children" ("Gli islamici rispettino i nostri valori," *Il Secolo,* 2004). Furthermore, other articles printed in *Il Secolo* are more explicit in expressing fear about the dangers of an aggressive Islamic minority developing in Italy. For example, in 1999, in criticising a proposed sanatoria on the part of the centre-left government, it warned against increasing Islamic aggression: "Italy will become more and more a geographic expression, inside which Catholicism is a relative majority pressed by an aggressive Islamic minority" ("Il duo Turco–Jervolino ha un chiodo fisso, il tornaconto elettorale," *Il Secolo,* 1999).

Ample space has also been given to members of the Catholic Church hierarchy in Italy who have expressed unease at the effects of Islamic immigration on Italy's Catholic identity—for example, the controversial statement by Cardinal Biffi of Bologna in 2000 to restrict Islamic immigration and favour Christian immigrants. This was supported by *Il Secolo*, which also gave space to these supporting words from Gianni Baget Bozzo (a clergyman close to Berlusconi and Forza Italia): "Only the cosmopolitan and multicultural prejudice which seeks to carve out the roots of Christianity which keep the West alive can be blind towards the Islamic question" ("La miopia della sinistra contro Biffi," *Il Secolo,* 2000).

Beside the leader of Forza Italia, Berluconi, even some of the conservative exponents of DC have expressed concern about Islamic immigration. Indeed, Rocco Buttiglione (then of CDU, latterly of UDC) contributed to the anti-Islamic debate launched by Cardinal Biffi on the dangers of Islamic immigration. He claimed that Muslims were more susceptible to crime because of their cultural difference:

This is how I see it: if when deciding the quota of workers coming to Italy you take into account the level of criminality of different national groups and their ability to integrate, you would discover that the groups creating less problems are the Catholics or Christian ones. This happens . . . because they have a culture more similar to ours and can count on networks such as the parishes. (Rocco Buttiglione, Udc; "La miopia della sinistra contro Biffi," *Il Secolo,* 2000)

In the debate on the Bossi–Fini law, it was also notable that, while the language was much more guarded than that used by LN or even AN, the UDC spokesperson also strayed onto antiimmigrant territory:

As experiences shows, it [multiculturalism] involves heavy costs for everyone, especially for the weakest social groups, who, not by chance, react by developing hostility and stronger ethnic and racial prejudice than the wealthy, who find other systems of social insulation. And costs are heavier the higher the cultural distance of the society of migration and the society of origin of immigrants is. . . . Corrections bear the sign of more sensibility towards the national community's ability (and indirectly to the European one) to be effective in controlling its own borders, to be more sensitive towards the responsibility towards one's citizens, to have more sensitivity towards the power of the national community to decide the means of expression of universal human brotherhood. (Gubert, UDC, Bossi–Fini Senate, February 19, 2002)

The documents of the centre-left (PCI-PDS-DS) demonstrate a strong repudiation of nationalist and negative ethno-pluralist frames. This is a constant in the evolution from PCI into PDS into DS. Although stressing the "fundamental principles and values" of Italian society, the centre-left documents stress the potential benefits of a "multicultural society" and the contribution that immigrants can bring to a new multicultural identity in which diversity can be valued and respected. The centre-left coalition displays more positive and inclusive attitudes towards immigrants. However these attitudes changed negatively since the 1990s. Their position in this respect has to do with their opposition to the centre-right coalition's negative propaganda against immigrants.

Employment and Welfare Issues

This frame is also used by the mainstream parties. The AN exponents, Maurizio Gasparri, said in a debate preceding the Turco–Napolitano law in 1997:

I think that right now an earthquake survivor in Nocera Umbra is worse off than an Albanian because in Albania, thank God, there are no civil wars nor earthquakes. There are unemployment and social problems, but, Right Honourable Minister of Home Affairs, there are also these problems in many parts of the South, with which you are very familiar. Also in the southern parts of Bergamo province or in the internal areas of Piedmont there will be some unemployed who would like to be treated as an Albanian unemployed! (Maurizio Gasparri, AN, Turco–Nap House of Representatives, October 23, 1997)

Moreover, in the same debate, other AN speakers also made statements similar to those of the Lega when discussing provisions which would provide immigrants with access to public housing and other social benefits. It was argued that such benefits were not even available for Italians and that therefore immigrants were being shown preferential treatment (Roberto Menia, AN, Turco–Nap camera, September 30, 1997).

It was notable that a similar complaint came from a senior Forza Italia spokesperson (and future European Commissioner), Franco Frattini:

Well, either all of this won't be given, and we do not want to put our signature on a deception on the good faith of the weakest, or we will give immigrants access to the services that our citizens, in the outskirts or in the slums of our cities, have never had. (Franco Frattini, FI, Turco–Nap Chamber of Deputies, October 23, 1997)

The welfare chauvinist frame was not one indulged in by DC. Indeed, in its newspaper *Il Popolo,* discussion of the positive contribution made in terms of social security contributions by immigrants can be found: "Thus we have today immigrants who contribute 800 billion lire to INPS (social insurance). Without rules we will damage even ourselves" (don Di Liegro, *Il Popolo,* September 15, 1994). The proimmigrant debates of the centre-left coalition are based more on its opposition to the centre-right coalition's antiimmigration propaganda. This means that their reaction is more to justify immigration as instrumentally good (in terms of the labour force) for Italy. Therefore, the centre-left emphasized "the need of the labour market" to have immigration. In a debate on the Turco–Napolitano law of 1998, the DS representative illustrated this:

Also, it seems to me, that a balance is struck between rigour and integration, legality and regulation: a rigour of rights and duties; an integration that links the right of security for the citizens with the needs of the labour market. (Antonio Di Bisceglie, DS, Turco–Nap camera, October 23, 1997)

Contributions of immigrants, in terms of tax revenue from immigrants' earnings, get referred to occasionally in *L'Unità.*

Law and Order Issues

This frame is used only occasionally by the mainstream parties. The linkage between crime and immigration was not made in the documents of DC. However, in the party press, *Il Popolo,* the need to combat the issue of 'illegal immigrants' was discussed. But it was in the context of the unfair exploitation clandestine migrants were subject to. Others, such as representatives of one the DC's more conservative successors, CCD (part of the centre-right bloc and later to form part of UDC), did make reference to the link between clandestine migrants and crime in a parliamentary debate on the Turco–Napolitano law:

> We are facing a dramatic lack of legislation, a legislative void that made our country the privileged landing place of the organisations responsible for illegal immigration. . . . .We think (we have been repeating this for months) that our country is in an unsustainable situation. . . . In relation to the most recent crime news, where non-EU immigrants were repeatedly involved, it has been discovered that many of these immigrants, both in Abruzzo and in Apulia, had already been condemned for atrocious crimes, but their expulsion had been blocked by an appeal to TAR [the Administrative Regional Court]. (Carlo Giovanardi, CCD, Turco–Nap camera, October 10, 1997)

With regard to the centre-left, the relationship between crime and immigration is discussed in party documents. It is stated that there is a security risk involved in allowing immigrants to enter Italy. This issue of risk comes particularly to the fore when discussing clandestine immigration, such as in the DC 2001 election manifesto: "The uncertainty and troubles the South as well as the North are facing depends on the link between the fear of crime and the fear that is provoked by illegal immigration." The centre-left government makes again a link between 'criminality' and 'the control of borders' in the same electoral manifesto: "Crimes are diminishing, cities are less violent, and the state has resumed the control of the territory" (DC, 2001).

Mass Media and the 'Others'

In addition to the analysis of party documents, speeches and parliamentary debates, an analysis was undertaken of coverage of the immigration issue by three national newspapers: the two leading 'quality broadsheets,' *Corriere della Sera* and *La Repubblica,* and a populist tabloid, *Il Giorno.* The analysis focused on the coverage of six events deemed as key to the evolution of coverage of the immigration debate in Italy since 1990: the landing on the coast of Puglia in August 1991 of thousands of refugees fleeing from Albania as the communist regime there collapsed, the passage of three key laws on immigration in Italy—the Dini law of 1995, the Turco–Napolitano law of 1998 and the Bossi–Fini law of 2002—and two international events with a major impact on the national debate in Italy, that is, the September 11 attacks of 2001 and the eastern enlargement of the European Union in May 2004. This analysis provided the opportunity to shed light on the space given by these newspapers to the xenophobic and ethno-populist discourse of the Lega and other actors, and on the general way in which immigration has been discussed and conceptualised in what are leading examples of the Italian press.

Corriere della Sera and *La Repubblica* are both 'quality' broadsheets and Italy's biggest selling daily newspapers with a circulation of around 600,000–700,000 each. *Corriere* is one of Italy's longest running dailies, being founded in the late 19th century. Though generally perceived as being more to the centre-right (however, not necessarily sympathetic to the centre-right coalition) it has a reputation for impartiality in the reporting of news events, giving space to diverse views in its comment and opinion pages. *La Repubblica* is a fairly late arrival on the newspaper market, having been founded in the 1970s, giving more space to comment and opinion (generally of a left-liberal character—the paper is perceived to be sympathetic to the positions of the centre-left.) than *Corriere*, and seeking to challenge the latter's leading position. Although no real mass market tabloid exists in Italy (along the lines of *The Sun* in the United Kingdom), *Il Giorno* was chosen as the third newspaper analyzed because of the contrast provided vis-à-vis the other two newspapers. Founded in the 1950s, it has developed a more populist outlook, with plenty of space devoted to gossip and showbiz news. News coverage is generally devoted to the mechanistic chronicling of domestic news, with little space for more profound comment. Its coverage of the news, however, appears slanted towards a general political orientation that can be located on the right of the political spectrum. Nevertheless, it sells only around 120,000 copies daily.

Landing of Albanian Refugees on Puglian coast, August 1991

With regard to a situation in which over 10,000 Albanians fleeing the collapsing communist regime in the summer of 1991 arrived on the Puglian coast, the *Corriere della Sera* and *La Repubblica* dealt with the situation in a similar way to each other, focusing on the economic hardships and deprivation of human rights suffered by these people. Thus, both newspapers demonstrated a compassionate, solidaristic and understanding approach. Nevertheless, there is a difference in the way that the two different newspapers structure articles, which is reflective of their differing styles of journalism. Whereas *Corriere* presents its coverage by means of reporting the words of politicians, trade unionists, members of the Church and other relevant actors by citing their words directly, *La*

Repubblica has a more 'involved' approach to reporting, giving greater space to the opinions of journalists and commentators. The perspectives adopted by the two papers in the articles have much in common. The frames that occur most frequently relate to conceptualisations of different political actors (i.e., the usual negative description by political actors of other political actors for their positions on the issue) or are those which either stress the need to welcome immigrants (expressing compassion and understanding for their motives) or the undesirability of allowing immigrants to enter and stay in Italy.

The tabloid paper, *Il Giorno,* meanwhile, uses sensationalist and "apocalyptic" language in its headlines, as illustrated by the following examples: "Boat people apocalypse" (August 9, 1991); "Cholera casts its shadow over the drama" (August 14, 1991); "Desperates' last assault" (August 14, 1991). The language used to describe the refugees in the articles is also patronising. For example, the following phrases were found: "poor devils"; "starving, rag-covered people"; "a bunch of hotheads is invading us"; "poor devils, we can't shoot them, can we?"; "those ones"; "an unrestrainable, unstoppable horde"; "the raft people." There is little doubt that the adjectives and locutions used conveyed sharply negative meanings.

Passage of the Dini Decree on Immigration, November 1995

The frame most prevalent in the three newspapers analyzed in relation to coverage of passage of the Dini decree on immigration in November 1995 was that relating to conceptualisations of political actors (i.e., criticism of political opponents). Political actors variously described each other as intolerant or excessively tolerant, inefficient, incapable or guilty of electoral opportunism. While the left accused the right of racism and intolerance, and the right accused the left of being excessively permissive and incapable of taking a firm stand to defend the country's interests, a great deal of coverage also related to criticisms of the government (the caretaker Dini administration which had been installed following the fall of the first Berlusconi government) for its use of a decree law. *Corriere* especially underlined the need to rethink the way in which the immigration issue had been traditionally dealt with. According to the newspaper, while the debate focused on a conflict between the left advocating a welcoming approach and stressing the rights of immigrants, and the right calling for exclusion and quotas, immigration would remain an issue to be exploited for electoral purposes. The view expressed in *Corriere* was that a meeting of minds was needed between the advocacy of tolerance and solidarity, and the need for security and the rule of law. Although more openly in favour of welcoming immigrants, similar views were expressed in the pages of *La Repubblica*.

The tabloid, *Il Giorno,* draws a rather balanced picture of the positions of those opposing the decree (because they thought it was too soft and that it might turn into a 'general amnesty'—like the Lega Nord), and those stating that the decree was discriminatory and violated human rights (because it envisioned the direct expulsion of immigrants caught in criminal acts). The paper presented interviews with actors from the various parties, as well as from the Catholic Church, in which criticisms of other political actors were commonplace.

Parliament Passes the Turco–Napolitano Law, March 1998

None of the three newspapers analyzed took a clear position on the 1998 law (and nor did they do so for the later Bossi–Fini law), although *Il Giorno* displayed a right-wing orientation in its tendency to focus on unpleasant news stories which served to minimize the impact of the antiimmigration position of certain politicians. In particular, during the month of August, examples of headlines filling *il Giorno* included the following: "Free to escape. The mockery of the expulsion order (*foglio di via*): hundreds of illegal immigrants will leave the detention centres . . . to stay in Italy and Europe"; "Immigrants and chaos, Bossi asks for Napolitano resignation"; "Parks scare us"; "Illegals will soon be free, government under fire." All these headlines tended to highlight the shortcomings of the Turco–Napolitano law and to increase the sense of panic across public opinion. *La Repubblica* tended to give space to a free exchange of opinions without linguistic exaggerations. For example, in relationship to the discussion on the link between illegal immigration and terrorism, Giorgio Napolitano (interior minister and one of the sponsors of the law) appeared to give credence to the immigration–terrorism link in his parliamentary speech: "Those desperate people lacking a perspective of positive integration in the Italian society are at risk of becoming a cheap workforce for terrorist groups" (*La Repubblica*, August 29, 1998). *Corriere della Sera*, for its part, followed a similar line, although it gave more space to representatives of the (centre-right) opposition with clear xenophobic ideas.

The Attacks on the World Trade Center and Pentagon in the United States, September 11, 2001

The attack on WTC in New York received a huge amount of coverage in the Italian media. It also sparked a deeper debate about questions of race, ethnicity and the immigration question in Italy, and particularly the implications of Muslim immigration. There were clear differences in the way that the three newspapers analyzed covered this debate. As per its traditional style, *Corriere* tended to provide a chronicle of the various statements and rebuttals made in the debate, with support for Berlusconi coming from within the parties of the ruling coalition, and denunciations coming from the opposition and the Arab League. Berlusconi's anti-Muslim statement on September 15, just a few days after the attack, created a hot debate in the mass media. In the wake of Berlusconi's statement, *La Repubblica* published a large dossier with a range of features on Muslim culture, data on the presence of Muslim immigrants in Italy, and discussion of possible consequences. Both *La Repubblica* and *Corriere* gave a lot of space to Berlusconi's declarations, whereas *Il Giorno,* too busy depicting the tragedy of the twin towers, did not mention the issue at all. The tabloid newspaper debated the "danger of Islamic fundamentalism" and its possible impact, both for Italy and the world. For example, the following statements were found: "Silence falls. Especially today. Especially after the American slaughter" (Andrea Brusa, *Il Giorno,* September 19, 2001), and "The recent days attacks have faced the world with some questions on the dangerousness—or at least on the nature—of Islam. Muslim culture . . . can also give birth to the monster of fundamentalism" (*Il Giorno,* September 14, 2001).

Parliament Passes the Bossi–Fini law, July 2002

As was the case for the 1998 law, the newspapers do not express specific positions, although in the case of *Il Giorno,* there seems, from reading between the lines, to be a tacit approval of the passage of the Bossi–Fini law. Both *La Repubblica* and *Corriere della Sera* try to give space to all the possible points of view, almost playing the role of an interested onlooker, although they provide significant pointers for reflection in different ways. *Corriere* in particular tends to focus on reporting the controversial declarations of various political actors, while *La Repubblica* seeks to provide the reader with 'alternative' perspectives and viewpoints in order to promote different evaluations. In *La Repubblica,* judgements on the centre-right government tend to be harsh. The paper gives a lot of space to the accusations by the centre-left that the government had acted in a racist and intolerant way, and that the law would damage workers and entrepreneurs alike and favour the growth of criminality (*La Repubblica,* June 4, 2002). *Corriere* makes an attempt to do two things simultaneously: on the one hand, reporting the opinions of all political parties, on the other hand, trying to set the problem of immigration in the framework of the related issues, such as integration: "Society is already multicultural, there is no point in setting up an apartheid" (Paolo Costa, formerly minister for public works in Prodi government, CdS, June 1, 2002). Also, anti-Muslim propaganda is a relevant issue in *Corriere:* "This kind of Islam is our enemy. It cannot be encouraged in any way, whereas this way we would encourage Islamic penetration in our territory" (Federico Bricolo, LN, CdS, June 30, 2002). Similarly, consequences on public security are a concern here: "Did you know that there are countries that empty their prisons sending us their criminals? The trip is paid by the governments. And Europe covers up for them. I stick to my old idea: we should throw them all into the sea" (Giorgio Marzi, LN activist, CdS, June 24, 2002).

Il Giorno for its part tends to underline how the Bossi–Fini law is consistent with the norms and opinions of Italy's European partners (as if to say, 'we are not alone') and that softer positions with regard to the immigration phenomenon carry risks: "A multiracial society between criminality and hope" (June 19, 2002). There is an attempt to destabilize public opinion, highlighting the dangerousness of immigrant people, pointing out the risks that they may carry dangerous diseases and that they might be terrorists planning biological attacks: "He compared Rom people with pilgrims who during the last centuries carried dangerous diseases" (Maurizio Pagani, responsible for Opera Nomadi, *Il Giorno,* June 19, 2002).

The Enlargement of the European Union, May 1, 2004

The 2004 enlargement of the European Union is probably the event dealt with most differently by *Corriere* and *La Repubblica* when compared with *Il Giorno*. The two broadsheets attach a great deal of importance to the issue, putting it on their front page. As the deadline gets closer, *La Repubblica* also presents a countdown towards 'the new Europe,' and in its editorials gives voice to eminent personalities such as Javier Solana, Council High Representative for CFSP, or the historian Timothy Garton Ash. Both newspapers provide interviews with Commission president, Romano Prodi, who expresses great satisfaction at the achievement and talks about the new challenges Europe has to face in the wake of enlargement.

However, *Il Giorno* gives a lot of space to the so-called 'Roma emergency,' suggesting that enlargement will encourage the arrival of Roms unwilling to integrate with the local culture and representing a risk for citizens' safety. On May 10, *Il Giorno*'s front page headline cries: "'Rom' invasion. Emergency—thousands coming from East: bag-snatchings, burglaries, and robberies multiply. People are scared. Nomads must respect the law." The paper also includes interviews with Milanese citizens expressing their fear and anger concerning what they define as an intolerable situation. Hence, in this paper we find a clear association between the enlargement of the European Union and the exponential growth of immigration from eastern countries, considered as the cause of an increase in the crime rate. The analysis of these elements leads to a dramatically different conceptualisation of the event by *Corriere* and *La Repubblica* on one hand, and *Il Giorno* on the other. While the two major broadsheets highlight the importance of the event, reflecting on its historical significance and its political, social and cultural innovation, *Il Giorno* underlines its negative aspects, drawing a parallel of sorts between the breaking down of frontiers and the breaking down of the rule of law.

Conclusion

The Italian XPP in general and LN in particular, played a central role in bringing down the party system of the 'first republic' at the beginning of the 1990s. LN's antiestablishment discourse, and particularly its attacks on the corrupt *partitocrazia,* captured the zeitgeist of the period in Italian politics and reflected the sentiments of many Italians. Moreover, in the early 1990s, LN commanded the support of over 20% of the electorate in the northern regions of Italy, and was a party of government briefly in 1994. Since then it has continued to be a significant influence in Italian politics. It captured a great deal of attention in 1996 with its theatrical campaign for the secession of the northern regions from the rest of Italy, returned to the centre-right coalition in 2000, and has played a central role in government since 2001.

The electoral success of LN provided it the possibility to make a direct impact on the mainstream parties and politics of the country. It has had a direct impact on the centre-right coalition through its participation in the government, as well as on the media, public opinion, and on the harshening debate on immigration (in particular, on the perceived need for more law and order). Media coverage reflects a political situation in Italy where the extremist discourse of LN has ensured that the immigration issue remains central to the political debate. It also reflects increasing public concerns over the number of immigrants in Italy and overtly links immigrants with criminality and threats to local and national identities. The fact is that these concerns are, in a symbiotic way, both shaped and followed by LN in particular and by other XPPs more generally, such as AN and FI. With regard to the influence of this debate on the frames adopted by other political actors, the effects are diverse. On the one hand, political actors of both the centre-right and centre-left have accepted the need for tougher control and the regulation of immigration, combating criminality (which was usually linked to immigrants), and enforcing law and order. On the other hand, LN's antiimmigrant discourse has moved the centre-left to adopt counterframes which strongly oppose the use of racist, xenophobic and ethno-populist discourses, stressing instead the positive contribution made by immigrants to the economy and the potential richness of 'multiculturalism.'

Despite the collapse of DC, the role of Italy's Catholic politicians remains central to the political debate on immigration in Italy. Those aligned with the centre-left have contributed to the solidaristic positions of this alignment, while those aligned with the centre-right have played a key role in reining in some of the more repressive policy options favoured by right-wing and populist actors.

THE CASE OF CYPRUS

The Political Context of Xenophobia in Cyprus

Cyprus is a tiny island, divided since 1974 with the Greek junta and EOKA B coup and the Turkish army invasion and occupation of the northern territories. Since independence from the British in 1960, the Republic of Cyprus has had a troubled history. The two main communities of the island, the Greek-Cypriots (78%) and the Turkish-Cypriots (18%), have collided over governance and the 'course' of the newly established republic: the Greek-Cypriot nationalist aspiration was to achieve union with Greece (*Enosis*) and the Turkish-Cypriot was partition (*Taksim*). Efforts to resolve the Cyprus problem have so far failed; the latest failure being the UN effort to provide a comprehensive plan (the Annan plan) resolving the problem on the eve of accession to the European Union in April 2004. Greek-Cypriots overwhelmingly rejected it. Turkish-Cypriots, on the other hand, overwhelmingly accepted it, leaving the issue in a state of limbo.

Since 1974, the southern territories under the control of the Republic have experienced a rapid economic growth, particularly in the tourism and service sector, which is sometimes referred as 'the Cyprus miracle.' By the 1980s, the economy was orientated towards Europe, acting as a bridge between the Middle Eastern neighbours and northern African countries (Wilson, 1993) and taking advantage of the cheap labour provided by refugees, as well as of regional and international. In the meantime, Cyprus increasingly began to turn towards EEC and then EU (particularly after Greece accession in 1980) as a means of resolving the Cyprus problem (Trimikliniotis, 2001). By 1990, the Republic had decided to open its doors to migrant labours to meet the labour shortages (Trimikliniotis, 2001). This is where the history of 'immigration' begins: currently there are over 50,000 migrant workers, and this is where the debates over immigration and modernization meet.

Given the specific historic-political context of Cyprus, and the protracted 'ethnic conflict' as a 'national problem' that maintains the divisions in this microstate, as well as the fact that the presence of migrants on a large scale is a very recent phenomenon stretching back only fifteen years, the political divide over the position of migrants and immigration does not correspond to other European contexts. Whilst it can be safely assumed that those forces on the traditional political right generally tend to be more xenophobic, racist and antiimmigrant, on closer examination this general observation is not necessarily accurate in all cases.

On the subject of immigration, there are *intra-party* differences of such a scale that one is able to observe *within the same political party* variations from the staunchly proimmigrant who are positively inclined to the immigrant contribution to economy, culture and society, to those who are outright hostile and express antiimmigrant sentiments. Generally speaking, the intellectual circles close to the political left (whose points of reference are the working class and internationalist solidarity), as well as some cosmopolitan and liberal circles of the centre-left, tend to be more sensitive towards immigrant rights. Tolerant sections of the centre-right and right-wing parties see them as 'necessary for the economy,' reflecting more the employers' positions; however, the left is divided as to effect on the welfare and employment rights of Cypriots, reflecting the trade unions' general reluctance over the presence of migrant workers as a source of cheap, docile and unorganized labour to be used by employers against the organized and class-conscious local working class. Nationalists and conservatives, meanwhile, are generally hostile to migrants, but the actual attitudes and frames with which they articulate these attitudes tend to vary considerably depending on their constituency, and their political leanings and reasons of expediency, as well as ideological grounds concerning the 'ethnic cohesion, purity and quality' of 'the nation,' 'the city,' and so on.

The political party system is sharply divided along left-right ideological lines but there are matters that complicate and distort the traditional left-right divide in the context of Cyprus. We ought to examine in some detail the different dimensions of the political divide between Greek-Cypriot political parties, if we are to understand the newly emerged 'politics of immigration.' We can see these as 'axes of the political divide' in Greek-Cypriot politics.

1. The 'radical' versus 'conservative' dimension (in relation to the socio-economic order): This more or less reflects the international ideological divide between the ideologies of the left (communism/socialism, social democracy, libertarianism, collective/class action), centre-left (social democracy, Keynesianism/welfare state, liberalism, libertarianism), centre-right (mixed economy, capitalism, Keynesianism/welfare state, but also stress on private initiative and enterprise) and right (capitalism, mixed economy, private initiative, individualism and enterprise, privatisation, 'less state'). In practice, consensus politics has meant that 95% of legislation is passed unanimously, and that the 'tripartite' system of industrial relations and advanced social dialogue between the social partners has kept some of the rhetoric alive but not resulted in much actual conflict (in terms of industrial disputes and direct action by workers).

2. The Cyprus issue dimension: One would assume that generally left-wing inclined parties, due to their internationalism (or at least their proclaimed internationalism), are more conciliatory towards the Turkish-Cypriots and are willing to live in peace with them. Historically, this was generally the case: Leftists and liberals tended to be proplace, procompromise and prorapprochement. Matters however, are distorted as the question of nationalism cuts across the ideological and party cleavages; apart from the extreme nationalist position, there has always been a social democratic and centrist hardline nationalism attached to the Greek-Cypriot controlled state. It is well-known from other contexts that nationalism is a complex phenomenon and takes different forms, affecting even those who

are on the left of the political spectrum, particularly in anticolonial and postcolonial contexts where national liberation and patriotism are motivating forces (Balibar, 1991). Furthermore, strands of the left who are anticapitalist and antiimperialist often see nationalism as a 'tactical ally' to achieve their goal, or may even adopt national-ism as part of their programme of 'self-determination of the nation' and 'national liberations.' Matters have become even more confus-ing since 1990 with the collapse of USSR and their allies, as some pro-Soviet left-wing parties have taken up nationalism to replace their now redundant dogmatic ideology.

3. Social issues: On these subjects the distinction is between 'conserva-tive' versus 'liberal/libertarian.' Cypriot society is generally conserva-tive; thus, on issues such as homosexuality, abortion, and freedom of religion, debates do not take place strictly on a left-right divide.

4. The immigration issue: This issue becomes an additional factor con-nected to nation formation and social and economic issues more gen-erally. Moreover, it is many times located within the context of the accession to the Europea Union, as well as the perception of a pro-longed state of 'national emergency' due to the 'intractable' Cyprus problem. However, most MPs interviewed suggested that the issue has not yet been a 'party issue' to be debated in detail.

Amongst the most nationalist are politicians drawn from the political par-ties whose ideological points of reference vary considerably (the centre-right DEKO, the social democratic EDEK, and the far-right segments of the traditional right-wing DESY). Paradoxically, some political actors who are openly anti-Turkish or who are, in some way, opposed to any reconcili-ation with 'the Turks,' on the grounds that "Ankara cannot be trusted" and "the Turkish-Cypriots are objectively mere 'extensions of Ankara'" may appear not to be particularly 'antimigrant.' Individual politicians from other parties, such as the vice president of DEKO, Mr. Pittokopi-tis (a former SEK trade unionist from Pafos), is amongst the most vocal antiimmigrant populists in Cyprus. Established political groups which are considered to be the far-right, such as *Neoi Orizontes* (NEO) and *Euro-paiki Democratia* (EvroDe) are more careful and reserved when making comments on immigrants, but there is a 'hidden racism.' The recently for-mulated party *Europaiki Democratia* (which split away from the broad party of the traditional right DESY following the decision of the leader-ship to support the United Nations plan to resolve the Cyprus problem in the referendum of April 24, 2004) apparently has not yet formulated a policy on the subject of immigration. In fact, these parties appear to be more focused on the subject of the Cyprus problem, voicing opposition to a federation-based settlement, and their rhetoric has anti-Turkish under-tones. They have very recently announced that they will merge into one party (see *Phileleftheros* May 11, 2005).

Both Greek-Cypriots and Turkish-Cypriots have been subjected to colonial racism, practiced by British colonialists during their rule of the island between 1878–1959, which has, in turn, shaped 'local' racisms. *Orientalism*, to use Said's concept (1978), as a colonial discourse underpins British colonialism. *Orientalist* perceptions of Cyprus and Cypriots are apparent in texts of British officials in Cyprus (see Storrs's *Orientations* [1930]). *Orientalism*, as the production of distorted and hegemonic knowledge by the colonist, justifies the conquering and exploitation of other countries. The characterisation and essentialist accounts of Cypriots as colonial subjects and versions of 'the noble savage' are found in these texts. However, these conceptions can better be found in the kind of policies practised by colonial authorities. The discourses of *Orientalism* concerning 'the nature' of Cypriots were instrumental in the ultimately oppressive rule of the British in Cyprus. Even in the postindependence period, the United Kingdom retains British bases and has international treaty obligation as a 'guarantor nation.' This racism underpins and, to a large extent, has *played a constitutive role* in the representations of Greek-Cypriots and Turkish-Cypriots shaping the intercommunal relations. The 'distorted' perception of the 'Other' by each of the two communities was certainly historically mediated by the political role of British colonial policy and a way in which one community was 'played against the other.' Also, the role of the two so-called "motherlands" or "mother-countries" (Greece and Turkey) in the construction of the two racialised communities' ethnic identities must be considered (Calotychos, 1998; Pollis, 1998, p. 85–100).

Historical reasons for the emergence and shape of social forces are crucial to understand the present; however, it would be equally problematic to shift the whole blame forever to the past, as it would obscure the current forces at play, as well as the elements of political choice, human agency and autonomy of the political action, which may well define 'new' social factors acting as current drivers of nationalism and racism in the perpetuation of the phenomena. The ethnic conflict may have been managed and manipulated by 'foreign powers,' but this, by definition, contains 'racialised relations' whose 'boundaries' are constructed and thus expand and contract in accordance with particular social, political and economic conjunctures. The levels and intensity of ethnic conflict are, by and large, regulated by the extent to which the 'racialised boundaries' are internalised by the communities in conflict.

As accession to the European Union approached over the course of the late 1990s, and up until the actual accession day on May 1, 2005, Cypriot 'debates' over immigration and arguments for 'tighter control' appeared to become increasingly 'Europeanized' (See also Trimikliniotis, 2001). Cyprus has, for some time, been in the process of transformation, and not only as a result of economic factors; state legislation and policy harmonisation with the Community acquire, and the political, social, cultural and interpersonal influence of accession, has become more immediate. Debated issues appear to assume a more European twist and there are direct European 'imports' in the everyday political debates, particularly with regard to racism, minority rights, antidiscrimination, immigration control, and trafficking.

Cyprus ought to be seen as a southern European country located in the periphery of the European Union, and, a country that started its Europeanization later than other European countries. It seems that Europeanization of the island went hand in hand with the 'import' of the worse traditions of European history. Adaptation of what may be called *'European apartheid'* (Balibar, 2004) is one of the consequences of such Europeanization. The Cypriots' Europeanization appeared to be one-sided, lacking the full incorporation of the traditions of social solidarity, tolerance, and coexistence.

The political context of Cyprus has not produced, at least so far, a political party whose defining characteristic is antiimmigration, nor has immigration policy become a great dividing line between political parties. Immigration has nonetheless become politicized, particularly since accession to the European Union, and the increasing 'Europeanization' of immigration policy is bringing the issue to the fore. Already some views are being heard that link the accession of Turkey to the European Union to the 'danger of being flooded by migrants,' giving a new 'Europeanized' twist to anti-Turkish sentiments. Many politicians invoke European Union policy and even call on the European Union to help in the management of immigrants and asylum seekers who stop over in Cyprus on their way to the heart of Europe.

Discursive Reconstruction of 'Us' vs. 'Them'

Xenophobia and racism takes particular, and (partly) internally differentiated, shapes and characteristics in Cyprus. This is mainly because of the partition of the island and the ethnic conflict between Greek-Cypriots and Turk-Cypriots. Anti-Muslim sentiments have been stronger than antiimmigrant ones. However, relatively high levels of immigration to Cyprus and European Union accession have contributed to an increase in antiimmigrant attitudes and policies.

Given the absence of a XPP similar to other countries examined in the research project, the study is based on ethno-nationalist parties and politicians holding strong anti-Turkish and antiimmigrant sentiments, and disseminating propaganda, in Cyprus. This makes a political axis of the extreme right parties, the *Neoi Orizontes* (NEO) and *Europaiki Demokratia* (ED) as well as ADYK, which is a one-person party in parliament. It was set up by a former Minister of Interior, Dinos Michaelides, and is a party with a nationalistic stance on the Cyprus problem and antifederation. The discourses of other parties, such as the centre-right Democratic Party (DEKO), the Social Democratic Party (EDEK), and the right-wing party (DESY), also contain ethno-nationalist elements.

The problem of the lack of a XPP and of party programmes to analyze, forced us to focus on the actual content of the political debates, speeches, parliamentary debates, and existing interviews with politicians of the two most nationalist, 'anti-Turk' and antiimmigrant parties (both recently established), NEO and ED. These two political groups have merged into a single party, Evropaiko Komma (European Party, EK) but a small group of the ED chose to continue on its own. They are considered to be the 'ethno-nationalistic' right, as they have the hardest line on the Cyprus problem and how they perceive relations with Turkey and the Turkish-Cypriots. Nevertheless, they appear on the whole to be rather 'reserved' in their public comments regarding immigration. On closer reading however, their public statements and their discourses in interviews do reveal much about their attitudes.

The main sources of analysis were the three right-wing parties' party documents and public declarations and debates, as well as, media interviews and completing interviews conducted by the Cyrus research team with the two party officials Nicos Koutsou, the leader of the NEO, and Taramountas, the former leader of ED and the current deputy president of the newly established party, EK. The following frames have been analyzed: (a) Collective Identity; (b) Employment Issues; (c) Welfare Issues; (d) Law and Order Issues; (e) Liberal Values; (f) Antiestablishment; (g) Immigrant Status; and (h) Legitimisation of Racism. However, not all frames were explicitly and frequently used in Cyprus. Those frames most frequently used are presented here.

Collective Identity

The frame is used as an instrument to make a distinction between Greek-Cypriots and Turk-Cypriots. Immigration is also related to this issue and is seen as 'culturally' different from 'Us.' Taramountas argues that settlers are a tool in Turkey's hands to put pressure on the Greek-Cypriot side by changing demographically the occupied areas (interview, February 22, 2005). He refers to Greek-Cypriots as a nation with specific cultural and historical roots. He conceives migrants, and especially settlers from the Turkish part of the island, as a major threat. According to Taramountas, the colonisation of the occupied territories and the resulting settlement is not only a war crime, but also a problem because "our society cannot absorb them culturally, as they are so different." The same rhetoric is repeated regularly, irrespective of his public, in speeches, interviews and TV programmes. Even Koutsou offers similar statements, though more covertly, making a connection between immigration and a need for the preservation and reproduction of the Greek-Cypriot culture and traditions.

As the leader of EK, Taramountas expressed the fear regarding civic values 'brought in' by migrants. He speaks of other cultures in terms or 'right' and 'wrong': "Some have the right attitude, others are unacceptable (as regards law)." He asserts:

> They sit on the pavement with an oriental style, drink until early in the morning, have very loud music, you think you are in an oriental

bazaar. Someone should point out to them that this is not the way that is done here in Cyprus . . . if the police go there every day.

This is an opinion widely shared and regularly repeated by antiimmigration politicians in Cyprus.

Employment and Welfare Issues

This frame is mainly used to demonstrate the 'burden' of immigrants on the labour market and the 'abuse of welfare' by NEO, ED, and EK. Labour force immigration was introduced in Cyprus in 1989. The shortage of labour in specific sectors of the economy was the determining factor that allowed the change of immigration policy in 1989/1990 with the consent of the trade unions. However, the resident permits were on a temporary basis. This and the crossborders movement of 7,000–10,000 Turkish-Cypriot workers to the South since April 2004 were upheld by NEO, ED, and EK as a danger to Cyprus. There are party declarations and addresses in the party leaders' speeches and interviews on the competition of 'law paid' immigrant workers with Greek-Cypriot workers, and the abuse of welfare.

Law and Order Issues

This frame is used by the right-wing nationalist parties, NEO, ED, and EK to relate the immigration of Turkish-Cypriots, Roma and other immigrants to southern Cyprus with criminality. The first issue is about 'illegal immigrants.' The leader of EK, Taramountas, stated that 'immigration is an open wound' and characterizes migration issues as a serious problem. Through the narrative of specific everyday events, he allowed for sweeping generalisations inferring that crime is an everyday part of the culture of specific migrant groups. By innuendo, he let it be known that their cultural attitudes and traditions are an 'obstacle' for their societal integration. He says that "migrants cannot share the same values as locals," and argued for "more policing." Even Koutsou utters its concern about the need for controlling "illegal immigration." He means that the European Union should pay for the control because Cyprus stands now as its southern border and controls the influx of immigrants and fights criminality.

Antiestablishment

This frame is almost totally absent from the political scene of Cyprus. Since all parties have either a hardline or a softline of ethno-nationalism, and political developments during the last decades have been favourable for Greek-Cypriots and for the establishment in the country, there is no place for antiestablishment propaganda. Although a few hardliner politicians from small parties have declared their satisfaction with the establishment's acceptance of the United Nations plan for reconciliation and a federal solution to the Cyprus problem, the opposition has been marginal.

The Dichotomy of 'Us' against the Muslim 'Others'

The ethno-nationalist right wing parties have depicted Islam and Muslims as a danger to the Greek-Cypriots' collective identity and indeed existence. The postcolonial history of the constructed conflict between Greek-Cypriots and Turk-Cypriots, with religious undertones, has been expanding anti-Muslim sentiments. The murder of Muslims during the civil war prior to the Turkish invasion of the island in July 1974, and the division of Cyprus by the Green Line which separates the two peoples from each other, has lead to a reinforcement of anti-Muslim sentiments and attitudes on the Greek side of the island. The anti-Muslim attitudes sometimes take the form of direct physical attacks on persons who are of Muslim appearance. Following the killing of two Greek-Cypriots in the village of Deryneia by Turkish soldiers in August 1996 (in demonstrations against the Turkish army occupation of the north of the island), a group of Pakistani and Bangladeshi workers in the same area were badly beaten up by a group of local youths, who also told their victims that the reason for this attack was because they were Muslims, like the Turks who had killed their covillagers a few weeks earlier. Another example is the attack in Ayia Napa, on August 29, 1996. Apparently, the students were brutally beaten with sticks and other instruments by a group of Greek-Cypriots threatening to kill them if they did not leave the country within 24 hours. The motive reported in the media was that the students were Muslims like the Turks. Politicians from the three mentioned parties have repeatedly presented Muslims, Turks, and immigrants with Islamic backgrounds (such as Pakistanis and Bangladeshis) as a danger to 'the culture,' 'the values,' 'the religion,' and 'the traditions' of Cyprus.

Assessing Impacts of XPP

The electoral system of Cyprus allows even small parties to get a mandate in parliament. There are some parties with only one representative in the parliament. This will give even the hardline ethno-nationalist parties the opportunity to participate in the parliamentary debates and decision makings. However, the small differences between the hardline ethno-nationalist parities and the mainstream parties on antiimmigration and anti-Turkish issues makes it very difficult to assess any possible direct, as well as indirect, effects of hardline ethno-nationalists on the major decision makings and opinion changes in Cyprus. In order to illustrate the framing of the 'Others' as a problem, and the same dichotomisation of

'Us' against 'Them,' the mainstream parties' use of XPP frames will now be presented.

The largest political parties are those of the traditional left and right. AKEL is a party that evolved from the Communist Party (Κομμουνιστικό Κόμμα Κύπρου) in the 1940s and is the oldest political party. It has consistently polled from one quarter to a third of the votes. Its communist ideology has not prevented it from acting as a moderate centre-left party in practice.

The main party in the centre-right alliance in Cyprus is DESY. The party is the traditional conservative party of the Greek-Cypriot nationalist right that was established in 1976. It encapsulated both a pragmatic/conciliatory wing and a far-right irredentist nationalist wing. It was organized from the remnants of the EOKA associations, the anti-Makarios nationalist segments, and others on the right, but its leader, Glafkos Clerides, had for years been an associate of the first president of Cyprus, archbishop Makarios. Essentially, he is a pragmatist and tactician and has been quite happy to play the nationalist card to gain power. In 1976, he found himself out of favour with Makarios and formed a party with 'disaffected' populations mainly drawn from the extreme right. It has links with both the employers' associations and SEK. Like AKEL, it polls about one third of the votes.

Moreover, the case of Cyprus is special, since the political parties are very much connected to trade unions. The trade union, PEO, is linked with the political party AKEL, while trade union DEOK is linked to the political party EDEK, and trade union SEK is linked to the political parties DESY and DEKO. Therefore, the declarations of such trade unions and their representatives (who have often become politicians) are also included in the analysis.

Concerning the party press, there is only one party newspaper, *Haravgi*, which is owned by AKEL, and is a political party that stretches from the far-left to the centre-left. There are a number of right-wing papers such as *Simerini, Alithia, Mahi*, which are owned by private companies but are loyal to specific segments of the right-wing political parties such as DESY. As already explained, the trade unions and their press are also connected to political parties; for this reason the PEO and SEK newspapers (*Ergatiko Vema* and *Ergatiki Foni*, respectively) were also included in the study.

The lack of party programmes and other party documents is compensated for by conducting interviews with party officials and politicians, as well as, using other sources of information, such as parliamentary debates and media interviews. The two 'party newspapers' selected are *Haravgi* (AKEL) and the right-wing *Simerini* (DESY). *Simerini* together with *Mahi* are the most antiimmigrant, anti-Turkish, and nationalistic papers in Cyprus. The trade union's press, with direct contact with and support for the two main parties (namely, AKEL and DESY), are also used in the analysis.

Collective Identity

This frame is highly related to the partition of the island. The traditional right-wing parties' nationalism was based on a desire for reunion with Greece. However, from the late 1980s onwards, significant ideological changes have taken place in Cyprus in the makeup of 'nationalism' and the shape of the wider political landscape. The old irredentist nationalism of 'Enosis' was transformed into something new. Greek-Cypriot or Helleno-Cypriot nationalism emerged which centred around a Greek-Cypriot controlled state in Cyprus rather than union with Greece: irredentist nationalism had mutated. However, the two ethno-nationalist flanges in the Cypriot politics are engaged in 'Otherization' of Turk-Cypriots. Moreover, since the early 1990s, the 'Otherization' has been extended to include even Roma and the migrant worker.

There is a consensus between the two political blocs and parties that the European Union should "help in the control of migrants inflow," since Cyprus is the bridge between the European Union and migrants (Asian, African and Arab) countries on their way to Europe (Parliamentary debate, February 1998). The right-wing political parties, in particular DESY, propagate that Turkey's membership in the European Union would mean the inflow of a great mass of Turkish migrants, a danger that will have negative economic, employment, cultural and religious impacts. For example, the Minister of Interior, Christodoulos Christodoulou, argued that migrants have a negative impact on "our liberal values and national identity" (*Simerini,* November 10, 2003). AKEL is a profederation party supporting the unification of Greek-Cypriots and Turkish-Cypriots as the primary means of opposing the partition of Cyprus. The party and its politicians refer often to the two people's "common needs," "common history," and the "solidarity between workers on both sides."

Employment and Welfare Issues

This frame has been used by the established party to 'evaluate' the position of the 'Others' in the Cypriot labour market and the welfare system. Since the mid-1990s, the issue of immigrant workers became a political issue for both political blocs. In 1997, *Simerini* published an article titled "Unemployment and criminality because of migrants employment" (March 17, 1997) in which the role of migrant workers in increasing unemployment among Cypriots and the indirect effect on the rise of criminality were discussed. The press continues to present immigrant workers as a problem (*Simerini,* March 11, 2003).

Out of the 52 items classified in this frame, 11 were from *Haravgi* referring to a negative impact on employment and welfare to articulate its fears and reservations over the 'inflow' of migrants. In 1989, *Haravgi* used a revealing subtitle: "Employers dismiss or do not employ Cypriots to create an artificial shortage of labour" (September 19, 1989). In 1996, in an article titled "Alien workers" asserts that migrant workers may be used by their employers against the national workers: "migrant workers and especially illegal aliens have become a problem to the Cypriot society" (*Haravgi*, November 10, 1996). Similarly, in 2001, Pontian Greeks are referred to as "job stealers" because they accept lower wages and benefits (July 22, 2001). PEO's newspaper *Ergatiko Vema* adopts a similar tone to support more policing in relation to migrants, since they are a threat to the society and economy. The titles used in two of its articles are illustrative: "Dangers due to the uncontrolled entry of migrant workers" (October 9, 1996) and "Whilst unemployment rises for Cypriots; Foreigners, Foreign workers everywhere" (September 8, 1993).

The parliamentary debates and politicians' articles in, and their interviews with, the mainstream press often present immigrants as being more or less a danger for the Cypriot labour market, although for different reasons. However, the issue of welfare is not, in this respect, as frequent as is the issue of employment.

Law and Order Issues

Diachronically, many politicians and government officials used arguments that fall under this frame to legitimise their negative attitude towards migrants' presence in Cyprus. In 1996, minister Mousiouttas claimed that among the social problems relating to the presence of migrants is the increase of criminality (*Simerini*, June 30, 1996). In 2003, the then head of Aliens and Immigration Department, Theodorou argued that prostitution and illegal immigration are the two main problems that police have to deal with (*Simerini*, March 11, 2003). In the same year, Justice Minister Doros Theodorou made the infamous statement about "50% of Eastern European women dreamed of becoming prostitutes" (November 27, 2003).

'Conflict' and 'criminality' are regularly invoked by ethno-nationalists and populist politicians, sometimes by narrating 'stories' they know involving migrants involved in crime. The MP Taramountas used this extensively. The most prominent and vocal example are the statements of the MP Pittokopitis, who argued that "crime is in their blood" (Project interview, February 18, 2005). His main political antiimmigrant stance is heavily based on the claim that "they are a threat to our society, culture and nation as they are inherently linked to criminality." Even the leftist press, *Haravgi*, links criminality with the presence of "foreign workers," especially the Pontians (January 25, 1991).

Mass Media and the 'Others'

The role of mass media in 'Otherization' of Turks and immigrants in Cyprus has barely been studied. However, a few studies show that the mainstream media are highly connected to different powerful actors, including the political parties, in Cyprus (Christophorou, 1984). In order to study the role of the Cypriot mainstream press in increasing xenophobia and racism, the following publications from the mainstream press are chosen: *Phileleftheros,* the most established 'broadsheet' of Cyprus; *Simerini* is the second newspaper, which, while a mainstream newspaper (it is the second most popular newspaper in Cyprus), is also a right-wing tabloid that is one of the main proponents of Greek-Cypriot nationalism and one of the main supporters of right-wing political parties; and the third newspaper is *Haravgi* which is AKEL's newspaper, but also a widely circulated mainstream paper. For the purposes of this study both *Simerini* and *Haravgi* were used twice, both as party press and as mainstream press. The 'critical events' that have been chosen in this study are:

1. the change of immigration policy, 1989/1990;
2. the killing of two Greek-Cypriots in anti-Turkish demonstrations in the village of Deryneia in 1996;
3. the attacks on the World Trade Center and Pentagon in the United States, September 11, 2001; and
4. the enlargement of the European Union, May 1, 2004.

The Change of Immigration Policy, 1989–1990

Following political debate criticising the government for not having an immigration policy between 1989 and 1990, a new law was passed under which migrant workers were allowed to work on a temporary basis on specific jobs and for specific employers. This is one of the most important changes concerning immigration up until that date. It coincided with the collapse of 'actually existing socialism' in Eastern Europe that had a twin impact for Cyprus: (a) migrant workers from South-East Asia, the Arabic neighbours and Eastern Europe were employed in certain, poorly paid jobs for which there was a shortage of labour, and (b) Eastern European businesses were set up in Cyprus, particularly in Limassol. The change of the migration law was widely discussed by all the three newspapers. *Phileleftheros* warned against unlimited and uncontrolled immigration from the east, and increasing criminality and lawlessness. *Haravgi* was more concerned about the competition of a 'foreign and cheap labour force' with the 'Cypriot workers.' The tabloid *Simerini*'s reports were more populist and alarming.

The Killing of Two Greek-Cypriots in Anti-Turkish Demonstrations in the Village of Deryneia

The reports of the three newspapers revolved around the killing of two Greek-Cypriots in an anti-Turkish demonstration in the village of Deryneia. Condemnation of the killing was the main angle of the newspapers' reports. The reports of *Phileleftheros* and *Simerini* included articles and reportages about some antiimmigrant and racist insults against immigrants being made after the event. Reports concluded that many immigrants who "looked like Turks" or Muslims were attacked. Even the Roma minority was alleged to be "Turkish spies." There were frequent reports in the three newspapers about the problems related to the immigration of the increasing numbers of Roma from the north.

The Attacks on World Trade Center and Pentagon in the United States, September 11, 2001

The attacks on the World Trade Center in New York have been frequently reported in the mainstream media. However, it did not produce an immediate anti-Arab or anti-Muslim public reaction in Cyprus as there is little pro-American sentiment amongst the Greek-Cypriots and Greeks in general. Nevertheless, the 'antiterrorist frenzy' which was widely circulated by the mainstream media, produced 'novel' stereotypes and incidents against individuals who suffered as a result of false accusations of 'looking like a terrorist.' It has certainly reinforced the anti-Turk and anti-Muslim attitudes in Cyprus. Some of the articles in the newspapers were accusing Islam and Muslims of being responsible for 'terrorism.'

The Enlargement of the European Union, May 1, 2004

The enlargement of the European Union in 2004 was a major media event in Cyprus. While the south became a member of the European Union, the north remained outside the union. This was among the most important aspect of reporting in the mainstream media. *Haravgi* warned, for instance, that the European Union membership risks giving the separation of the island a permanent status. There were warnings in the two other newspapers too, but this time concerning the risks of increasing immigration for the island. The accession to the European Union on May 1 was even presented in *Phileleftheros* and *Simerini* as a victory for Greek-Cypriots and a defeat for Turk-Cypriots.

In general, the conclusion that can be safely extracted from the study of the mainstream newspapers' reactions to the selected events is that *Phileleftheros* mostly adopts an antiimmigrant, ethno-nationalist approach. The *Harvagi* is more moderate and, in many cases, shows more proimmigrant attitudes. The tabloid *Simerini* usually takes an antiimmigrant position to events and reports them dramatically.

Conclusion

In the context of Cyprus there is a serious problem of defining XPP in the same way as in other European countries. The 'national issue' (i.e., the 'Cyprus problem') is the determining factor in defining whether a party is 'ethno-nationalist' or 'radical right.' The determination of who belongs to the 'nation' is premised on how 'the nation' is defined. For the ethno-nationalist Greek-Cypriots, the 'state' is the 'instrument' for the reproduction of the 'nation' and the 'protection of the national territory,' as well as the 'protection' from other 'threats' to its well-being (health, welfare, internal security, the ethno-national order, customs, ethics, traditions, and moral standards). Immigration is normally articulated as a 'threat' to the south. Such views are regularly aired in the political arena and across the media.

However, the immigration issue has always been subordinated to the 'main problem,' or the main 'enemy,' what many Greek-Cypriots have referred to as 'the main front' (*το κύριο μέτωπο*)—namely, Turks. In Cyprus, there is an 'ever present' discursive frame, the Cyprus problem, which is the point of reference in defining the strategy for the 'ethnos,' the 'nation.' The 'Other' is primarily the 'Turk'; however, the 'Other' is increasingly multiplying beyond the Turk, to include Turkish-Cypriots, Roma and migrant workers. For Greek-Cypriot nationalist ideology, the Turkish-Cypriots are depicted as the mere 'appearance' or smokescreen for a more powerful and sinister force. Similarly, Roma, who are considered to be a part of the Turkish-Cypriot community, are viewed with suspicion as 'spies,' 'criminals' and 'vagabonds.' These are primarily media-generated images which have become part of popular knowledge in creating what can be called 'common sense' racism and xenophobia.

A particular property of xenophobia in Cyprus is the role that antiimmigrant and xenophobic populist politicians play. In a small society such as Cyprus, the role of individual politicians in acting as 'carriers' of antiimmigrant populist opinions, and as 'articulators' of xenophobic-loaded ideologies, is of particular importance as the media amplifies such views in an alarmist fashion. This is confirmed by international reports on xenophobia and racism in Cyprus. The Second ECRI Report (2001) refers to "a growing tendency towards the perception of the immigrant and the foreigner as a potential threat to the Cypriot standard of living." A cultural racism appears to be especially strong amongst those nationalist 'intellectuals' who are in positions of power and are usually considered to be men or women of letters—teachers, for instance, or ministers, or university professors.

Individual ministers and other political leaders play a decisive role in making comments that find their way into becoming media headlines. Even the second ECRI Report on Cyprus (2001) criticized the "inflammatory speeches" by certain politicians against immigrant workers. ECRI deplores instances of racially-inflammatory speech by public figures targeting these groups. ECRI strongly encourages the Cypriot authorities to take all possible

measures to prevent such a trend from evolving into more overt and generalised manifestations of hostility vis-à-vis members of minority groups.

This study shows that there is a web of politicians, political parties, and
mainstream media that together are 'Otherising' both Turks and migrants.
Racism and xenophobia is a part of 'political correctness' and often hidden
behind 'anti-Turkish,' anti-occupation, and nationalist sentiments.

THE CASE OF POLAND

The Political Context of Xenophobia in Poland

The national borders of Poland as a country have many times been changed
in its modern history because of wars, occupations, and revolutions. After
1945, with the shift in frontiers and the displacement of inhabitants,
Poland became relatively ethnically homogeneous and minority problems
were radically marginalised in internal politics. After the fall of the Berlin
Wall in 1989, the Polish state (rather than Polish society, which had already
acknowledged the existence of minorities under the socialist regime) discovered the political significance of ethnic minorities in Poland. Pressure
from the European Union, and the increasing social salience of national
minorities with their political and cultural organisations that challenge the
traditional perception of Poland as 'an ethnic homogeneous country,' make
the need for a new policy necessary.

Poland between the two World Wars was polyethnic. According to the
first census in 1921, national minorities constituted at least one third of the
total population of the country. These were Ukrainians (more than 14%),
Jews (7.8%), Byelorussians (3.9%), Germans (3.8%), and other groups such
as Russians, Lithuanians, and Czechs (approximately 1%). The Polish state
was faced with a challenge to manage a country beyond ethic divides. The
interwar Poland attempted different variants, starting from the federation-
national model, and ending with a homogenous model of the nation state.
Politicians and ideologists today like to refer to the heritage of the inter-
war years. Although the period between the two World Wars was not only
a positive experience concerning ethnic relations in Poland, it created a
model of tolerance and generalised respect for ethnic minorities and for
heterogeneity. This is used now, even by the contemporary state elites, as a
model for organising ethnic relations in the country.

The systemic change of 1989 in Poland has created not only a public
arena within which various visions of a new social order—for example,
democratic, liberal, and conservative—are contended. It has also recreated
a 'grey zone' of radical, especially *national,* ideologies typical of the inter-
war period. The past decade has not only been a period when peaceful
building of the new democratic order and the nurturing of the ideas of an
'open society' took place, but also a period when extremist, nationalist,

and quasi-fascist groupings (so-called 'leader's teams') had emerged. They strived to justify their political existence by invoking traditions of the inter-war Polish nationalism. Simultaneously, it was the time when completely new nationalist milieu appeared, these attempting to create a new integral nationalism out of the frustrations and resentments of various 'losers' of the systemic transformation.

After 1989, many parties and political organisations were formed which labelled themselves as 'nationalist parties,' and were characterized by small membership, paramilitary organisational structures, the use of aggressive ideological rhetoric, and, what is most important, their acting within the legally defined margin of the public sphere. They presented themselves as 'true national parties' in opposition to parties of the centre and of the left. It should be emphasized that the aggressive nationalism of such small parties and extraparliamentarian groupings has marginalised them in the public sphere. Until 2001, when the 'Polish Families' League' (LPR) was founded and won parliamentary seats in the elections, the parliamentarian right-nationalist groupings (PC, PK) and nationalist-Christian ones (ZCHN, KPN) attracted much less attention from the public because their pro-state attitudes and activities (aiming at strengthening their presence in parliaments and cabinets) constituted dominant elements in their political rhetoric and activities.

The extraparliamentarian nationalist right included '*Stronnictwo Narodowo-Demokratyczne, Stronnictwo Narodowe,*' '*Ojczyzna,*' '*Polska Wspólnota Narodowa,*' '*Polskie Stronnictwo Narodowe,*' and '*Narodowe Odrodzenie Polski.*' They were supported significantly by paramilitary, mainly youth, organisations that swelled all over the country. Their members and followers were unified by a conviction that they do not belong to the recently formed political establishment. Running into a conflict with the established legal order was one of the permanent elements of their political game (violating the law of freedom of speech in general and the law of establishing associations, in particular). Representatives of such parties and groupings 'legitimized' their 'political existence' by violating civil and criminal laws and by declaring hostility towards the new state, its elites and politics. However, the overt xenophobic propaganda and rhetoric entered into the Polish political sphere in the electoral campaign of 1997. Yet, while xenophobia and racism existed among many parliamentary and extraparliamentary parties and political associations, it was not the main ideological property of those parties and associations. This is mainly because of the particularity of the Polish history.

Poland has a specific situation concerning the discourses of the 'Others' or of immigrants. Given the country's socialist past, there is not any significant number of immigrants in the country. An estimation of a precise number of immigrants is a difficult task, since there are many groups with an immigrant background who are living in Poland without official registration. The last general census that was carried out in 2002 has indicated that 49,221 foreigners had received a permanent residence permit in Poland. This number constitutes less than 0.1% of the country's population. However, there are other categories of foreigners who should be added to this number, that is, immigrants who come to Poland with tourist visas and get involved in seasonal work, immigrants who stay in Poland illegally, immigrants who have a temporary residence permit, and those with immigrant backgrounds who have been granted Polish citizenship. Public opinion surveys conducted in September 1999, August 2004, and February 2005 by the Public Opinion Research Centre in Warsaw (CBOS) shows that less than one-third of the adult population of Poland knows a foreigner living in the country. The proportion increased between the years 1999 and 2004 by 5%. Residence size, education and age all affect the probability that a person will know a foreigner. People living in big cities are more likely to know them than are residents of small towns and rural areas. Young people most often declare they know people from other countries who live in Poland.

Besides the real number of immigrants in Poland, immigrants make up the category of the 'Others' who are living among 'Us.' The same surveys show that one third of the population disagree with the principle of the right for everyone to come and settle in Poland. A vast majority think that Poland does not need immigrants. The respondents who think Poland does need immigrants are less than a fifth of the adult population. Positive attitudes towards immigrants mainly concerns immigrants from east and central European countries. Immigrants from non-European countries, in particular Muslims, are increasingly seen to create 'cultural clashes' and terrorism.

Discursive Reconstruction of 'Us' vs. 'Them'

Following the 1991 elections, the core group of nationalist parliamentarian parties was constituted by: (a) *Zjednoczenie Chrześcijańsko-Narodowe* (Christian-National Union, CNU), which was the focal party of Wyborcza Akcja Katolicka (Catholic Electoral Action, WAK) with 8.7% of the votes; (b) *Polskie Stronnictwo Ludowe* (Polish Peasant Party, PSL), with 8.7% of the votes; and (c) *Konfederacja Polski Niepodległej* (Confederation of Independent Poland, KPN), with 7.5% of the votes.(KPN was founded in 1979 as the first independent political party in Poland.) The features they all shared in common were their pro-state orientation, their antisocialism, and their protection of continuity and national traditions, as well as their promulgating 'ethical and moral Catholic values.' It was only since 1997, during the campaign preceding parliamentary elections that the significant xenophobic elements in political activities at the national level came to the fore. However, xenophobia and antiimmigrant attitudes were not translated into the political programmes and ideological credos as yet formulated by the parties. Overt racism and xenophobic political programmes and activities emerged overwhelmingly in 2001 when the *Liga Polskich Rodzin* (Polish Families' League, LPR) and the xenophobic youth organisations of the extreme right, *Młodzież Wszechpolska* (All-Polish Youth, MW), were established. The European debate concerning Poland's membership in the European Union, and, related to it, discussions concerning the need to defend the nation's and the state's cultural and economic sovereignty against 'the European threat,' became important elements in crystallising the tendencies.

The appearance of LPR in the public sphere in 2001, and the relatively high level of electoral support that it won in the parliamentary elections radicalised nationalist tendencies, including revitalising the 1930s tradition of radical nationalism, invoking Dmowski, his 'national camp' and the tradition of anti-Semitism. For the first time since 1989, a political party appeared in the Polish parliament that openly voiced its affinity to radical nationalism, without proclaiming extreme xenophobic messages at the level of its basic programmatic declarations. These were the reasons why, in this study, LPR is classified in the Polish political context as a XPP.

LPR unites more than 20 small parties, many national-Catholic groupings, such as *Stronnictwo Narodowe* (a political party), *Rodzina Warszawska or Stowarzyszenie Polskiej Racji Stanu* (associations), and the MW (a xenophobic youth organisation). Father Rydzyk, who is the well-known director of the 'Radio Maryja' (a xenophobic radio station), initiated LPR. The league was even joined by some right-wing oriented politicians under the leadership of Zygmunt Wrzodak who was the leader of a radical nationalist right wing group within the workers' Solidarity during the Marshal Law period and afterwards. From the beginning, the key role in the party was played by the Giertych family—Maciej Giertych (father) and Roman Giertych (son)—who proclaimed themselves to be heirs to Roman Dmowski's national camp tradition of the 1930s. Roman's grandfather, Jędrzej Giertych, was one of the founders of the 'national camp.'

Despite the fact that this was its first time running in parliamentary elections, LPR won the support of 7.87 % of voters and introduced its members both to Sejm and Senate. It was represented by 38 MPs (against the total number of 460) and by two senators (against the total number of 100), and Roman Giertych became head of LPR's parliamentary club. Currently, since some MPs have now left, the club counts 25 members. LPR MPs participate in standing for Sejm committees but, despite the club's efforts, none of its members managed to be elected as the Sejm Vice-Speaker because they were not considered by other parties as 'important actors' in parliament.

During the local government elections, which were held in October 2002, LPR put up electoral lists together with other 'rightist' groupings, such as *Zjednoczenie Chrześcijańsko-Narodowe and Komitet Wyborczy, Rodzina i Ojczyzna*. It (LPR) was supported by 14.29% of voters and altogether won 92 seats in regional assemblies. In September 2003, during LPR's II

Congress, Maciej Giertych was elected the party chair. Marek Kotlinowski became president of the party's Main Board, while Zygmunt Wrzodak was elected chairman of LPR's Political Council. Despite its clearly anti-European Union orientation, LPR participated in the elections for the European Parliament and gained 16% of the votes, granting them 10 seats (compared to the total number of 54 Polish EMPs). LPR's Eurodeputies joined the *Independence and Democracy Group*. In its *Deklaracja Ideowa* (Ideological Declaration) and its *Program* the LPR presents itself as a nationalist and Catholic party and points to ideological linkages with the extreme right national-democratic formation of Roman Dmowski, which was active before World War II.

The following sources of data have been selected in order to analyze the framing of 'the Others' by LPR and its influence within the Polish political sphere:

* Program ideowy Ligi Polskich Rodzin z 5 kwietnia 2002 r. (Ideological programme of LPR, April 5, 2002);
* Odzyskać polską samorządność"—Program samorządowy Ligi Polskich Rodzin (To regain Polish self-governance—LPR Programme for the local government);
* Ramowy program LPR dla wyborów samorządowych, 2002 r. (Framework programme of LPR for the local election, 2002);
* Skrót programu gospodarczego, trwałego rozwoju, wykorzystującego naukę, wiedzę oraz zasoby przyrodnicze, zmierzające do samowystarczalności kraju dla niepodległej Polski oraz suwerennego Narodu Polskiego, LPR, Warszawa, 3 maja 2003 r. (The abridged version of the economic programme of sustainable development, use of science, knowledge and natural resources for self-sufficiency of the state, for independent Poland and sovereign Polish Nation, LPR, Warsaw, May 3, 2003);
* Stanowisko II Kongresu LPR w sprawie sytuacji politycznej Polski po zaakceptowaniu w referendum przez Naród wejścia Polski do UE, wrzesień 2003 (Standpoint of the Second Congress of LPR on the political situation of Poland after the acceptance by the Nation of the accession of Poland to EU); and
* Program posłów LPR do Parlamentu Europejskiego, 2004 (Program of the LPR Members of European Parliament, 2004).

For the analysis of LPR party press, two titles were selected: '*Informator Parlamentarny LPR*' (Parliamentary Bulletin of LPR) and '*Opoka w kraju*' (Bedrock in the State). *Informator Parlamentarny LPR* (*IP*) is a periodical which comes out once a month or once in every two months. The first issue appeared in 2003. It is edited by the Press Office of LPR Parliamentary Club. Each issue contains information about the activities of the parliamentary club, submitted legislative initiatives, bill proposals, statements and speeches made by the MPs from LPR, and the club's stances on legislative proposals, as well as information about the activities of the MEPs from LPR. The other LPR journal, *Opoka w kraju* (*OK*), is a journal edited solely by Maciej Giertych who is an ideologue and nationalist politician, currently an MP from LPR, a member of LPR Political Council and the LPR candidate for the President of Poland. It has been published at irregular intervals since 1993, usually at the rate of three to four issues a year. It is distributed free of charge to selected people (among those to Polish bishops), and also available at the national and local offices of LPR as well as on the internet. Each issue contains analyses and comments on the current political, economic, social, cultural and religious events. The issues of *IP* and *OK* in the period 2001 to 2004 were selected for the analysis.

The speeches and central political declarations of the LPR party leaders and key representatives Roman Giertych, Janusz Dobrosz, and Stanisław Gudzowski, from between 2002 and 2004, have been analyzed. In addition, the parliamentary debates of the representatives of LPR on the issues on immigration from 1998 to 2005 have been included in the analyses.

The same frames of analysis that have been used for the other countries in the study—namely (a) Collective Identity; (b) Employment Issues; (c) Welfare Issues; (d) Law and Order Issues; (e) Liberal Values; (f) Antiestablishment; (g) Immigrant Status; and (h) Legitimisation of Racism—have also been used for Poland. The most frequently used frames in Poland are presented here.

Collective Identity

LPR's party programme as a whole is formulated within the frame constituted by references to two most important values: the *Nation* (interpreted in ethno-cultural terms, as an organic community) and the *State* (perceived as a political representation of the Polish nation). They claim to guarantee the welfare of Poles, the demographic growth of Poles, preservation of the national tradition and culture, maintenance of territorial integrity, and the reformation of the state's structures. The rhetoric inherent in the discourses of the party indicates a strong sense of belonging to the 'Polish nation' presented, in ethno-cultural terms, as the only lawful owners of the Polish land. Land becomes here the key element of the Polish cultural identity, the basis for the Polish nation's sovereignty and independence. Protecting the Polish land becomes a patriotic duty, a type of acting in defence of the culture and identity of Poles. Hence, already in the first political programme formulated by LPR, a postulate was found that the ownership of the Polish land must be in the Polish hands.

In the party press there are several articles and editorial notes that warn against "multiculturalism" and the "mixture of cultures and different folks":

> Even in a country of so racial uniformity like Poland, they try to make
> a Polish man of E. Olisadebe or to emphasize the presence of collared
> children in music bands. It can be already foreseen that after entering
> the EU we will be forced to accept (open borders) masses of multi-col-
> lared immigrants who are so numerous in the Western Europe entering
> Poland. (*OK*, 2002, Vol. 43)

However, it is not only 'coloured immigrants' who are considered by LPR
as 'a threat' to the Polish nation, but also, to some degree, Germans and
Jews. The Germans are mentioned both as a German minority inhabiting
Polish territory and the German nation as a neighbouring country.

LPR leaders' and politicians' statements clearly indicate the belief that
national, cultural and religious differentiation within a single state leads
to tensions and is a source of threat to the Pole's national identity, as well
as to the stability and independence of the state in cultural, political and
economic spheres. For this reason, the state should implement a policy of
strong control over immigration and over all forms of 'foreign penetration'
in Poland, such as foreign capital and foreign cultural fashions. The party
leaders and politicians present Poland and the Polish nation as the victims
of aliens, endangered by Germanization and Balkanisation. LPR considers immigrants to be 'strangers' (*innych obcych*). This category refers to
the group of non-Polish people—not only foreigners but also the members
of national minorities who live in Poland. Such an attitude results from
the party employing a narrow understanding of the ethno-cultural concept of the 'Polish Nation.' The party, its politicians' and the party press,
frequently refer to the danger being imposed on the national and cultural
identity by all the 'strangers.' LPR presents itself as a guardian of the Polish family, which is defined as a union of a man and a woman with Polish
background exclusively. The tenets are clearly related to the social doctrine
of the Catholic Church, even to traditional conceptions of Catholic morality with overt anti-Islamic sentiments. Until May 1, 2004, LPR publicly
opposed the European Union, claiming that the accession would result in a
threat to the Catholic faith and to national identity.

Employment and Welfare Issues

LPR's party programmes lack comprehensive references to this frame. Generally, immigrants are seen as welfare competitors and those 'stealing our jobs'
or endangering the stability of the Polish labour market through 'wage drain.'
In a parliamentary debate in 2003, the MPs of LPR make a statement that:
"The Job Office has estimated the number of illegally employed foreigners to
be approximately a million; hence it refers to a million workplaces that cannot
be taken up by our citizens." However, the negative discourses of the party
towards 'strangers' living in Poland imply constant indications of 'culture'
and 'civilising distinctiveness,' while referring to immigrants of African or

non-European origin. Thus, the frame of 'employment and welfare' is often used in combination with the fear of 'immigrants as noncivilized elements of distinct cultures' who constitute a 'potential danger' to the Polish society, including to its labour market and welfare system. The underdeveloped Polish welfare state, in comparison to other older member states of the European Union, makes this frame less important in the Polish context.

Law and Order Issues

This frame was used mainly by LPR when addressing immigrant groups and the Roma minority group. In many cases immigrants are addressed by LPR as "smugglers" of illegal commodities and services. In this respect, Roma, Russians, Ukrainians, Armenians, and other eastern neighbours are particularly singled out by LPR politicians. Other groups, such as the Vietnamese, have been accused of "not paying taxes." For instance, in a parliamentary debate of September 2002, an MP of LPR argues that "Vietnamese working in Poland are normally chased by police, among other things, for not paying taxes," and are considered to be criminals. Many other migrant groups alongside the Vietnamese, such as the Chinese, Africans, Muslims, and other non-European migrants, are used by LPR in its political propaganda surrounding the "defence of the Polish national identity" against the "foreign threat" and their criminal acts.

Antiestablishment

LPR used this frame in its party programs and leaders' speeches in order to present itself as the only "true defender of the Polish nation, Polish families" and "Catholic and Polish cultural values." The party has particularly criticized the government for not doing enough to protect Polish people's interests both in the country and abroad. The governing elites were also criticized by LPR for introducing a specific law on the rights of national minorities; this was described as an attempt to "open a Pandora's box" in Poland. The party means that Poland is treated unfairly by the European Union, whereby the country obliged to fulfill the criteria that other, older European Union countries do not fulfill.

The Dichotomy of 'Us' against the Muslim 'Others'

Poland was a country of the 'Eastern Block' for many decades and, as such, a part of the Cold War ideology and attendant political arrangements. Alongside this, it was not a major colonial power. These historical circumstances are among the reasons for there being less institutionalised anti-Muslim ideas and racism. However, this does not mean that anti-Muslim attitudes and politics do not exist in the country. The attacks on the World Trade Center in New York and Washington, D.C. evoked centuries long prejudices and anti-Muslim ideas and sentiments in Poland. The political discourse of 'security' came to be also related to the 'war against terrorism' and 'the control of potential terrorists' in Poland. The word 'terrorism' came to be connected to and interchangeable with 'Muslims.' LPR has in its parliamentary debates and party press presented Muslims as a potential threat to Poland's security. The party press, *OK*, and the parliamentary journal of the party, *IP*, have, in several articles and editorial notes, presented Muslims as a 'problem' for the country. In many cases the indirect references to 'worried Poles' have been used to frame the 'threats from Muslims and the Muslim culture.' In a comment supporting the anti-Muslim journalist, Oriana Fallaci, *OK* writes:

> The strongest anti-Islamic reaction was forwarded by 70-year old lady of Italian journalism, Oriana Fallaci, with a demand of expelling illegal Islamic immigrants from Italy and waging an open war with Islamic culture transgressing into Christian countries. She was claimed to be a fascist, a racist, a European disgrace. (*OK*, 2001, Vol. 40)

The events of September 11 were the beginning of the politicisation of the 'Muslim question' and revealed the anti-Muslim, anti-Islamic attitudes among many Polish politicians and journalists. LPR was one of the main political agents in the 'Otherization' of Muslims. The party did not shy away from using overt racist comments in presenting Muslims both as a demographic threat to the west and also as the counterpart of the 'Nordic' people. The party warns Poles against allowing the country to be drowned in the same problems as Germany and the US with their large Muslim and 'negro' populations respectively:

> In Germany it can be clearly seen that Nordic Germans are being replaced on a mass scale by German citizens of Turkish or Arabian origin (of Islamic religion). Negro, single mothers have the biggest families in USA. And here in Poland? (*OK*, 2001, Vol. 39)

Poland's alliance with the United States and its 'war against terrorism,' particularly its participation in the war in Iraq, was supported and considered important for the country's place among the 'civilized western countries.'

Assessing Impacts of XPP

LPR has access to parliamentary seats and has made alliances with the mainstream parties concerning many different questions. It has also been part of different coalitions both with the centre-right and with the centre-left parties. Some of its direct impacts can be observed in the visa restrictions for people coming in from the eastern borders, such as Ukrainians, and in discussions concerning the rights of national minorities. However, it also has an indirect impact on Polish politics. The assessment of the impact of LPR upon Polish mainstream party politics was analyzed, including the two main political parties or alliances, namely *Polskie Stronnictwo Ludowe* (Polish Peasant Party, PSL) and *Sojusz Lewicy Demokratyczne* (Left Democratic Alliance, SLD) (the latter of which is an alliance of many small social democratic parties). The largest party of the leftist alliance was *Socjaldemokracja Rzeczypospolitej Polski* (Socialdemocracy of Republic of Poland, SdRP). PSL was founded in 1990 as a direct result of the reformation of *Zjednoczone Stronnictwo Ludowe* (United Peasant Party) who had been active in 'socialist' Poland. The party presents itself as an heir to the former PSL, a party which was created in the interwar period under the leadership of W. Witos and which was, in the period of 1945–1947, headed by Stanisław Mikołajczyk (who was Polish Prime Minister of the émigré cabinet during World War II and deputy Prime Minister after the war in the Lublin cabinet). Throughout the 1990s, and remaining so today, PSL is a political party which enjoys one of the most numerous membership in Poland. According to the party sources, the membership includes ca 140 thousands of people. PSL has well developed organisational structures at the regional and local level. Owing to this, and despite the fact that it does not win very much support in parliamentary elections, it was frequently asked to form governing coalitions with other parties, and has played the role of a linchpin. It has formed alliances both with post-Communist parties and with post-Solidarity parties. Even LPR, along with other xenophobic political groups and associations, declared their willingness to form governing coalitions with PSL. For instance, in the local and regional elections of 2001, the coalition between PSL and LPR was formed. Members of PSL play an important role in Polish parliament, often becoming its speakers. In 1993, PSL noted their biggest election success, gathering 15.4% of votes.

The leftist party/alliance SLD is the main social democratic party in Poland. After the disbandment of the Polish Communist Party (*Polska Zjednoczona Partia Robotnicza*) in January 1990, many small social democratic and leftist parties built a coalition later that year; this gradually became a political party uniting Polish social democrats—SLD. The decision was made by Leszek Miller, one of the leaders of the party who became prime minister in 2001. We may say that SLD is continuation of SdRP, because their leadership and party structure are the same. The main success of SLD came in 1995 when its leader Aleksander Kwasniewski defeated Lech Walesa, the legend of Solidarity, in the presidential election. Between 1995 and 1997, two members of SLD became the prime ministers, Jozef Oleksy and Wlodzimierz Cimoszewicz. In the last parliamentary election, SLD gained 41.04% of the votes, which was the highest result for a party in the postsocialist history of Poland. Miller became the prime minister and announced the new era of SLD rule. Miller was, however, to be proven wrong, and since the beginning of 2003—when a newspaper, *Gazeta Wyborcza*, revealed that the SLD politicians were engaged in corruptions and scandals (so called 'Rywin-Gate')—the support for the party continuously decreased. Gradually, the party broke apart, because one of its leaders Marek Borowski decided to organise his own party excluding politicians connected to scandals. In a national opinion poll published in May 2005, only 7% of respondents in May 2005 declared an intention to vote for SLD in the forthcoming parliamentary election.

The following party programmes and documents of SdRP and, later, SLD were analyzed in this study:

- *Deklaracja SdRP 1990* (Declaration of SdRP, 1990);
- *Uchwała Programowa Kongresu Założycielskiego SdRP 1990* (Programme of the Foundation Congress of SdRP, 1990);
- *Polska postępu, prawa i demokracj–program społeczno-gospodarczy 1991* (Poland of Progress, Law and Democracy–socioeconomic programme, 1991);
- *Polska Sprawiedliwa, Demokratyczna, Bezpieczna–Program SdRP 1992* (Poland–a Just, Democratic, Secure Country–Programme of SdRP, 1992);
- *Socjaldemokratyczny Program dla Polski–deklaracja przed II kongresem SdRP 1992* (Socialdemocratic programme for Poland–declaration before the Second Congress of SdRP, 1992);
- *Tak dalej być nie może. Polsce potrzebny jest nowy program–program koalicji SLD 1992* (It can't go on like that. Poland needs a new programme–programme of the SLD coalition, 1992);
- *Socjaldemokracja wobec przemian współczesności. Jednostka-Polska-Europa-Świat. Deklaracja III kongresu SdRP 1997* (Social-democracy in the face of changes of the present day. Individual-Poland-Europe-World. Declaration of the Third Congress of SdRP, 1997);
- *Program SdRP przyjęty na III Kongresie SdRP w dniach 6–7.12.1997* (Programme of SdRP approved at the Third Congress of SdRP on 06–07.12.1997);
- *Nowy wiek–nowy SLD. Socjaldemokratyczny Program dla Polski 1999* (New Century–New SLD. Socialdemocratic programme for Poland, 1999); and
- *Program wyborczy SLD-UP 2001* (Election programme of SLD-UP 2001).

The following party programmes of PSL has been analyzed:

- *Polskie Stronnictwo Ludowe wobec najważniejszych problemów kraju 1991* (Polish Peasant Party in the face of the major problems of the state, 1991);
- *Deklaracja ideowa Polskiego Stronnictwa Ludowego 1993* (Ideological declaration of Polish Peasant Party, 1993a);
- *Polskie Stronnictwo Ludowe wobec węzłowych problemów państwa 1993* (Polish Peasant Party in the face of the key problems of the state, 1993b);

- *Deklaracja ideowa PSL 1997* (Ideological declaration of PSL, 1997);
- *Program społeczny PSL 1997* (Social program of PSL, 1997);
- *Czas na zmianę . . . Program społeczno-gospodarczy PSL 2001* (Time for a change . . . Social-economic programme of PSL, 2001); and
- *Tezy programowe 2004* (Programme theses, 2004).

For the analysis of the PSL's party press the main party weekly newspaper *Zielony Sztandar* (The Green Flag, ZS) was chosen. It has been on the market since 1931. It is known as an official voice of PSL and has a nationwide distribution. The samples chosen for the analysis were a random two issues for every year from 1989 until 2003. Neither SdRP nor SLD have a regular party newspaper. However, several random issues of the two newspapers connected to the parties, namely *Biuletyn Informacyjny* (*BI*) and *Przegląd Socjaldemokratyczny* (*PS*), starting in 1990 up until 2003, were chosen for the analysis. Alongside this, the parliamentary debates of the two mainstream parties have also been analyzed.

Collective Identity

One of the central concerns in Poland of the two mainstream parties, as well as LPR, is the fear of 'selling out the country' to 'foreigners.' The new economic system, capitalism, which was introduced after 1989, attracted foreign capital to the country. The fear of the increasing control of foreign capital in the country, and of European Union interference, has been a part of the political frame of Polish collective identity. Regarding immigrants, in particular non-European immigrants, the political concern of the mainstream parties has surrounded 'cultural difference.' For example, PSL declares in its party program of 1997 that: "Cultural politics of the state have to be characterized by: the protection of the most precious values of national culture." The PSL programme is a mixture of traditional, collective values (in terms of culture and society), neo-agrarian ideas, and limited state interventionism in the economy. The party emphasizes in its party programmes the Polish national and Christian values that invoke traditional patriotism as a foundation of political, economic and social order.

Nevertheless, despite the pro-European or even universalistic orientation it declares, the party increasingly stresses over time elements of loyalty to the Polish national tradition in its programmes and activities. Besides references in its party programmes and speeches, this is evidenced, for instance, by the fact that, during electoral campaigns, SLD deploys traditional national symbols, while its leaders use national celebrations as occasions for party celebrations. The PSL collective identity is very much related to a traditional conception of the Polish nation that, in turn, is related to issues of language and land. Language and land are treated as especially valuable symbols of national wealth, and constitutive of the

Polish national identity, thus requiring special protective measures on the part of the Polish state.

In addition, the mainstream parties, in line with LPR, take an anti-Muslim attitude, particularly after September 11, and declare themselves to be protecting 'western democracy' against nondemocratic and 'terrorist Muslims.' Politicians use the frame of 'Collective Identity' to refer to the necessity of engagement in the 'war against terrorism' (meaning mostly support for the United States in the Iraq war, but also in terms of introducing some sort of internal security measures, which are not specified). This was combined with 'warnings' about 'potential threats' to Polish and European interests. Among these is the necessity to be sensitive to potential problems that national minorities might cause in Poland and allegedly are creating throughout Europe, a veiled hint that western Europe is slowly turning into a mosaic of culturally incompatible immigrant communities who will prove to be also incompatible in terms of legal and political norms.

Employment and Welfare Issues

How the political parties used this frame has changed during the period under study. Initially, in most cases reference is made to problems that the inflow of illegal migrants from the east (mostly the Ukraine, Byelorussia, and Russia) create for the Polish labour market and welfare system. Such arguments are used both by politicians of the mainstream and governing SLD (most frequently) and by the politicians of the oppositional PSL, as well as by LPR (less frequently). SLD politicians frequently raise the issue of the need for legal regulation of 'illegal immigrants' and their activities. By this is meant that the illegal employment of immigrants, and illegal trade and production activities in Poland, without paying taxes and other fees, is an unfair competition with Poles. The introduction of a new visa regime was sometimes presented as a solution to the problem.

Over recent years, the two mainstream parties, PSL and SLD, have used the frame of 'employment and welfare' in relation to non-European refugees and illegal migrants who abuse the Polish health services. However, the discourses on welfare issues are less frequent in the debate (in terms of both the party press and parliamentary debates), which might be a consequence of the still small number of immigrants in Poland and the perceived lack of need for legal and institutional regulations in this area.

Law and Order Issues

This frame is frequently used by the mainstream parties. The usage of the frame evolves over time: up to the mid-1990s politicians focused predominantly on the alleged import of crime (of both mafia-type and ordinary petty crime) from 'our eastern border' (i.e., Ukraine and Russia in particular), coupled with a fear that the import will grow when the visa regime is abolished. They stressed the importance of the role of the police for combating criminality. The eastern border is presented as a special case. Using stereotypes, politicians from mainstream parties presented immigrants from the ex-Soviet states as criminals. Towards the end of 1990s, and in 2000s, the frame appears in the context of legal regulations concerning the introduction of new border traffic and visa regimes related to Poland's accession to the European Union. They are focused on regulating illegal migration, smuggling, and organized crime. Also, the issues of corruption, breaking intellectual property rights, and copyright (in respect of computer software) are raised. Quite often they are mixed with assessment of the negative economic effects of immigrants' criminality.

In contrast to the early 1990s, at the end of 1990s and in early 2000s the problems of criminal activities and violating taxation and social security laws are ascribed more often to immigrants from Vietnam and China than to immigrants from the ex-Soviet countries. In the aftermath of the September 11 attacks in the United States, there is a significant increase in anti-Muslim and/or anti-Arab utterances by politicians from mainstream parties. Politicians and official authorities declare the need for combating the 'potential terrorist threat' in the country. Police and Internal Security Agency use stereotypes of Arabs and Muslims in their frequent reports about restrictive measures taken to deal with terrorism. SLD declares in the parliamentary debate of September 2003 that: "If there is any risk that the number of foreigners is increasing, in particular those foreigners that are generally not welcomed in Poland, the current immigration shall be significantly restricted."

Mass Media and the 'Others'

Mass media are very much engaged in the formation of public opinion. They are not only elaborating their own political affiliations to influence people, but are also providing space for politicians and debaters, mainly of the same ideology, to form public opinion. The mass media in Poland were under state-control for a long time. The new, free media came into existence after the 1989 political change. However, it is not only the state-control of mass media that is a problem, but also the media's political affiliations, participation in power constellations in society, and their established prejudices against the 'Others.'

For the purpose of the analysis of antiimmigrant discourse on the selected "important" domestic and foreign events, four daily newspapers were selected—the two biggest opinion-making dailies *Gazeta Wyborcza* (GW) and *Rzeczpospolita* (RZ), and two tabloids *Super Express* (SE) and *Fakt* (F). GW was launched on May 8, 1989 during the election campaign for the first partially free parliamentary election. It was founded by a group of journalists from the independent underground opposition press descending from

KOR (Workers Defence Committee). The editor-in-chief was Adam Michnik, who has held the post ever since. GW is considered to be the main opinion-making daily in Poland as well as the key source of information about domestic and foreign events. It is believed to be prodemocracy and procivil society, pro-European, and of centrist and centre-left affiliations. Its turnover is approximately 450,000 copies a day. RZ is a daily newspaper with a tradition dating back to the 1920s. The newspaper has several times changed its ideological profile. Before the outbreak of World War II, it was affiliated with the right-wing Christian-National Party (*Stronnictwo Chrześcijańsko-Narodowe*). After 1945, the title was taken over by the communist authorities. In the period of 1980to 1989, the newspaper officially started playing the role of the main government daily. At the moment, RZ is the forth (in terms of sales) national daily and is considered to be the main competitor of GW. After 1989, it has changed its political affiliation and became a pro-centre-right newspaper that defines itself as the defender of the anticommunist block.

SE came into existence at the end of 1991 as an outgrowth of an earlier newspaper, *Express*. It was the first high circulation daily with sensational news. From the beginning, it was edited in the form of a tabloid with colourful, lavishly illustrated layout. The circulation of the paper is 300,000 copies during the weekend 700,000 at the weekends. Since its main competitor, F, entered the market, the sale and readership of SE have declined markedly. F has been on the market since October 22, 2003. Its low price, colourful layout and a wide advertising campaign contributed to the fact that by the December of that year the title already reached the sale of 539,000 copies a day, which was the highest monthly average in ten years for the daily press in Poland. The newspaper has a distinctly tabloid character, modelled on the German *Bild* daily (the owner of both of the papers is the same German press concern owned by Axel Springer). But apart from the typical tabloid content of sensation and gossip, there is also information, comment and opinions on political and social characters. On Wednesdays, the main edition is supplemented with a secondary publication, *Weekly of Ideas*.

The events that have been chosen in the study of the role of mass media in reinforcing 'Otherization' and xenophobia in Poland are as follows:

1. the fall of communism, August 24, 1989;
2. the riots in Mława, June 21, 1991;
3. the Polish debate about Jedwabne murders during World War II;
4. the attacks on World Trade Center and Pentagon in the United States, September 11,2001;
5. the introduction of visas for Ukrainians, Byelorussians, and Russians, November 1, 2003; and
6. the enlargement of the European Union on May 1, 2004.

Since the first tabloid newspaper, SE, did not appear in Poland until 1992, they are included in the study of the four following events only: Riots in

Mława, Jedwabne case, the introduction of visas for the citizens of the Russian Federation, Belorus and Ukraine, and the attack on WTC on September 11. As soon as *F* entered the Polish press market in October 22, 2003, it was used instead of '*Super Express*' in the analysis. Therefore, the *F* is the only tabloid included in the analysis of the last event, namely the enlargement of the European Union on May 1, 2004.

The Fall of Communism, August 24, 1989

The date for the fall of communism in Poland is chosen in this study as August 24, 1989, when Tadeusz Mazowiecki became prime minister. There was not any discussion on immigration in Poland at that time. During the 1980s, Poland was a country of mass emigration because of the political and economic crisis. The situation begun to change slowly, because of reforms conducted by Mazowiecki's cabinet in 1990. The mainstream media did not discuss immigration issues, but did discuss some related subjects, such as the position of national minorities in Poland and of the Polish minorities in other countries. The discussions on minorities in the newspapers were simultaneously a critique of the former Polish Communist propaganda advocating a view of Poland as a homogenous country. However, the debate and articles in the newspapers were mostly about Pole migrants in other European countries, such as Germany. It was reported in both the mainstream newspapers, *GW* and *RZ*, that Lech Walesa (leader of Solidarity) is concerned about the status of Polish immigrants in Germany and had discussed it with German authorities. At that time, then, it was mainly emigration that was the public issue rather than immigration.

Riots in Mława, June 21, 1991

In the small town of Mława, situated in northeast part of Poland, a man died and another was seriously injured as a result of a car accident caused by a driver of Roma background. A group of people subsequently attacked Roma's borough. None of the Roma people was injured as the fury was focused mainly on their properties. The majority of opinions from the two mainstream newspapers have an informative character including detailed description of the event. There are also articles about the Roma culture and style of living, with some discursive stereotypes. The underlying economic background of the conflict was also discussed in a way that presented Roma as 'rich' in comparison with 'Poles.' The dualism of Poles and Roma was frequently presented in the reports. No tabloid was analyzed because none existed at that time.

The Polish Debate about Jedwabne Murders during World War II

In April 2000, a book by Jan Tomasz Gross called *Sasiedzi* (The Neighbours) was published that was about the Polish community of the town

Jedwabne who, in 1941 (during the German occupation of Poland), murdered their Jewish neighbours. The review of the book published in *GW* on November 18, 2000 started enormous public discussion about Polish anti-Semitism. Before this, there had been no public discussion of the fact that Poles were not only victims of World War II but sometimes also offenders. *RZ* frequently provided articles to many intellectuals who could not agree that Poles took part in the murder of Jews. Many historians attacked Gross saying that his book is biased and that its only source is the memory of one Jew, who ran away before the murders started. *RZ* cited people saying that even Poles were forced by German Nazis to kill their neighbours. Both *GW* and *RZ* provided evidence for others who stressed the existence of Polish anti-Semitism. Following the discussion of the intellectuals, the case became a political one, when president Kwasnkiewski decided to apologize to Jews in the name of Polish nation. Newspapers reported voices of the politicians from the Right who argued that the whole nation cannot apologize for the deeds of individuals.

The Attack on the World Trade Center and Pentagon in the United States, September 11, 2001

The mainstream newspapers were analyzed for two weeks before and for two weeks after the attack against WTC in New York on September 11, 2001. The attack was covered by the mass media in an informative manner mostly. There appeared a few large essays in the two mainstream newspapers in order to inform the public about the reasons behind the attack. However, Islam and Muslims were held responsible for the attack and, in some cases, the established 'Otherising' theories—such as the 'clash of civilisation' offered of Samuel Huntington, and Bronisław Geremek's theory of Islam as the 'Others'' religion with completely different messages from Christianity and the west—were widely discussed in the two mainstream newspapers. Even references to these kinds of ideas were addressed in the tabloid SE. The newspapers had almost daily reports of the attack and there were editorial expressions of solidarity with the United States and with building alliance against terrorism. All the newspapers frequently debated the need for forging a U.S.-led coalition to fight terrorism. There also appeared a short essay in GW, whose author asked whether the war against terrorism would result in a new wave of refugees in Europe. There reports and articles also appeared in the mainstream newspapers concerning the aftermath of the September 11 attacks, such as the incident in Gdańsk where a few youngsters threw stones at a local mosque, an incident at the Balice airport where an Algerian was arrested, an interview with a few Arab students who claimed to have been discriminated against because of September 11, and an investigation related to Polish connections of some Arabs suspected of participation in the September 11 attacks. RZ (September 21, 2001) published a letter from Samir Ismail, president of Muslim Students Association in Poland, who accused Polish society of having turned against Muslims in Poland and having supposed the guilt of Muslims for the terrorist attacks even earlier than did the United States. Articles with sensational and threatening titles, such as SE's article on September 27/28, 2001, "A terrorist in Krakow" (discussing the arrest of an Algerian at the Krakow airport), were frequently circulated, including in the other mainstream newspaper, RZ. It writes on October 3, 2001 that:

(The Polish) *Agencja Bezpieczeństwa Wewnętrznego* (Internal Security Agency) explains that the Algerian arrested at the airport in Kraków is being investigated to establish if the suspect has planned a terrorist attack in Poland or what else has been his intention to arrive in Poland.

Introduction of Visas for Ukrainians, Byelorussians, and Russians, November 1, 2003

The introduction of a new visa regime for non-EU eastern neighbours of Poland was one of the conditions of Polish accession to the European Union. The Polish government first announced the introduction of visas in 2001 (together with Czech Republic and Slovakia) but kept postponing it until the last deadline negotiated with Brussels. An analysis was conducted of the two mainstream dailies RZ and GW, and the tabloid SE, covering the period of 4 weeks (2 before and 2 after the introduction of the new visa regime). There are articles and news concerning the 'costs,' as well as the contribution of eastern immigrants. One of the related issues is the cost of illegal immigrants upon the Polish health care system. An illustration of such media debates is an article published in RZ on September 23, 2003 with the title: "No one pays for those who run away." It writes that representatives of public hospitals complain that they are—by law and by moral codes—forced to treat foreigners even if they are not insured. It continues that the majority of the foreigners simply run away when the treatment is approaching its successful end or otherwise give false data concerning their identities. This causes a major increase in the cost of the public health care system. There are other articles addressing the position of Poles towards immigrants. For example, RZ on September 29, 2003 publishes as article with the title "Unwanted people," which is a report on Chechnyans who have a dream of emigrating to western Europe through Poland, not realising that no one wants them there.

The Enlargement of the European Union on May 1, 2004

There were a number of articles that analyzed future consequences of Poland's accession to the European Union. Some articles pointed out the opportunities that the European Union membership will bring for Poland, while others indicated some of the fears related to membership. The economic and political dimension of the accession dominated the press. There were also a few articles concerning the cultural and 'civilisational' aspects to the debate. In this discourse, the debate concerning the 'problem' of immigration was marginal. One could barely find in the mainstream newspapers about the politicians' and political parties' opinions on this concern. The fear of accession was rather directed towards the foreign investment in Poland that could eliminate the Poles' control over their land and market. However there were different opinions expressed in the mainstream journals (such as *RZ, GW,* and *SE*) by various political parties. The ruling party, SLD, represented by the Speaker of the Sejm, indicated that such fears are groundless and unfounded. The opposition party, PSL, along with the populist *Samoobrona* and rightist party, LPR, were ready at that time to form a Polish coalition against the denationalisation of Polish land. Those parties appealed to the conviction that it is in the Polish national interest to maintain the ownership of Polish land solely in the hands of the Polish people.

Conclusion

The discourse analysis on the xenophobia and racism in the Polish political system is not well-developed. This study shows that the Polish political system and public sphere have an ambivalent position towards questions of racism, xenophobia, and immigration. Since the country has been mainly a country of emigration, and it is only since the late 1990s that we are witnessing an increase in immigration to the country, the discourse on immigration is not elaborative. However, the adaptation of the 'west' or 'western European' socioeconomic and political systems has entailed not only the positive democratic politics, but also the negative European tradition of 'Otherism,' xenophobia, and racism. The relative small size of immigrants to the country makes the real phenomenon of immigration not a political slogan or a part of the Polish political parties' electoral strategy. Notwithstanding this, the 'Otherization' processes, which are taking place both as part of identification with *a country* (Poland) and as identification with *the European community,* make immigrants and other minority groups (such as Roma people) politically interesting. The question of belonging to a nation or to Europe creates several 'Others' in the Polish context. For example, the German minority in Poland did not constitute a part of the Polish nation prior to the accession to the European Union. This was mainly a result of World War II occupation of the country by Nazi Germany and the later problematic relationships between the two countries. Roma people living in the country for many years are another minority group which has constituted the visible 'Other' in the country and which has been discriminated against.

New immigrant groups, such as the Chinese, Vietnamese, Africans, and Arabs/Muslims, are the new groups who are defined as the 'Others' and subjected to discrimination—and, in the case of Muslims, even demonisation. It is not the number of non-Europeans, and in particular Muslims, that makes this 'category of people' politically interesting for Polish politicians, but the *symbolic power* of 'Muslim Others' for the creation of the new democratic and Western Poland. It seems that the 'Otherization' of Muslims in other Western European countries is imported to Poland in order to reinforce the Polish European identity. Political parties and mass media are the core group in the 'Otherization' of immigrants and minority groups as the counterpart of the Polish nation.

LPR is a party with strong nationalistic and xenophobic attitudes. The party put the questions of national minorities and Polish nationalism and protectionalism on the political agenda. It also introduced political issues related to immigration as a problem for Poland. Its access to parliamentary seats and its coalition with mainstream parties gave them opportunity to directly influence political decisions and debates. However, its *indirect* impact on the mainstream parties (such as PLS and SLD), as well as on public opinion, through its access to mainstream media is more important than is their direct impact. The party is close, in many cases, to the ideas of the mainstream party, PLS. In particular, there is a clear cooptation between the two parties on the issues related to traditional conceptions of the Polish nation, Polish culture, Polish religion, and so on. The study shows that even some of the political programmes of LPR, such as protecting Polish financial and economic interests, have been accepted and defended by PLS.

However, the political situation of the last decade has also had an impact on LPR, forcing them to change their attitudes and programmes. One such change concerns the moderation of the party's opposition to the European Union. This is mainly due to the Polish parties' national and European reorientations. The still uncompleted task of Polish nationalism remains a problem for nationalists since Poland became a part of the European Union. This creates many problems for, or solutions to, collective identification. Poland has become a country between the 'problematic east' and the 'nonproblematic west.' Mainstream political parties define themselves, and Poland, as a European country, a part of the western European family gathered in the European Union. Europeanization of Poland means also the import of new forms of 'Otherization' and of racism against the 'Others' that have been in effect in many western European countries for centuries.

SUMMARY AND CONCLUSIONS

The analyses of the impact of different countries' XPPs on their mainstream parties and politics shows a variation in impact across countries. Depending on the political systems and the threshold for entering, the decision-making organs—such as parliaments and local assemblies—influence the impacts of such parties on mainstream political parties, institutional discrimination (such as law making), and public opinion. The impacts of XPP can be categorized into two 'types,' the direct and the indirect impacts.

The *direct* impact takes place when a XPP gets access to parliamentary seats, which can be used for influencing and changing laws both alone and through alliance with other parties. This is the case in Austria, Italy, France (in mid-1980s), Cyprus, and Poland. The direct impacts of XPP are not normally long lasting. This is due to the following factors:

1. the periodic alliances with mainstream parties;
2. mainstream parties' 'take over' of XPP's politics and party programmes;
3. lack of reliable political programmes; and
4. difficulties in the institutionalisation of their charismatic leadership.

XPPs are often unable to rule by their own majority and are forced to make alliances and coalitions with other mainstream parities. Some of them make tactical alliances when in opposition in parliament. This means that they support political suggestions and propositions in cooperation with mainstream parties over those issues that interest them and serve their slogans and programmes. Others, such as the Italian XPP, Liga Nord, make more lasting alliances with other, mainstream parties and participate in governmental coalitions. In both such cases, coalitions and alliances with other parties, while having some benefits to a XPP, create some obstacles to realising their policies. They are forced often to compromise with their coalition partners and therefore reduce their overt 'Otherising' slogans and politics; this is seen by their voters as a 'retreat' from a 'radical' position.

The second reason for XPPs' relatively short-standing political success is the mainstream parties' adoption of those political programmes and slogans that are attractive to voters. There is a clear tendency for the electoral success of XPP to make many mainstream parties interested in the issues, such as migration, that are often politicized and presented as a major political question to the public. The alignment of mainstream Swedish parties (such as the Social Democratic Party and the Moderate Party) to the XPP Nydemokrati at the beginning of 1990s is among such examples. Nydemokrati's programmes and slogans, such as restrictions on asylum seekers, limiting family reunion, helping refugees in conflict areas, and restricting foreign development aid, are almost entirely realised by the conservative right-wing government led by the Moderates and by the leftists Social Democrats since then. The party lost its attractive position and disappeared from the political scene of the country.

The third reason behind the decreasing popularity of XPP is these parties' lack of a comprehensive socioeconomic program. Such parties are often 'one-question' parties which make 'Otherism,' xenophobia and racism their main political agenda. Although they normally belong to the right-wing political camp of the European countries, they lack reliable programmes to deal with the complex socioeconomic problems of the country. Simplification of socioeconomic problems by framing immigrants and minorities as the sources of those problems proves its ineffectiveness when such parties seize or share the political power and become a part of the establishment. This eliminates such parties' antiestablishment agenda, which had helped them to gain political influence in the mainstream politics and attract voters.

The fourth reason for such parties' loss of popularity after a major electoral success is the focus of the party on their often charismatic leaders and difficulties with institutionalisation of charismatic leadership in the long run. As is shown in country specific studies, the frequent speeches and declarations of charismatic leaders of XPP, which tend to include several instances of typically discriminatory use of language, and which have rather 'free' structures and are very frequently filled with very direct rhetoric (e.g., offensive linguistic forms directed at specific representatives of migrants and minority groups), are the most effective means of mobilising antiimmigrant and racist sentiments. Demonising of immigrants is recurrently supported with various other linguistic features which help the leaders to reach the audience and transmit their populist views.

On the other hand, the party programmes and other programmatic documents rarely use any direct rhetoric and, contrary to the speeches, tend to be often characterized by a high degree of 'political correctness,' as well as by the legal-technical, 'objective-like,' and, thus, less strictly populist language. It is these seemingly-neutral party programmes, and not speeches, which often find their way to official parliamentary and other legislative proposals and official state-acts. This marginalizes often the relatively 'free' role of the charismatic leader and forces him/her to transform their charisma into an 'office charisma' of the party. This reduces the party's popularity, which is mainly based on its 'radical' anti-immigrant rhetoric.

However, the *indirect* impact of XPP on the mainstream politics of each country is much more extensive than is their direct impact. Although occurring in various ways, the following are the major characteristics of the indirect impact:

- impact on public opinion;
- impact on mainstream parties; and
- legitimisation of xenophobia and racism.

Although new in their political organisation as a party, XPP have often developed from small xenophobic, nationalist, and racist organisations (depending on the country's political context and history). In some countries, such as Sweden, strong nationalist attitudes and ideas have never developed to become a strong nationalist movement. However, in other countries, such as Germany and Cyprus, there have, on the contrary, been and still are relatively strong nationalist movements with clearly xenophobic and racist perspectives. Such movements have developed to new political parties aiming at seizing political power and influencing political decision making. Participation in their countries'—as well as the European Union's—democratic systems and elections provides them opportunity to be seen and heard by the public. They appear in the mainstream media, such as TV, radio, and newspapers, and propagate their 'simple solutions' to 'complex problems.' The simple way of framing immigrants and minorities as 'problem,' and stopping or excluding them from being a 'solution,' has, during the period studied in this research (1980–2005), become a focus of such groupings' and parties' political agenda. XPPs' democratic legitimisation provides them access to democratic channels for influencing 'a public,' who as members of other institutions, such as the educational system, are already familiar with considering the 'Others' as inferior to 'Us.' (This will be discussed in more detail in the next chapter.)

The electoral success of XPP alarms the mainstream parties, who worry about losing their part of the electoral pot, and makes them aware of the political potentiality of immigration. This research shows that this is one of the major reasons behind the politicisation of the question of immigration. Thus, political discussions and debates with XPP provide XPP more possibilities for influencing public opinion. Their very existence as a 'debate partner' largely sets the agenda for the debate and gives it a xenophobic and 'immigration focus.' The fear of losing votes forces many mainstream parties on many occasions to 'admit the problem of immigration.' 'Immigration,' 'immigrants,' and 'problem' become almost synonymous in the public debates with XPP. Thus, the politicisation of immigration issues is combined with framing immigrants as 'problem.' There is also another side to this impact. Some mainstream parties, in order to reduce the influence of XPP and of losing votes to them, raise counterissues to framing 'immigrants as problem'—for example, welfare and employment and increasing criminality—and also present 'immigrants as solution' for, for example, the needs of the national labour market and health care system. This makes 'immigrants' a double-sided 'instrument' which is either 'bad' *or* 'good' for 'Us.' The study shows clearly that mainstream parties overall are influenced by XPP in a negative way. Many of XPPs' political propaganda and programmes are realised by the mainstream parties in power. Among such measures against immigration and immigrants are restrictions on immigration, restrictions concerning family reunion, restriction of asylum right, and increasing security control of non-European immigrants (Muslims in particular). Such impacts have taken place, in many cases, without the direct participation of a XPP in the parliamentary decision-making.

Enjoying mass media attention, XPP politicians and leaders get opportunity for influencing the public debate and change the borders of the 'public political correctness' so that it becomes more xenophobic. Many xenophobic and overt racist public utterances about immigrants, in particular their 'foreign cultures and religion,' becomes normalised and tolerated in public debate. Increasing demonisation of Muslims and Islam by XPP, mainstream parties, and mass media is one of the major illustrations of this phenomenon.

Demonisation of Muslims in Europe

Increasing immigration of Muslims and the attacks on the World Trade Center in New York and on the Pentagon in Washington, D.C. have been two reasons behind the increasing demonisation of Muslims and anti-Muslim actions in all the eight countries which were explored in this project. Muslims are increasingly becoming the most 'visible Other' in Europe. Increasing concern about security and the engagement of many countries in the 'war against terrorism' have increased discrimination and racism against Muslims in all the eight countries. It has gone so far as some politicians making reference to the 'Muslim question' in Europe.

The tradition of Orientalism is highly relevant in political discourses in Europe today. It is not only XPP, but also the mainstream parties and media that 'Otherize' and demonise Muslims. They are presented as 'deviant,' 'culturally different,' 'antimodern,' 'security problem,' 'patriarchal,' and 'honour killers.' It seems that anti-Muslim sentiments and actions have nothing to do with each country's specific history, but is rather a common problem in all the eight countries. Cyprus, for example, has a history of conflict with the Turkish population of the north of the island who are Muslims. The religious difference between south and north plays a role in the conflict, and anti-Turk attitudes in the south is directly connected to the ethnic/national conflict between the two populations. Thus, anti-Muslim attitudes and discrimination may be partly related to the ethnic conflict on Cyprus. However, Muslim groups have not been engaged in ethnic or national conflict in any of the other countries engaged in the research (namely Austria, France, England, Italy, Germany, Poland, and Sweden), but there they are also demonized and discriminated against.

The Dualism of 'Us' against 'Them'

The research shows that 'Otherism' in its institutional forms (which entail systematic differentiation, discrimination and exclusion), is also a part of the political systems of the countries engaged in the research. Such sociopolitical categories of the population used in political discourses make 'immigrants' an *object*, that is, a defined and differentiated social fact or reality. The analysis of how categories are constructed and applied, their cognitive basis, and their role in identity (and distinctions between identities) is central to our analysis. Although there are many forms of 'Otherism,' and they arise through a variety of political, social, and psychological mechanisms, political 'Otherism' is one of the most important ones with long-standing effects for 'Otherised' groups. Making public issues of negative attitudes, prejudices, feelings of revulsion, about particular categories of persons and groups provide the conditions for political 'Otherism.' 'Otherism' is shaped by the logic of distinction and exclusion, the separation of the 'Us' from the 'Them,' and the construction of adversarial frames, requiring a negative identification by which the 'Them' becomes not only a 'feared other' but an *enemy*. However, the transition from negative attitudes and prejudices to exclusion and, in turn, to adversity is a very subtle one. Most groups are based on a sense of 'Us-ness' as distinct from the 'Others.'

The potentiality for 'Otherization' mechanisms to become adversarial is always present. Reproduction of 'Us-ness' often needs the 'Others.' This creates normal means of coping with this necessity for boundary maintenance against the 'Others.' In this respect, xenophobia and racism are particular expressions and acts of 'Otherism.' It may derive from an anxiety or perceived threat associated with the presence, appearance or behaviour of the 'Others.' XPPs use the mechanisms of 'Otherism' in order to reinforce a sense of a familiar 'Us' against a foreign 'Them' who are threatening 'our existence.' The differences, real or imagined, between 'Us' and 'Them' becomes central to XPPs,' and even the mainstream political parties' and mass media's, discourses of 'immigrants.'

In sum, the emergence of XPP as political parties and forces in the democratic scene of the countries engaged in this research has reinforced a xenophobic and racist discursive climate that conditions what is politically correct or incorrect. They have framed 'immigrants as problem' and have influenced even mainstream parties and politicians in taking a more xenophobic position. The counterdebate of some parties that frames immigrants as 'solution' to 'our problems' has unintentionally reinforced the established dualism of 'Us' and 'Them.' Thus, the discourses of XPP, and the mainstream parties' and mass media's adaptations to those discourses, have created some crucial barriers for the equal distribution of rights and resources to all citizens in many European countries.

4 Institutional Discrimination in the Labour Market and the Educational System

INTRODUCTION

In the institutional perspective guiding this research, otherization and discrimination operate not only in particular interpersonal encounters but also in and through institutions that reproduce power relations in society. Discriminatory practices produce and reproduce differential access to resources, positions, careers, and so forth. Thus, as mentioned earlier, any given society consists of an elaborate 'web of institutions' that in their routinized daily actions discriminate against the 'Others' and make for unequal life chances.

As mentioned earlier, institutional discrimination operates through operative norms, laws, regulations, and procedures that determine differential access to resources in society. It implies the categorisation of some groups as inferiors through widely shared systems of stereotypes, prejudices, and norms that reproduce the dualism of the superior 'Us' against the inferior 'Them.' It is not only 'biological differences' between 'Us' and 'Them' that is the focus of 'Otherization,' but 'cultural differences' too. There are theories based on essentialised 'cultural differences.' Culture is often treated as fixed, and in many cases, contradictory, properties. The established paradigm of 'cultural difference' is among many European countries' 'cultural motives' that reproduce and legitimizes the institutional discrimination in those societies. Thus, many European countries' modus operandi that are not formed based on intentional discrimination, can discriminate against immigrant and minority groups.

Institutional discrimination implies that it is possible for any individual occupying a position of institutionalized decision making to discriminate or combat discrimination. This includes even individuals with immigrant backgrounds who are agents in the reproduction of the institutional arrangements of society and who discriminate and practice racist treatments of the 'Others' of the same background. Amongst those individuals with institutional power engaged in discrimination of the 'Others' are: in France, the president, Nikolas Sarkozy, and two of his ministers with immigrant backgrounds, Rachida Dati (minister of justice) and Fadela

Amara (minister of housing); in the United States, Gonzales (minister of justice); and in Sweden, Nyamko Sabuni (minister of integration). This means that it is not the discriminators' personal attitudes or intentions that must be the focus of the studies of institutional discrimination, but the consequences of their actions.

For the purposes of this research, we distinguish analytically two general types of institutional forms of discrimination, which can be investigated and analyzed using the tools of institutional case studies:

1. *General institutional discrimination*, which entails the routine operation of rules and procedures that reproduce the privileges of the 'Us' and disadvantage the 'Others';
2. *Institutional agentic discrimination*, which pertains to the acts of powerful institutional agents. Such acts are carried out by individuals in institutional positions of authority or power in the form of discriminatory decisions or practices that disadvantage the 'Others' compared to 'natives.' That is, incumbents can use their positions, exercising their rights and authority, to make a difference in the lives of people. We are particularly interested in agents who play *gatekeeping roles*, determining opportunity structures and life chances. First, however, we shall examine pure institutional discrimination before moving onto a consideration of institutional agentic discrimination.

In this part of the book the results of the research on institutionalised 'racial' discrimination in the labour markets, workplaces, and the educational systems of the eight countries engaged in this study are presented.

METHODOLOGY AND RESEARCH DESIGN

This part of the research has been conducted using a variety of methods. Each of the partner teams in the eight countries made use of official documents, data banks, and existing research reports on institutional discrimination, as well as conducting in-depth informant interviews (a minimum of 20 in each country). In their choice of informants, the research teams were to focus on generalists and specialists. Generalists comprised: (a) leaders/spokespersons of minorities, as well as key persons in engaged nongovernment organisations (NGOs) dealing with immigrant issues such as antidiscrimination matters; (b) policy makers, labour unionists, journalists, and social scientists with expertise on migrant groups (or particular minorities) and on patterns of discrimination and exclusion in workplaces and schools in the cities to be investigated. These interviews provided leads and insights relating to discriminatory patterns of labour markets, workplaces, and educational systems.

Research was also conducted in particular in organisational settings such as workplaces, schools, and employment or recruitment offices.

Interviews were carried out during 2004 (March to October) in 32 workplaces, 32 employment agencies, and 16 schools in 16 different cities in the eight countries. In each workplace, two to three key persons involved in personal administration and recruitment were interviewed (a head of personal administration, a CEO, and a key union representative); in addition, five employees (qualified and unqualified, immigrant and 'native') in each workplace were interviewed. In each city interviews were conducted at one public and one private employment agency. And finally, in each city a school (with children of immigrant background) was selected and interviews conducted at the school; interviews were conducted with three key persons in the school (teachers, particularly those in positions of responsibility, and school counsellors). Also, three interviews were conducted with representatives of parent–school associations and immigrant organisations or other NGOs involved with the school. More than 500 interviews were conducted, more than 65 in each country. As mentioned earlier, the research aimed to identify and analyze mechanisms of discrimination and exclusion operating in labour markets, workplaces, and schools.

INSTITUTIONAL DISCRIMINATION IN THE LABOUR MARKET

Institutional discrimination and exclusion takes place daily and systematically in European labour markets and are inextricably linked to—and have further effects on—immigrants' opportunities in relation to careers, continuing education, housing, and their participation in democratic society. In any such setting, decisions are made, resources are allocated, opportunities given (or denied), persons granted or not granted voice, entire groups included or excluded. Our focus has been on the labour market. Our questions concerned which migrant and minority groups are being discriminated against and excluded, and how, that is, through what mechanisms are they being excluded, and where this exclusion is taking place?

The following table (Table 4.1) is an illustration of the position of immigrants in the labour market of the eight countries engaged in this research, namely Austria (A), Cyprus (C), Germany (D), Italy (I), France (F), England (GB), Poland (PL), and Sweden (S):

The principal finding of the national case studies is that non-European migrants (mainly otherised groups) tend to be employed in positions characterized by low wages and a low status, no matter in which sector of the economy. Even in high-tech industries, they are, as a rule, employed as unskilled workers for hard, inconvenient, dirty, or dangerous jobs. In general, migrants work on short-term contracts in precarious, part-time positions in agriculture, heavy industry and the service sector. Many of them are also often employed at the fringe of legality. In particular the service sector directed towards households (domestic help, child care)

Table 4.1 Positions of individuals with immigrant background in the
European labour market

	Low-status job/low wages	1. Seasonal	Highly qualified job	Self-employment (employment of migrants, illegal networks)	Public services
Tertiary sector	Gas stations (I) Taxi drivers (S, GB, D) Hairdressers (D, S) Cleaning business (A, C, D, I, F, GB, PL, S) Catering business (I, A, S) Casual, insecure, part-time (A, C, D, I, F, GB, PL, S) Restaurants (A, C, D, I, F, GB, PL, S)	Tourism (I) Food distribution Geriatric care (I,D) Family care: assistance/ cleaning, Child-/ geriatric care (I, S, F)	Multinational companies (D, F, PL, in lesser extend S) Medical services (S, F) Dentists, physicians and nurses (S, GB, F)	Service sector (I) Building trades (I, C) Restaurants (S, GB, C) Food distribution (GB, S)	'Cultural mediation' (I, S)
Secondary sector	1. Unskilled positions: Automotive and electronic industry (D, F, S) 2. Manual work: Shoemaking (I) 3. Dangerous/dirty: Construction work (A, C, I, F)				Social work (GB, F, S); Police (F, GB)
Primary sector		Agricultural work (I,C,D)			

appears to be the stronghold of the employment of female migrants, with a high rate of illegal employment. Although it can be assumed that this illegal sector is primarily targeted at illegal migrants, 'foreigners' with work permits can also be found there due to the lack of alternative forms of employment. Ethnic and gender stereotypes play here a very efficient role in defining positions where the presence of a migrant will be acceptable, and even expected.

This equation of migrant work with low skilled, hard, low-paid and low-status jobs should not make us disregard the fact that many migrants in those countries are actually highly educated, and, in some cases, manage to find qualified positions. Case studies indicate that large, multinational companies are likely to hire employees with a migrant background either because they fill quotas defined by antidiscrimination procedures, or because it is their 'multicultural' background which is needed for a particular position, rather than solely on the basis of formal qualifications. For instance, multinationals like Siemens in Germany will hire employees with a specific ethnic background because they think they possess 'cultural expertise' which will be helpful to the company. Migrants often have to emphasize their 'exotic' skills or 'cultural competence' to achieve success both in multinational enterprises, private companies and public sectors, and when they try to escape discrimination by turning into self-employed business people running 'ethnic' restaurants, supermarkets, furniture stores, or translation offices.

This research indicates that in all countries we studied work-permit and job access-granting official authorities are major institutions of discrimination. Moreover, of the eight case study countries, six have discriminating laws and/or regulations barring migrants either from access to work in general or access to particular types of work. With some minor exceptions, these six countries reserve their civil service sector for citizens only. In two countries (Cyprus and Germany), explicit discriminatory laws keeping migrants away from the labour market are absent and instead it is agentic discrimination (by authorities and/or employers) that plays a major role in barring immigrants from access to jobs.

Legal Frames of Institutional Discrimination

Research and historical experiments show that laws and their institutional applications in society provide an important ground for institutional discrimination against the 'Others.' Apartheid laws and regulations, in the United States prior to antiracist movements of 1950s and in South Africa before the abolition of the apartheid system, are illustrative of the role of the law in the reproduction of racism and discrimination. Therefore, we looked at the laws and regulations that could reinforce and even prevent discrimination of individuals with immigrant and/or minority background.

Table 4.2 Legal frames of discrimination in the European labour market

Country	Priority law or regulation	Only 'natives' in public institutions	Restrictive naturalization law	Title (non) recognition	National anti-discrimination law
Austria	■	■	■	■	▨
Cyprus	■	▨	□	□	▨
England	□	□	□	□	□
France	■	■	▨	■	▨
Germany	■	▨	■	■	▨
Italy	■	▨	□	□	▨
Poland	■	▨	■	□	□
Sweden	□	■	□	■	▨

■ Nationwide (strong)   ▨ Nationwide (weak)   □ Does not exist

The following table (Table 4.2) is an illustration of the legal frameworks of discrimination in the eight countries engaged in this research:

Priority Laws and Their Equivalents

As Table 4.2 shows, the most important discriminatory factor are laws and regulations that in many cases constitute or legitimize barriers for 'Others' who are today European Union-citizens and long-term residents of those countries, barriers which deny them access to jobs in accordance with their competence, qualifications, and merits. We find these laws and regulations in six of our eight case study countries. In France, Germany, Austria, Poland, Italy, and Cyprus, employers and/or work mediation officials have to take on the burden of proving that no person privileged by laws or regulations can fill the vacant position. By these laws and regulations, recent migrants and non-European Union-migrants find themselves excluded, to a greater or lesser extent, from access to the national labour market. For instance, France introduced a ban on migration in 1974 and then linked migration to the labour market situation in 1984; Germany, meanwhile, introduced a law giving priority to Germans as employees in 1993. The revised German law, denying migrants work permits unless no Germans, European Union-citizens or long-term migrants can be found for the job, was passed in 1998 and a similar law was passed in Italy in 2002.

Moreover, 'labour force migrants' and/or their employers carry the burden of renewing the work permit, as well as a residence permit which can be received only when the work permit is in place. Both the work and the residence permit have to be renewed at frequent, regular intervals, and the renewal process is extremely cumbersome and uncertain. This means that permit-granting institutions, with their bothersome rules and procedures as well as their discriminating decision makers, make their own contribution to discrimination.

Job Access Laws—Civil Service

Secondly, we note that in six of our case study countries—Austria, France, Italy, and, with some minor exceptions, Poland, Germany, and Cyprus— through laws or regulations, only citizens are entitled to work in the civil service. In a seventh country, Sweden, this is a matter of an established practice in some areas, rather than an explicit law.

Since citizenship is a key precondition for access to the labour market and to public service in six case study countries, it has to be noted that restrictive naturalisation laws, which grant more weight to citizenship by descent (*jus sanguinis*) than to citizenship by birth place (*jus soli*), reinforce the outcome of excluding noncitizens and non-European Union-nationals. Such restrictive naturalisation laws are most pronounced in Austria and Germany, but even in France in 1993 citizenship ceased to be an automatic right of every 'foreign' child born and living (at least five years) in France and instead became a matter of a special declaration (see also Wodak & Van Dijk, 2000; Brubaker, 1996). In some countries, restrictive naturalisation laws and regulations pose obstacles to acquiring citizenship even for the children and grandchildren of migrants, and thus make their access to national labour markets more difficult while also barring them from the civic service sector.

Title (Non)Recognition

The next heavy-weighing piece of legislation concerns title-recognition. We found that at least in five of our eight cases—Germany, Austria, Italy, France, and Sweden—either law requires, and makes difficult, the conversion of qualifications acquired abroad (Germany, Austria, Italy, France) or this is a national praxis without clear support in law (Sweden). Many immigrants and naturalized citizens face difficulties in getting recognition for their merits and qualifications earned in their countries of origin. This nonrecognition concerns not only with respect to educational merits, but also immigrants' work experience attained in other countries.

Other laws and regulations pertaining to job announcements leave room for discriminatory practices, even if they do not contain antidiscriminatory clauses. In Cyprus, the fact that advertisements are in Greek and ask for citizenship or proficiency in the 'native' language discriminates not only against various migrant groups, but also the largest minority of Turkish Cypriots. Antidiscriminatory laws, which put a legal ban on such practices, do help to limit them. Noteworthy is that only four of the eight countries engaged in this research have specific antidiscrimination laws or regulations, namely France, Sweden, Italy, and Germany, although European Union antidiscriminatory laws are to be institutionalized in all member states.

Antidiscrimination Law

Concluding the presentation of some key laws contributing to discrimination, it is crucial that we mention that virtually all of our interviewees were of the opinion that antidiscrimination laws are ultimately ineffective. They exact 'politically correct' or legal conduct from the discriminating decision makers, but cannot counteract discrimination. Even so, it is important to note that only three of eight case study countries—France, Great Britain, and Austria—had such laws. Cyprus has an antidiscrimination law only for the private sector of employment. Germany's antidiscrimination law (found in the *Betriebsverfassung*) protects only against discrimination within private and public enterprises. The European Union-antidiscrimination law is supposed to cover even many other aspects of social life, but NGOs and their experts are not even aware of this and such interviewees kept pointing out that no German antidiscrimination laws help protect migrants.

Furthermore, if we are to address discrimination we would do well to first question the point of departure of traditional approaches to antidiscrimination law and the way they take for granted a liberal view of 'difference' and the inequalities that follow. The issue, however, is not only one of difference, but of how difference is constituted through hierarchies and the meanings attached to it. These find their articulation in the more subtle forms of institutional, structural and cultural norms and are often part of the taken-for-granted fabric of everyday life for those who belong to the 'Us' category. However, the majority society's claim to neutrality and sameness—as an expression of supposed objectivity—fails to capture the experiences of 'Others' and see its own role in the 'objective discrimination' of the 'Others.' Neutrality and objectivity would perhaps make sense if the challenge was simply one of *differentiation*. But because the problem is one of *hierarchy*, and the meanings attached to these so-called 'objective differences,' the response of neutrality is not only inadequate, but also serves to promote the continued existence of these hierarchies of difference.

Institutional Agentic Discrimination

Institutional discrimination can take place through the actions of persons who possess institutional power and influence. This is referred to in this research project as 'institutional agentic discrimination.' Therefore, one goal of the research is to identify decision makers in key institutions—such as schools, work mediation offices, or work enterprises—whose routine decisions lead to discrimination against, or the exclusion of, migrants and their children. These decision makers can be conceptualized as gatekeepers since they decide which categories of persons will gain access to specific resources. These decision makers have the power to categorize human beings, to grant permits and/or access to jobs or other resources. It is when they exercise their agentic power that these gatekeepers create certain disadvantaged groups. And their decisions create *systematic biases in the allocation of premiums and penalties through institutional mechanisms.*

As far as the labour market is concerned, officials in charge of granting work and residence permits play a major role as discrimination agents in at least six of the eight countries we studied, namely, Sweden, Germany, France, Italy, Austria, and Cyprus. Based on this and previous research phases, we can say with a reasonable degree of certainty that they serve as the major gatekeepers who work to exclude migrants and their children from the mainstream of national institutional life. The Polish case is interesting. Immigrants from the 'west' encounter positive discrimination and easterners from the Ukraine, Lithuania, or White Russia, negative discrimination. This is more or less the same in other countries also, and is an indication of the eight countries understanding of who belongs to the category of 'Us' and who to the category of the 'Others.' Thus, the concept of 'immigrants' should be modified in terms of 'desired western migrants' and 'undesired and otherised migrants' from 'nonwestern' countries.

An equally important role is played by enterprises. The research shows that there is quite a bit of national variation in who are the key decision makers in enterprises. In some countries, such as Italy, only the bosses or their forepersons have a say in hiring, while in others, such as Sweden, several decision makers—such as supervisors, heads of personnel office, key union functionaries, and key employees—decide who will be hired. This, on the one hand, reflects the democratic and egalitarian values of Swedish society. On the other hand, it also permits more subtle and insidious kinds of discrimination that may be more difficult to trace because discriminatory practices permeate several 'gatekeeping' levels.

Although employers, subcontractors or forepersons play a more exploitative and abusive role in the illegal labour market of Italy and Poland than is the case in the six other countries, their findings can be generalized. Often the subcontractors and forepersons belong to the same ethnic group as the employees, rely on network-hiring, and are as abusive and exploitative as the bosses. Illegality makes migrants vulnerable. Part of their income is kept by their employers, or by subcontractors or forepersons, on the grounds that they hire them in the first place, help them with the formalities, or provide them with housing.

Returning to the legal labour market, it seems that some 'ethnic networks' and NGOs play a key role in counteracting discrimination. 'Ethnic networks' help spread information about openings and support the hiring of members of the same ethnic group for certain jobs. Such networks are said to play a key countering role in four out of the eight countries. When they have a chance to develop, 'ethnic networks' help to mitigate the worst types of discrimination in hiring.

It should be noted, however, that, in general, our research does not find (except in Italy for certain areas) the type of "ethnic networks" found in America, which, as Tilly and Tilly (1994, p. 302) show, reverse the discrimination criteria and use their networks to monopolize control over hiring for certain jobs, departments, trades, or professions. The presence of such mostly "white ethnic networks," organized by Italians, the Irish, Poles, and Jews in specific trades and professions in the United States, led Alejandro Portes (1998, p. 15) to speak of ethnic groups as possessing certain—positive or negative—social capital. We have found a certain fear of such networks but only when, for example, German managers fear that Turkish networks may actively try to expand the number of Turks working for their company. NGOs try to play the role of benevolent employers or of advocates for migrants, but are mentioned only in two cases, namely Poland and Italy. Trade unions are also mentioned as supportive of migrants but only in two countries, namely Italy and England. In Cyprus, trade unions are mainly xenophobic and only a minor group builds bridges to non-Greek Cypriots. In Germany and Sweden, they express their fear of migrants and new European Union members as competitors for jobs, while they fight against illegal labour, sometimes in the name of compassion for the exploited workers. In many cases arguments concerning unemployment are linked to immigration policies and mobilized to hinder immigrant networks and discriminate against immigrants in terms of accessing employment.

Intersections: Ethnicity, Religion, Gender, and Class

Compounding the discrimination based on people's belonging to other imagined 'races' or 'ethnicities' are clear gender, religious, and class dimensions. The issue of Muslim girls' and women's headscarves appears in various contexts as a specifically gendered and symbolic challenge to native-dominated workplaces and the established norms of belonging and 'correctness.' In Germany and Austria, the discrimination is most overt; however, in many other countries, Muslim women are targeted, stereotyped, and stigmatized for wearing headscarves, and this includes the drawing of patronising parallels between the lives of Muslim and non-Muslim women. These foremostly rely upon crude gendered stereotypes that typically posit 'western culture' and 'western women' as 'free' and 'autonomous' and consequently relegate immigrant girls and women as 'victims' of their culture. Thus, one of the common excuses presented by many employers for not employing Muslim women is that customers and clients feel uncomfortable facing venders, sellers, and other company employees if said employees are wearing a headscarf.

However, women with immigrant backgrounds, whoever they are and however they are categorized, are highly racialised and 'Otherised.' When immigrant women do find employment, trends indicate an increasingly feminized and gender-segregated labour market underpinned by crude stereotypes. In many European countries entire populations of immigrant women are categorized as being 'caring,' 'clean,' 'obedient,' and so forth. Whether they be from Eastern Europe or the Philippines, the discriminatory images and effects are similar; entire categories of women are stereotyped in gender specific ways, essentialising their caring 'nature' as women and their suitability as domestic servants as if such women had an *a priori* disposition to cleaning and caring.

These stereotypes are reproduced in a variety of practices and also intersect with particular constructions of women as 'sexual.' In Cyprus, for example, the requirement for so-called '*nice looking foreign women that are healthy and clean*' (quote from interview), ensures that female candidates for particular occupations are only recruited after their appearance has been examined via photograph. Such practices accentuate the parameters of power which permit racialised (and gendered) discriminatory behaviour through the construction of women as aesthetically attractive and sexual. These forms of recruitment are not unique to Cyprus but are also practiced in Italy and other European countries. The Cyprus case, however, reveals particularly disturbing forms of sexual exploitation against immigrant women who are violently taken advantage of in their role as domestic 'servants,' where they have been required to sexually service the children of the household. Whilst such an extreme case might represent the 'exception' rather than the rule, it does point to a troubling intersection of 'race,' gender, and sexuality in the exploitation of a particular ethnic minority. In other words, women's bodies become racialised, sexualized, and 'Otherised.'

Just as 'race' and ethnicity intersect with gender and sexuality, so too does class factor as an important dimension in the power relations between immigrant groups and majority society. While, as we have seen, there are multiple factors that intersect and function to marginalize immigrants living in all European countries, an attention to class can help, in many respects, to highlight *the differences between* different immigrant groups and their positions in European societies. It is important also to stress the intersections of ethnicity and class in the labour market in those cases where immigrant families are of lower and working class background. The intersection of class and ethnicity certainly does contribute to a marginalized status for immigrants in the labour market.

The 'Market' Constructed as a Discriminatory Mechanism

In many countries the 'market' and the perceived demands and values of clients and customers govern the norms of what candidates are considered suitable for employment. Stereotypes by employers, opportunistic exploitation of migrant workers in a vulnerable position, and employers' so-called objective 'concerns' about what other employees or clients might think about immigrant employees are used to deflect and externalize the prejudices underpinning these practices. Here, the 'market' is constructed as a kind of force *per se,* and responsibility for prejudices is shifted off individuals and into this 'sphere.' There is a kind of circular logic through which immigrants are denied access to labour markets. The claim that clients and customers might react against immigrant employees permits gatekeepers to position themselves as benevolent and well-intentioned by *not* employing immigrants and thus 'protecting' them from such reactions and experiences.

Assumptions Concerning the 'Others'

Discrimination is a process of noting, perceiving, constructing a difference or distinction between members of an in-group ('Us') and members of an out-group ('Them') and deciding that these differences should qualify for differential treatment and justify the exclusion of the out-groups. In our study of the eight countries' labour markets, we found that in daily interactions, migrants and members of some minorities are stereotyped as lacking language and 'cultural competence,' or as being unreliable, lazy, devious, and criminal. On the basis of such judgements, they are then 'sentenced' either to unemployment or to menial, hard, repetitive, dirty, and low paid tasks; in both ways they are denied equal opportunities with 'natives' when it comes to accessing a job or position.

In the best case scenario, specific 'skills' or 'talents'—such as being flexible, being able to take on hard workloads or the worst working times—become attributed to migrants or members of some minorities. In Europe, these 'skills' or 'talents' are then referred to in order to justify why they are given the jobs which hardly any 'natives' want to do. There are similarities between Europe and the United States in this respect. Tilly and Tilly (1994) show that American employers attribute specific skills, work experience, and traits to specific ethnic groups, and, based on these attributions, they decide against hiring them at all or assign them to different departments in their enterprises which results in ethnic segregation within these enterprises. Comparable to this would be the conviction, spread throughout much of Europe, that Turks are only suitable for unskilled jobs in industry, while Albanians or Ukrainians are willing to take on dirty or backbreaking, low-paid seasonal jobs in agriculture (picking strawberries, wine grapes, asparagus, or apples) or the construction industry. Another belief that is found in our study is that even in the irregular labour market there are stereotyped and discriminatory assumptions among 'Europeans' about the 'Others' that influence the latter's chances in the labour market. For example, many believe that Polish women make 'great nurses,' whereas women from the Philippines are ideal as loving and caring babysitters.

Our perhaps most important finding from six of the countries (the exceptions are Cyprus and Italy) is that directly racist statements are hard to come by these days. Instead of being confronted with outright racism, interviewers came across an entire series of rather 'innocent' views in the name of which migrants and their children were excluded from access to jobs or consigned to inferior jobs and career paths. In a rather trivial way, most gatekeepers in enterprises argued that their hiring decisions are based on such criteria as 'qualifications,' 'fitting in,' 'communicative skills,' and 'a well-structured CV and interview.'

The statements smelling strongest of prejudice were rather innocuous and 'common sense.' Experts and gatekeepers all agreed that language competency is a must for immigrants to be able to get a job or position in society. The claim to one's own linguistic (and so implicitly, cultural, national, and even, in some cases, racial) superiority has to be read into this job requirement, since it is not explicit. More explicit in its national bias is the demand for 'native' educational titles or work experience, which are believed to be superior in everyone of the countries except in Poland. But a discerning discriminating mind does not stop at making distinctions between citizens and noncitizens, recent and new migrants. It is irritated by and rejects anything 'foreign.' It demands 'local knowledge' (GB) or familiarity with 'national cultural codes' (S, D) from a suitable job candidate.

Even if the first set of belief patterns amongst gatekeepers and employers (concerning language competency and 'native' titles and work experience) seem innocuous and only mildly nationalist, its effects are discriminatory. These belief patterns make the practice of setting priority on 'native citizens' in hiring legitimate at the same time as they legitimate rejecting noncitizens and 'nonnatives.' Yet one could argue that titles and work experience constitute 'hard data' whose comparability can be precisely defined.

The second, subtle set of requirements (calling for 'local knowledge' or the knowledge of 'national cultural codes') is even more discriminatory because it makes the possession of nontangibles into a job prerequisite. This kind of discrimination is accordingly harder to prove and to counteract. One such example of this is that Swedish employers—as with many others—seem to seek to recruit people who do not differ too greatly from the perceived 'majority culture.' One informant expressed this dilemma as follows: "They say that they are neutral and objective, but they are not. They belong to the same culture, the majority culture, with its own values and stereotypes, and they want to reproduce this majority group."

In this sense, the 'goal posts' are constantly shifting for immigrants. The image of a homogenous 'majority culture' shared by 'native individuals' belonging to 'the nation' is reproduced in relation to groups of people, called 'immigrants,' who are considered outsiders in relation to 'the nation.' Thus, immigrants are asked, in many cases, to mimic the image of 'being' Italian, Swedish, German, and so forth, but just how these qualities are to be defined relies heavily on the construction of the immigrant as the 'Others' and as 'lacking' the value and qualities that are perceived to epitomize 'being' within the nation. In both Sweden and England, there are clear examples of the importance of the 'Other' in the constitution of the image of 'the nation' as a homogenous 'Us.' 'Swedishness' and 'Britishness' are constituted through defining what the immigrant 'Other' is *not*. In Italy too, the immigrant 'Other' is described as deviating from Italian norms and values. What immigrants are seen to lack in many cases is some form of undefined 'cultural competence,' expressed in Sweden, for instance, as 'feeling for work' and 'personal chemistry,' and, in Cyprus, as 'character.' More generally, in these kinds of descriptions, both the majority society and immigrants are essentialised as belonging to essentially different cultures. The homogenized dichotomy of 'majority culture' and 'immigrant cultures' are presented as real and fixed. At the same time, there is a denial that discrimination takes place at all. In seven of the eight countries engaged in this research, namely Austria, Cyprus, France, Italy, Germany, Poland, and Sweden, discrimination and racism are viewed simply as 'exceptions' and "kinds of frictions between immigrants and the majority culture and as a matter of individual cases and individual personalities." It is only England that has accepted that there is institutional discrimination against immigrants and minorities in the country. The study shows that in the denial of discrimination lies a purification of the discourse of 'Us' from the negative properties of racism and discrimination. The blame of racism and discrimination in the labour market is put either on immigrants themselves (such as in lacking 'right competence,' 'ability to apply correctly,' 'applying for wrong jobs,' and 'not fitting in the group'), or on particular individuals acting without institutional support. As Cowlishaw (1997, p. 233) puts it, the concept of "national identity" is often used to authorize exclusionary discourses that invariably embrace racist dialogue in order to achieve a sense of "national self."

Following on from this, we can appreciate employment policies and practices as a part of a continual nation-building exercise. Through the practice of reproducing hegemonic cultural norms, the political imaginings of nations, and the use of cultural hierarchies, the labour market contributes to the exclusion of various populations from the space of 'belonging' within the nation. It is important to appreciate, however, that these practices are not necessarily entirely new, and have not simply appeared in response to 'challenges' posed by increasing flows of migrants. Hierarchical views of culture have often underpinned the historical liberal view that the laws and hegemonic culture of the majority society justify the exclusion of those not adhering to the 'majority culture's' view of the world. Furthermore, universalist claims, such as 'equality before the law,' 'all should apply and compete for a job,' and 'majority's democratic rule,' have often served to silence claims of discrimination from subjects not conforming to the so-called established universal norms, values, and assumptions of the majority that discriminate against them. Whilst the established institutions of the eight countries engaged in this research do, based on 'universal norms,' claim to include all subjects in the 'body nation,' we are witnessing simultaneously the fact that employment, educational, cultural, and citizenship practices exclude daily 'undesirable' and 'Otherised' individuals.

The study shows that discrimination and exclusion of the 'Other' that is taking place in the labour market is a way of reproducing 'the nation' by excluding the 'Otherised' groups from access to jobs and positions of influence. As Isin (2002) puts it, various subjects and populations are excluded and 'Otherised' in the very name of inclusion. Thus, universal citizenship is not universal because it actually encompasses all subjects, but because "citizenship is that particular point of view of the dominant which constitutes itself as a universal point of view" (Isin 2002, p. 275). Indeed, populations that have eventually been 'included' by naturalisation, such as immigrant groups, are still often viewed as the 'Other' and their constituents deemed by the state to be failed or 'not-quite-capable' citizens. And so citizenship and 'Otherness' are, then, not really two different conditions, but two aspects of the ontological condition that makes politics possible (Isin, 2002). In this sense, nations are invented as familiar spaces, and as places of comfort and belonging, by the majority culture only through recognising that there are some people who are not familiar, who are not part of the majority society, and who will always remain 'foreign' (cf., Silverman, 1992).

After reviewing the material, we can thus identify various forms of reconstruction of a nationalist view of 'Us' by a belief in the superiority of one's own educational merits and work patterns existing in all countries engaged in this study. Even educational merits and work experiences attained in European countries by immigrants are not considered and evaluated equally with those attained by individual applicants with 'native' background in hiring processes. The belief in the superiority of 'Us' over the 'Others' reproduces and reinforces the processes of 'Otherization' by excluding the 'Others' from those jobs which are commensurate with their actual level of competence. Even where there are laws and regulations that aim at preventing discrimination of immigrants, there are other means which are used to legitimate discrimination. For example, discriminatory subtle demands for 'local knowledge' or 'cultural competence' are used in countries such as Sweden and the United Kingdom where (a) the naturalisation laws are more liberal, (b) priority laws or regulations do not set up a barrier to the hiring of migrants, and (c) antidiscrimination laws exist.

The case studies can be divided into two categories with two different discrimination emphases: Germany, Austria, Italy, Cyprus, Poland, and France have discriminatory laws or regulations concerning work permits, and so gatekeepers and their beliefs can mainly play a reinforcing or miti-gating role. Great Britain and Sweden have no such laws and therefore gate-keepers, operating in such a legal context, become one of the major agents of discrimination of immigrants. Alongside this, in all countries permit or access granting institutions, such as the police, the *Ausländerbehörde* or the work mediation office, play a clearly discriminatory role.

INSTITUTIONAL DISCRIMINATION IN THE EDUCATIONAL SYSTEM

The modern education system has been formed, amongst other things, to reinforce the sense of belonging to a nation. The teaching of a country's history, culture, and religion, has been an inseparable part of modern edu-cation. Emile Durkheim, in his classical work on integration from the early 20th century, *The Division of Labor in Society,* presented the modern edu-cation system as a central actor in promoting national integration. Mod-ern education should create and reinforce modern norms as substitutes for religious norms and values. Durkheim, who was of Jewish background, was concerned about the Jewish minority's situation and discrimination in France, and saw secular education as a way out of racism and discrimina-tion against religious minorities. He underestimated, however, the role of the modern education system as the *reproducing* agent of modern norms, in reproducing a sense of, and internalised believe in, the superior 'Us' against the inferior 'Them.'

All countries have more or less a package of 'equal rights' and 'protec-tion' for their citizens, including antidiscrimination laws. However, the dec-laration of rights does not automatically entail 'equal treatment.' There are still many cases of direct and indirect discrimination against immigrants, for instance, in the educational system. In practice, across Europe, there is evidence that immigrants have more limited access and fewer opportuni-ties with respect to education than do the 'natives' of these countries. How-ever, the patterns are complex and there is considerable variation among immigrant groups. In general though, immigrant children are less likely to enter or to finish the higher levels of education (upper secondary school and beyond). There are pervasive reports of language difficulties and of special classes whose intent may be laudable but which serve also to stigmatize. Par-ticularly common is stigmatisation and generalisation around 'problems' of males from poor social backgrounds; while these problems extend to 'native' youth as well as immigrants, typically the latter suffer more. These instances are not necessarily linked to legal discrimination—although in some they clearly are—but, in most cases, more subtle forms of discrimination are at work, through institutional, structural, and cultural norms.

Clearly, there are multiple factors or mechanisms affecting the opportuni-ties and life chances of immigrants or their children in the school system and on the labour market. Being an immigrant or a member of an 'Otherised' minority explains some, but not all, of the variances between immigrants and 'natives' in the educational system. Social class and social background, gender dynamics, the educational level of the parents, the quality of the school, and the nature of the neighbourhood are also important factors. Mapping out and analysing this complexity could provide a solid basis for effective policy and programs in order to mitigate the European dilemma: the gap between the ideal of a Europe with a human face and a democratic and egalitarian body, on the one hand, and the practices of differentiation, discrimination, and exclusion that the research presented here suggests. Above all, what the research implies is the immediate and dire need for the majority society to reflect over its own position of power in the constitution of structural, institutional, and cultural norms and actions that underpin educational systems, and the way this necessarily discriminates against the 'Others.'

There is considerable research suggesting serious problems of institutional discrimination in education systems. Some, albeit limited, research has been devoted to trying to explain these patterns, and in particular to what extent, and through what concrete mechanisms, institutional discrimination takes place (Operario & Fiske, 1998; Kamali, 2006a; Dance, 2006; James, 2006). Although laws and regulations forbid direct discrimination in countries such as Sweden and England, informal rules, deep cognitive structures, and established practices pervade the educational institutions in discriminatory ways. For instance, established classification and interpretative schemes typically operate in a discriminatory manner. Both in its formal and informal expressions, the term 'immigrant' serves to maintain and reproduce certain discriminatory concepts and practices—for instance, those conducted in a paternalistic fashion that see pupils of immigrant background as inferior to 'native' pupils and which 'clientise' them.

In general, the reports here suggest that there is considerable discrimination and exclusion in educational systems in all European countries, although the extent of this discrimination and exclusion varies markedly according to country. Several of the major patterns that are identified in the study concern institutional patterns of ethnic discrimination—what we call the *mechanism of ethnic discrimination*. The following discussion provides an illustration of the mechanism of discrimination in the field of education.

Discrimination in educational institutions continues to be an important factor underlying the lower degree of educational achievement among students with nonmainstream background in all countries studied in our project. This pattern is reported in a substantial literature concerning institutional discrimination in the educational system of many European countries (in particular, England, France, and Germany; Fitzgerald, Finch, & Nove, 2000; Osler & Morrison, 2000; Derrington & Kendall, 2004; Pye, Lee, & Bhabra, 2000; Wright, Weekes, & McGlaughlin, 2000; Judge, 2004; Reuter, 1999, 2001; Schewe, 2000). As mentioned earlier, there is a powerful tendency for the majority society to perceive immigrant or minority (e.g., black) children as 'problem students' (Glasgow, 1980; Wilson, 1987; Anderson, 1990). This is associated with the 'dropout' of students with black and/or immigrant backgrounds from mainstream schools in the USA.

Discrimination as a Societal and Interinstitutional Phenomenon

Racism and discrimination in schools is not isolated from other social structures and institutions. The phenomenon of discrimination has many 'spill-over' mechanisms. Discrimination in one institution has 'spill-over' effects on other institutions, as was discussed earlier. Along with this mechanism go the discursive processes of denying institutional discrimination by addressing 'equal treatment' of everybody. The school systems, for instance, are presumed to be open to all, meritocratic in theory and practice.

In our study, it was clear that inferiorization of immigrant pupils goes hand in hand with narratives of the 'normal' and 'superior' 'native' pupils. There are widespread, established institutionalized 'stories' in classroom discourses and in schoolbooks about 'foreigners' or 'immigrants,' which tend to reinforce 'Otherism' and xenophobia at the same time that there are institutionalized discourses which self-servingly reinforce the view that the better educational achievement of 'native' pupils is due to their 'better quality.' Interviews with school leaders and teachers show that many of them do categorize immigrant pupils in a very prejudiced and discriminatory way. The process of categorisation and, relatedly, demonisation, is part and parcel of analysing xenophobia and 'Otherism' in a broader scientific perspective. Problematically, these kinds of mechanisms are enacted by teachers themselves, which impacts on the life chances and opportunities of immigrant groups.

Social and educational policies in Europe have also been influenced by racist categories that generalize and divide people into different groups and associate those groups with specific qualities. School systems and schoolbooks contribute to the reproduction of overall sense of 'difference' between 'Us' and 'Them,' by which 'Them' puts, culturally, in lower position than 'Us.' The hierarchisation of cultures along a continuum maintains the enlightenment view that some cultures are constantly superior to others. Our case studies in the eight countries show that this ethnocentric view of the world finds clear articulation and robust reproduction in the school system.

In the majority of the case studies, we have found that discriminations against pupils of immigrant background are unintentional. Intentionality is more obvious in the case of Cyprus and France. In Cyprus, the overt stress on the Cypriot language, culture and descent is common among school teachers and other staff. In France, the stress on secular education is a way of denying many immigrant pupils' claim of the problems with a system that openly excludes Muslim girls from public education. In all countries engaged in this research, pupils of immigrant background are portrayed and categorized as 'different.'

In those cases where measures have been formulated in response to immigrants it is not uncommon to justify certain policies and actions within educational systems by referring to perceived differences between 'natives' and 'immigrants.' Indeed, the idea that fixed cultural differences exist has underpinned many variations of the so-called 'cultural explanation' of immigrant pupils' problems in schools, such as lower levels of success. For the most part it is the case that these explanations are based not on the findings of empirical research, but are grounded instead in preconceived ideas about life in the typical "Muslim," "Oriental" or "Southern European" family (Bender-Szymanski & Hesse, 1987, p. 37). Even when empirical evidence is provided, many methodological objections can be raised concerning the design of these studies and the interpretation of the findings. For example, Leenen, Grosch, and Kreidt (1990) claim that Turkish families cling to a "traditional" understanding of learning and teaching: learning by heart, unquestioned acceptance of the material, and seeing teachers as absolute authorities (Leenen, Grosch, & Kreidt, 1990, pp. 760–761). This encourages what they call a "receptive orientation" (Leenen, Grosch, & Kreidt, 1990, p. 761). For these authors, this type of 'traditional' understanding stands in sharp contrast to the "modern," that is, instrumental and individualistic understanding (Leenen, Grosch, & Kreidt, 1990, p. 762). The latter exemplifies the aims and methods of learning and teaching advocated, for example, in the German educational system. This typical and crude division between immigrants as 'premodern' and the norms enshrined in the majority society's education system as 'modern' (and incompatible with 'Other' cultures) perpetuates a hierarchical view of both peoples and cultures. As Bhabha (1996, p. 55) puts it, there is a kind of logic of "culture-as-difference," and of culture as 'Other' (see even Bhabha, 1994).

Immigrants are not homogenous groups with the same properties contrary to what many countries try to confirm. Indeed, our and other research in the field of education shows that important differences exist among immigrants. For example, in compulsory education in Sweden, some immigrant children do very well compared with both immigrant and ethnically Swedish students, and in university, some ethnic groups are more highly represented compared to others. However, in many countries differences between immigrant and minority groups are conflated, as if these populations were homogenous. In Sweden, there are clear differences between the higher education enrolment levels between groups of immigrants: Students with Iranian background have a normal representation whilst Somalian students are clearly underrepresented. Statistics and broad generalisations about 'immigrants,' as if they were one group, tend to render these differences invisible. In Italy, the experiences of 'foreign' youngsters differ greatly from one another. There are differences, for example, between such children based on how old they were when they came to Italy—namely, those who came before starting their education in their country of origin and those who came after a few years of education.

In the case of Cyprus, the 'homogenisation' of differences between immigrants is enshrined in the Constitution itself, where the rigidity of the Constitution fixes ethnic identity in such a way that the two communities of Greeks and Cypriot Turks must be kept apart. Anyone not belonging to either of the two categories, such as members of smaller religious groups, must opt to belong to either of the two main communities. This entails not only a binary division between the two majority cultures in Cyprus, but also forces all minorities to conform and identify within this binary.

'Otherization' Processes in School

The case studies show that the educational systems and practices of the eight countries are a part of a continual nation building exercise. Through the practice of reproducing cultural norms, the political imaginings of nations, and the use of cultural hierarchies, educational systems contribute to the exclusion of various populations from the space of 'belonging' within the nation. The educational system, including school books and classroom discourse, is an important instrument in this respect. The case studies show that 'national culture' and 'national identity' are discourses that are used by school personnel in order to legitimize 'Otherization' of pupils of immigrant background.

In Austria, history books still clearly draw on national and cultural stereotypes. For instance, the Viennese Siege by Turks (of the year 1683) is a predominant story retold that draws upon a very negative picture of the Turks as 'invaders.' As one Turkish interviewee remarked: "Me and my Turkish school mates often felt insulted and got angry when listening to the comments in our history books." Even politicians who are responsible for the educational system use such discourse to reinforce a sense of belonging to a nation of 'Us,' one which is culturally homogeneous, historical, and 'different' from the 'Others.' For example, this is framed In the United Kingdom as 'our historical heritage,' in Germany as 'our German culture,' and in Sweden as 'our established norms.' The 'Others' are seen as 'foreign elements' to the homogenous and historical nation. The recognition of the 'difference' between 'Us' and 'Them'—sometimes demonstrated by the term of 'multiculturalism'—is often a means of making and reinforcing the distinction between 'Us' and 'Them.' Migrants or the 'Other' are used to define and determine what the very nature of, for instance, 'Englishness,' 'French-ness,' 'German-ness' and 'Swedish-ness' are. Educational system is one of the most important agents in the production and, particularly, the reproduction of 'national' sentiments, prejudice, racial stereotypes, myths, discourses and attitudes about ethnic minorities, migrants and the 'Other.'

In other worlds, building a homogenous nation by education goes with making distinctions towards the 'Other.'

In France, the debate on the access of Muslim girls who wear headscarves to education shows a clear connection between the exclusion of Muslim girls from public education and the defence of traditional 'French-ness' and the French nation. Even recognition of increases in urban segregation, violence, and exclusion of immigrants is used to legitimize such exclusionary actions by emphasising the integrative role of the French Republican schooling system. In Sweden too, reactions over 'multiculturalism' and 'difference' in schools as threats to the Swedish secular and 'normal' educational system are clearly and freely articulated by teachers and politicians. Such expressions are not only deeply concerning for their discriminatory implications, but also highlight how inextricably linked education is to the majority society's own view of the nation as a space of belonging; consequently, education is an integral part of 'Otherization' processes.

Even the colonial past of France is glorified in some text books and presented as modernization efforts of the French in America, Africa, Asia, and the Middle East. Colonialism is not properly discussed in any country. Although not all countries have been colonial powers (Cyprus itself was an English European colony until after World War II) and some countries, like Sweden, to a much lesser extent than England, France, Italy, and Germany, the colonial image of 'Otherised' people are common to all countries. For example, pedagogical textbooks contains negative images of the 'Others,' such as Africans and Muslims. Another common feature in all countries' textbooks are the existence of dichotomies of 'Us' against 'Them.' As the results of expert interviews show, almost everything is presented from a western perspective where everything that relates to 'Us' is 'correct' and glorified and everything that belongs to the 'Others' (such as culture, history, and religion) is inferiorised.

In England too, besides some improvement in recent years, most informants could draw on some aspects of the curriculum that they felt presented the 'Others' in a negative, or at least inaccurate, way. Some informant interviewees indicated the ethnocentrism of many school textbooks. The concepts used here, such as 'The Far East,' was used as an example. As a British informant said: "Far or east from where exactly?" and "Britain still thinks of itself as a powerful Empire, and to some extent you can see that in the way subjects like history are taught." However, most informants identified a shift in this regard. One claimed, for instance: "One could say in general terms that the books we use now are more 'politically correct' [than in the past] as they don't assume everyone is white or British-born."

There is also a tendency in England to use class-explanations as a way of denying claims of discrimination against immigrants. Schools with a relatively high proportion of migrant pupils tended to be in poorer areas and have a large pupil to staff ratio, and were underfunded in general. The argument presented by those working in such schools was that differences in resources should not be explained with reference to the number of pupils with a migrant background, but the other way around; in other words, due to social inequalities outside the education system, some migrant pupils are within the catchments areas of poorly resourced schools. As migrants tend to be concentrated in urban areas, with more recent migrants to the country, and often in poor quality housing stock in less affluent inner-city areas, the suggestion from some interviewees was that children of migrants, and especially some more recent migrants to England, will tend to be in less-well resourced schools whose catchments areas to draw pupils from are the inner city areas. Those working in schools also suggested that these schools tend to have a higher turnover of staff than is average, which compounds many of the issues outlined here. However, whilst inequalities associated with social class certainly play a role, it is absurd to deny the relationship between schools being segregated between migrant and nonmigrant pupils as having also to do with the fact that immigrants are also discriminated against. Those working in the education sector, though, were reluctant to identify segregation *per se* in schools.

All interviewees in Italy agreed that the school textbooks do reflect and reproduce the views of the majority society. When 'diversity' is used it is as a sign of 'difference.' In many cases the more diversity is underlined, the more this is used to marginalize the 'Other.' The informants mean that there is marginalisation through 'diversification' (read, distinction) of immigrants from majority society. The result of this study is supported by another study conducted by 'The network of *Centri Interculturali*.' The network analyzed school programmes and textbooks in Italy and showed that all texts analyzed are markedly Italian-centred, not even European-centred.

In Sweden too, the interviewees claimed that it is still quite common to dichotomize 'the west and the Orient,' the civilised and the uncivilised. Almost everything is presented from a Swedish/western perspective. One interviewee expressed the following concern:

> What we can read in the books sometimes is about what happened with the Jews in Germany. There is a displacement of the problem to another place and to another time. This cultural racism that exists in our time is the problem, it has a great influence on how you feel and what kind of plans you have for your future.

Another interviewee expressed a concern about the textbooks that was also mentioned in interviews in other countries: "When I look at my daughter's schoolbooks, I do not find anything about immigrants. These positive models that the Swedish children have . . . their parents are in powerful positions. Children of immigrant parents have nothing to be proud of; this is a pattern, a stigmatized pattern."

The interviewees from Germany and the study of the textbooks show that the presentation of immigrants is very rare in schoolbooks and that when there is any such presentation, it is in a highly stigmatising manner. Although teachers can use their own additional materials, they rarely use texts which present the 'Others' in a fair or favourable way. The 'Others' are presented as 'alien' to 'Us.' Interviewees also said that schoolteachers frequently ask pupils of migrant background to present on 'their own countries' or, together with their parents, to organize cooking sessions with ethnic foods and 'theme weeks' about themselves in schools. This highlights, according to interviewees, a disturbing 'exoticisation' of immigrants. Such activities are based upon, and contribute towards, the established assumption that the cultures of the 'Others' are 'exotic' and do not belong to 'Us.'

The question of 'Otherization' of pupils of immigrant background is not explored in Poland. This study is one of the first ones addressing the question of 'Otherization' through education. According to the interviewees, school textbooks are highly ethnocentric and deal exclusively with the needs of Polish pupils. Pupils of immigrant background are not considered as a question to be discussed. There are some minor addresses in the textbooks about the historical relations between Poles and Jews, but nothing about other groups. Even the concept and discussions concerning 'multiculturalism' in schools are totally lacking in the Polish school system. However, there are some acts of 'Otherization' by 'exoticisation' of immigrants in schools. There are a few teaching themes dedicated to the learning of 'other cultures and nations.'

Equality and Difference

Many of the tensions described in education systems throughout Europe reflect not only an overt practice of cultural racism and nation building, but also more subtle forms of political discourse. The 'equality-versus-difference' debate is one such political discourse that can work in various ways to create difference, silence difference, conflate sameness with equality, and even justify segregation through difference. Regardless of the various outcomes, what all of these debates rely upon is a binary opposition that creates a scenario as if it were a choice of one or the other, that is, either endorsing 'equality' or its presumed antithesis 'difference': "In fact, the antithesis itself hides the interdependence of the two terms, for equality is not the elimination of difference, and difference does not preclude equality" (Scott, 2001, p. 258).

Examples of these debates in Europe may not always take the explicit form of this binary, but the assumptions remain the same. In France and Sweden, this debate finds its articulation in the political discourses of 'republicanism' and 'equality' (everyone to be treated the same) respectively. French Republicanism, through its proud division of state from church, manages to justify a kind of authoritarian republicanism through 'upholding' the values of secular society, as the recent cases with the girls who wished to wear the *hijab* to school indicated. Where the religious symbol of the *hijab* here is seen to challenge the republican model, differences are suppressed in the name of equality within the school system. As is the case in the majority of the other European countries engaged in this study, the education policies and practices dealing with the position of so-called ethnic minorities in France have historically depended upon broad sociopolitical, institutional and economic factors, while remaining intricately linked to the Republican values of equal treatment, secular education, and universality. However, equal treatment and universality are far from objective terms; they provide the majority society with the tools to deny the recognition of difference and the rhetoric through which minority claims are effectively silenced. In Sweden, research on 'multiculturalism' in schools has focused on discussions of *values*, that is, different values between 'immigrants' and 'Swedes' in relation to education. The discourse of 'our human values' is frequently used to make a 'distinction' between 'Us' and 'Them.' In the Swedish debate on '*Värdegrund*' (Basic values) in schools, pupils with immigrant backgrounds, along with their parents, are presented as 'undemocratic' and 'traditional,' and as not sharing 'our *värdegrund*' (see also Parszyk, 1999; Kamali, 2006a).

What is important here is how meaning is constructed in schools and how understandings of culture, particularly students' cultures, are constructed in relation to the key term of *equality*. The Swedish case, which is common for many other countries (such as Austria, France, Italy, and Germany), discussed how teachers often interpret equality as similarity, which means providing children with a *similar* education. Teachers' interpretation of *equality as meaning similarity*, or treating students similarly, has discriminatory effects on students of immigrant background. Thus, school actors' norm-sustaining practices have discriminatory effects.

In England, whilst experts recommend that schools develop a 'multicultural approach' to school inclusion, both in the curriculum and across other areas of school life (e.g., Local Education Authorities should include the specific needs of ethnic minority groups *as distinct groups*), this can 'Otherize' pupils of immigrant background as 'essentially different' from 'Us.' On the other hand, the policy of 'equality' of Austria, France, and Sweden, for instance, helps to reproduce the discriminatory mechanisms included in the 'normal' practices of those countries' educational systems.

Segregation and Language

In many countries there are consistent and staged points at which institutional discrimination takes place. Most school systems consist of several decisive moments in which students' educational careers are determined; in the case of the immigrant student, these decisions are overwhelmingly based on judgements made concerning their language skills. In those countries where language policies exist, many immigrant students are segregated into special classes that may be, in some cases, well-intentioned, but are essentially paternalistic and sometimes quite damaging to the future educational prospects of these students: Too often they reinforce already existing segregation. There are also many schools that openly refuse to admit immigrant students for fear of damaging the perceived reputation of the school, whilst at the same time maintaining a façade of benevolence. These are just some of the many complex ways in which discrimination is played out.

There are examples of blatant discrimination by Italian head teachers who tell immigrant children that the school is full. The present Italian regulative norms require that there should be no more than five 'foreign' students in a class; however, today people of 'foreign' background in Milan make up 30% of the population and this quota is clearly no longer adequate. In neighbourhoods of Milan with high immigrant concentration, kindergartens, primary schools, and lower secondary schools are attended by a large number of pupils of immigrant background. Such trends are seen to damage the 'image' of those schools. Italian parents are concerned because they believe the presence of 'foreign' pupils will inevitably slow down teaching activities. For this reason, a tendency towards separation between Italian and 'foreign' students is currently emerging: The former are sent to the school chosen by their parents and the latter (together with the children of the poorest Italian households) are sent to the nearest school, that is, the one in their neighbourhood. As a consequence, in recent years, new kinds of classes have developed, the so-called 'dustbin' classes, made up almost entirely of immigrant pupils. In these classes the only Italian pupils are, very often, those that had to repeat the school year. As a result, there is a concentration of 'problematic' cases within the same school and the same class.

Additionally, immigrants are excluded from classes that have a certain historic prestige, such as bilingual classes, because it is believed that they should concentrate on learning Italian. Initially, teachers assumed that 'foreign' students might not know the language but would have the same learning approaches and schools systems as in Italy. However, cases have been reported of 'foreign' children being sent out of the classroom simply because they cannot understand their lessons. This is a case of 'push-out' that can gradually force pupils of immigrant background to leave public education.

Similar strategies of segregation and 'push-out' mechanisms are apparent in Germany. Segregation of classes based on pupils' ethnic background was particularly popular during the 1980s. School classes were kept homogeneous, while children from immigrant homes were sent to special preschools and 'problem-catching' classes. However, the ministries of education and cultural affairs in several federal states began to notice increases in expenditures on education associated with these practices and took measures to prevent them. Indeed, most people within and outside of schools find it plausible, even necessary, to subject migrant children to special treatment, a need for which is justified by stereotypes held about "other cultures" (cf., Gomolla

& Radtke, 2002). Since it is widely accepted that both their grasp of German and level of development is inferior, that they have a different mentality and that they do not receive enough support from their parents, there is no resistance to the school praxis of excluding them from regular schools shortly after their enrolment. Many in Germany believe that a concentration of migrants in certain schools could damage a schools' image.

Both Poland and Sweden suffer from similar politics where the fear exists that immigrant children will lead to an increase in problems at school and a decrease in the standard of education. In general, interviewees in Sweden claimed that school segregation has a negative effect on the quality of education. Schools with a high proportion of immigrant pupils are perceived as 'messy' when compared to 'white' schools. It also appears, according to statistics, that pupils in these kinds of schools receive lower degrees. One of the main effects is that, more frequently, the pupils in segregated schools do not continue with their education after elementary school. In Poland, the fact that schools try to be ranked as best as they can in a variety of school rankings (which matters in big cities such as Warszawa and Lublin) leads to segregation of immigrants. As one of the informants said: "A school director who takes pains to be ranked high, won't admit foreigners to his school, perhaps with the exception of [a few] exceptional Vietnamese." The fear that a school's ranking could deteriorate because immigrants are admitted may also produce negative reactions from the parents of other students, especially it is a so-called 'good school' in question.

In Austria, parents also express concerns over increasing numbers of immigrants in schools and the perceived associated decrease in educational standards at those schools. Correspondingly, language requirements are very strict: immigrant students must either pass a difficult entrance examination or prove that they have undertaken at least eight years worth of German lessons. The efforts made by the Austrian Ministry of Education, Science, and Culture to diminish discriminating effects within the school system in favour of an increasing 'multiculturalism' are mainly additive measures which do not question the existing system itself. Generally, a distinction can be made between structural and additive measures. Structural measures result in changes of the system, whereas additive measures only supplement the status quo (cf., Gomolla and Radtke, 2002). Ironically, whilst traditional languages such as English, French and Italian are available at all levels of schooling in Australia, the two foreign language groups that are spoken most frequently, namely Turkish and Bosnian/Serbian/Croatian, are not promoted and not even available at some levels of the education system.

Discourses of Deficiency

Linked to the aforementioned processes of segregation are a variety of discourses concerning language skills, and a concentration on the importance of learning the majority society's language. One of the most clearly articulated discourses concerning immigrants, language and culture is that of *deficiency*. There is, however, an important distinction between a material deficiency in resources—in so far as schools require additional resources to meet the needs of immigrant pupils—and *discourses of deficiency*, which are concerned to describe and explain the lack of skills held by immigrants students. In Germany and Italy, we see clear examples of both: a lack of resources and teachers to teach extra language classes on the one hand, and, on the other hand, the pervasive idea that immigrant children and families are somehow 'lacking' in required skills. This is taking place in a situation where resources available for schools are decreasing, whereas the migrant school population is increasing. The mechanism of deficiency (and the lack of resources it entails) and discourses of deficiency (seeking to describe immigrants as 'lacking' in knowledge/skills), certainly work together in educational systems to further marginalize immigrant students. The concern of this section, however, is to address the ways in which the latter stigmatizes immigrants.

Whilst there has been a general shift in discourse from that of cultural imperialism to that of recognising 'cultural diversity,' the vested interest remains the same—that is, the power to name, know, and describe ethic 'cultures' and ethnic 'Others' as a field of knowledge, and ultimately as a governable domain of transformation and intervention. The issue is how discourses about immigrant culture, whether they are a romanticisation about the 'exotic,' a claim to acknowledge the diversity of competing cultures, or derogatory accounts of culture and cultural groups as 'lacking' and deficient in language skills, are being deployed and drawn upon as bodies of knowledge and expertise. How are immigrant people constituted as a population with knowable, cultural characteristics and skill levels? How are particular claims made about their capacities as individuals? How do these various discourses rationalize and justify the deployment of certain techniques that claim to build upon the capacities of immigrant people? How are the ways in which immigrant people are encouraged to regard themselves as certain kinds of cultural subjects linked to various ideas about 'deficiency' and part of policies that promote transformative practices?

A liberal and 'rational' assumption of 'improvement' often underpins discourses of deficiency, dichotomising 'native' and 'immigrant' cultures. The common use of the argument that immigrant people are lacking in language skills, and that they need to meet specific language criteria in order to participate in school, exemplifies this process. A scale of capacities is constructed against which immigrant people are implicitly deemed to be deficient. Within these programs, immigrant people are encouraged to recognize themselves as lacking particular skills, as if this lack were a natural or inevitable outcome of their position in the category 'immigrant.' In Germany, for example, many social scientists, as well as educators, have argued that 'foreign' pupils are strangers to the German society, its institutions and its values. Because of "their cultural heritage," they have deficits in what is considered to be the "normal equipment" of a (German) child from the same age group (Gogolin, 2003, p. 264). Pedagogical practice based on these ideas about normality has defined it as necessary to aid 'foreign' children in overcoming their deficits by means of all kinds of organisational measures—for example, the introduction of preparatory or special classes. These measures, and the premises they are based on, have been summarized under the label of 'foreigner pedagogic' (*Ausländer-pädagogik*) even though 'foreigner pedagogic' has been sharply criticized in many quarters (Hebenstreit, 1988; Lutz, 1991).

Thus, in German schools, children from migrant families who do not have a good knowledge of the German language become equated with not being 'fit' for school. They become categorized as lacking in maturity and developmentally delayed. The exclusion of migrant children through their relegation to special classes or to special schools is still a widespread and unquestioned practice in Germany. Within this reasoning, the fact that immigrants' are overrepresented in 'special' schools is maintained as a logical consequence of the deficiency of immigrants. What this kind of approach fails to address is the actual institutional structures that discriminate against immigrants and any other non-German way of experiencing and seeing the world.

Similarly in Austria, school teachers can influence a pupil's school career by misjudging—whether consciously or unconsciously—the pupil's scholarly performance based on negative stereotypes. There are two pivotal points in the Austrian school system: one after elementary school when pupils have to choose between HAUPTSCHULE (regarded as easier and less demanding) and AHS (a school which secures a pupil's place on the further education track up to university studies). Furthermore, if there is segregation in Austrian schools, it would have to be regarded as structural, insofar that pupils of migrant background are often forced into 'special schools.' There are also examples, both in Austria and in other countries, of immigrant students being advised by teachers to pursue vocational training rather than attempting to continue with higher academic learning because of the presumption that immigrant children are lacking in requisite skills and knowledge. This is apparent in the Swedish case where immigrant pupils are overrepresented in 'practical' educational programs at upper-high school level. This is, however, also linked to class divisions and traditional segregation between working class populations continuing into practical vocations and middle-upper class generations continuing into professional and academic careers.

Likewise, immigrant students in Italy are more likely to choose technical or professional schools, because it takes fewer years to complete them and they allow quicker access to the labour market. All these cases indicate a form of 'structural discrimination' because, regardless of statistics, their decision to choose professional schools is forced on them as a result of their 'ethnic essential.' Similarly in Germany, immigrant males tend to choose practical programs, and in Poland also, there tends to be an emphasis on 'concrete professions' for immigrants. In France, many children of immigrant parents are not encouraged to go onto university because of the perception that they will fail. They advise immigrant students to undertake short-term and technical studies. However, the same attitudes and advice is not apparent with regard to 'native' French pupils who have difficulties.

Underpinning many of these practices is a sustained belief that immigrant parents are less enthusiastic, less involved and less concerned with the outcomes of their children's education. Key stereotypes in Germany pertain to the parents of migrant children. For instance, they are judged as insufficiently supportive of their children in school and, in some cases (e.g., with African immigrants), even pathologised as 'bad parents.' This echoes the kind of sentiments found in Sweden and Italy. The involvement of parents at parent–teacher meetings is seen to be indicative of parent enthusiasm but attendance might be much lower in the case of migrant parents for several reasons: For instance, both parents need to work in order to make a living, or because parents, mothers in particular, do not speak the language sufficiently. However, in Germany, the role of parents is institutionalized as recommendations given by primary school teachers for their pupils' transmission from primary to secondary education do not depend on their grades only, but also on the characteristics of a specific pupil's private surroundings, which are regarded as achievement prerequisites. The most important of these characteristics is a 'parental home that is willing and able to support the child's educational efforts' (*unterstützendes Elternhaus*). This is exactly what is often suggested not to exist in the case of migrant children, so that their grades are weighed down by a negative factor that is not usually applied to German children. This is, of course, biased, and, moreover, it ignores the structural reasons for immigrant children's home lives; recent studies show that many immigrant parents with a high level of education are *degraded* and *disqualified* in many European countries, being forced to work in low-paying branches of employment which do not require higher education, and consequently living in marginalized areas (see, among others, Similä, 1994; Kamali, 2006a).

Another important set of stereotypes pertains to migrant children themselves. The much broader *discourse of deficiency revolving around migrants* also reflects on their position in schools where they are perceived as problematic. Immigrant boys, for instance, are often seen as 'macho' and 'trouble makers,' whereas immigrant girls, especially if wearing headscarves, have an image of being overly restrained. Often being less articulate, less self-confident and having habits not understood by teachers, they may be perceived by them to be on a lower level than their 'native' costudents. This is also linked to the general tendency for schools to have lower expectations of immigrants' competencies and potential.

Language is clearly the focus of many debates concerning immigrants. In Austria, the German language is enforced as the national language both legislatively and normatively. If an immigrant student's language problem is particularly serious, teachers may suggest that it is better the student attend another, simpler school, to avoid the student repeating a year. This kind of paternalistic benevolence justifies a 'special' kind of support and treatment, but it is questionable if immigrant students actually benefit from a system that undervalues their competency.

In Italy, 'dustbin' classes indicate a kind of deficiency discourse and practice, whereby immigrant students are relegated to classes with 'native' children who have learning disabilities. In general, a 'foreigner' is seen as a person lacking in something (first and foremost, in their knowledge of Italian). In German schools, the trends are similar. Since the 1970s there had been a steady increase in the proportion of 'foreign' children in special schools for children with learning disabilities (Trommer & Köhler, 1981, p. 130). This trend continued, so that in 1999, 15% of all pupils going to special schools were 'foreigners,' though their share of all pupils in the German school system was only 9.4%. This means that 'foreign' children were overrepresented by the factor of 1.56% (Powell & Wagner, 2001). With regard to the overrepresentation of 'foreign' children in schools for students with learning disabilities, a slogan, 'Special schools—schools for foreign children?' was coined to indicate that 'foreign' children were pushed into special schools for all kinds of reasons, but not because higher proportions of them than of German children had learning disabilities.

Intersections: Ethnicity, Gender, and Class

Even despite the benevolent intentions of some school systems in their attempts to address 'language' challenges, students with immigrant background consistently achieve lower grades in compulsory school and leave without completing their education at higher rates than do other students. Particularly striking are the gender aspects: in Sweden, for example, every fourth boy from a 'foreign' background does not have the necessary grades to continue onto a national program in upper secondary school. Compounding this is the fact that many gatekeepers in Swedish schools automatically identify immigrant boys as 'problem' pupils. When employing multiple variables, 'foreign' young men from working class backgrounds are particularly vulnerable both in schools and in the employment market. Here, there are multiple factors at work: class, ethnicity, gender, and age intersect and function to marginalize immigrants living in Sweden and in other European countries.

The issue of headscarves appears again and again, in various contexts, as a particularly symbolic challenge to European countries' educational systems. In Germany, the indications suggest that it will most likely be forbidden for teachers to wear headscarves at school in the near future. As mentioned earlier, in many countries, immigrant girls are targeted, stereotyped and stigmatized for wearing headscarves. They are considered and presented as 'victims' of their culture.

In England, the intersection and interaction of ethnic background and class play an important role in explaining differences, both between 'whites' and immigrants, and between various immigrant groups. However, an attention to class can also help to stress the importance of the intersections of ethnicity and class in those cases where immigrant families are of lower- and working-class background. In the case of Sweden, the combination of immigrant background and lower social class has a crucial impact, influencing pupils' choices concerning higher education. Likewise, in Italy, the future of immigrant children often mirrors the experiences of lower-class Italians: A limited parental income often forces students to leave school once they have completed the compulsory education period. However, in Germany, it has been argued that whilst the intersection of class and ethnicity certainly do contribute to a marginalized status for immigrants, it is overwhelmingly the position of immigrants within a particular 'ethnicity' that determines the discrimination experienced.

In Poland, class and ethnicity also intersect whereby the education system privileges those students coming from upper-class families who have the capacity to pay the high fees necessary to send their children to fee paying private schools. Children from better educated families also stand much higher chances of making good educational choices than other children, including immigrant children, and most specifically children of refugees. However, another portion of immigrants in Poland, constituted as the 'foreign elite,' are very much a part of this privileged contingent who are able to afford to send their children to private schools. In Poland, in general, immigrants from western countries who are mainly employed by multinational companies and within finance are very much associated with higher status and educational success.

CONCLUSION

The studies of institutional discrimination in the eight countries' labour markets and educational systems show that discrimination is not a 'deviant' behaviour of individuals but an inseparable part of the structural and institutional arrangements of those countries. The question of intentions—of individuals, or of institutions and organisations—is not of any particular importance in understanding the *outcome* of discriminatory actions against people with immigrant and/ or minority background. Our structural perspective has identified and analyzed several major institutional mechanisms underlying discrimination in labour markets, workplaces, and schools of the eight countries. Institutional discrimination functions through multiple mechanisms. The following is a selection of key mechanisms that were presented in the chapter:

1. *Institutionalized category systems and stereotypes* that are widely and persistently applied to immigrant groups. Stereotypes, like other categories, entail some combination of prototypical features, concrete exemplars, and theory-like causal knowledge. They obey the principle of cognitive economy, which means that categories are utterly central to seeing and thinking, as they are to talking and acting (Brubaker, 2004). Like categorising, stereotyping is deeply rooted in ordinary cognitive processes, and countering or correcting stereotypes is a costly process involving sustained effort (Brubaker, 2004). Thus, ethnic and other groups subject to differentiation and discrimination are socially constructed. Structurally oriented research is focused on 'group making' and 'grouping' activities as a function of classification, categorisation, and identification in institutional settings.

   In these processes, ethnic groups, 'races,' religious groups, and nationalities come to be treated as things-in-the-world, as real, substantial entities with their own cultures, their own identities, their own interests; they are formed and considered as fixed 'cultural blocks.' These stereotyped cultural blocks are also *hierarchical*. Not only do immigrant groups find themselves a part of a group that is deemed to be 'lesser' that the norm, but immigrant groups are often divided along a hierarchical continuum. This is commonly based upon geographical origin, religion, or skin colour, in which people from Africa, for example, or Muslims, are placed at the bottom of the chain, and those coming from countries more similar to 'host countries' are placed highest and closest to the 'norm.'

2. *The application of established norms of language, appearance, and behaviour* is a common basis of differentiation and discrimination against people with immigrant background. These norms are often applied in relation to job recruitment, career advancement, and so forth, even when, for instance, high language competence is not especially relevant to the type of job or career. The 'deviant' accent or less-than-perfect language are often considered as deficiencies on the part of immigrants. Similarly, 'deviant' appearance, (especially, but not only, Muslim women) and 'deviant' behaviour are frequently the basis for blocking or side tracking those of immigrant background who are seeking a job, career advancement in the workplace, or to progress in education. More than this, however, immigrants must prove that they are *exceptional*, as one Italian informant stated: "If you are a migrant you must be an angel, to be accepted you have to be above the norm. In other words it's like they tell you: Consider yourself lucky to be here."

3. *Legal and normative restrictions* discriminating against immigrants are widespread across Europe, relating to, amongst other things,

employment and careers. Formally or informally, 'natives' tend to be favoured ahead of immigrants. This is particularly the case in economies with tightly regulated wage structures. Under such conditions, there can be little difference between the labour costs of 'natives' and immigrants, therefore reinforcing the selection of 'natives.' In systems allowing more variation in wage setting (e.g., in England and Italy), recruitment conditions for immigrants are more open and favourable. A number of European Union countries (e.g., Austria, France, Germany, Italy, and Poland) have laws which give a certain priority to 'natives' or to European Union citizens in obtaining jobs. For example, employers or work mediation officials have the burden of proof to show why recent migrants or non-European Union migrants should fill a vacant position before a 'native.' In a number of these countries, only citizens are allowed to work as civil servants. But there are also other mechanisms operating to ensure that priority tends to be given to 'natives' over those of immigrant background.

4. *Biases in judging experience and certification* impacts on immigrants applying for jobs or applying for admission to educational institutions. There are often legal requirements for certification for many jobs or academic courses but there are multiple constraints on certifying immigrants (legal, resources, lack of interest or goodwill) to translate certification of qualifications acquired abroad, whether this relates to education or work experience. For instance, degrees and diplomas may not be legally recognized; similarly, work experience abroad may be ignored. There is a widespread tendency to favour education and work experience in the 'host society.'

5. *Gatekeeping discrimination* on the part of institutional agents relating to gatekeepers who utilize category systems, stereotypes, and value judgements which are differentiating and discriminatory. Such agents are found in all institutions, including government agencies and political parties. Officials granting access to work, education, and residence permits are among the most powerful agents with gatekeeping functions in this respect. Gatekeepers have institutional power and are important agents in discrimination processes against individuals and groups of immigrant background. Gatekeepers may generalize on the basis of a few cases to an entire group of persons concerning their 'lack of skills and competence' and 'improper value orientations' (e.g., 'they are not interested in education' or 'they don't do well as academic subjects').

6. *'Fitting-in' discrimination* appears when gatekeepers such as employers take into account the reactions (or imagined reactions) of clients and/or employees against an 'Otherised' person as coworker or colleague. Work groups may complain that those with immigrant background 'don't fit in,' 'don't know or understand our social behavioural or social codes,' or that 'they lack cultural competence' quotes from expert interviews).

'Fitting-in' discrimination reflects a type of 'collective' gatekeeping and may be justified in the name of workplace 'democracy.'

7. *'Spill-over' mechanisms* are also engaged in the institutional discrimination of immigrants. Due to limited educational opportunities, selective channelling, and differentiated programs of study, job opportunities and career possibilities are narrowed. Or only finding housing in certain stigmatized areas may limit job access and opportunities, as employers (and employees) react negatively to persons coming from certain areas. What makes integration even more difficult, not only for immigrant parents but also for their children (both those who were born here and those who have come here afterwards), is the development, in big European cities, of neighbourhoods where most immigrants live. The fact that adult immigrants are often offered only those (unskilled) jobs that the majority society no longer want to do, the fact that their educational qualifications cannot be acknowledged, and the fact that their working conditions are precarious all become reasons behind the 'internal colonisation' which creates marginalized and poor urban areas. Poor educational possibilities and discrimination in schools lead often to worse educational outcomes for children of immigrant background. In other words, such children are less likely to complete higher education at the rate of their peers, and as such their employment prospects are considerably reduced. These children have thus less chance of competing for jobs and positions in society. This is called 'spill-over' discrimination, a discrimination that carries over from urban structural discrimination to the educational system and the labour market.

8. *The formulation and diffusion of denial discourses* is a major mechanism which tends to block awareness of the existence of institutional discrimination and reform efforts (cf., Van Dijk, 1992, 1998; Kamali, 2005). Many interviewees of 'native' background were concerned to declare that they were not discriminating against immigrants: "of course, we do not discriminate; we are not racists"; "we always apply our norms, laws, procedures and programs in a fair and proper way." Across countries, institutions, and workgroups, denial among politicians and journalists, or distorted and low reflectivity, is commonplace. Discriminatory judgements and patterns are revealed through contradictions in statements and through astute observations. Typically, the biased attitudes, stereotypes, and negative talk and actions toward immigrants contradict the norms and values of "equality," "democracy" and "humanitarianism" that are part of the positive self-conceptions of modern, European societies and most of their citizenry (cf., Van Dijk, 1998, p. 323). It is striking how the salience of discrimination is played down in many countries. Inequalities, such as higher unemployment rates, are argued to be partly natural as migration is accompanied with status losses and disadvantages in many cases.

Within this logic, and against the statistical facts, these trends would gradually disappear. Discrimination is still clearly affecting individuals with immigrant background, that is, those who never migrated, but are born in Europe and are called "2nd, 3rd, and 4th generation immigrants" because their parents or grandparents once immigrated to Europe. Systematic denial of discrimination and racism legitimizes and normalizes the institutional discrimination of the 'Others.'

Institutional discrimination and their 'spill-over' effects operate through very complex mechanisms and form a highly robust system. If one mechanism is blocked or fails to operate, others fill the function. There are redundant and reinforcing mechanisms discriminating against, and excluding those, of immigrant background. General pronouncements, information campaigns, and antidiscrimination legislation are not likely to move far such a system—however, such gestures are important in terms of expressing interest and normative concern. Nonetheless, more radical types of policies and regulations are necessary.

5   Beyond the European Dilemma and the Categorisation of 'Us' and 'Them'

INTRODUCTION

Europe faces a dilemma of presenting itself as the forte of humanism and democracy in the modern world, on the one hand, and, being a site of systematic discrimination and racism against the 'Others' (in Europe and elsewhere), on the other. European modernization is meshed with colonialism, slavery, genocide, and wars that have insulted and harmed the majority of human beings in the world. European colonial expansion was helped by 'scientific racism' in becoming a 'fair' and legitimised military action by which the modern world and its inequalities have been formed.

The connection of the concept of 'race' with 'racism' is one of the matters helping to *mask* the real racism with its *institutional* patterns in Europe today. Although biological interpretations of the concept of race can be in effect, these are marginal to the social mechanisms of 'Otherization' of individuals and groups with non-European/nonwestern background. The concept of 'culture,' which assumes also 'belonging' and defines the boundaries between 'Us' and 'Them,' is of more substantial and methodological interest to defining the study of racism and discrimination in contemporary Europe. Belonging to 'our culture' or 'their culture' provides different status to groups living in a European Union country. Symbolic boundaries based on 'race' have been replaced by those based on religion, language, and culture (Goldberg, 1993; Lamont, 1999). Those belonging to 'Us' are ranked with higher status in different social systems and institutional settings than those belonging to the 'Others.'

The cultural conception of 'Us' versus 'Them' includes racialised ways of thinking and acting through identification with a 'group' based on such properties as shared language, religion, and place of birth. The connection of 'race' with religion and language is not new; it existed already in the 14th century against Muslims and Jews in Spain. Even belonging to a language could be used as a way of racially identifying different people. By the 18th century, European linguists did not use physical markers to classify 'races,' but rather used people's belonging to different language groups. In 1808, Friedrich Schlegel argued that the German, Greek, Latin, French, and English were commonly rooted in Sanskrit that indicated the superior Aryan origin of

Europeans. This made Europeans "rational, moral, civilised, and capable of abstract thinking" (Goldberg, 1993, p. 71).

In earlier chapters of this book, we have discussed the role of 'geographical thinking' in racism. Place of birth provides a ground for racist judgements and treatment, and for the categorisation of 'Us' and 'Them.' The early European colonialism, which created a 'racial map' of the world, came to form our understanding of 'differences.' 'Racial' differences came to be presented in an interplay of biological and cultural properties with well-defined geographical locations. More recently, global movements and migration increasingly challenge the European countries' geographical self-definition and homogeneity, forcing them to revitalize the 'lines of distinction' by reinventing concepts as 'European culture,' 'European heritage,' and 'belonging.'

European modern history, including its racisms, colonialism, and discrimination, is institutionalised and part of Europe's structural properties that harm many 'Otherised' people. Institutional discrimination and racism is increasingly causing problems for social integration by 'Otherising' people of immigrant or minority background and excluding them from access to jobs, to power and to influence in society. Discrimination, racism, 'Otherization,' and exclusion of individuals and groups based on their 'racial' attributes are serious problems in each of the countries that participated in this research project. Although, these frequently tend to be expressed in patterns that contain remarkable consistencies across national boundaries, these exclusionary and racist practices tend to be legitimised somewhat differently based upon the specific societal context. The processes of discrimination and exclusion, and the various forms of racism and xenophobia from which they derive, are diverse, multilayered and densely interwoven. They are expressed in institutionalised form in the social structures through which selection takes place and through which resources, rewards and sanctions are distributed. They are also apparent in what could be called European 'racist culture' (Goldberg, 1993; or the modern 'otherising, racist, and narcissist culture,' Lawrence, 1997), the cultural forms that define 'Us' and 'Them,' the practices which are 'proper' and 'inappropriate' (or 'normal' and 'abnormal') in society, and in general, how the 'Us' and 'Them' are perceived. Both institutional and cultural factors are mediated by human agents—particularly societal elites and individuals in gatekeeping roles, who occupy key roles or positions relatively high in social hierarchies which are invested with power. Together, these factors form a complex and robust matrix that powerfully influences individuals' life chances based on their ethnicity, 'race,' 'culture,' national origin, and other factors related to migration.

VOICES OF IMMIGRANTS IN EUROPE

Institutional discrimination is directed at 'Otherised' groups in general, and at persons of immigrant background in particular. Since denial of discrimination and racism is very common, our research team decided in a very early stage of the research project to collect the voices of those who are, on a daily basis, subjected to discrimination and racism in Europe. We chose a discourse-centred method that would facilitate this. Focus groups have been previously used to good effect in a number of key social scientific studies addressing racism and discrimination, such as Gamson (1992), Essed (1991), Wodak, DeCillia, Reisigl and Liebhart (1999), and Lamont (1999). Thus, two cities (one large and one small) were used in each country for the purposes of conducting a focus group element to the study. Each focus group was supplemented with in-depth interviews with a few members of the group. Although it is very difficult to make anything stronger than general conclusions about focus group research, it is possible to identify some recurring themes and ideas that resonated in each country's focus groups, and these recurrent themes reinforced other findings of the research. However, further research must be conducted concerning the experiences of the 'Others' in Europe in order to get deeper insight into the forms of 'everyday racism' that are a major problem in European societies.

The study of 'voices of immigrants' was undertaken mainly because of the lack of 'microdata' in research on institutional discrimination. This was a way to provide individuals who are on a daily basis subject to discrimination and racist insults with the opportunity to voice their own experiences. Significantly, the national reports contain few stories of racist *violence* directed against participants—although there might have been a reluctance on their part to talk about it in the particular research context. Rather, the vast majority of participants reported incidences of what Philomena Essed has termed *'everyday racism.'* This form of racism involves "systematic, recurrent, familiar practices. The fact that it concerns repetitive practices indicates that everyday racism consists of practices that can be generalised" (Essed, 1991, p. 3). Essed categorizes "everyday racism" as insulting actions against the 'Others' that "involves socialised practices and behaviour" (Essed, 1991, p. 3). Nearly every participant described encounters with attitudes that could be considered in this way, with incidences occurring predominately in public spaces such as bars, restaurants, schools, labour offices, police stations, public transport, shops, and in the street.

The strategies employed by the participants for dealing with such encounters tended to be based on presenting a challenge to the protagonist's ignorance. This subverts the widespread assumption that a person of migrant or minority background is the disempowered 'victim,' an inferiorised individual in need of help and care. Participants also spoke about challenging the daily utterances of majority societies' racist assumptions of cultural superiority. The face-to-face nature of many of these 'everyday' encounters dictates that resistance to racism and discrimination also takes place at an individual level; a significant number of participants across all eight countries described highly individualised resistances to such prejudice. It is also important to state that 'subtle' forms of racism, such as Euro/ethno-centric value systems, stares, jokes, and insults in the mass media and in public spaces often led participants to wonder whether they should actually stay in Europe, although many had no choice other than to do so.

Many considered themselves as not being full citizens of their countries of residence, but still human beings worthy of receiving equal treatment. This was a crucial concern of many participants, in particular youths, who were questioning their sense of belonging. They were not sure to which country they belonged. Questions such as: 'Am I German or Turk?,' 'Am I French or Arab?,' 'To where or which nation I belong?' were frequently asked and reflected upon in group discussions.

Challenging racism and other forms of discrimination at a bureaucratic level poses a very different problem to tackling individual racism. In general, there was a high level of awareness of how discrimination operative at an institutional level can be subtle, covert, and difficult to prove. Some of the participants had found ways to challenge large government bureaucracies by becoming experts in immigration policy and the appeals system. There were stories of successful challenges to racist individuals within institutions, where participants had lodged complaints or gathered evidence against a prejudiced individual. However, there was awareness of the limitations of such actions against established institutions. There were also a significant number of stories from migrants who had engaged in 'situation testing' (e.g., changing their 'foreign' surname to a 'native' one on an application form or a piece of academic work, to assess how far their treatment could be considered discriminatory) as a way of challenging the culture of institutional racism that exists in a range of services and organisations.

A recurring frustration for many of the participants across the partner countries was the difficulty many had faced in transferring professional skills, educational qualifications and other competencies to the country to which they had migrated. It often seems that ethno- and Euro-centric ideologies serve to undervalue and undermine the frequently considerable skills that migrants bring with them. In many countries, the participants suggested that hostile headlines and hysterical reports of asylum seekers have led to a public which is misinformed about migration, and hostile and defensive about any inward migration at all. Language was flagged as an important issue in every country, and frequently referred to by the participants as *the* key skill to facilitate access in a range of social sectors, perhaps most significantly in the labour market. Certainly participants emphasised the importance of 'language competence' not only for securing a job, but also for more general 'acceptance' in the host society. It is revealing, however, that some participants with a high level of language competency still told of prejudiced comments directed at them due to, for example, a slight accent. There were also those who believed that the demand for 'language competence' is a cover for the legitimisation of discrimination and racism. There were stories about those who speak the language perfectly, such as immigrants' children born in European countries, but are still being discriminated against and subjected to racist treatment because of their 'ethnic attributes,' religion, and assumed 'culture.'

Participants in focus groups felt in general that they had been discriminated against in a range of ways. Although the actual forms of discrimination varied substantially, it seems reasonable to divide these experiences into categories of individual racism and institutional racism. Although it is theoretically difficult to draw a dividing line between the two 'types' or levels of racism, we can use the categories to explain the experiences of persons of immigrant background. They face racism in their daily lives, but they know that while they may be able to challenge some of the individual and face-to-face forms of racism, this is not so for indirect and subtle institutionalised mechanisms of racism.

CONCLUDING REMARKS OF THE STUDY

The study of the European Dilemma presented in this work aimed to examine (a) taken-for-granted, institutionalised forms of racism and xenophobia that result in discrimination against, and exclusion of, immigrants; (b) the political, manifest forms of racism and xenophobia and the emergence of sociopolitical movements and parties with xenophobic messages and proposals for discriminatory policies; and (c) the impact of (b) upon (a), as was mentioned in the introduction to this work. The study of the uprising and electoral success of the Xenophobic Populist Party (XPP) shows that there is a common trend in almost all European countries to frame immigrants as a major national problem and as an 'enemy within.' The antiimmigrants' xenophobic ideas and slogans have proven themselves to be very effective means for political mobilisation in societies with established institutional discrimination and 'Otherization' mechanisms. XPP does not really create a new paradigm, but builds on already established prejudices and negative ideas about the 'Others' and reinforces majority societies' narcissism. However, this is not to say that XPP has no effect on the institutional discrimination and 'Otherization' of immigrants. The study shows that XPP has influenced and reinforced institutional discrimination in Europe in variety of ways. The following figure (Figure 5.1) is an illustration of the impact of the established institutional 'Otherization' and discrimination on the emergence of XPP and the impact of XPP in reinforcing already existing institutional discrimination.

Existing institutional discrimination provides the ground for the uprising of XPP in all countries. XPP leaders and politicians use xenophobic and racist ideas that already exist in the eight European countries which participated in our research, and thereby mobilize political support for their parties. They influence the public debate and change 'political correctness' to be more xenophobic and racist. This is one of the main indirect impacts of XPP on the established political spheres of these countries.

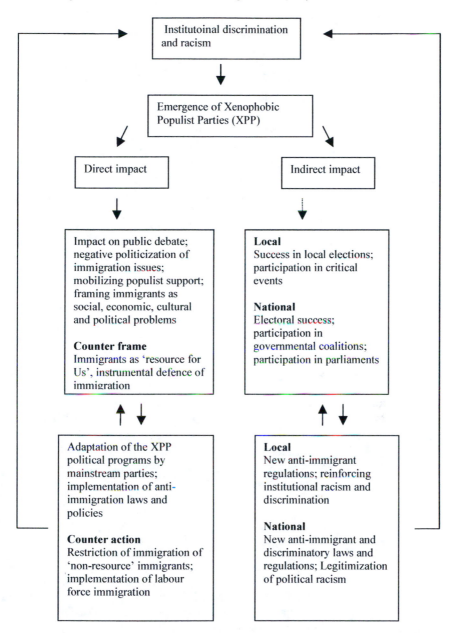

Figure 5.1 The role of XPP for the reinforcement of the institutional discrimination

By framing immigrants as a major problem for the national interests of the countries, and so creating a xenophobic and racist discursive context, XPP influences the mainstream political parties and mass media that use the same frames and further 'Otherize' immigrants. The mainstream parties and media show no difficulty in adapting to the antiimmigrant and racist discourses of XPP.

However, there are parties, politicians, and journalists who try to counteract XPP's antiimmigrant discourses. Such discourses have an instrumental structure and try to frame immigrants as 'a resource for Us.' These discourses lead often to further 'Otherization' of immigrants as a category of people 'essentially' different from 'Us.' Thus, the 'good intentions' of some parties and politicians result in unintended negative consequences for many groups categorised as immigrants and minorities. They have to be 'useful' or an 'instrument' for the well-being of majority society. It seems that 'immigrants' cannot be like many groups in majority society, such as children, unemployed, employed, healthy, sick, workers, politicians, teachers, passengers, drivers, criminals, police, and so on. Belonging to the 'immigrant category' sees some groups automatically categorised as different and separated from 'Us'; they can either be a 'problem' or 'resource' for 'Us.'

The electoral success of XPPs helps them to directly influence political decision making and to introduce and reinforce discriminatory laws and regulations concerning the 'Others.' Participation in local and national parliaments provides them good opportunities to impact on mainstream parties and political decisions. In many cases, the mainstream parties and media argue for a restriction on immigration and a change in 'kindness politics' (Sweden) towards immigrants in order to not give a XPP the opportunity to mobilize popular support. This has led to the change of some mainstream parties' programmes and the adaptation of antiimmigrant and anti-'Other' slogans and programmes. Therefore, the electoral successes of XPPs during the last decade in the European countries have reinforced institutional discrimination and racism, thereby creating many new obstacles for the development of integrated societies with equal opportunities for all, irrespective of place of birth, skin colour, religion, ethnicity, and so forth.

INSTITUTIONAL DISCRIMINATION, SOCIAL BOUNDARIES, AND INTEGRATION

Social development and modernization in Europe have created many institutional arrangements that, alongside other possible consequences, discriminate against 'Otherised' peoples. The scientific thought of the Enlightenment was a precondition for the growth of a modern racism based on physical typology in combination with cultural assumptions of 'inferiority.' The modern sciences and scientific scholars have been engaged in the 'scientific' 'Otherization' of non-European or nonwestern individuals and groups. The institutional arrangements of many European societies form the basis for the reproduction of racism, discrimination, and exclusion of 'Otherised' groups from access to power and influence in society.

Institutional discrimination is routinized, systematic, and a part of the daily function of many European structures and institutional arrangements. This includes established laws, procedures, and practices that systematically reflect and produce inequalities between those who are assumed to belong to 'Us' and those who belong to 'Them.' If institutional laws, procedures, and practices lead to the reproduction of 'white supremacy' and the inferior-ised positions of the 'Others,' the *institution* itself is racist whether or not the individuals maintaining those practices have racial intentions. In institutional discriminatory practices, intentions are not of focal importance because it is the consequences of the action that should be judged. As mentioned earlier, this Weberian theory of action is a useful means of judging and evaluating institutional discrimination. Although institutions can behave in ways that are overtly racist, they routinely operate in a covertly racist fashion through inherently racist and exclusionary actions, such as adopting policies that while not specifically directed at excluding the 'Others' result in their exclusion.

Therefore, institutions can respond to 'Us' and 'Them' differently and be racist in outcome if not in intent.

As Fredrickson (2002) argues, racism originates from a mindset that regards 'Them' as different from 'Us' in ways that are permanent and unbridgeable. He includes two important components in his discussion of racism, namely, 'difference' and 'power.' The distinguishing of groups of immigrant background from 'Us' is a process of 'Otherising' based on marking *difference,* which is already going on in many European countries with or without the presence of the 'Others.' As shown in Figure 2.1 (see Chapter 2), those in power, through their monopoly over power-means—such as control over political, economic, bureaucratic, and legal systems, as well as control over labour markets and the mass media—make the dis-crimination a permanent and inseparable part of the reproduction of soci-eties' main institutions.

Discrimination and racism are experienced by those who are subjected to discrimination, namely the 'Others'; and those discriminated against are institutionally inferiorised and disempowered (Kamali, 2005). The lack of access to powerful positions in society by the 'Others' is one of the main rea-sons behind the institutional reproduction of discrimination and racism.

Institutionalised discrimination and racism is a major obstacle to social integration. There is a conflict between political declarations for the inte-gration of immigrants in the member states of the European Union, on the one hand, and the existing 'Otherization' and racialisation of those who are supposed to be integrated in European societies, on the other. The con-cept of 'Us' is supposed to relate to the 'same group' belonging to the 'same nation,' as 'a race' or 'a culture.' Therefore, even the traditional social sci-entific discussions on general and modern integration have been changed to be valid only in relation to 'immigrants.'

Social integration has been one of the major discussions in the social sciences. Social scientists of the early modern age discussed the need for social integration in a society going through rapid modern changes and huge movements of displaced people who were leaving their traditional areas for work in other places. Industrialisation led to social differentiation and challenges to what Emile Durkheim (1984) called the existing, traditional 'mechanical solidarity.' There were two antagonistic responses to the problem of the lack of social integration, namely those of Hebert Spencer and Karl Marx. Spencer argued that the capitalist market would solve the problem and create social integration because all are forced to sell what they have and buy what they need in the market. The market's invisible hand would help fill the gap of traditional values and norms which had helped to establish 'mechanical solidarity' in society. Marx had a more radical answer, namely a revolution by which the basis of disintegration (according to Marx, economic inequalities) would disappear. Durkheim presented a compromise, namely a 'soft socialism' (Aron, 1970), which was a combination of market economy and welfare state. He argued in *The Division of Labor in Society,* that modern integration, or, in his words, 'organic solidarity,' is possible by reducing economic inequalities between different groups through redistribution of resources in order to create national 'social boundaries.' This is may be the best articulated theoretical discussion in the area of social integration.

The national state here becomes the major actor for integration through its control over economic resources (thorough a proportional tax system) and over modern educational systems that, according to Durkheim, provide and reproduce the common values and norms necessary for social integration. As mentioned earlier, what Durkheim ignored was the discrimination and racism inherent in the modern institutions of the welfare state and education. The creation of a sense of belonging to 'Us,' framed as the 'Nation,' went, in many cases, hand in hand with the creation of 'Them,' who were supposed to not belong to the 'mother nation.' Thus, minorities immigrants were excluded, subjected to racialisation, and discriminated against. However, Durkheim was aware that social integration was not possible without social justice, which is more than having a job or making one's living in a society. It is also about individuals' and groups' own feelings of *belonging,* which is highly influenced by the established institutional arrangements in society.

Social boundaries are also based on conceptual distinctions used to construct notions of 'Us' and 'Them.' The importance of such divisions for the construction of social identities has for a relatively long time been recognised and discussed (Barth, 1969; Eriksen, 1992; Jenkins, 1996). Integration is seen in connection to national social boundaries influenced by different policies and 'philosophies of integration' (Favell, 1998). In England, the concept of 'race relations' has been central in discussions of integration, and a form of 'multiculturalism' prizing *differences* between Britons and 'immigrants' has been promoted. An opposite position can be find in France, where the use of 'racial categories' or 'ethnic categories' is prohibited under the tenets of republicanism (Weil, 2002). Neither the English 'multiculturalism of race relations' nor the 'Laïcité' of French republicanism have been successful in their efforts for integration since there is established institutional discrimination in both countries that is not truly being challenged. Racist beliefs which expanded and became deeply rooted during the colonial era continue to exist to this day (Bleich, 2005). However, it must be mentioned that the situation is worse in France compared to England because the French government still denies the existence of institutional discrimination and racism. Since institutional discrimination takes place in a web of institutionalised rules, norms, and behaviours, it is more powerful and effective in dividing society than 'politically correct' declarations of the will to 'include the Others' are at uniting it.

The resurgence of XPP during the last decades has, through their direct and indirect impacts, reinforced institutional discrimination against, and the 'Otherization' of, immigrants in Europe. This may be is one of the reasons behind the resurgence of the term, and the claim to, 'assimilation' in the public debates of European countries. More recently, Brubaker (2003) has identified a strong resurgence of assimilationist rhetoric spurred by the success of XPP in France. Similar, although perhaps less virulent, debates about assimilation have emerged in Britain (Bleich, 2003; Favell, 2001) and Germany (Kastoryano, 2002). The debate of 'tolerance' and 'respect for difference' legitimised by the term 'multiculturalism' is now replaced by assimilationist claims to 'adjustment' and 'like it or leave it.' Harshening of the public debate concerning the 'Others,' implementing of new antiimmigration laws and regulations, and frequent and intensive insults against Muslims are among the signs of the reinforcement of institutional discrimination and racism in Europe. This is one of the major obstacles to social justice and the facilitation of integration in Europe.

INSTITUTIONAL DISCRIMINATION AND SYMBOLIC VIOLENCE

The claim to assimilation is not only put forward by political actors, such as the politicians, debaters, and journalists of majority societies, but also by individuals with immigrant and minority backgrounds. The established racialisation of the 'Others' in general, and Muslims in particular, has created a suitable situation for the use of 'experts of and on the Others' in the established political systems in many European countries. These 'experts of and on the Others' are increasingly becoming important 'ethnic allies' of majority society in reinforcing institutional discrimination by exerting symbolic violence against the 'Others.'

The French sociologist, Pierre Bourdieu has, in several of his sociological works, developed a theory of symbolic power and symbolic violence. He argues that the definition of state by Max Weber—in which it is defined as an organisation that successfully claims the monopoly of the legitimate use of physical and symbolic violence (Weber, 1969)—is still valid but should be elaborated upon. According to Bourdieu (1999):

> If the state is able to exert symbolic violence, it is because is incarnates itself simultaneously in objectivity in the form of specific organisations, structures and mechanisms, and in subjectivity in the form of mental structures and categories of perception and thought. (p. 56)

The symbolic power of the state is manifest through its control of a modern education system that creates and reproduces mental structures and categories necessary for the state's legitimised control over the means of violence (Bourdieu & Passeron, 1977). However, the established power of the state and those favoured by the state power, that is, other socioeconomic privileged groups, leads to 'symbolic struggles' between the privileged and less privileged groups in a relatively 'autonomous' way. As Bourdieu (1989) puts it:

> These symbolic struggles, both the individual struggle of everyday life and the collective, organised struggles of political life, have a *specific logic* which endows them with a real autonomy from the structures in which they are rooted. (p. 21)

This autonomy makes the exertion of symbolic power, and its major form, symbolic violence, difficult to trace back to its 'structures in which they are rooted.' Symbolic violence is violence wielded with tacit complicity between its victims and its agents, insofar as both remain unconscious of submitting to or wielding it (Bourdieu, 2001).

Bourdieu (1977, pp. 188–191) originally introduced the term "symbolic violence" in *Outline of a Theory of Practice* and defined it as a complement to domination which is necessary in societies which, in contrast to our own, cannot rely on the money economy, courts and the legal system, politics, police, and so on to help legitimate, conceal and reinforce the prevailing forms of domination. In these societies, material and symbolic bonds conceal the relation of exploitation and domination which in fact prevails. Bonding practices call on the 'master' or the leader to be generous and respectful, extending material and symbolic protection to his 'clients' or 'servants.' Language is an effective means of symbolic violence and the reproduction of exploitation and domination. Symbolic violence is inherent in the ordinary language, in particular in the system of concepts by means of which the members of a given group provide themselves with a representation of their social relations, since these concepts constitute the thinkable, the doable, the permissible, thus reproducing the social practices which reinforce the rule of the dominating group (Bourdieu (1977, pp. 21–22). In the Algerian villages that Bourdieu studied, the ordinary language of kinship and familiarity masked the fact that the 'master' and the 'client' were not friends but employer and employee, a creditor, and a debtor. Bonding practices and the ordinary language created an 'enchanted relationship,' which euphemised the true unequal and exploitative relationships. Symbolic violence means then that gentle, hidden exploitation, which is never recognised as such, exists whenever overt, brutal exploitation is impossible (Bourdieu, 1977, p. 192).

Symbolic violence, as an essential means for the reproduction of a dominant group's privileges, is equally important in the modern European countries of today. Domination in this context is *masked* by a system of legitimisation and 'softening.' By exerting symbolic violence, the real domination of institutional racism and discrimination is hidden. In this respect, many racist and discriminatory actions are concealed within 'politically correct' language and presented as something 'good for you.' This entails 'enchanted relationships' between 'Us,' the masters, and 'Them,' the clients. This is also reinforced by the demands of antiracist movements that have forced 'masters,' in an 'antiracist fashion,' to legitimize their racist actions as 'not-racist' and 'necessary for all.' One of the best ways of doing this is to make use of persons with immigrant and minority backgrounds by giving them 'gifts, credit, confidence, obligation, personal loyalty, hospitality, gratitude, and piety,' which helps construct a 'gentle, hidden form' of racism.

Individuals of immigrant background are frequently used in the political and public arena of many European countries in order to legitimize majority societies' discrimination against immigrants and minorities. This 'action of masking racism' by symbolic violence is increasing as racism and discrimination continues to grow. In Sweden, this is known as 'kravpolitik' (the policy of demand). This means that some established parties, such as Folkpartiet in Sweden (which followed its Danish counterpart, Danske Folkepartiet), claim that the failure of integration of immigrants is due to their lack of will to be integrated based on their cultural deficiencies. This became an official and effective electoral slogan in the last election (2006). They have made use of many racialised discourses to legitimize racist policies as 'good for you.' In their 'Otherization' efforts, Folkpartiet used politicians with immigrant backgrounds, such as Maricio Rojas (a Chilean born politician) and Niamko Sabuni (a Congolean-born politician). Rojas became their representative in parliament, and Sabuni was positively sanctioned and upgraded, being minister of integration in the new right-wing government since 2006.

In France, Nicolas Sarkozy, who himself is of immigrant background, has proven to be tough on immigrants since coming to office as Prime Minister. On winning his position, he immediately chose two people with immigrant backgrounds as ministers in his cabinet—a woman of Moroccan-Algerian background, Rachida Dati, as justice minister, and a woman of Algerian background, Fadela Amara, as minister for urban policy. Dati and Amara are both ministers who have subsequently been engaged in the inferiorization of immigrants. Dati has argued for harsher punishment for youth criminality, always relating this to youths with immigrant backgrounds, and Amara has consistently presented immigrants in terms of 'honour killers' and as being 'culturally inferior' to French 'natives.' She has also supported more recently DNA tests for immigrants to prove their family bonds for family-reunification. Not surprisingly the immigrant allies of majority society have mostly Islamic backgrounds. Our research shows that in many countries, there is a discriminatory and racist discourse of the 'Muslim problem.' This is maybe the best way of exerting symbolic violence against Muslims in Europe.

Almost in all older member states of the European Union, such as England, France, Germany, and Sweden, individuals of immigrant or minority background are used to defend and legitimize majority societies' racist and discriminatory actions and privileges. This should be changed. As Bourdieu (1989) puts it: "To change the world, one has to change the ways of world-making, that is, the vision of the world and the practical opportunities by which groups are produced and reproduced" (p. 17). As long as majority society, in control of structural and institutional power, do not change their way of thinking about and conceiving the world, that is, in terms of the 'Otherization' of people with immigrant backgrounds, and the dependency on an 'Us' and 'Them' dichotomy, institutional discrimination will continue to create major problems for the realisation of a better society for all.

COMBATING INSTITUTIONAL DISCRIMINATION
AND RACISM IN EUROPE

Racism and discrimination, in all their forms, are reproduced by established structural and institutional rules and norms crystallised in systematic discriminatory behaviours against the 'Others.' Racism and 'Otherization' have a long history in Europe and are an inseparable part of modern European history. Although 'racial' 'Otherization' takes different forms, and appears in various densities, depending on the sociocultural and political contexts of each country, it has the same enduring content and mechanisms. The category of 'Us' needs the 'Others' in order to reproduce majority society's socioeconomic and cultural privileges.

The historical and modern division of a 'European Us,' and 'non-European Others,' or 'the west and the rest,' is increasingly being challenged by globalisation and increasing movement beyond national borders and boundaries. New supranational organisations, such as the European Union, challenge the concept of 'sovereign national identities' as well as creating the ground for a new exclusive identity: 'Europeans against the Others.' This is even visible in new European Union countries, such as Cyprus and Poland, as was shown in our study. Our research shows that all countries engaged in the study display institutional discrimination in their labour markets and educational systems. School systems and schoolbooks contribute to the overall sense of *difference* and *Otherness*. For instance, school history books see the world divided between the 'West and the rest' by which the west is the centre of science and civilisation beginning with Greece, and 'the rest' are the 'Others' that are largely 'primitive,' 'irrational,' 'uncivilised,' and have little or nothing to do with the actual development of Western civilisation or global modernization. Of course, their cultures may be 'exotically' interesting (Sawyer & Kamali, 2006; James, 2006; Dance, 2006).

Existing explanations about inherent prejudice and discrimination toward individuals of immigrant background and minorities in key institutions refer to deep 'cultural components,' institutional inertia, and power groups with other agendas and ideologies (see, amongst others, Operario & Fiske, 1998; Van Dijk, 1997, 2006; De Los Reyes & Kamali, 2005). In particular, earlier research on institutional discrimination identifies a number of factors that help to explain the great difficulty in bringing about effective reforms (Feagin, 1980; Knowles, Prewitt, & Blank, 1969; Ohri, Basil, & Curno 1982; Williams, 1985; Wilson, 1973). The results of our study provide additional insights along these lines.

Institutionalised racial categorisations, judgements, and practices in responding to and dealing with the 'Others' provide a basis for systematic forms of discrimination, marginalisation and exclusion of persons and groups that differ from the 'imagined community's' perception of itself and the 'Others,' from its norms and ideals, and are perceived as a threat. Not all arrangements that discriminate and exclude may have been designed for this particular purpose. Discrimination may be unintended, the result of pursuing other goals, but nevertheless it results in the negative treatment of 'Otherised' groups. Therefore, as stressed earlier, not all patterns of difference between 'natives' and immigrants are the result of intention or conscious discrimination. Some differences that constitute a form of discrimination may be the result of established practices and understandings operating in labour markets, workplaces, and schools to the systematic disadvantage of 'Otherised' groups.

From a broadly instrumental perspective, racism and xenophobia contribute to and legitimize discrimination, which squanders or underutilizes the skills, competencies, energies, and imagination of citizens or residents of European Union countries who are marked as *different* by virtue of their 'ethnic' appearance or/and properties, such as skin colour, religion, language, accent, clothes, and place of birth. Disproportionately higher rates of unemployment, lower wages, and social exclusion among workers of an immigrant background—differences which can be attributed to discrimination and not differences in competencies—contribute to greater numbers of individuals and families lacking essential disposable income, thus generating poverty and segregation, and reducing the amount of resources that are put back into national and overall European Union economies. Established institutional discrimination also contributes to creating the very problems for which the 'Otherised' groups, immigrant and ethnic minorities, are blamed.

Racism and discrimination hinder integration and the development of communities (national or European), the residents of which enjoy common membership in a shared collectivity. At the margins, specific policy failures vis-à-vis immigrants provide a convenient scapegoat for xenophobic groups and XPP, creating new and divisive societal wedges at the same time as they distract attention from root problems.

This research has identified a broad array of practices and policies that contribute to racial discrimination. Among those are:

- *The stereotyping and categorisation of immigrant minorities as 'Others':* Human behaviour is guided in part by categorisation. While this is an ongoing process, specific categories may become especially resilient as they become formalised and institutionalised, and thereby become a basis for the distribution of life chances to those who populate such categories. The European crusades, Enlightenment, colonialism, imperialism, and the way Europe is engaged in the 'Europeanization of Europe' in postcolonial manners are the basis for ongoing racial 'Otherization' and institutionalised discrimination.
- *The denial of discrimination:* In each of the eight countries, there is a complex set of accounts that tends to justify or obscure discriminatory practices. Justifications frequently refer to stereotypical traits (such as 'cultural difference') and/or vague standards (such as 'language competence,' 'skill competence,' and 'different merits') that are argued to be important. Another form of denial occurs when the source of discrimination is externalised, such as when 'the market' in held responsible for dictating the exclusion of immigrants.
- *Resistance:* This occurs in relation to the development of a robust system of enforcement of antidiscrimination law, based in part on a generally unwillingness to acknowledge discrimination in general, and institutional discrimination in particular, as a phenomenon that is present in society.
- *Exclusive attention on extreme forms of racism:* This is at the expense of attention to structural and institutional obstacles to integration, and tends to obscure the forms of discrimination (such as structural discrimination) that may prove more harmful overall.

A variety of concrete institutionalised practices appear to contribute towards, justify, or legitimize discrimination, racism, and xenophobia, in spite of intentions or pretensions to support integration. When these categorisations are accepted as facts, discrimination is legitimised on the basis of 'objective' qualifications. These work in different ways in settings of the labour market, the educational system, and in the political system.

In the labour market:

- *Preferential treatment* exists for 'natives' over immigrant groups. Immigrants' merits and work experience are given secondary place to those of 'natives.' This is legitimised as the assumption of 'better education' and 'better work experience' in 'our country.' In other words, "we know what we have, but do not know what we get" (quotes from interviews).
- *Language competence requirements frequently exceed the requirements of the job.* It is often not only immigrants' knowledge in language that is judged, but also their accents. For instance, Arabic and Swahili accents are often considered a negative property for applicants in some countries.
- There is *an absence of systematic practices for evaluating and taking into consideration competence and education from outside the country in question,* or resistance to doing so.
- There is *the pretence of a merit-based system of selection when, in practice, it is frequently the individual's contact network that generates and determines opportunities.* The wider and better contact networks of the 'natives' gives them better opportunity to successfully find a job which matches their qualifications. The chances of immigrants to find a job in accordance with their qualifications reduce not only by the lack of effective networks among them, but also because many employers collect their employees through networking. The employers 'native background' and increasing social segregation between 'natives' and people of immigrant background increases 'networking discrimination' on the labour market.
- There is *a demand for 'fitting in' within the working group.* This is often used for excluding 'undesirable applicants' who may create problems for the group. Employers can legitimise decisions to exclude immigrant applicants by claiming to be addressing the 'opposition of other employees.'

In the educational system:

- *'Programme segregation'* exists, whereby immigrant students are channelled into 'practical programmes' (which can lead to employment in manual professions) and advised to not continue onto theoretical programmes because they would not then have chance of getting a job. This follows ethnic stereotypes among teachers and other school officials.
- *School segregation* occurs on the basis of 'native' language or immigrant status. Segregation also takes place between different schools, such as those in poor areas and those in rich areas, and between 'native' students and those with immigrant backgrounds in the same school.
- There is *an underrepresentation of persons of immigrant background in 'role model' or gatekeeping positions,* such as teachers

and school counsellors, combined with an overrepresentation of the same group in low-status professions, such as lunchroom workers and janitors.

In the political system:

- There is *an underrepresentation of immigrants in regular political positions,* or in positions of political leadership.
- *Excessively long residency requirements* exist prior to migrants being permitted to participate in democratic processes, thus denying them an important outlet for channelling grievances.
- *XPP is legitimised* by adopting its programmes, discourses and formulations which identify immigrants as the cause of socioeconomic and cultural problems.
- *Mainstream parties' parliamentary and local 'tactical' cooperation with XPP* for political advantage, such as forming a government.

STRATEGIES AND REMEDIES FOR COMBATING RACISM AND DISCRIMINATION

Institutionalised racial discrimination is one of the major obstacles to the development of fair and integrative European societies. Integration is not possible without combating institutional discrimination and racism in the member states of the European Union. Drawing on both our own and others' empirical research, we can identify several general factors that can counter racial discrimination, exclusion, racism, and xenophobia.

At the European Union level:

- *Political declarations that admit the existence of institutional discrimination in Europe.* As discussed in this work, the denial of the existence of institutional 'racial' discrimination is one of the reasons for its reproduction. As long as the existence of the problem is denied, there can be no systematic solutions.
- *Declaring racial discrimination as a violation of human rights that cannot be tolerated, by changing the political landscape of the member states.* 'Racial' discrimination based on individuals' and groups' inferiorised 'attributes' should be prohibited and treated as a violation of human rights. The electoral success of XPP should not be allowed to violate the human rights of anyone, in particular those persons of immigrant and/or minority background.
- *The reinforcement of antidiscriminatory directives to the member states.* Our research shows that there are many differences between the member states' antidiscrimination laws. This should be harmonised by

the European Union. Alongside this, the existing laws against discrimination should be broadened to include mechanisms of institutional discrimination. Although the law cannot cover many subtle mechanisms of discrimination and racism, an enforcement of antidiscrimination laws—such as an obligation for employers to 'publicly announce a position' and allow external agents (trade unions, for instance) to participate in the process of hiring—can be a good sign to 'gatekeepers' and other officials with institutional power to consider and change discriminatory institutionalised mechanisms.

- *Establishment of a European research centre for comparative research in the area of institutional discrimination, with the duty to inform the European Commission of its findings in annual reports.* Existing research shows that institutional discrimination and racism takes different forms in different contexts and is changeable across time and space. Therefore a research centre with broad competence on discrimination and racism is needed to develop a knowledge base concerning discrimination and racism. In addition, many researchers who are working with such research agendas face institutional difficulties in conducting their work. These can be funding problems, administrative opposition, and institutional cultural obstacles. A research centre can eliminate such problems and guarantee the generation of new knowledge in this area.

- *The establishment of a central European authority for promoting equal opportunities, to continuously investigate whether or not each member state follows European Union antidiscriminatory directives and guidelines.* All actions against institutional discrimination should be evaluated by an independent central authority which can move beyond the administrative and legal limits of different European Union organs. Our own and others' research shows that many institutional mechanisms have consequences that exceed their institutional limits and have *spill-over effects* onto other institutions and areas of society. For example, poor social services and residential problems in marginalised geographical areas lead often to poor results in schools that, in turn, negatively affect a person's chances in the labour market. The authority of equal opportunity should hence provide recommendations for combating spill-over effects and other transinstitutional impacts of institutional discrimination in each area.

At the national level:

- *Political declarations that admit the existence of institutional discrimination in each member state.* Nation states should equally accept the existence of institutionalised 'racial' discrimination because of existing evidence in the research area and declare the will for change.

- *The establishment of an independent authority for promoting equal opportunities in each member state of the European Union, to continuously investigate the mechanisms of institutional 'racial' discrimination and suggest countering policies.* The same argument that was provided above for the necessity of the existence of such a central organ for the European Union is also valid for each nation state.
- *Reinforcing antidiscrimination laws and regulations.* As mentioned above, there are many differences between the member states of the European Union concerning their antidiscrimination laws and regulations. With the exception for England, there are no laws and regulations against institutional discrimination in the case study countries; therefore, the antidiscriminatory laws and regulations should also include institutional patterns and politics.

In the labour market:

- *Introducing affirmative action for residents in marginalised areas where the majority of inhabitants have immigrant or minority backgrounds.* One of the major consequences of institutional discrimination and racism is increasing marginalised residential areas in the major cities of European Union countries. The socioeconomic problems of such areas have been shown to be one of the main reasons behind the uprisings and revolts that have taken place in recent years. Many people, in particular youths, are denied the opportunity to receive a good education and to enter the labour market. This makes them disappointed and kin to adopting radical ideologies and violent behaviour. A change in this concern is of great importance for everybody and not only for the youths and residents of those areas. What is frequently addressed as 'internal colonialism' should be changed by making easier the entrance of residents in poor and marginalised areas into the labour market. One of such solutions is affirmative action, based not only on 'ethnicity,' but on a combination of 'ethnicity' and class. Therefore, some variables such as income, residential areas and ethnicity can be used for the application of affirmative action for poor people living in marginalised areas.
- *A recruiting equality goal for public authorities.* National governments must encourage, if necessary through law enforcement, public authorities and organisations to give priority to hiring applicants of immigrant or minority background so that the approximate proportion of their employees reflects the proportion of different groups in society.
- *Educating 'gatekeepers' in the labour market.* The importance of the role of 'gatekeepers' in reproducing and combating discrimination has been discussed in this work. However, 'gatekeepers' themselves are often not aware of this essential matter. Educational courses in

public and private companies can help 'gatekeepers' to recognise the place they have in combating institutional 'racial' discrimination.

- *New laws and regulations for countering 'network hiring.'* As discussed earlier, many employers often use their own networks in order to hire employers. These networks are often closed to persons of immigrant background for many reasons. This should be changed through new laws and regulations, such as the obligation of 'public announcement of a vacancy' and increasing control of the trade union in the hiring process.
- *Engaging trade unions in the entire process of hiring.*

In the educational system:

- *The establishment of a national research centre for investigating mechanisms of institutional discrimination,* informing nation states of its findings, and cooperating with the European Union research centre for comparative studies of discrimination. The arguments presented for the necessity of the establishment of such a research centre at the European Union level is also valid for nation states. There is an urgent need for new knowledge in the area of institutional 'racial' discrimination. This research centre can gradually include work on other mechanisms of discrimination, for instance, those based on gender or class.
- *Declarations of antidiscriminatory 'values' that should be added to so-called 'majority values' and norms that guide the national educational systems,* by central educational authorities. In many countries there are declarations about the guiding values of the official educational politics. There is often an ignorance of the antidiscrimination values in those declarations. Research shows that even neutral declarations, such as those of democracy and human rights, are often used by teachers and other school personnel to mark a distinction, that is, to address the lack of democratic thinking and the tradition of human rights on the part of pupils of immigrant background. Therefore, anti-discrimination values should be included in the official declarations of 'majority values' that guide public education, and existing declarations—that can be discriminatory against pupils with immigrant backgrounds—should be revised.
- *The education of 'gatekeepers' in schools and universities concerning their role in promoting and combating discrimination.* As mentioned with reference to the labour market, 'gatekeepers' in schools, and in the educational system as a whole, should be educated about their important roles in the reproduction and combating of institutional discrimination.
- *The revision of schoolbooks and curriculum in order to eliminate 'racial Otherization' through education.* Structuration of minds

through education is one of the main consequences of the modern educational system. However, if not critically evaluated and controlled, education can be used for increasing nationalism, 'Otherism,' and racism. Our and others' research show that schoolbooks and the curriculum are one of the means of 'Otherization,' categorisation, and reproduction of the dualism between a superior 'Us' against an inferior 'Them.' The way schoolbooks present, for instance, the history and religion of 'Us' in comparison to the history and religion of 'Them' should be changed in order to combat cognitive 'Otherization.'

In the political system:

- *Rejecting any cooperation with XPP by mainstream parties.* Some mainstream parties in many European democracies cooperate with XPP in their efforts to gain governmental power or reinforce their influence in parliaments. This research show that such cooperation results in reinforcement of institutional 'racial' discrimination, legitimizing racist beliefs, the reinforcement of the duality of 'Us' and 'Them,' and harshening attitudes against the 'Others.' If this is not a democratic goal or in line with the policies of mainstream parties, then they should avoid any cooperation with XPP in order to not legitimise their xenophobic agenda.
- *Combating 'symbolic violence' by encouraging and implementing engagement of politically active 'critical voices' of immigrant background in political parties.* The increasing political 'Otherization' of citizens and others of immigrant and minority background in a context in which an antiracist movement is combating racism, has resulted in a new phenomenon on the political scene of many European countries. Many political parties increasingly use persons with immigrant or minority backgrounds in order to legitimize their overt and covert racism and discrimination. This should be observed, debated and changed. In addition to mainstream parties' own ethical responsibilities, one of the ways of combating such a phenomenon is to open up possibilities for those of immigrant background who see the problem of institutional discrimination and have a strong will to promote a better society for all. These are often 'critical voices' combating the silencing efforts of mainstream parties and their mass media allies.
- *Rejecting simplifications of complex socioeconomic problems by adopting XPP's major strategy of presenting 'immigrants as problem.'* Mainstream parties and mass media agents should be aware of the impact of giving simple answers to complex questions, in particular concerning socioeconomic and cultural problems relating to immigrants and minorities. For example, the degradation of many countries' welfare systems or increasing criminality are issues often

been used by XPP (and some other politicians and journalists) to scapegoat immigrants. Mainstream parties should avoid using these xenophobic frames, which provide wrong and simplistic answers to problems which are generated by a variety of reasons, such as globalisation, reduction of a nation state's tax income, and demographic changes in Europe.

These are just a few suggestions directed at combating institutional discrimination in some areas. It is quite apparent that a broad array of activities will be needed to counteract and revise historical beliefs and enduring prejudices, social norms and practices, as well as the societal structures that contribute to or cause 'racial' discrimination. Some such activities have occasionally been put into practice and merit significant expansion. However, consequential and systematic actions against institutional 'racial' discrimination are still lacking. When taken together, the suggestions for change that are presented here aim at systematically combating institutional discrimination. The role of nation states and European Union organs are of great importance in this concern, since one of the major inventions of modernization has been the 'primacy of politics' (Eisenstadt, 1987b; Kamali, 1998). The importance of nation states and modern politics for the reorganisation of societies, for better and for worse, has been recognised by almost all scholars of the social sciences. The European Union, as a modern supranational actor, can, together with member states, play a crucial role in combating institutional 'racial' discrimination, since political organisations and institutions are paradoxically one of the actors behind the reproduction of, as well as the solution to, institutional 'racial' discrimination.

Notes

NOTES TO THE INTRODUCTION

1. The concept of 'extended Europe' includes those countries that have been established by European colonial powers in accordance with European models, i.e. the US, Canada, New Zealand, and Australia.
2. Concerning race specifically, see Miles (1989, p. 40); Anthias & Yuval-Davis (1992, p. 2).

NOTES TO CHAPTER 1

1. For more discussion about Heller's 'master narratives' concept, see Heller (2004, 1994).
2. See also the influential work of Edward Said, *Orientalism;* also Daniel (1960) and Southern (1962).
3. See, for instance, Max Weber's arguments about the relationship between Protestantism and the development of the European capitalist system in (1992) *The Protestant Ethic and the Spirit of Capitalism.*

NOTES TO CHAPTER 2

1. Mark Mazower (1998) in his book, *Dark Continent,* explores the role of European nation states in the wars which formed the history of Europe during the 20th century.
2. Although Memmi (2002) uses 'oppression' and 'aggression' (these being understood as deployed by a group for a certain end) as important factors specifically in the definition of racism as a concept, I think that these variables, together with 'power,' could also be used for the definition of 'Xeno-otherism.'
3. The tradition of 'one people, one religion' was a part of the Treatise of Wesphalia (1648) which guaranteed the 'prince' the right to decide about the religion of his subjects. It was in a time when the 'Others'—for instance, the Ottoman Empire—were a multi-religious and multi-ethnic empire.
4. See also the following reports about discrimination in France: Human Rights Documentation Centre (2001) *Racial Discrimination: The Record of France,* (http:www.hrdc.net), and *The National Consultative Committee on Human Rights (Commission nationale consultative des droits de l'homme, CNCDH)* (1998).

5. Compare with Philip Lawrence's discussions on the narcissism of modern culture in his book (1997) *Modernity and War*.
6. See, for instance, the International Helsinki Federation for Human Rights' Report, *Intolerance and Discrimination against Muslims in the EU: Are Muslims 'An Enemy Within'?* (2005).

NOTES TO CHAPTER 3

1. Cf. www.sora,at/wahlen/wahlanalysen/analyse_nrw02, 2005
2. Cf. www.sora.at/objects/Presse%20NRW%202002%20PK.pdf,
3. The report can be find on http://www.coe.int
4. Cf. Reisigl & Wodak, 2001, Chapter 4, for further details and an in-depth analysis of the petition.
5. Migrant is not used here as a synonym for 'ethnic minority' (which, in itself, is also a problematic term).
6. The control of borders against immigration has continued and indeed has now become an important electoral slogan for the Labour Party. On the homepage of the Party one can read: 'Labour believes in strong and protected borders—they are fundamental to Britain. Within this framework, we are committed to continuing our proud history of welcoming legal migrants who can benefit Britain; and to a just asylum system which provides a safe haven for refugees. We must continue to ensure that only those truly in need of refuge, or those who can contribute to the success of the nation, come to Britain.' (http://www.labour.org.uk/asylum_and_immigration)
7. In order to distinguish the part of the five new states of the reunited Germany from the former GDR, we refer to "east Germany" instead of "East Germany."
8. Source: http://lexikon.idgr.de/k/k_a/kameradschaften/kameradschaften.php#fn1 (March 31, 2005)
9. "Ignatz/Michel" is a reference to the chair and the vice-chair of the Jewish National Committee, Ignatz Bubis and Michel Friedman, respectively.
10. Integrationsverket: Rapport integration, 2004; Rapport integration, 2005.

References

Aftonbladet. 1991, September 20
Aftonbladet. 1991, September 11
Aftonbladet. 1986, March 2
Aftonbladet. 1986, March 3
Aftonbladet. 1989, November 12
Aftonbladet. 1989, November 17
Aftonbladet. 1991, September 19
Aftonbladet. 1996, December 2
Aftonbladet. 2001, September 12
Aftonbladet. 2001, September 5
Aftonbladet. 2004, April 21
Aftonbladet. 2004, April 27
Aftonbladet. 2004, April 29
Al-Azmeh, A. (1981). The articulation of Orientalism. *Arab Studies Quarterly,* 3(4), 384–402.
Alexander, N. (1990). *Education and the struggle for national liberation in South Africa: Essays and speeches.* Braamfontein, South Africa: Skotaville.
Alexander, N. (2001). *Language, education, and race relations.* Paper prepared for the United Nations Research Institute for Social Development (UNRISD), Conference on Racism and Public Policy, Duban, South Africa, September, 2001.
Algar, H. (1969). *Religion and state in Iran 1785–1906.* Berkeley, CA: University of California Press.
Al-Hamawi, Y. A. A. (1974). *La España musulmana en la obra de Yaqut (s. XII–XIII) : repertorio enciclopédico de ciudades, castillos y lugares de al-Andalus, extraído del Mu'yam al-buldan (Diccionario de los países).* Granada: Islamica Occidentalia.
Alibhai-Brown, Y. (2002). *Who do we think we are? Imagining the New Britain.* London: Penguin.
Ålund, A., & Schierup, C. U. (1991). *Paradoxes of multiculturalism: Essays on Swedish society,* Aldershot, UK: Avebury.
Ålund, A., & Schierup, C. U. (1992). Kulturpluralismens paradoxer. *Kulturella perspektiv,* 1, 8–20.
Ålund, A. (1997). *Multikultiungdom, kön, etnicitet, identitet.* Lund, Sweden: Studentlitteratur.
Ambrosini, M. (2001). *La fatica di integrarsi. Immigrati e lavoro in Italia.* Bologna, Italy: Il Mulino Contemporanea.
Anderson, E. (1990). *Streetwise: Race, class, and change in an urban community.* Chicago: University.

Ansley, F. L. (1989). *Stirring the Ashes: Race, class and the future of civil rights scholarship.* Reprinted in R. Delgado & J. Stefancic (Eds.) (1997), *Critical white studies: Looking behind the mirror.* Philadelphia: Temple University Press.

Anthias, F., & Yuval-Davis N. (1992). *Racialized boundaries: Race, nation, gender, colour and class and the anti-racist struggle.* London: Routledge.

Appiah, L., & Chunilal, N. (1999). *Examining school exclusion and the race factor.* London: The Runnymede Trust.

Arjomand, S. A. (1984). *The shadow of God and the hidden Imam.* Chicago: University of Chicago Press.

Aron, R. (1970). *Main currents in sociological thought, Vol II.* Harmondsworth, UK: Penguin.

Aula. 1999, March Issue

Aula. 2000, October Issue

Aula. 2000, September Issue

Aula. 2004, November Issue

Balibar, E. (1991). Es gibt keinen Staat in Europa: Racism and politics in Europe today. *New Left Review,* 186, 5–19.

Balibar, E. (2002). *Politics and the Other Scene.* London: Verso.

Balibar, E., & Wallerstein, E. (1991). *Race, nation, class: Ambiguous identities.* London: Verso.

Barth, F. (Ed.). (1969). *Ethnic groups and boundaries: The social organization of culture difference.* Oslo, Norway: University förlaget.

Batelaan, P., & van Hoof, C. (1996). Cooperative learning in intercultural education. *European Journal of Intercultural Studies,* 7(3), 5–16.

Bauman, J. F. (1995). The truly segregated? Exploring the urban underclass. *Journal of Urban History,* 21(4), 536–548.

Bayernkurier. 2000, no. 9

Bayernkurier. 1982, no. 10

Bayernkurier. 1995, no. 9

Bayernkurier. 1992, no. 10

Bayernkurier. 1992, no. 36

Bayernkurier. 1995, no. 9

Bayernkurier. 1999, no. 35

Bayernkurier. 2002, no. 36

Bayernkurier. 2004, no. 36

Beck, U. (2000). *What is globalization?* Cambridge, UK: Polity Press.

Beetham, D. (1985). *Max Weber and the Theory of Modern Politics.* Oxford, UK: Polity Press.

Behtoui, A. (2006). Nätverksrekrytering, infödda och invandrare, i Neergaard Anders (red) (2006) *På tröskeln till lönearbete: Diskriminering, exkludering och underordning av personer med utländsk bakgrund.* Stockholm: Fritzes.

Belorgey, J.-M. (1999). Rapport sur la lutte contre les discriminations, Paris: Ministére de l'emploi, du travail et de la cohesion sociale.

Bender-Szymanski, D., & Hesse, H. G. (1987). *Migrantenforschung.* Darmstadt, Germany: Bohlau.

Bernal, M. (1991). *Black Athena: The Afroasiatic roots of classical civilization.* London: Free Association Books.

Bhabha, H. K. (1994). *The location of culture.* London: Routledge.

Bhabha, H. K. (1996). Culture's in-between. In S. Hall, & P. Du Gay (Eds.), *Questions of cultural identity.* London: Sage Publications.

Bhattacharyya, G., Gabriel, J., & Samll, S. (2001). *Race and power: Global racism in the twenty-first century.* London: Routledge.

Bild. 2001, September 14

Bild. 2001, September 21.

Bild. 2004, April 16

Biorcio, R. (1997). *La Padania Promessa.* Milano: Il Saggiatore

Bleich, E. (2003). *Race politics in Britain and France: Ideas and policymaking since the 1960s.* New York: Cambridge University Press.

Bleich, E. (2005). The legacies of history? Colonization and immigrant integration in Britain and France. *Theory and Society, 34*(2), 171–195.

Bourdieu, P. (1977). *Outline of a theory of practice.* Cambridge, UK: Cambridge University Press.

Bourdieu, P. (1989). Social space and symbolic power. *Sociological Theory, 7*(1), 14–25.

Bourdieu, P. (1996). *The State Nobility: Elite Schools in the Field of Power.* Cambridge: Polity Press.

Bourdieu, P. (1999). Rethinking the state: Genesis and structure of the bureaucratic field. In G. Steinmetz (Ed.), *State/culture: State-formation after the cultural turn.* Ithaca, NY: Cornell University Press.

Bourdieu, P. (2001). Television. *European Review, 9*(3), 245–256.

Bourdieu, P., & Passeron, J.-C. (1977). *Reproduction in education, society and culture.* London: Sage Publication.

Bovenkerk, F., Miles, R., & Verbunt, G. (1990). 'Racism, Migration and the State in Western Europe: A Case for Comparative Analysis', in *International Sociology,* Vol. 5, No. 4, pp. 475–490.

British Conservative Party (1983) 'The Challenge of Our Times', UK: Conservative Party Programme.

British Conservative Party (1987) 'The Next Moves Forward', UK: Conservative Party Programme.

British Conservative Party (1992) 'The Best Future for Britain', UK: Conservative Party Programme.

British Conservative Party (1997) 'You can only be sure with the Conservatives', UK: Conservative Party Programme.

British Conservative Party (2001) 'Time for Common Sense', UK: Conservative Party Programme.

British Conservative Party (2005) 'Are You Thinking What We're Thinking?', UK: Conservative Party Programme.

British Labour Party (1983) 'Labour Manifesto'. UK: Labour Party Programme

British Labour Party (1987) 'Britain Will Win with Labour', UK: Labour Party Programme.

British Labour Party (1992) 'It's Time to Get Britain Working Again', UK: Labour Party Programme.

British Labour Party (1997) 'New Labour Because Britain deserves better', UK: Labour Party Programme.

British Labour Party (2001) 'Ambitions for Britain', UK: Labour Party Programme.

British Labour Party (2005) 'Britain Forward Not Back', UK: Labour Party Programme.

British National Party (1987) 'British National Party Manifesto', UK: British National Party.

British National Party (1997) 'British National Party Manifesto', UK: British Natoinal Party.

British National Party (2001) People Just like You Striving for a Better Britain', UK: British National Party.

British National Party (2005) 'Rebuilding British Democracy', UK: British National Party.

Brubaker, R. (1996). *Nationalism reframed: Nationhood and the national question in the New Europe.* Cambridge, UK: Cambridge University Press.

Brubaker, R. (2003). The return of assimilation? Changing perspectives on immigration and its sequels in France, Germany, and the US. *Ethnic and Racial Studies, 24*(4), 531–548.

Brubaker, R. (2004). *Ethnicity without groups.* Cambridge, MA: Harvard University Press.

Brune, Y. (1998). *Mörk magi i vita medier: svensk nyhetsjournalistik om invandrare, flyktingar och rasism.* Stockholm: Carlsson.

Brune, Y. (2004). *Nyheter från gränsen: tre studier i journalistik om "invandrare," flyktingar och rasistiskt våld.* Göteborg, Sweden: Göteborg University.

Burckhardt, J. (2001). *The civilization of the Renaissance in Italy.* Kitchener, Ontario: Batoche. (Original work published 1860)

Butterwegge, C., Griese, B., Krüger, C., Meier, L., & Niermann, G. (1997). *Rechtsextremisten in Parlamenten. Forschungstand. Fallstudien. Gegenstrategien,* Opladen.

Calotychos, V. (1998). The role of foreign powers in structuring ethnicity and ethnic conflict in Cyprus. In A. Pollis, *Cyprus and its People: Nation, identity, and experience in an Unimaginable Community 1955–1997,* Boulder, CO: Westview Press.

Camauer, L., & Nohrstedt, S. A. (2006). *Mediernas vi och dom: mediernas betydelse för den strukturella diskrimineringen.* Stockholm: Fritzes.

Castro, A. (1971). *The Spaniards: An introduction to their history.* Berkeley, CA.

Chilton, P. (2004). *Analysing political discourse: Theory and practice.* London: Routledge.

Chilton, P., & Schäffner, C. (Eds.). (2002). *Politics as text and talk: Analytic approaches to political discourse.* Philadelphia: John Benjamin Publications.

Christlich Demokratische Union Deutschland (1987) 'Election Manifesto', Germany: Christlich Demokratische Union Deutschland.

Christlich Demokratische Union Deutschland (1989) 'Christlich Demokratische Union Partei Manifesto', Germany: Christlich Demokratische Union Deutschland.

Christlich Demokratische Union Deutschland (1994) 'Christlich Demokratische Union Partei Manifesto.

Christlich Demokratische Union Deutschland (1998) Christlich Demokratische Union Deutschland Partei Manifesto', Germany: Christlich Demokratische Union Deutschland.

Christlich Demokratische Union Deutschland (2002) 'CDU/CSU Wahl Manifesto', Germany: Christlich Demokratische Union Deutschland.

Cocker, M. (1998). *Rivers of blood, rivers of gold: Europe's conflict with tribal peoples.* London: Jonathan Cape.

Cohen, E. G., & Lotan, R. A. (Eds.). (1997). *Working for equity in heterogeneous classrooms: Sociological theory in practice.* New York: Teachers College Press.

Cohen, J., Howard, M., & Nussbaum, M. C. (Eds.). (1999). *Is multiculturalism bad for women?* Princeton, NJ: Princeton University Press.

Cooper, F. (1977). Plantation slavery on the East Coast of Africa. New Haven, CT: Yale University Press.

Cooper, F. (1996). Decolonization and African Society: The labor question in French and British Africa. Cambridge, UK: Cambridge University Press.

Constable, O. R. (1994). *Trade and traders in Muslim Spain: The commercial realignment in Iberian Peninsula, 900–1500.* Cambridge, UK: Cambridge University Press.

Corne, P. (2004). *Medieval Islamic political thought.* Edinburgh, UK: Edinburgh University Press.

Cowlishaw, G. (1997). Where is racism. In G. Cowlishaw & B. Morris (Eds.), *Race matters: Indigenous Australians and "our" society.* Sydney, Australia: Aboriginal Studies Press.

Crenshaw, K. W. (1998). Race, reform, and retrenchment: Transformation and legitimation in antidiscrimination law. *Harvard Law Review, 101.*

Dagens Nyheter. 1986, February 2

Dagens Nyheter. 1986, February 17

Dagens Nyheter. 1986, March 1

Dagens Nyheter. 1989, October 26

Dagens Nyheter. 1989, November 3

Dagens Nyheter. 1989, November 10

Dagens Nyheter. 1989, November 17

Dagens Nyheter. 1989, November 19

Dagens Nyheter. 1991, September 11

Dagens Nyheter. 1991, Sepember 17/19

Dagens Nyheter. 1991, September 20

Dagens Nyheter. 1996, December

Dagens Nyheter. 2001, September 2

Dagens Nyheter. 2001, September 13/14

Dagens Nyheter. 2004, May 6

Dance, J. L. (2004). Racial, ethnic and gender disparities in early school leaving. *The Consortium on Race, Gender and Ethnicity, Issue 2,* Maryland: University of Maryland.

Dance, J. L. (2006). The land of the free, världssamvetet och olärandet av invandrarelever och elever från etniska minoriteter: betraktat i det sociala kapitalets perspektiv. In L. Sawyer, & M. Kamali, Masoud (Eds.), *Utbildningens dilemma: Demokratiska ideal och andrafierande praxis.* Stockholm: Fritzes.

Deutsche Stimme. 1980, no. 2

Deutsche Stimme. 1980, no.3

Deutsche Stimme. 1980, no. 9

Deutsche Stimme. 1981, no. 3

Deutsche Stimme. 1981, no. 9

Deutsche Stimme. 1982, no. 9

Deutsche Stimme. 1984, no. 4

Deutsche Stimme. 1985, no. 3

Deutsche Stimme. 1986, no. 3

Deutsche Stimme. 1986, no. 9

Deutsche Stimme. 1988, no. 9

Deutsche Stimme. 1989, no. 3

Deutsche Stimme. 1990, no. 9

Deutsche Stimme. 1991, no. 9

Deutsche Stimme. 1992, no. 9

Deutsche Stimme. 1993, no. 3

Deutsche Stimme. 1994, no. 3

Deutsche Stimme. 1995, no. 9

Deutsche Stimme. 1999, no. 3

Deutsche Stimme. 2000, no. 9

Deutsche Stimme. 2001, no. 9

Deutsche Stimme. 2002, no. 9

Deutsche Stimme. 2003, no. 9

Deutsche Stimme. 2004, no. 4

de los Reyes, P. (2001). *Mångfald och differentiering: diskurs, olikhet och normbildning inom svensk forskning och samhällsdebatt.* Solna, Poland: SALTSA.

de los Reyes, P., & Kamali, M. (Eds.). (2005). *Bortom Vi och Dom: Teoretiska reflektioner om makt, integration och strukturell diskriminering*. Stockholm: Fritzes.

de Los Reyes, P., & Mulinari, D. (2005). *Intersektionalitet: Kritiska reflektioner över (o)jämlikhetens lanskap*. Malmö, Sweden: Liber.

Derrington, C., & Kendall, S. (2004). *Gypsy traveller students in secondary school: Culture, identity and achievement:* Stoke on Trent, UK: Trentham Books.

Doane, A. W., & Bonilla-Silva, E. (2003). *White out: The continuing significance of racism*. New York: Routledge.

Drei-Säulen-Konzept (1997). This is a programme declared by NDP and means 'three pillar strategy' which was declared in 1997).

Du Bois, W. E. B. (1996). *The souls of black folk*. Charlottesville, VA: University of Virginia Library.

Durkheim, E. (1987). *The division of labour in society*. Basingstoke, UK: Macmillan.

Dustmann, C., & Preston, I. (2002). *Racial and economic factors in attitudes to immigration* Centre for Economic Policy Research at http://www.ucl.ac.uk/~uctpb21/pdf/Comp1_08.pdf

Eatwell, R., & Mudde, C. (2004). *Western democracies and the new extreme right challenge*. London: Routledge.

ECRI (2001). European Commission against Racism and Intolerance. *Annual Report of Council of Europe*. Strasbourg.

Ehlich, K. (2000). Diskurs. In: H. Glück (Ed.), *Metzler Lexikon Sprache*, Stuttgart, Germany: Metzler.

Eisenstadt, S. N. (1966). *Modernization: Protest and change*. New York: Englewood Cliffs.

Eisenstadt, S. N. (1987a). *Patterns of modernity*. London: Pinter.

Eisenstadt, S. N. (1987b). *Patterns of modernity. Vol II: Beyond the West*. London: Printer.

Eisenstadt, S. N. (1999). *Fundamentalism, sectarianism and revolution: The Jacobin dimension of modernity*. Cambridge, UK: Cambridge University Press.

Eisenstadt, S. N. (Ed.). (2002). *Multiple modernities*. New Brunswick, NJ: Transaction Publishers.

Eisenstadt, S. N. (2003). *Comparative civilizations and multiple modernities*. Boston, MA: Brill.

Ekberg, J., & Gustafsson, B. (1995). *Invandrare på arbetsmarknaden*. Stockholm: Studieförbundet näringsliv och samhälle (SNS).

Eriksen, T. H. (1992). *Us and Them in modern societies: Ethnicity and nationalism in Mauritius, Trinidad and beyond*. Oslo, Norway: Scandinavian U.P.

Essed, P. (1991). *Understanding everyday racism: An interdisciplinary theory*. Newbury Park: Sage.

EUMC (2000). European Monitoring Centre for Racism and Xenophobia, Vienna: EUMC (http://www.eumc.at/eumc/index.php).

EUMC / Eurobarometer (2001). *Attitudes towards Minority Groups in the European Union*. Vienna EUMC.

European Council Decision, 2000/750/EC, at http://ec.europa.eu/employment_social/news/2001/jul/200750_en.htm.

European Council Decision, 2000/750/EC, at http://eurlex.europa.eu/lexUriServ.do?uri=CELEX:31996F0443:EN:NOT.

Eze, E. C. (Ed.). (1997). *Race and the Enlightenment: A reader*. Oxford, UK: Blackwell.

Fairclough, N., & Wodak, R. (1997). Critical Discourse Analysis. In T. Van Dijk (ed) *Discourse as Social Interaction*. London: Sage.

Favell, A. (1998). *Philosophies of integration: Immigration and the idea of citizenship.* In M. Featherstone, (1995), *Global modernities.* London: Sage.

Favell, A. (2001). *Philosophies of integration: Immigration and the idea of citizenship in France and Britain.* Basingstoke: Palgrave.

Feagin, J. R., & Eckberg, D. L. (1980). Discrimination: Motivation, action, effects, and context. *Annual Review of Sociology, 6,* 1–20.

Featherstone, M. (1995) *Undoing Culture: Globalization, Postmodernism and Identity.* London: Sage.

Fekete, L. (2000). *Racism: The Hidden Cost of September 11.* London: Institute of Race Relation.

Fekete, L. (2001). The Emergence of Xeno-Racism. *Race and Class, 43*(2), 23–40.

Feuer, L. S. (Ed.). (1971). *Marx and Engels: Basic writings on political philosophy.* London: Fontana Books.

Fine, M. (1991). *Framing dropouts: Notes on the politics of an urban public high school.* New York: State University of New York Press.

Fitzgerald R., Finch S., & Nove, A. (2000). *Black Caribbean young men's experiences of education and employments.* DfEE Research Report No. 186, London: DfEE.

Foucault, M. (1977). *Discipline and punish: The birth of the prison.* London: Penguin Books Ltd.

Frankfurter Algemeine Zeitung. 1986, September 15.

Frankfurter Algemeine Zeitung. 1986, September 20.

Frankfurter Algemeine Zeitung. 1989, November 1.

Frankfurter Algemeine Zeitung. 2002, September 21.

Fredrickson, G. M. (2000). *The comparative imagination: On the history of racism, nationalism, and social movements.* Berkeley, CA: University of California Press.

Fredrickson, G. M. (2002). *Racism: A short history.* Princeton, NJ: Princeton University Press.

Freiheitliche Partei Österreichs (1986) 'Burgenland Resolution'. Austria: FPÖ.

Freiheitliche Partei Österreichs (1989) 'Lorenzener Resolution'. Austria: FPÖ.

Freiheitliche Partei Österreichs (1993) 'Parteiprogramm der FPÖ'. Austria: FPÖ.

Freiheitliche Partei Österreichs (2001) '10-Punkte Programm der FPÖ: Österreich ist kein Einwanderungsland' (10 theses of the FPÖ: Austria is not an immigration country). Austria: FPÖ.

Front National (1998) FN Regional Party Programme, France: Front National

Front National (2002) FN Party Programme, France: Front National

Front National (2004) FN Party Programme, France: Front National

Furedi, F. (1998). *The silent war: Imperialism and the changing perception of race.* New Brunswick, NJ: Rutgers University Press.

Gamson, W. A. (1992). *Talking politics.* Cambridge, UK: Cambridge University Press.

Gazeta Wyborcza (Poland). November 18, 2000

Giddens, A. (1987). *The nation-state and violence.* Berkeley, CA: University of California Press.

Giddens, A. (1990). *The consequences of modernity.* London: Polity Press.

Giddens, A. (2002). 'The Third Way can beat the Far Right Politics', in *Guardian,* Friday May 3, 2002.

Giddens, A. (2007). 'A Liberty in the Balance', in *Guardian,* Thursday July 26, 2007.

Gilroy, P. (1987). *"There ain't no black in the Union Jack": The cultural politics of race and nation.* London: Hutchinson.

Glasgow, D. G. (1980). *The black underclass: Power, poverty, unemployment, and entrapment of ghetto youth.* New York: Vintage Books.

Glover, S., et al. (2001). *Migration: An economic and social analysis.* Occasional Paper No. 67. London: Home Office.

Gogolin, I. (2003). *Pluralismus unausweichlich? Blickwechsel zwischen verglei-chender und interkultureller Pädagogik.* Berlin, Germany: Waxmann.

Gogolin, I., Graap, S. & List, G. (eds.). (1998). *Multilingualism.* Tuebingen: Stauffenberg.

Goldberg, D. T. (1993). *Racist culture: Philosophy and the politics of meaning.* Oxford, UK: Blackwell.

Gomolla, M., & Radtke, F.-O. (2002). *Institutionelle Diskriminierung. Die Herstellung ethnischer Differenz in der Schule.* Wiesbaden, Germany: VS Verlag.

Gordon, D. C. (1989). *Images of the West: Third world perspective.* New York: Rowman and Littlefield.

Griffin, N. (2001). Interview with BBC Radio 4, *Today,* June 30, 2001. http://news.bbc.co.uk/hi/english/static/in_depth/programmes/2001/bnp_special/the_leader/beliefs.stm.

Gurr, T. R. (1993). *Minorities at risk: A global view of ethnopolitical conflicts.* Washington, DC: United States Institute of Peace.

Hall, S. (1996). The West and the rest: Discourse and power. In S. Hall, D. Held, D. Hubert, & K. Thompson (Eds.), *Modernity.* Oxford, UK: Blackwell.

Hall, S. (2002). Race, articulation, and societies structured in dominance. In P. Essed & D. T. Goldberg, *Race critical theories,* Oxford, UK: Blackwell.

Hall, S., Held, D., & McGrew, T. (1992). *Modernity and its future.* Cambridge, UK: Polity Press.

Hannaford, I. (1996). *Race: The history of an idea in the West.* Baltimore, MD: Johns Hopkins University Press.

Hargreaves, A. G., & Leaman, J. (1995). *Racism, ethnicity, and politics in contemporary Europe.* Aldershot, UK: Edward Elgar.

Hebenstreit, A. (1998). *Language Attitudes of Austrian Pupils towards British and American English.* Unpublished Magister Thesis. Vienna.

Hegel, G. W. F. (1975). *Lectures on the philosophy of world history: Reason in history.* Cambridge, UK: Cambridge University Press.

Hegel, G. W. F. (1997). Race, history, and imperialism (1882–1888). In E.C. Eze (Ed.), *Race and the enlightenment: A reader.* Oxford, UK: Blackwell.

Heller, A. (1994). *A theory of history.* Oxford, UK: Blackwell.

Heller, A. (2004). *A theory of modernity.* Paper presented in Beyond East and West Conference in Elmau, Germany, April 4–7, 2004.

Hine, D. (1993). *Governing Italy: The politics of bargained pluralism.* Clarendon: Oxford.

Hoexter, M., Eisenstadt, S. N., & Levtzion, N. (Eds.). (2002). *The public sphere in Muslim societies.* Albany, NY: State University of New York Press.

Hömberg, W., & Schlemmer S. (1995). Fremde als Objekt. In: *Media Perspektiven,* No. 1, pp. 11-20.

Huff, T. E. (2003). *The rise of early modern science: Islam, China, and the West.* Cambridge, UK: Cambridge University Press.

Hume, D. (1964). Of national characters. In T. H. Green & H. Grose, *The philosophical works,* Aalen, Germany: Scientia Verlag.

Identity. The British National Party press. 1993, September Issue

Identity. The British National Party press. 1996, September Issue

Identity. The British National Party press. 2004, March Issue

Identity. The British National Party press. 2004, April Issue

Integrationsverket (2003). *Rapport integration* (Integration Report). Norrköping: Integrationsverket.

Isin, E. F. (2002). *Being political: Genealogies of citizenship.* Minneapolis, MN: University of Minnesota Press.

Jackman, R., & Volpert, K. (1996). Conditions favouring parties of the extreme right in Western Europe. *British Journal of Political Science,* 26(4), 501–521.

Jäger, S. (1993). *Der Groß-Regulator*. Duisburg: Institut für Sprach- und Sozialforschung.

James, C. E. (2006). Rasifierad profilering och utbildning av rasifierade ungdomar med minoritetsbakgrund. In L. Sawyer & M. Kamali (reds) *Utbildningens dilemma: Demokratiska ideal och andrafierande praxis*. Stockholm: Fritzes.

Jantzen, G. (1998). *Becoming Divine: Towards a Feminist Philosophy of Religion*, Manchester: Manchester University Press.

Jenkins, R. (1996). *Social identity*. London: Routledge.

Joint Action European, 96/443/JHA, at http://www.legaltext.ex/text/en/T71556. htm.

Joas, H. (1999). The modernity of war: Modernization theory and the problem of violence. In *International Sociology, 14*(4).

Judge, H. (2004). The Muslim headscarf and French schools. In *American Journal of Education*, 111, November.

Kamali, M. (1997). *Distorted integration: Clientization of immigrants in Sweden*. Uppsala, Sweden: Multhiethnic Papers.

Kamali, M. (1998). *Revolutionary Iran: Civil society and state in the modernization process*. Aldershot, UK: Ashgate.

Kamali, M. (2001). Civil society and Islam: A sociological perspective. *European Journal of Sociology, XLII*(3), 457–482.

Kamali, M. (2002). *Kulturkompetens i socialt arbete: Om socialarbetaren och klientens kulturella bakgrund*. Stockholm: Carlssons bokförlag.

Kamali, M. (2005). Ett europeiskt dilemma: Strukturell/institutionell diskriminering. In P. de los Reyes & M. Kamali (Eds.), *Bortom Vi och Dom: Teoretiska reflektioner om makt, integration och strukturell diskriminering*. Stockholm: Fritzes.

Kamali, M. (2006a). Skolböcker och kognitiv andrafiering. In L. Sawyer & M. Kamali (Eds.), *Utbildningens Dilemma: Demokratiska ideal och andrafierande praxis*. Stockholm: Fritzes.

Kamali, M. (2006b). Den segregerande integrationen. In M. Kamali (red), *Den segregerande integrationen: Om social sammanhållning och dess hinder*. Stockholm: Fritzes.

Kamali, M. (2006c). *Multiple modernities, civil society and Islam: The case of Iran and Turkey*. Liverpool, UK: Liverpool University Press.

Kastoryano, R. (2002). Negotiating identities: States and immigrants in France and Germany. Princeton, NJ: Princeton University Press.

Katz, S. R. (1999). Teaching in tensions: Latino immigrant youth, their teachers and structure of schooling. *Teacher College Record, 100*(4).

Kaya, I. (2004). *Social theory and later modernities: The Turkish experience*. Liverpool, UK: Liverpool University Press.

Kedourie, E. (1993). *Nationalism*. Oxford, UK: Blackwell

Kierman, V. G. (1981). *The lords of human kind: Black man, yellow man, and white man in an age of empire*. New York: Colombia University Press.

King, R. (1999). *Orientalism and religion: Post-colonial theory, India and the Mystic East*. New Delhi, India: Oxford University Press,

Kingston-Mann, E. (1999). *In search of the True West*. Princeton, NJ: Princeton University Press.

Knowles, L. L., Prewitt, K., & Blank, O. (Eds.). (1969). *Institutional racism in America*. Englewood Cliffs, NJ: Prentice-Hall.

Krais, B. (1993). Gender and symbolic violence: Female oppression in the light of Pierre Bourdieu's theory of social practice. In C. Calhoun, E. LiPuma & M. Postone (Eds.), *Bourdieu: Critical perspectives*. Cambridge, UK: Polity Press.

Lamont, M. (1999). *The cultural territories of race: Black and White boundaries*. Chicago: Chicago University Press.

302   *References*

La Padania. 1999, Feb. 9
La Padania. 2000, July 25
La Padania. 2000, September 14
La Padania. 2000, November 5
Lawrence, P. (1997). *Modernity and war: The cread of absolute violence.* New York: Macmillan.
Le Blanc, P. (Ed.). (2003). *Black liberation and the American Dream: The struggle for racial and economic justice: Analysis, strategy, readings.* New York: Humanity Boods.
Leenen, W. R., Grosch, H., & Kreidt, U. (1990). Bildungsverständnis, Plazierungsverhalten und Generationenkonflikt in türkischen Migrantenfamilien. *Zeitschrift für Pädagogik, 36*(5), 753–771.
Lega Lombarda (1983) Statuto della Lega Lombarda da Lombardia Autonomista n. 14 settembre 1983
Lega Nord (1994) PROGRAMMA ELETTORALE, 1994 SEGRETERIA POLITICA FEDERALE LEGA NORD
Lega Nord (1996) Programma Politica, Lega Nord Programma Elettorale Per La Padania Elezioni Politiche Del 21 Aprile 1996
Lega Nord (1999) Per una Padania libera in una libera Europa", programma per le europee 1999
Lega Nord (2001) Ragionamenti per la campagna elettorale", programma per le politiche 2001
Lega Nord (2002) "Ragionare sull'immigrazione: la nuova legge Bossi", testo specificatamente dedicato alle politiche della Lega per l'immigrazione 2002.
Lega Nord (2004) LEGA NORD PER L'INDIPENDENZA DELLA PADANIA, ELEZIONI EUR Programma per le elezioni europee 2004OPEE 2004
Lemke, J. L. (1995). *Textual Politics: Discourse & Social Dynamics.* London: Routledge.
Lewis, B. (1993). *Islam and the West.* New York: Oxford University Press.
Lewis, B. (2002). *What went wrong?: Western impact and Middle Eastern response.* London: Phoenix.
Liga Polskich Rodzin. (2001). 'Odzyskać polską samorządność—Program samorządowy Ligi Polskich Rodzin' (To regain Polish self-governance—LPR Program for the local government), Poland: LPR.
Liga Polskich Rodzin (2002a) 'Program ideowy Ligi Polskich Rodzin z 5 kwietnia 2002 r.' (Ideological program of Polish Family League, April 5, 2002), Poland: LPR
Liga Polskich Rodzin (2002b) Ramowy program LPR dla wyborów samorządowych, 2002 r.' (Framework program of LPR for the local election, 2002), Poland: LPR.
Liga Polskich Rodzin (2003a). 'Skrót programu gospodarczego, trwałego rozwoju, wykorzystującego naukę, wiedzę oraz zasoby przyrodnicze, zmierzające do samowystarczalności kraju dla niepodległej Polski oraz suwerennego Narodu Polskiego, LPR, Warszawa, 3 maja 2003 r.' (The abridged version of the economic program of sustainable development, use of science, knowledge and natural resources for self-sufficiency of the state, for independent Poland and sovereign Polish Nation, LPR, Warsaw, May 3, 2003), Poland: LPR.
Liga Polskich Rodzin (2003b). Stanowisko II Kongresu LPR w sprawie sytuacji politycznej Polski po zaakceptowaniu w referendum przez Naród wejścia Polski do UE, wrzesień 2003' (Standpoint of the Second Congress of LPR on the the political situation of Poland after the acceptance by the Nation of the accession of Poland to the EU), Poland: LPR.

Liga Polskich Rodzin (2004) Program posłów LPR do Parlamentu Europejskiego, 2004' (Program of the LPR Members of European Parliament, 2004), Poland: LPR.

Lindgren, C. (2002). *Etnisk mångfald i arbetslivet i Norden*. Norrköping, Sweden: Integrationsverkets rapportserie, No. 10.

Lindqvist, S. (1992). *Utrota varenda djävel (Exterminate all the Brules)*. Stolkholm: Bonniers.

Linné, C. V. (1964). *Systema naturae, 1735: Facsimile of the first edition*. Nieuwkoop, The Netherlands: B. de Graaf.

Loomba, A. (1998). *Colonialism/Postcolonialism*. London: Routledge.

Lutz, H. (1991). *Welten verbinden: Türkische Sozialarbeiterinnen in den Niederlanden und der Bundesrepublik Deutschland*. Frankfurt: Verlag für Interkulturelle Kommunikation.

Lybyer, A. H. (1913). *The government of the Ottoman empire in the time of Suleiman the magnificent*. Cambridge.

Mannoni, O. (1964). *Prospero and Caliban: The psychology of colonisation*. New York: Fredrick A. Praeger.

Marsden, C. (2001). 'Britain: Oldsham riots sparked by deliberate cultivation of racism' at World Socialist Webside, May 29, 2001 (http://www.wsws.org/articles/2001/old-m29.shtml)

Martin, J. J. (2004). *Myths of Renaissance individualism*. New York: Palgrave.

Martinot, S. (2000). Introduction. In M. Albert, *Racism*. Minnesota., MN: University of Minnesota Press.

Marx, K. (1954). *Capital: A critique of political economy. Book 1, The process of production of capital*. London: Lawrence & Wishart.

Marx, K. (1956). *Capital: A critique of political economy. Book 2, The process of circulation of capital*. London: Lawrence & Wishart.

Marx, K., & Engels, F. (1973). Manifesto of the Communist Party. In K. Marx, *The revolution of 1848*. Harmondsworth: Penguin.

Massey, D. S., & Denton, N. A. (1996). *American apartheid: Segregation and the making of the underclass*. Cambridge, MA: Harvard University Press.

Mayer, N., & Perrineau, P. (1989). *Le Front national à découvert*. Paris: Fondation Nationale des Sciences Politiques, cop.

Mazower, M. (1998). *Dark continent: Europe's twentieth century*. London: Allen Lane.

McLaren, P. (1993). *Schooling as ritual performance: Towards a political economy of educational symbols and gestures*, London: Routledge.

McNeill, W. H. (1983). *The pursuit of power*. Oxford, UK: Basil Blackwell.

Medborgaren. 1996, No. 2

Medborgaren. 1996, No. 6

Medborgaren. 1999, No. 4

Medborgaren. 2002, No. 1

Medborgaren. 2002, No. 5

Memmi, A. (1969). *The coloniser and the colonised*. Boston: Beacon Press.

Memmi, A. (2000). *Racism*. Minnesota, MN: University of Minnesota Press.

Miles, R. (1987). *Capitalism and unfree labour: Anomaly or necessity?* London: Tavistock.

Miles, R. (1989). *Racism*. London: Routledge.

Miles, R. (1993). The articulation of racism and nationalism: Reflections on European history. In J. Wrench & J. Solomos, (reds), *Racism and migration in Western Europe*. Oxford, UK: Berg.

Mills, C. W. (1997). *The racial contract*. Ithaca, NY: Cornell University Press.

Mills, C. W. (1998). *Blackness visible: Essays on philosophy and race*. Ithaca: NY: Cornell University Press.

Mills, C. W. (2003). White supremacy as sociopolitical system: A philosophical perspective. In A. Doane & E. Bonilla-Silva, (reds), *White out: The continuing significance of racism.* New York: Routledge.

Moderata samlingspartiet (1984) 'Moderata samlingspartiets partiprogram' (The Moderate Party Programme), Sweden: M

Moderata samlingspartiet (1993) Moderata samlingspartiets valprogram' (The Moderate Party Election Manifesto), Sweden: M

Moderaterna (2001). 'Moderaternas parti program' (The moderates Party Programme), Sweden: M

Mohanty, C. T. (2003). *Feminism without borders: Decolonizing theory, practicing solidarity.* Durham, NC: Duke University Press.

Montesquieu, C. D. S. (1989). *The spirit of the law.* Cambridge, MA: Cambridge University Press.

Moore, N. M. (2000). *Governing race policy, process, and the politics of race.* Westport, CN: Praeger.

Mudde, C. (2007). *Populist radical right parties in Europe.* New York: Cambridge University Press

Myrdal, G. (1944). *An American dilemma: The negro problem and modern democracy.* New York: Harper & Brothers.

Nasr, S. H. (1976). *Islamic science: An illustrated study.* London: World of Islam festival publications.

Nationaldemokratische Partei Deutschlands (1973) 'Nationaldemokratische Partei Manifesto', Germany: Nationaldemokratische Partei Deutschlands

Nationaldemokratische Partei Deutschlands (1977) 'Nationaldemokratische Partei Manifesto', Germany: Nationaldemokratische Partei Deutschlands

Nationaldemokratische Partei Deutschlands (1997) 'Nationaldemokratische Partei Manifesto', Germany: Nationaldemokratische Partei Deutschlands

Natriello, G., McDill, E., & Pallas, A. (1990). *Schooling disadvantaged children: Racing against catastrophe.* New York: Teachers College Press.

Neergaard, A. (Ed.) (2006). *På tröskeln till lönearbete: Diskriminering, exkludering och underordning av personer med utländsk bakgrund.* Stockholm: Fritzes.

Norman, D. (1960). *Islam and the West: The making of an image.* Edinburgh, UK: Edinburgh University Press.

North, D. C. (1990). *Institutions, institutional change, and economic performance.* Cambridge, UK: Cambridge University Press.

Nydemokrati (1990) 'Det här är vårt program' (This is our programme), Sweden: ND

Nydemokrati (1994) 'Nydemoratins parti program' (New democrates' Party Programme), Sweden: ND

Nydemokrati (2004) 'Nydemokratins valprogram' (New democracy's Election Manifesto), Sweden: ND

Ohri, A., Basil, M., & Curno, P. (1982). *Community work and racism.* London: Routledge and Kegan Paul.

Okin, S. M. (1999). Is multiculturalism bad for women? In J. Cohen, M. Howard & M. C. Nussbaum (Eds.), *Is multiculturalism bad for women?* Princeton, NJ: Princeton University Press.

Operario, D., & Fiske, S. T. (1998). Ethnic identity moderates perceptions of prejudice: Judgments of personal versus group discrimination and subtle versus blatant bias. *Personality and Social Psychology Bulletin, 27*(5), 550–561.

Opoka w kraju. 2001, Vol. 39

Opoka w kraju. 2001, Vol. 40

Opoka w kraju. 2002, Vol. 43

Osler, A., & Hill, J. (1999). Exclusion from school and racial equality: An examination of government proposals in the light of recent research evidence. *Cambridge Journal of Education, 29*(1).

Osler, A., & Morrison, M. (2000). *Inspecting schools for race equality: OFST-ED's strengths and weaknesses: A report for the Commision for Racial Equality.* Stocke on Trent, UK: Trentham Books.

Österreichische Volkspartei (1972/1995) 'Salzburger Programm' (Salzburg Program). Austria: ÖVP.

Österreichische Volkspartei (1985) 'Das Zukunftsmanifest der ÖVP: Österreich hat Zukunft (The Future Manifesto of the ÖVP: Austria has a Future). Austria: ÖVP.

Österreichische Volkspartei (1995) 'Grundsatzprogramm neu' (New Party Program). Austria: ÖVP.

Österreichische Volkspartei (1999) 'Der bessere Weg. Programm der ÖVP am Beginn des 21. Jahrhunderts' (The better Way. ÖVP Program at the Beginning of the 21st Century). Austria: ÖVP.

Österreichische Volkspartei (2002) 'Das Österreich-Programm der Volkspartei' (The Austria-Programme of the ÖVP). Austria: ÖVP.

Österrichische Volksparteir (2003) 'Regierungsprogramm. (Government Programme), Austria: ÖVP.

Parszyk, I.-M. (1999). En skola för andra: *Minoritetselevers upplevelser av arbets- och livsvillkor i grundskolan.* Stockholm: HLS förlag.

Party Socialiste (1997) 'Party Socialiste Manifesto' France: PS

Party Socialiste (2002) 'Party Socilaste Manifesto', France: PS

Petterson, B. (2006). *Stories about strangers: Swedish media construction of sociocultural risk.* Lanham: University Press of America.

Pettigrew, T. F., & Taylor, M. C. (1992). Discrimination. In E. F. Borgatta & M. L. Borgatta (Eds.), *The Encyclopedia of Sociology,* Vol. 1. New York: Macmillan.

Pieterse, J. N. (1994). Unpacking the West: How European is Europe?. In A. Rattansi & S. Westwood, *Racism, modernity and identity.* Cambridge, UK: Polity Press.

Pincus, F. L. (1994). From individual to structural discrimination. In F. L. Pincus & H. J. Ehrlich (Eds.), *Race and ethnic conflict.* Boulder, CO: Westview.

Pincus, F. L. (1996). Discrimination comes in many forms: Individual, institutional, and structural. *American Behavioral Scientist, 40*(2), 186–194.

Pollis, A. (1998). *Cyprus and its people: Nation, identity, and experience in an unimaginable community 1955–1997,* Boulder, CO: Westview Press.

Polskie Stronnictwo Ludowe. (1991). 'Polskie Stronnictwo Ludowe wobec najważniejszych problemów kraju 1991' (Polish Peasant Party in the face of the major problems of the state 1991), Poland: PSL.

Polskie Stronnictwo Ludowe. (1993a). 'Deklaracja ideowa Polskiego Stronnictwa Ludowego 1993' (Ideological declaration of Polish Peasant Party 1993), Poland: PSL.

Polskie Stronnictwo Ludowe. (1993b). 'Polskie Stronnictwo Ludowe wobec węzłowych problemów państwa 1993' (Polish Peasant Party in the face of the key problems of the state 1993), Poland: PSL.

Polskie Stronnictwo Ludowe (1997a). 'Deklaracja ideowa PSL 1997' (Ideological declaration of PSL 1997), Poland: PSL.

Polskie Stronnictwo Ludowe. (1997b). 'Program społeczny PSL 1997' (Social program of PSL 1997), Poland: PSL.

Polskie Stronnictwo Ludowe. (2001). 'Czas na zmianę. . . Program społeczno-gospodarczy PSL 2001' (Time for a change . . . Social-economic program of PSL 2001), Poland: PSL.

Polskie Stronnictwo Ludowe. (2004). 'Tezy programowe 2004' (Program theses 2004), Poland: PLS.

Portes, A. (1998). Social Capital: Its origins and applications in modern sociology. *Annual Review of Sociology, 24,* 1–24.

Powell, J. J. W., & Wagner, S. (2001). Daten und Fakten zu Migrantenjugendlichen an Sonderschulen in der Bundesrepublik Deutschland. Selbständige

Nachwuchsgruppe Working Paper 1/2001. Berlin: Max-Planck-Institut für Bildungsforschung.

Pred, A. (2000). *Even in Sweden: Racisms, racialized spaces, and the popular geographical imagination.* Berkeley, CA: University of California Press.

Pye, D., Lee, B., & Bhabra, S. (2000). *Disaffection amongst Muslim pupils: Exclusion and truancy.* London: IQRA Trust.

Rassemblement pour la République and Union pour la Démocratie Française Party Programme (1997) 'RPR and UDF Election Manifesto', France: RPR/UDF

Rattansi, A. (1994). "Western" racisms, ethnicities and identities in a "postmodern" frame. In A. Rattansi & S. Westwood, *Racism, modernity and identity: On the Western front.* Oxford, UK: Polity Press.

Rattansi, A., & Westwood, S. (1994). *Racism, modernity and identity.* Cambridge, UK: Polity Press.

Reisigl, M., & Wodak, R. (2001). *Discourse and discrimination.* London: Routledge.

Reuter, L. (1999). Schulrechtliche und schulpraktische Fragen der schulischen Betreuung von Kindern und Jugendlichen nichtdeutscher Erstsprache. *Recht der Jugend und des Bildungswesens*, 1/99, 26–43.

Reuter, L. (2001). Schulrecht für Schüler nichtdeutscher Erstsprache. *Zeitschrift für Ausländerrecht*, 3/2001, 111–119.

Richards, G. (1997). *'Race,' racism and psychology: Towards a reflexive history.* London: Routledge.

Rivera, A.-M. (2003). *Estranei e nemici. Discriminazione e violenza razzista in Italia.* Rome: Derive Approd.

Runfors, A. (2003). *Mångfald, motsägelser och marginalisering: En studie av hur invandrarskap formas i skolan.* Stockholm: Prisma.

Ruzza, C., & Schmidtke, O. (1993). Roots of success of the Lega Lombarda: Mobilization dynamics and the media. *West European Politics*, 16(2), 1–23.

Rzeczpospolita. 2001, September 21

Rzeczpospolita. 2001, October 3

Rzeczpospolita. 2003, September 29

Sabila, G. (2007). *Islamic science and the making of the European Renaissance.* Cambridge, MA: MIT Press.

Said, E. (1978). *Orientalism.* New York: Pantheon Books, cop.

Sardar, Z. (1984). *The touch of Midas: Science, values and environment in Islam and the West.* Manchester, UK: Manchester University Press.

Sardar, Z. (1999). *Orientalism.* Philadelphia: Open University Press.

Sawyer, L., & Kamali, M. (Eds.). (2006). *Utbildningens dilemma: Demokratiska ideal och andrafierande praxis.* Stockholm: Fritzes.

Schewe, S. (2000). Migration, Arbeit und Diskriminierung in Deutschland. *Gewerkschaftliche Praxis: Gegen Diskriminierung und Fremdenfeindlichkeit,* 1, 15–17.

Schmitt, C. (1985). *Political theology: Four chapters on the concept of sovereignty.* Cambridge, MA: Mitt Press.

Schönbach, K. (1977) *Trennung von Nachricht und Meinung.* Munchen: Freiburg.

Scott, J. W. (2001). Deconstructing equality-verso-difference, or The uses of poststructuralist theory for feminism. In A. C. Herrmann & A. J. Stewart (Eds.), *Theorizing feminism: Parallel trends in the humanities and social sciences.* Boulder, CO: Westview Press.

Scott, R. W. (1995). *Institutions and organizations.* Thousand Oaks, CA: Sage.

Silverman, M. (1992). *Deconstructing the nation: Immigration, racism and citizenship in modern France.* London: Routledge.

Similä, M. (1994). Andra generations invandrare i den svenska skolan. In R. Erikson & J. O. Jonsson (Eds.), *Sortering i skolan.* Stockholm: Carlssons.

Simpson, L. (2002). "Race" statistics: Their's and our's. *Radical Statistics, 79*. (See also at: http://www.radstats.org.uk/no079/simpson.htm)

Sivanandan, A. (2001). Poverty is the new Black. *Race and Class, 43*(2), 1–5.

Smith, A. D. (1991). *National identity*. London: Penguin.

Smith, S. D. (2006). *Slavery, family, and gentry capitalism in the British Atlantic: The world of the Lascelles, 1648–1834*. Cambridge, UK: Cambridge University Press.

Sniderman, P., & Carmines, E. G. (1997). *Reaching beyond race*. Cambridge, MA: Harvard University Press.

Sniderman, P., & Piazza, T. (1993). *The scar of race*. Cambridge, MA: Harvard University Press.

Snowden, F. M. (1970). *Blacks in antiquity: Ethiopians in the Greco-Roman experience*. Cambridge, MA: The Belknap Press of Harvard University.

Socialdemokratiska arbetarpartiet (1975) 'Det socialdemokratiska valprogrammet' (Socialdemocrate's Election Manifesto), Sweden: SAP

Socialdemokratiska arbetarpartiet (1990) 'Det socialdemokratiska programmet' (The Socialdemocrat Party Manifesto), Sweden: SAP.

Socialdemoratiska arbetarpartiet (1993) 'Det socialdemokratiska programmet' (The Socialdemocrat Party Manifesto), Sweden: SAP.

Socialdemokratiska arbetarpartiet (2000) 'Socialdemokraternas valprogram' (The Socialdemocrat's Election Manifesto), Sweden: SAP.

Socjaldemokracja Rzeczpospolitej Polskiej (1990a) 'Deklaracja SdRP 1990' (Declaration of SdRP 1990). Poland: SdRP.

Socjaldemokracja Rzeczpospolitej Polskiej (1990b) 'Uchwała Programowa Kongresu Założycielskiego SdRP 1990' (Program of the Foundation Congress of SdRP 1990), Poland: SdRP.

Socjaldemokracja Rzeczpospolitej Polskiej (1991) 'Polska postępu, prawa i demokracji—program społeczno-gospodarczy 1991' (Poland of Progess, Law and Democracy—socio-economic program 1991), Poland: SdRP.

Socjaldemokracja Rzeczpospolitej Polskiej (1992a) 'Polska Sprawiedliwa, Demokratyczna, Bezpieczna"—Program SdRP 1992' (Poland—a Just, Democractic, Secure Country—Program of SdRP 1992), Poland: SdRP.

Socjaldemokracja Rzeczpospolitej Polskiej (1992b) 'Socjaldemokratyczny Program dla Polski—deklaracja przed II kongresem SdRP 1992' (Social-democratic program for Poland—declaration before the Second Congress of SdRP 1992), Poland: SdRP.

Socjaldemokracja Rzeczpospolitej Polskiej (1992c) 'Tak dalej być nie może. Polsce potrzebny jest nowy program—program koalicji SLD 1992' (It can't go on like that. Poland needs a new program—program of the SLD coalition 1992), Poland: SdRP.

Socjaldemokracja Rzeczpospolitej Polskiej (1997a) 'Socjaldemokracja wobec przemian współczesności. Jednostka-Polska-Europa-Świat. Deklaracja III kongresu SdRP 1997' (Social-democracy in the face of changes of the present day. Individual-Poland-Europe-World. Declaration of the Third Congress of SdRP 1997), Poland: SdRP

Socjaldemokracja Rzeczpospolitej Polskiej (1997b) 'Program SdRP przyjęty na III Kongresie SdRP w dniach 6-7.12.1997 (Program of SdRP approved at the Third Congress of SdRP on 06-07.12.1997), Poland: SdRP.

Socjaldemokracja Rzeczpospolitej Polskiej (1999) 'Nowy wiek—nowy SLD. Socjaldemokratyczny Program dla Polski 1999' (New Century—New SLD. Social-democratic program for Poland. 1999), Poland: SdRP.

Socjaldemokracja Rzeczpospolitej Polskiej (2001) Program wyborczy SLD-UP 2001' (Election program of SLD-UP 2001), Poland: SdRP.

Solomos, J., & Back, L. (1996). *Racism and society*. Basingstocke, UK: Macmillan Press.

Southern, R. W. (1962). *Western views of Islam in the Middle Ages*. Cambridge, MA: Harvard University Press.

Sozialdemokratischen Partei Deutschlands (1973) 'Sozialdemokratischen Partei Manifesto', Germany: Sozialdemokratischen Partei Deutschlands.

Sozialdemokratischen Partei Deutschlands (1985) Sozialdemokratischen Partei Manisfesto', Germany: Sozialdemokratischen Partei Deutschlands.

Sozialdemokratischen Partei Deutschlands (1997) 'Sozialdemokratischen Partei Manifesto', Germany: Sozialdemokratischen Partei Deutschlands.

Sozialdemokratischen Partei Österreichs (1978) 'Das neue Parteiprogramm der SPÖ' (The New Party Program). Austria: SPÖ

Sozialdemokratischen Partei Österreichs (1998) 'SPÖ Parteiprogramm' (Party Programme of the SPÖ), Austria: SPÖ

Sozialdemokratischen Partei Österreichs (2002) 'Wahlprogramm: Projekt 19' (Election Programme: Project 19). Austria: SPÖ

Sozialdemokratischen Partei Österreichs (2003) 'Argumente 9': Integration ist kein Thema (Argument 9: Integration is not an issue). Austria: SPÖ

SPÖ-2003/2 Argumente 15: Aktive Integrationspolitik, 2003 (Argument 15: Active Integration Politics)

Spencer, H. (1851). *Social statica*. London: John Chapman.

Spencer, H. (1852). A theory of population. *Westminster Review*, April.

Spencer, H. (1857). Progress: Its law and cause. *Westminster Review, 67*, 445–485.

Spencer, H. (1862). *A system of synthetic philosophy*. London.

Spencer, H. (1878). *Study of sociology*. London: Kegan Paul C. & Co.

Super Express. 2001, September 27/28.

Svanberg, I., & Tydén, M. (1992). *Tusen år av invandring: En svensk kulturhistoria*. Stockholm: Gidlund.

Svenska Dagbladet. 1986, February 16

Svenska Dagbladet. 1986, February 25

Svenska Dagbladet. 1989, November 21

Svenska Dagbladet. 2001, September 14

Sverige Kuriren. 1990, No. 11

Sverige Kuriren. 1998, No. 2

Sverige Kuriren. 2003, No. 51

Sverigedemokraterna (1989) 'Sverigedemokraternas program', (Sweden Democrates Program), Sweden: SD

Sverigedemokraterna (1999) 'Sverigedemokraternas parti program', (Sweden Democrates Party Program), Sweden: SD

Taylor, C. (1989). *Sources of the self: The making of modern identity*. Cambridge, MA: Harvard University Press.

Taylor, P. J. (1999). *Modernities: A geopolitical interpretation*. Minneapolis, MN: University of Minneapolis Press.

Thompson, L. A. (1989). *Romans and Blacks*. London: Routledge.

Tilly, C., & Tilly, C. (1994). Capitalist work and labor markets. In N. J. Smelser & R. Swedberg (Eds.), *The handbook of economic sociology*. Princeton, NJ: Princeton University Press.

Tränhardt, D. (1999). Ausländer im deutschen Bildungssystem. In M. Krüger-Potratz, (Ed.), *Interkulturelle Studien*. Münster, Germany: Westfälische Wilhelms-Universität Münster.

Trimikliniotis, N. (1999). Racism and new migration to Cyprus: The racialisation of migrant workers. In F. Anthias & G. Lazarides, *Into the margins:Exclusion and migration in Southern Europe*. Avebury.

Trimikliniotis, N. (2001). Europeanisation and modernisation: Locating Cyprus in the Southern European context. *The Cyprus Review, 13*(2), 47–74.

Trommer, L., & Köhler, H. (1981). *Ausländer in der Bundesrepublik Deutschland. Dokumentation und Analyse amtlicher Sttistiken: Reihe Materialien zur Ausländerabeit.* München: Verlag Deutsches Jugendinstitut.

Turner, B. S. (1974). *Weber and Islam.* London: Routledge and Kegan Paul.

Turner, B. S. (1978). *Marx and the end of Orientalism.* London: George Allan and Unwin.

Turner, B. S. (1994). *Orientalism, postmodernism and globalism.* London: Routledge.

Turner, H. R. (1997). *Science in medieval Islam: An illustrated introduction.* Austin, TX: University of Texas Press.

Tyndall, J. (2004). "The Party I Want", *Spearhead* at www.spearhead.com/0409jt2.html.

Uion pour un Mouvement Populaire (2002) 'Union pour un Movement Populaire Party Programme', France: UMP

van der Veer, P. (1993). The foreign hand: Orientalist discourse in sociology and communalism. In V. Ware (1992), *Beyond the pale: White women, racism and history,* London: Verso.

van Dijk, T. A. (1984). *Prejudices in discourses.* Philadelphia: John Benjamin Publications.

van Dijk, T. A. (1991). *Racism and the press.* London: Routledge.

van Dijk, T. A. (1992). Discourse and the denial of racism. *Discourse and Society,* 3(1), 87–118.

van Dijk, T. A. (1993). *Elite discourse and racism.* Newbury Park, CA: Sage.

van Dijk, T. A. (1996). *Discourse, racism, and idelogy.* La Laguna: RCEI Ediciones.

van Dijk, T. A. (1997). Political discourse and racism: Describing Others in Western parliaments. In S. H. Riggins (Ed.), *The language and politics of exclusion. Others in discourse.* Thousand Oaks, CA: Sage.

van Dijk, T. A. (1998). *Ideology: A multidisciplinary approach.* London: Sage.

van, Dijk, T. A. (2000). New(s) Racism: A discourse analytical approach. In S. Cottle (Ed.), *Ethnic minorities and the media.* Milton Keynes, UK: Open University Press.

van Dijk, T. A. (2005). *Racism and discourse in Spain and Latin America.* Philadelphia: John Benjamin Publications.

van Dijk, T. A. (2006). Elitediskurser och instiutionell racism. In P. de los Reyes & M. Kamali, *Bortom vi och dom: Teoretiska reflektioner om makt, integration och strukturell diskriminering.* Stockholm: Frtizes.

Vilhelmsson, R. (2002). *Wages and unemployment of immigrants and natives in Sweden.* Stockholm: Institutet för social forskning.

Voigt, Udo (2004) 'Speech at the NDP Congress on October 30, 2004', in *Deusche Stimme,* 2004, No. 8.

Vorwärts. 2000, No. 9

Wacquant, L. (1997). For an analytic of racial domination. *Political power and social Theory,* No. 11. Symposium on "Rethinking Race" with Ann Laura Stoler, Patricia Dominguez, David Roediger, and Uday Singh Mehta, 221–234.

Wacquant, L. (2003). *Urban outcasts: Towards a sociology of advanced marginality.* New York: Blackwell.

Wacquant, L. (2004). Body & soul: Ethnographic notebooks of an apprentice boxer. Berkeley, CA: University of California Press.

Wadensjö, E. (1997). Invandrarkvinnornas arbetsmarknad. In I. Persson & E. Wadensjö (reds), *Glastak och glasväggar?* Stockholm: Fritzes.

Wallerstein, E. (1974). *The modern world system.* New York: Academic Press.

Wallerstein, I. (2006). *European universalism: The rhetoric of power.* New York: New Press.

Ware, V. (1992). *Beyond the pale: White women, racism and history.* London: Verso.

Weber, M. (1978). *Economy and society.* Berkeley, CA: University of California Press.

Weber, M. (1992). *The Protestant ethic and the spirit of capitalism.* London: Routledge.

Weber, M. (2002). *The Protestant ethic and the spirit of capitalism.* Oxford: Blackwell.

Weil, P. (2002). *Qu'est-ce qu'un français?: Histoire de la nationalité français depuis la revolution.* Paris: Grasset.

Weiss, G., & Wodak, R. (Eds.). (2003). *Critical discourse analysis. Theory and interdisciplinarity.* Basingstoke, UK: Palgrave.

Wieviorka, M. (1995). *The arena of racism.* London: Sage.

Williams, E. (1944). *Capitalism and slavery.* London: Deutsch.

Williams, J. (1985). Redefining institutional racism. *Ethnic and Racial Studies, 3.*

Willis, P. (1991). *Fostran till lönearbete.* Göterborg: Röda bokförlaget.

Wilson, C. A. (1996). *Racism: From slavery to advanced capitalism.* London: Sage.

Wilson, R. (1993). *The external economic relations of the Republic of Cyprus.* London: Oxford University Press.

Wilson, W. J. (1973). *Power, racism and privilege: Race relations in theoretical and sociohistorical perspectives.* New York: Macmillan.

Wilson, W. J. (1987). *The truly disadvantaged: The inner city, the underclass and public policy.* Chicago: Chicago University Press.

Winant, H. (2000). Race and race theory. *Annual Review of Sociology,* 26(1), 169–185.

Wodak, R., & Chilton, P. (Eds.). (2005). *New agenda in (critical) discourse analysis: Theory, methodology, and interdisciplinary.* Philadelphia: John Benjamins Publications.

Wodak, R., De Cillia, R., Reisigl, M., & Liebhart, K. (1999). *The discursive construction of national identity.* Edinburgh, UK: Edinburgh University Press.

Wodak, R., & Pelinka, A. (Eds.). (2002). *The Haider phenomenon in Austria.* New Brunswick, NJ: Transaction Publishers.

Wodak, R., & van Dijk, T. (Eds.). (2000). *Racism at the top.* Klagenfurt/Celovec: Drava.

Wrench, J., & Solomos, J. (Eds.). (1993). *Racism and migration in Western Europe.* Oxford: Berg.

Wright, C., Weekes, D., & McGlaughlin, A. (2000). *'Race,' class and gender in exclusion from school.* London: Falmer Press.

Yack, B. (1997). *The fetishism of modernities: Epochal self-consciousness in contemporary social and political thought.* Notre Dame, IN: University of Notre Dame Press.

Index